ROBERT CARVER is the auth[...] [...]
The Accursed Mountains: Jou[...] [...]
shortlisted for the Thomas C[...] Award. Born in
England, he was brought up in Cyprus, Turkey and India.
Educated at the Scuola Medici, Florence, and Durham
University, where he read Oriental Studies and Politics, he
taught English in a maximum security gaol in Australia,
and worked as a BBC World Service reporter in Eastern
Europe and the Levant. Four of his plays have been broad-
cast by the BBC. He reviews for the *Daily Mail* and *TLS*,
and has written for the *Sunday Times*, the *Observer*, and the
Daily Telegraph, among other papers.

Visit www.AuthorTracker.co.uk for exclusive information
on your favourite HarperCollins authors.

From the reviews of *The Accursed Mountains*:

'A memorable debut. Robert Carver has fulfilled the dream
of every travel writer to find somewhere strange, remote
and unvisited, and to pin it to the printed page. *The Accursed
Mountains* is a tale at once endlessly diverting and pro-
foundly tragic'
WILLIAM DALRYMPLE

'One of the most exciting travel books for a generation'
Spectator

'A classic'
JUSTIN CARTWRIGHT, Books of the Year, *Observer*

'A dazzling account of a journey – always bizarre, often comic, and increasingly nightmarish – through one of the most dangerous backwaters currently to be found anywhere'

PETER HOPKIRK

'A splendid account of a courageous journey'

DERVLA MURPHY

'Required reading'   PATRICK LEIGH FERMOR

'Enviable writing skills . . . fresh horrors on every page'

JUSTIN WINTLE, *The Times*

'A gripping account of Albania in the 1990s'

JAMES OWEN, *Daily Telegraph*

───────────────

By the same author

Ariel at Bay: Reflections on Broadcasting and the Arts (ed.)
The Accursed Mountains: Journeys in Albania

ROBERT CARVER

Paradise with Serpents

TRAVELS IN THE LOST WORLD OF PARAGUAY

HARPER PERENNIAL

London, New York, Toronto and Sydney

Harper Perennial
An imprint of HarperCollins*Publishers*
77–85 Fulham Palace Road,
Hammersmith, London W6 8JB

www.harperperennial.co.uk

Published by Harper Perennial 2007
2

Map © HarperCollins*Publishers*, designed by HL Studios, Oxfordshire

Robert Carver asserts the moral right to
be identified as the author of this work

A catalogue record for this book is
available from the British Library

ISBN 978-0-00-257096-1

Set in PostScript Minion by
Rowland Phototypesetting Ltd, Bury St Edmunds, Suffolk

Printed and bound in Great Britain by
Clays Ltd, St Ives plc

Contents

Unhappy is the nation in need of heroes

Bertolt Brecht

Cada uno hace su propia aventura
Everyone makes his own fortune

Miguel Cervantes de Vedra

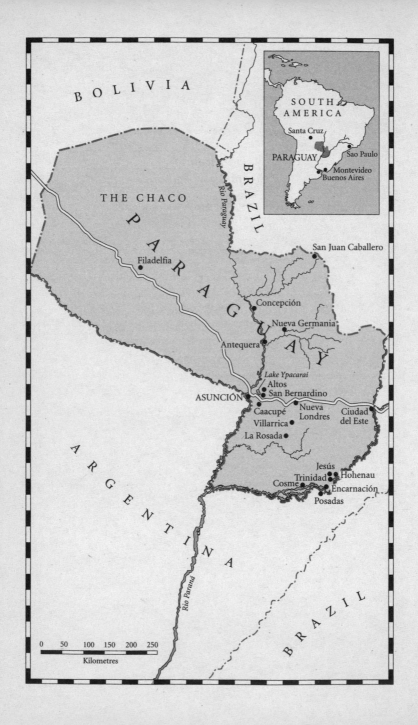

I

VOICES IN THE DARK

'When I first came to Asunción from Spain, I realised that I'd arrived in paradise. The air was warm, the light was tropical, and the shuttered colonial houses suggested sensual, tranquil lives. At night we'd go out walking the streets and I'd be aware of two things; the smell of jasmine and the sound of voices in the dark. But like any paradise, this one had serpents.'

Josefina Plá, Spanish poet

One

The Silver of the Mine

In the closing years of the 19th century a forgotten man returned to his home town in the Midlands of England, after an absence of more than thirty years. He had long been given up for dead. His father had been a wealthy man, an industrialist who owned lace factories and coal mines. This man had two sons, one who stayed at home and entered the family businesses, the other who went off to seek his fortune in the United States of America; he was never heard of again, and when the head of the family died his great fortune was left to both of his sons, in equal parts, though one of them had vanished, apparently for ever. In his will he had specified that advertisements in every English-language newspaper around the world should be run, each week, for a year, to inform the lost son of his new fortune, so that he could return to claim it, if he was still alive. At the end of that period, if the missing son had not appeared, his half of the family fortune was to go to charity, to found a theatre and a public hospital. His will was done. No one stepped forward to claim half of the great fortune. As a result, at the end of the year, the Nottingham Playhouse and the Nottingham Free Hospital came into being, founded and funded by half this man's wealth.

Then, years later, sensationally, a man returned from abroad, claiming to be the missing son. My grandfather Roy, at the time a schoolboy, recalled this event vividly. In his sixties, in the 1950s, Roy told me about this prodigal returned: a tall, massively built man who dressed in 'the American style', with broad-brimmed hat, long coat, embroidered high-heeled boots, silver Mexican spurs, and a fancy multicoloured waistcoat. He spoke with a marked American drawl, though spoke little but listened attentively to what others said. This man was Charlie Carver, my great-great-grand-uncle. He had returned home, at last, and he had a very strange tale to tell.

He had left England as a restless young man, determined to seek his fortune in the post-1845 gold and silver diggings of Western America. He had taken ship for San Francisco, and had arrived safely. Several letters had been received by the family back in England. Then nothing – silence for over thirty years. What had happened was as follows: in a bar-room brawl Charlie had been hit over the head, and was knocked unconscious. When he came to he could not remember who he was. He had been robbed and had no papers or possessions to give him any clues as to his identity. He found that he had been shanghai-ed and was on board a sailing clipper bound for Australia, enrolled by persons unknown for a bounty, as a common seaman. For the next five years he served, first as an ordinary seaman, then as ticketed mate, on board the big sailing vessels that crossed the Pacific. For all this time he still had no idea who he was, nor where he came from. He acquired an American accent and mannerisms. Then, tiring of the sea, and taking his savings, he disembarked in the States, determined to seek his fortune on land. He tried many trades and moved from town to town, one of the legion of homeless men drifting around the West in the 1970s and 1980s as the frontier closed in. Finally, he found a good position as a mining supervisor, south of the border, in Mexico. He still had no idea who he was, and was known to many simply as 'Jack', or *el hombre sin nom* – the man with no name. One day, inspecting a shaft deep inside the mine, a distant rumble was heard; it could mean only one thing – a fall. The miners, including Charlie Carver, alias 'Jack', all rushed for the distant pinpoint of light that was the entrance. They were too late. Dust, rock, pit props rained down upon them. Amid curses and cries of terror they fell to the ground, crushed under the weight of debris. More than twenty men died in that fall, but Charlie Carver was not one of them. He had a broken wrist and a dislocated shoulder, was bruised and cut about the head, but when the rescue party finally managed to dig the survivors out of the rubble, a shocked, semi-delirious voice cried out, in English, for he could no longer recall any Spanish, 'I'm Charlie Carver from Nottingham – what am I doing here?' The blows to his head caused by the rockfall had brought back his knowledge of who he was – and erased his memories of the previous thirty years. He had no idea at all what he had done or where he had been in the missing decades. His last memory was of a fight in a low saloon on the Barbary Coast of San Francisco. This time, however, there were clues – his bankbook, his mate's ticket and discharge papers, his clothes with their tell-tale maker's labels from San Francisco and Sydney. And there were people at the mine who had known where he had been, where he had worked before, because he had told them before the accident.

After he recovered his health he became a detective on the trail of his own past. He retraced his steps, back to San Francisco. There, in the shipping offices and newspaper stacks where the back-numbers were kept, he was able to trace his life as an anonymous seaman from the arrivals and departures of the grain ships, the muster lists and crew signings-on; on his mate's ticket he was described simply as 'Jack of England, Full Mate and Master-Mariner'. He had made his mark on the ticket, not signed it, indicating that in that other life he could not write. Somewhere in his travels he had learnt to use a knife and revolver. He found a keenly whetted blade in a leather sheath hidden in his left boot, and a pair of old, battered, but very serviceable Navy Colt .45 revolvers wrapped in oilskins. On his own body he found scars which he had a doctor examine: they were from the cat-o'-nine-tails, from fist fights, from knife wounds, and at least two puckered

scars were old bullet wounds. On his back the doctor also discovered a tattoo of a Polynesian type then only found in Tahiti,
made with native ink. It was in the newspaper offices in San
Francisco that he saw the advertisements placed for him all those
years ago, after his father died. He said afterwards, when he returned to England, that this was the only moment he lost himself,
when, alone and surrounded by mounds of yellowing newsprint,
he broke down and wept uncontrollably. He said he could still
remember the bay rum lotion his father had used after shaving,
the memory of it driving him to despair in his loss and pain.

He was now two men. In his mind he was still the young,
foolhardy, naive Englishman Charlie Carver, who had only just
got off the boat in San Francisco to seek his fortune, but in his
body he was the scarred, muscular, hard-bitten middle-aged man
who had lived rough across the Pacific for decades, an experienced
seaman who had lived under the lash, and a silver mining engineer
to boot. The latter persona had been illiterate, nameless and
left-handed; the former discovered he had genteel manners, was
well-spoken and wrote in a fine, educated hand. He even recalled
French poetry and Latin oratory he had learnt at school. He had
saved some money – not a fortune, but enough to return to
England. He had spoken fluent, colloquial Spanish after his years
in Mexico, Texas and California, but the blows to his head in the
mine accident had erased all that – and he had become right-
handed once again. But he still spoke English with an American
accent – and he could still use his weapons. My grandfather Roy
was one of several family members who were shown his prowess
as he blew a line of empty bottles off the top of a wall, using both
his revolvers. He had not missed a single bottle, my grandfather
recalled – twelve bullets had hit twelve bottles.

The return of Charlie Carver caused a sensation. His family
recognized him immediately: he had changed, of course, but was
still in essence the same man in voice and body. When the two
brothers saw each other for the first time in three decades they

both spontaneously burst into tears. Charlie was now more or less broke. His half of the great fortune had long ago been disbursed to charity, but his brother Bertie then made an outstandingly generous move. He split his own half of the inheritance in half, and gave one half to his brother.

There, by rights, the story should have ended. Now a wealthy man, with enough money to last him the rest of his days, Charlie Carver should have settled down to comfortable provincial obscurity. But he didn't. He was still gripped by the fever of the silver mines. He had become convinced, like many others, that there was still a hidden Inca city lost in the jungles on the borders of Bolivia, Paraguay and Brazil, a city founded on the wealth of one of the richest silver mines in the Americas. In the 1780s the revolt of Tupac Amaru, a direct descendant of the last Inca rulers, caught the Spanish authorities by surprise. The whole eastern province of what is now Bolivia, then part of the viceroyalty of Peru, was closed to the Spanish for several years. Systematically, the rebels destroyed the extensive gold and silver mines of the region, the survivors retreating eventually into impenetrable jungle to escape the revengeful Spanish. There they founded an Inca city-state which had as its currency and metal of utility the great hoard of gold and silver that the rebels had seized. Iron and copper had they none, so their plates, their knives and forks, their tools and implements were all made of either silver or gold; they also blended these two elements, making that precious metal known to the ancients as electrum. The Spanish never found the lost mines. Those who had known of their existence had been murdered in the rebellion, and the rebels had hidden and destroyed the entrances to these once profitable enterprises. Unlike El Dorado, these mines were not a myth – they had been producing gold and silver under Spanish tutelage before Tupac Amaru's rebellion. Using old maps, a North American had found one of these hidden mines in the late 19th century, which when opened up began to produce huge quantities of rich gold ore. So, if the quest was a fantasy, it was a least a fantasy with a strong basis in factual history.

Charlie Carver had acquired a map. He would not show it to anyone, would not tell anyone where he had got it, nor would he even say in which London bank vault he had deposited it. He made his plans calmly and carefully. Now, thanks to his brother's generosity, he had the money to equip a serious expedition. He interviewed a number of candidates for his proposed venture into the jungle to search for Tupac Amaru's lost city, sometimes called Paititi. One of the young hopefuls was a certain Fawcett, later to be known as Colonel Fawcett, who was to lose his life in the South American jungles looking for just such a lost city of gold. The two did not hit it off. Charlie Carver found Fawcett excessively romantic – a dreamer caught up in a web of fantasy involving a lost Atlantis in the depths of the South American rainforest. Also, and perhaps as pertinently, Fawcett had no money to contribute to the expedition. Eventually a suitable, tough, hard-bitten American was found, equipped with dollars instead of romance, and the two of them set off for Buenos Aires by ship, then up the Paraguay and Parana rivers on the Mihailovich steamer to Asunción, Concepción and eventually up into the tropical wilderness, still unmapped, right on the borders of Bolivia and Brazil.

The old pattern repeated itself. At first, regular letters were received by the family at home in England – then silence, nothing. A long, an overlong silence. Enquiries began to be made by anxious relatives and the British Embassy in Asunción was stirred into action. There was no news. Once again, Charlie Carver had simply vanished into the blue. This time, though, there was to be no miracle, no reprieve. The last people who had seen Charlie and his American partner alive were a small group of Spanish Catholic missionaries, working with Indians only just contacted by whites, on the very edge of known territory. The two explorers had stayed with the priests for several days before departing for the interior, into a region no whites were thought to have ever penetrated before. The smoke of their camp fires had been seen in the distance, coiling up into the sky for several days – then nothing. Some six months later, newly contacted semi-Christianized Indians appeared at the mission with several objects of European manufacture, shreds of cloth, buttons, and a smashed gold-plated, full-hunter pocket watch – manufactured in New York, with Charlie Carver's name engraved inside it, together with his family address in England. It was all that remained of the expedition. Somewhere in the interior the two men had been killed by hostile Indians. The Indians who brought in the pathetic remains did not even know the tribe which had carried out the attack – they had traded the objects with another tribe, who had had them from yet another. The watch was returned to England, and was even repaired. My grandfather Roy showed it to me when I was a young boy, flicking open the front to show me Charlie's name engraved in Victorian copperplate script. It still had many dents and bruises on its shell which no amount of repair could ever redress. Somewhere in the jungle the remains of Charlie Carver and his partner lay for ever lost to the outside world. Like so many Europeans they had searched for treasure in America only to find death.

That, too, should have been the end of the story. But it wasn't quite. Colonel Fawcett, the rejected candidate, got a job as a boundary surveyor in South America, and after his experiences there returned again and again to try to find the lost city of gold and silver, until he too lost his life in the attempt. But before he died he told his great friend the author Sir Arthur Conan Doyle about his theories, about a lost Atlantis in the jungle, Phoenician traders on the River Amazon, about the lost city of Paititi, and about Charlie Carver and his expedition. This information, as we shall eventually see, Conan Doyle eventually put to very good use.

After my book on Albania had been published the distinguished author and former *Times* foreign correspondent Peter Hopkirk, who had been instrumental in getting my first book published, asked me 'Where are you going next? You can go anywhere now, you know.' I replied that I was going to go to Paraguay. 'Why?' I explained to him about my great-great-grand-uncle Charlie Carver. 'To do an "in-the-footsteps-of" book, then?' he asked skeptically. 'The trail will be a bit cold after, what, a hundred years.' No, I replied, not at all. I had no interest in 'in-the-footsteps-of' travel books. Besides, Charlie's footsteps were only too well known – he walked into virgin jungle and was killed by Indians, end of story. What I was interested in were the half-made, half-abandoned places in the world, like Albania and Paraguay – and one could see Paraguay as a sort of South American Albania – lawless, piratical, bandit-ridden and corrupt, where neither tourists nor travel writers usually penetrated. And there was something else. South America had attracted the Spanish and countless other European adventurers who hoped to make their fortunes out of the river of silver and gold that had flowed, at such cost in human misery and suffering, after the Conquest. Yet quite another vision of America had also seized the imagination of the European mind. America could become a place of redemption, a place where the human spirit could be reborn, remade and refined. From its first discovery America had been a realm where imaginary Utopias could be set, and a place European dreamers could actually set sail for, arrive in and set up ideal communities which would, it was hoped, become beacons to mankind. Paraguay, from the first, had been a place which attracted Utopians and idealists. First the Jesuits had experimented with their *Reducciones*, theocratic communities of Christianized Indians ordered by a multinational caste of Jesuit priests; later 19th-century German nationalists, *fin de siècle* Australian communists, Mennonites, Moonies, and even renegade Nazis had all tried to set up their colonies in Paraguay. You could make a case that what New England was to Cotton Mather – a place where the exiled English Puritans could attempt to build the City Upon a Hill, which would be a light to lighten the gentiles – so was Paraguay the South American equivalent. In a strange sense the bifurcation of the human mind was reflected in the European's Manichean obsession with America – a place from which to loot and steal gold and silver, to pillage, rape and plunder, and a place to found ideal communities which would redeem mankind, straighten the crooked timber of humanity, and to build the Perfect City.

Both Charlie Carver and I were heirs to this dual, paradoxical, contradictory tradition, for we were both descended, after all, from John Carver, a Puritan gentleman from the English Midlands who in 1620 procured a vessel in Holland that was renamed the *Mayflower*, and who was then elected Master of the company of Pilgrims for the voyage, and on arrival in New England was elected first Governor of Plymouth Colony, Massachusetts. Though the English settlement eventually prospered, the first Governor did not. He was shot with an arrow by an Indian while out ploughing the land and died of his wound, leaving behind his wife and children, and his brother who had accompanied him on the Atlantic crossing, one Robert Carver. His descendant, Jonathan Carver, a captain in the Massachusetts Militia, had taken the Union flag of Great Britain to its furthest point west in the years immediately before the Revolution of 1776. He had been the first anglophone to overwinter with the Lakota Sioux, had made detailed plans to cross the Rockies and reach the Pacific coast, and whose travel book – published in London on his return – had proved a sensation all over Europe, translated into at least seven languages. He became a figure in literary London and at Court, and never returned to America. He was a disciple of the French *philosophes*, and in his tolerant appreciation of Indian culture and *moeurs* was a century and a half ahead of his time. Our family, I argued, had made a habit of going to America on quests – mine would be in the tradition.

I explained all this over several cups of cappuccino in a London coffee bar to Peter Hopkirk. He thought about it and gave a slight smile of approval. 'It does sound like an interesting quest. But remember, two Carvers have already been killed by American Indian arrows. Just make absolutely sure you are not the third. Always remember, you can't write a book if you are killed while researching it. Jonathan Carver is clearly the one to emulate. Steer well clear of silver mines, I should.' This was very good advice, and I often thought about it later when I found myself in much hotter water than I would ever have thought it possible to get into – and then get out of alive.

Two

An Ambassador is Born

At Sao Paulo airport the passengers in the transit lounge slumped forward like the dead, eyes shut, their heads resting downwards, caught in metal and canvas cradles, motionless, their arms hanging limply beside them. Above, around, and all over them hovered lean, lithe, intense young girls dressed in white t-shirts and jeans, with bare suntanned midriffs, their fingers, fists and elbows kneading their clients' skulls, backs, shoulders, torsos and feet. This service, unlocking flight-tautened muscles and imparting spiritual calm, cost five US dollars, and took place in full view of everyone; a whole line of these modern penitents were slumped as if in prayer between the coffee stall and the newspaper stand. The newspapers and magazines on sale were all from the Americas – from all over Brazil, Argentina, Uruguay, Peru, Bolivia and Venezuela, as well as Mexico and the US. There was nothing from Europe – and nothing, of course, from Paraguay: sometimes known optimistically as the Switzerland of the continent, it was more like the Tibet. You could get no information on the place anywhere. I was in a new continent, a new hemisphere, and a New World – and one in which my destination was as invisible as it had been in England.

The transit passengers, mostly Brazilians waiting for internal flights, whether upright, prone or at all angles between, were uniformly young, elegant and beautifully dressed. Wasp-waisted black men, ranging from double espresso to palest *café au lait*, drifted past me dressed in impossibly stylish suits of pastel hues. They were shod in elegant patent shoes which looked like Milan

13

goes Carnival in Rio. There was a calm, almost Zen atmosphere to this hyper-modern airport, hi-tech tranquillity, *luxe*, *calme* and *volupté*. By definition, only the richest could afford to fly in this huge but deeply divided society. The chaos, the colour, the poverty of the *favelas* was nowhere in evidence. Problems? What problems? you might ask yourself. But the newspapers reminded you every time you glanced at their headlines. Argentina, Brazil, much of South America was in deep crisis. Argentina had withdrawn from its commitment to value the peso on par with the dollar. Foreign currency reserves had vanished in unexplained circumstances. The banks had shut their doors. Now outside the angry protesters, already known as *los ahorristas*, hammered at the roller-shutter doors with sticks and batons, while the police looked on sympathetically – they too had lost their savings: this was a middle-class and middle-aged protest. They wanted their money back. They had trusted their government but their government had, in effect, stolen their money, promising to honour an exchange rate, then reneging, then closing the banks by fiat, refusing to allow savers access to their own money. Who would ever trust their money to an Argentine bank again? How could you run any sort of economy when the banks were untrustworthy and closed the doors on their own customers? Argentina could not, would not service its international debts. It had borrowed and borrowed and borrowed, but the money had all been stolen or wasted. No new loans could be negotiated until the country agreed to start repaying the interest on its old loans. There were already food shortages, medical supplies running out, layoffs and bankruptcies. Kidnapping and gunlaw had proliferated. The demonstrations in the streets against the government were turning ugly. One of the richest – in theory at least – countries in the world was behaving like one of the poorest. In Brazil the situation teetered on the edge of crisis. And what of Paraguay? It was hard to find anything out about that secretive and isolated country. I would simply have to go and find out for myself.

Initially, I had favoured the classic approach into the country
– via Argentina – to Buenos Aires, and up the River Plate and
River Paraguay to Asunción. It was the route everyone had always
taken from the first Spanish conquistadors to the exiled Argentine
President Perón. But the old Mihailovich steamers had passed out
of service, and Paraguay itself had started to look away from
Argentina, from the south and its past, instead looking east to
Brazil, and north to Miami and the USA. So I decided to fly to
Asunción via Sao Paulo. There was another reason, apart from
chaos, that I did not want to go via Argentina. It is no secret that
the relations between Paraguay and Argentina have always been
poor. Every Argentine I had met in London – and I had met dozens
of them – had expressed a low opinion of Paraguay and Paraguayans. I was not going to get any helpful information from such
entrenched and biased enemies of the country I wanted to explore.
They seemed to regard the Paraguayans as backward natives,
Indians in tents, almost savages. Their contempt was palpable.

From time to time, from the tannoy, a soft, sibilant voice
would whisper departures in Brazilian-accented Portuguese to
destinations from a poet's lexicon – Manaos and Rio de Janeiro,
Bahia de San Salvador and Cartagena de las Indias, Valparaiso
and Tegucigalpa. However, there was just one flight to Paraguay
and I would have to wait six hours for it. I found the departure
gate and read the notice posted in front of it in Spanish, Portuguese and English: 'Passengers are advised that all revolvers,
automatics, rifles and other firearms must be unloaded with
ammunition and packed inside luggage that has been checked in.
No person carrying loaded or unloaded weapons will be allowed
on to the plane. Thank you for your co-operation.'

With a sinking heart I realized that this was an official indication of what I had been warned of before – that Paraguayans
have a love affair with powder and shot, pistol and lead, that knows
no bounds. 'Do they all carry pistols?' I had asked a seasoned old
Paraguay hand in London. 'Well, I wouldn't say all – no, not by

a long chalk. However, it is fairly common. I mean, there are shootings all the time – I mean every day, everywhere. And knife fights, of course. It's as well to be very polite to people. That generally pays off. Unless they want to kill you, in which case no amount of politeness would help.' This was useful advice, I suppose: I had made a mental note to be more than usually polite. In the event, there might have been some Paraguayans I met during my eventful trip who were not armed with some sort of pistol, sub-machine gun, machete or knife, but I couldn't actually swear to it. Often we find ourselves the embarrassed witness of other people's intimate little moments when they think they are not being observed – the surreptitious scratch of the groin, the furtive pick of the nose, the fart eased out apparently unnoticed. In Paraguay these moments always revolved around someone's jacket falling open to reveal a gleaming or matt-black automatic peeping out coyly from waistband or shoulder holster; a drawer opened by mistake to display a cluster of Uzi sub-machine guns, a brace of pump-action sawn-off shotguns, or a vintage Luger with an embossed swastika on the wooden handle. As tea is to China, chocolate to Switzerland or red wine to France, so are firearms to Paraguay.

The first group of Paraguayans I saw, clearly waiting for the same flight as myself, were obviously *vaqueros* or *gauchos* – cowboys in jeans and stetson hats, sprawled on the bench seats near the departure gate. Each of them had a tan cowhide grip out of which protruded the butts of their rifles. They all wore empty leather pistol holsters and belts with empty bullet holders. They had obviously read the same notice I had and would check their luggage in when the counter opened. I was tempted to go and talk to them, but didn't. They looked tired, many of them actually kept falling asleep. They had clearly driven a herd of cattle across the border from Paraguay to Brazil, and were now returning home the quickest way possible. They would have sold their horses along with the cattle – it would make no sense to ride them back.

Besides a certain natural diffidence in pushing myself forward into such an uncompromising bunch, there was a question of language. If the word 'Indian' did not convey political incorrectness, one would have said these were Indians. They had coppery skins and hooked noses, dark lank hair and tight, compact bodies. They were *cholos, campesinos* or *indigenos*, though, that was what one called them. *Indio* was considered by many a term of abuse and never used politely, though the first morning I walked through the central square in Asunción a very drunk man approached me from the *favela* below the Presidential Palace, cackling and swaying – '*Yo soy indio, señor,*' he shouted at me. It was 7.30am and he was well away.

There was also the question of what language one should use in speaking to people. Graham Greene, who had visited Paraguay in the depths of the Stroessner dictatorship, had been warned that if he spoke in Spanish in the countryside, he might be assumed to be being patronizing and so run the risk of being shot. On the other hand, if he spoke Guarani, the language of the predominant ethnic group, he might be assumed to be insulting, considering them to be low, ignorant fellows. There was a third lingo, too, called Jalape, which was a mixture of Spanish and Guarani, just to make things clear as mud. I asked my Paraguay expert in London about this. 'Well, you could always try speaking to them in English – that wouldn't cause any offence. Not that they'd understand you, of course. In the Chaco the locals speak a version of 17th-century plattdeutsch. They learnt it from the Mennonites who farm out there. So you can find this chappie who knows where the *alcalde's* office is but the only language he can give you instructions in is his own tribal palaver and 17th-century Low German. I suppose you speak that fluently, of course?' I mumbled something about French and Italian. 'Well, those won't be much use. The other Germans, the Third Reich lot, don't actually say "Heil Hitler" any more, but rather "*Grüss Gott*". You could manage that, I suppose?' Surely now that Stroessner, the half-Guarani, half-

Bavarian dictator who had had a signed photograph of Hitler in his office and wore a pair of Goering's boots, had been expelled from the country, things were rather better? 'Rather worse, if anything. He ran a tight ship, did Don Alfredo. If you were a communist he had your balls cut off with a chainsaw to the sound of Guarani harp music. But if you were white, reasonably prosperous looking and apolitical he gave you no grief. Asunción in those days was a frightened town but a safe one. Now it's frightened and very unsafe. No one is really in charge, no one has been paid for months, in some cases for years. Tempers are short, so is cash, and with the poor even food. In the last year things have gone downhill badly. There's talk of a coup in the offing – or a revolution. Keep your head down is my advice.' Advice I fervently hoped I was going to be able to keep.

The flight was all but empty. I had been earnestly quizzed by the security staff about my armoury. Was I certain I didn't have any little *amuse-gueules* tucked away in my boots, sleeves, or hat? No little derringer pistols, ladies' handguns, odd trifles I might in my haste have forgotten? No plastic guns, like the Glock, which wouldn't have shown up in the X-ray machine? We were all frisked and turned over, very politely, three times before we were allowed on board. The group of cowboys sat at the front and got merry on beer. I sat at the back and concentrated on Argentine red wine. The plane went on afterwards to Cordoba in Argentina – Paraguay was just an embarrassing little stop to be got over as quickly as possible. The flight seemed very quick. Before I knew it we were banking over the river, below us a tropical city of low-rise red-roofed houses, much dark green foliage, and a few taller buildings in the centre. My stomach knotted up tightly. Why on earth was I going into one of the most dangerous countries on Earth? I let the cowboys – indeed let all the other passengers – get off first, then I ambled slowly in late-afternoon tropical heat across the tarmac. The airport building was shabby concrete, low and small.

You walked to the terminal on foot. I had had to fill in an old-fashioned white immigration card, exactly the same size and type as I'd filled in as a child in colonial Cyprus. 'I've flown back into the 1950s,' I thought, as I made for the Customs Hall.

Inside, under a high ceiling, a strange scene was being enacted. Several passengers with open suitcases were in deep argument with uniformed Customs officials. Between them were being passed a collection of automatics, pistols, rifles, sub-machine guns and boxes of ammunition that had clearly come out of the luggage. They were arguing, politely but forcefully about how much duty should be paid on these items. All the Customs men were engaged in this task. I kept walking.

A young woman in a smart uniform darted forward and smiled at me. '*¿Diplomatico?*' she asked.

This threw me. '*Yo soy inglés,*' I stammered.

'*¡Bravo!*' she said. '*¡Bravo – el embajador británico!*' even more loudly, and started to applaud me, clapping her hands. The Customs men looked up at me from their deliberations, and gave me great big smiles. Unnervingly, they and their clients with the weaponry all started to applaud me, clapping their hands and calling out. '*¡Bravo . . . ! ¡Bravo! ¡El embajador británico!*' I had only a small bag on wheels: I bowed to the left and to the right of me, and gave what I thought might pass as an ambassadorial benediction with my free hand, and kept on my way.

Another man stepped forward, took my immigration card, stamped my passport, and gave me a smart salute. 'Any firearms, Your Excellency?' he asked in Spanish.

'*No, señor, nada de nada,*' I replied. '*Pasar, pasar, Excelencia,*' he said, motioning me with his hand. I moved out into the arrivals hall, which was already all but empty. I was in Paraguay, reborn as an ambassador. I kept walking until I saw the *aseos* [toilets], and then darted in. I was now in a muck sweat, and it wasn't the heat. I had arrived all right, but what the hell had I got myself into?

*   *   *

The queue at the Cambio was short but the wait interminable. In front of me was a young North American banker and his girlfriend, here on business. 'She speaks German so we should be OK,' he told me. We exchanged cards. They were staying at Madame Lynch's old *estancia*, now the best hotel in Asunción. Eliza Lynch is one of the few people connected with Paraguay known to the outside world. She was the mistress and *éminence grise* of the mid-nineteenth-century dictator López, who ruined the country with his insane war against Argentina, Brazil and Uruguay all at the same time.

When my turn came I asked the cashier behind the counter to change US$100 into guarani. He look at me as if I was crazy. 'You want to change all of this into guaranis?' His expression told me that whatever else Paraguay was going to be it was not going to be expensive. My glance fell lightly on the automatic pistol in a shoulder holster under his arm, and a large revolver he was using as a paperweight to hold down mounds of ancient and dirty bank notes from being blown all over the place by the fan. My eyes slid, unavoidably, to the security guard who was sitting on a chair, the chair high on a desk, at the far end of the room. He was in uniform and had a bazooka on his shoulder. It was pointed straight at me. There was a heavy metal grill between me and the man counting and re-counting hundreds of thousands of guarani notes, but the bazooka and the man's stare made it hard for me to concentrate on the transaction. I did have the wit to ask for one of the ten thousand notes to be broken down into thousands. I hate the airport taxi rip-off, and always get the bus into town if there is one. I knew already the bus driver wouldn't be able to change a thousand guarani note. The man with the bazooka wasn't South American theatricals, I later discovered. The current method of bank robbery in Paraguay and Brazil was with an armoured car; these military vehicles simply ploughed into the banks and smashed through whatever bars were there. Bitter experience had taught the Paraguayans that a man with an antitank weapon was the only way of stopping these heists. Every bank I went into had one of these characters, as well as the run-of-the-mill fellows with sub-machine guns, pistols and grenades. Bank robberies were as common as thunderstorms and as violent. One of the current scandals in the papers, I discovered, was the use of a Paraguayan army armoured car in a bank robbery just across the border in Brazil. The Minister of Defence and the President were accused of having rented out the armoured car to the mob who carried out the raid, in return for a share of the proceeds. The Brazilians claimed they had photos of the armoured car during the raid, and then afterwards, back in its army park in Paraguay. They claimed US$15 million had been stolen, but the Paraguayan press claimed this was an exaggeration – more like $8 million, they thought. When asked why he robbed banks, Butch Cassidy had replied: 'It's where they keep the money.' He had been gunned down in Bolivia, eventually, just next door to Paraguay.

I evaded the lurking taxi-drivers who I knew might cheat – and possibly rob me – and walked out to the bus stop. A couple of obviously quite poor locals were waiting for the bus into town. They eyed me cautiously, but then looked away. A more hopeful fellow carried a briefcase, wore a smart watch and had a shirt with a tie. I fell into conversation with him, and explained I was new to the country – did one buy a ticket on the bus, from a driver, or from a kiosk? He was helpful and informative and I was pleased to discover that I understood his Spanish and he understood mine. The bus arrived, empty, and my new friend helped me get my ticket. We sat together, and I asked him about the state of things as we rolled towards town.

Luis Gonzalves was a Customs official, just coming off duty. Mercifully he had missed my apotheosis as fake ambassador. He gave me a thorough rundown on everything. Things were very bad. Fifteen banks had gone bust taking almost everyone's savings with them. The government was both weak and deeply corrupt.

You could trust neither the police nor the army – both were corrupt and criminal. Civil servants hadn't been paid for six months, some not for a year. The police hadn't been paid for three months, and if they weren't paid soon there would be a revolution. Foreigners were leaving the country in droves – every plane out was packed to capacity, every plane in virtually empty. The only people making money were the *cocaleros* who exported cocaine, and the mafia who stole from everyone. What about crime? Very bad, he said, and getting worse. Buses held up and the passengers robbed, even in central Asunción, every day. Shootings and kidnappings. Bank robberies and stick-ups. Everyone was sick of it. Many wished Stroessner was back in power. 'That was a paradise then, but we didn't know it,' he said, a view I heard echoed by almost everyone I met. No one I spoke to stood up for what passed for 'democracy' in Paraguay.

As he talked and I plied him with questions I looked out through the window, intrigued by my first sight of Paraguay on the ground. The earth was deep, laterite ochre red, the road pitted and ancient tarmac. As we came closer to the centre of Asunción the gardens grew lusher with tropical foliage, glossy green, sometimes studded with bright flowers. There were fine stucco houses of an Italianate style with red tile roofs, though everywhere was an air of decay and dereliction. The cars were surprisingly modern and the traffic busy. My premonition at the money changer at the airport that the bus fare would be tiny was correct. The fare turned out to be 1,300 guarani – about 25 US cents. Luis had told me that a 5,000 guarani note was 'too big' to expect the driver to change for a ticket. In the end Luis had put in 100 guaranis of his own money for my ticket, as I had only two hundreds.

I asked Luis what he thought of the hotel I had selected. It was near the Plaza Independencia. He made a face. 'Not good. A very bad area. Much crime, robberies, prostitution, drugs, alcoholics.' I rapidly changed my plans. The Hotel Embajador met with slightly more approval. 'A better area – near the business district.' There's nothing like local knowledge and a local warning. He was kind enough to get off the bus by the Embajador and show me where it was. We shook hands and he departed. Just before he left he said, 'Oh, and by the way, tomorrow is the annual census. Everything will be shut – everything. Everyone has to be off the streets for the whole day. No buses run, no taxis, nothing.' As we had been talking on the bus he had asked me casually 'Which part of Brazil do you come from?' I said, 'I'm English. From England.' He creased up his face as if in slight pain and waved his hand in front of his chest, 'Ohh – so far away . . .' First an ambassador, then a traveller from Brazil. Paraguay was very different to anywhere I had ever been before. It was quite simply one of the most remote countries in the world, about which almost no one knew anything, which almost no one went to, and almost no one came from – or indeed ever came back from. I felt heartened by this, but also daunted. I felt very much alone and friendless. If anything happened to me out here no one would know or care. Paraguay was a place in which one could disappear without trace.

Three

Counting Paraguay

The heat of the tropical night faded after midnight; the dull roar of traffic was replaced by an absolute calm. I slept fitfully and woke at dawn, faint pale light creeping down the yellowing wall of my room, the shutters casting a shimmering tracery of dark and pallid shadow, a mobile set of bars ominously like those of a prison. I dressed and went out into the open patio. The pot plants and creepers snaked up towards the pale, faintly azured sky, still star-flecked. Leprous walls peeled and sagged, dead plaster like the mummified flesh of a long-buried corpse. Old, decrepit chairs sprawled as if cast away in some deserted, abandoned Spanish *posada* of a hundred years ago. Dust lay thick on the tiled floor. The shutters' grey-ochre paint had blistered and flaked, the colour bleached away by heat and sun. The air smelt cool and earthy; I could hear birds twittering.

The Hotel Embajador had seen better days. It felt like something out of a Graham Greene novel – a place in old West Africa, pre-war Liberia, perhaps. I seemed to be the only guest. This was the sort of place Scobie had committed suicide in, I reflected. There was no air-conditioning and the electric bulbs had no shades. The walls were smeared with squashed mosquitoes and I had itched all night; I suspected bedbugs.

The young lad who had booked me in the night before was asleep on a couch in the foyer, fully dressed, with his shoes off. The hotel was on the first, second and third floors of a city centre building. I tiptoed to the open window and glanced out – the shutters were pulled back and the window open. The street below was deserted. A large Paraguayan flag hung idly from a 19th-century Parisian-inspired corner-building opposite, and on the top of the flagpole squatted a vulture, hunkered down, apparently asleep. Inside the hotel, on the wall opposite, above the sleeping boy, hung a gold-coloured plastic representation of Don Quixote, Sancho Panza, and the Don's horse Rosinante. Windmills were the backdrop. Wherever you travel in the Hispanic world, you are sure to meet Don Quixote, not just as wall decoration, but in person, and Paraguay was to prove no exception.

The lad awoke with a start and gave me a sleepy, friendly smile. I beckoned to the list of refreshments advertised on the wall. Coffee, rolls, cheese sandwiches, soft drinks – what was available, I asked? He looked sheepish. 'The woman who does the coffee and rolls and sandwiches won't be in today – because of the census. No one can move. I have to stay here all day.' I tried to persuade him to make me a cup of coffee – surely that at least was possible? But it wasn't. He didn't know how, or where the things were. I settled for a Coca-Cola, then went downstairs and out on to the silent streets.

The capital of Paraguay was as empty as if a nerve gas strike had wiped out the entire population in their sleep. Not a soul stirred, not a car, not a bus or taxi moved. It was now 6.30am. On a normal day in such a tropical city the place would already be bustling. I took my black bag with me and my cameras. The best photographs I was ever going to get without being disturbed or harassed would surely be today.

It was by now 7.30, and the first groups of students carrying clipboards began to move about from building to building. These were the sharp-end censors who did the actual counting. On the corners of the blocks, soldiers and armed police had appeared, standing in pairs. Trucks drove around dropping them off. I noticed the soldiers were all small and dark, and when I strode by they avoided my eyes and instead looked at the ground or into the middle distance. With my purposeful air, my black bag and my camera, it was evident that they thought I was something to do with the census, and a figure of authority. Much later, when I asked Gabriella d'Estigarribia what impression I made on the local people she had smiled and said, 'They think you are a German from the Technical Service. You stride about, and look angry, and stare at people. Johnny Walker! Very gringo and dangerous. You frighten them.'

This was a blow, I confess. I had thought I made a slightly better impression. The Technical Service was the euphemism given to the secret police who did the torturing under General Stroessner's regime, and who had not gone away after his fall. What was evident on this my first morning's walkabout was that at six foot I was very tall, and also very white, and the ordinary soldiers and police were very small and dark, and that the small dark people shrank from the tall white people in Paraguay, when they thought they had power. You wear your continent's history on your face, in your build, and in your skin colour. Whether I was Brazilian, German or British did not particularly matter: I was a white European in a country and a continent that had been conquered by tall white people, and whose descendants still largely owned, controlled and dominated it to this day, along with much of the rest of the world. It was not a comfortable realization. However liberal, however multicultural one felt oneself to be, in this continent one's safety, even one's continued physical existence depended upon being defended by a corrupt and unjustifiably empowered regime's police force, of which one felt afraid oneself. It is possible to forget you are white if you live in Europe: in the Third World it never is.

As I roamed about taking photo after photo, I wondered whether I, too, was supposed to be indoors along with everyone else. No one challenged me, but if they did I had a feeling that simply saying I was a *gringo turista* was not going to be a good enough excuse. But I wasn't challenged, far from it – I was obviously avoided and ignored, and so I wandered about with increasing confidence. There simply were no tourists in Asunción, I realized, so my movements were interpreted as being in some inscrutable way official. Better not to ask, they would be thinking – I might make trouble for myself.

I had spent a long time looking for a café that was open where I might be able to get a coffee and some breakfast, but the whole city was completely shut – not so much as a kiosk or corner store open. Later, the next day, in the newspaper *Ultima Hora*, I had seen a cartoon of a shivering Paraguayan family indoors trying to hide from view their smuggled TV set, fridge, freezer, hi-fi and so forth. Outside was a burglar wearing a black mask and carrying a swag bag, knocking on their door. 'No thank you – we know who we are,' the head of the household was saying. In Paraguay, as in Turkey, the censors actually entered every house and counted the people in every room, and noted down all the things they possessed. Each property had a sticker pasted on the outside door to prove they had been inspected. 'Smuggling is the national industry of Paraguay,' Graham Greene had observed, when he visited the country in the *stronato*, as the Stroessner years were called. 'Contraband is the price of peace,' Stroessner had stated, defining it as official policy. With the second lowest per capita income in South America, Paraguay imported more Scotch whisky than all the rest of South America put together. It was almost all immediately re-exported to neighbouring Brazil, Bolivia and Argentina. Paraguay was sometimes known as 'the Switzerland of South America' not because of its non-existent mountains or ski slopes, but because it was the regional haven for hot money, millionaires on the run, shady enterprises of all kinds, numbered bank accounts and smuggled luxury goods. As in Switzerland, there were a lot of cows and a lot of pastureland – but you didn't make much of a living out of those. 'Switzerland is where all the big criminals come together to hide the profits of their swindles and thefts,' Juan Perón, dictator of Argentina had said in the 1950s, before being ousted. He should have known: he had sent Eva Perón across to Europe in 1947 to bank their own ill-gotten gains in Geneva. The bankers had put on a special celebratory dinner for her. The British government had refused her a visa and denied her entry as a harbourer of fugitive Nazis and handler of stolen Jewish gold. It was estimated by the Allied Enemy Property Bureau after the Second World War that the Nazis laundered 80% of the loot they had stolen from the Jews and the countries they occupied through Switzerland, with the full knowledge of the Swiss, and the remaining 20% through Argentina, Paraguay, Egypt and Syria, all sympathetic to the Nazi cause. It was the Swiss authorities who had suggested the Nazis add a 'J' on to the passports of German Jews before the war, so the Swiss could tell who they were and refuse them entry. 'Few things have their beginnings in Switzerland,' observed Scott Fitzgerald, 'but many things have their endings there.' Seedier, poorer, more evidently corrupt and oppressive, Paraguay was a downmarket latino, South American tropical version, more like Albania in ambience. Already in my strolls around the city centre I had seen the empty shells of many monumental steel and glass banks, their doors locked and shuttered, beggars sleeping on cardboard under their massive porticoes. Inside you could see the desks and tables covered in dust, with empty cartons on the floors from where the computers and office equipment had been taken away. Like desecrated cathedrals, I thought, these were modern temples of money that had failed, abandoned by their priests, acolytes and devotees, who now worshipped abroad, in Miami and the Cayman Islands.

The night before, although tired after my 18-hour journey from London, I had gone out into the city centre, curious and impatient to get some first impressions. The broken pavements, sandy soil spilling out, potholed streets and grime-stained walls suggested a city down on its luck, and slipping into dereliction. Closed shops, broken windows, beggars, dirt, unpainted walls, shutters falling off their hinges: no one had spent any money on this city for a long time. There were armed police everywhere, hanging around, and the 19th-century stucco buildings suggested a derelict Andalucian provincial town in Spain during the early years of General Franco, just after the Civil War. But the Indian women crouched on the pavements selling tropical fruit and vegetables, herbs, potions and unknown fruit drinks were from the New World, not the Old. I had been recommended the nearby Lido restaurant by the hotel clerk. Right opposite the Pantheon of Heroes, this was an atmospheric 1950s-style soda fountain, with pink granite counter top at which one sat, huge fans churning the air above one's head. The place was run by capable, sensible Paraguayan women of a certain age, who wore pink uniforms with little pink caps. I ordered a veal escalope à la Milanese, with salad and bread, and a Pilsen beer. I had inwardly groaned when the waitress had appeared carrying the beer, and a bucket of ice with a glass inside it. Ice in beer is a favourite – and disastrous – tropical invention I had experienced in Malaysia and Indonesia. But I need not have worried. The glass rim had not touched the ice, and the bottle of beer was opened and thrust into the bucket in place of the glass, up to its neck in frosty coldness, as if champagne in an ice bucket. This was a hot country where they understood cold beer. I had last tasted an iced beer glass straight from the freezer in Australia, a country where they also understand the needs of thirsty, heat-choked men. The Paraguayan beer, brewed to a German lager recipe, was very cold and very good. The food was excellent too: the salad had a flavour completely unavailable in Europe today unless you grow your own vegetables without pesticides and fertilizers. Native pessimism led me to abstract about a third of the escalope and secrete it inside a paper napkin in my bag, together with a couple of slices of bread. I had a feeling there would be no food available on the morrow for any price. I was right, too. Together with an apple I had left over from my flight, and some boiled sweets, this was all I had to eat until the day after the census.

It was dark by 6pm. The night fell suddenly, like a curtain. Wood fires started up, pinpricks of light, from the shanty town on the sandbanks by the river. A breeze from the river wafted up the characteristic Third World smell of sweat, smoke, excrement and spices. By day I had been in Franco's Spain, but by night it was Java or Malaysia. There were small children everywhere, ragged, energetic, vociferous and hungry. The Lido had two private armed guards in khaki uniform, one inside by the cash desk, the other outside by the door. The children begged for coins as the customers left. There was a charity box by the cash desk which bore the printed label: 'Give generously for the lepers of Paraguay'. I just hoped none of them worked in the kitchens. In England, I had asked my local medical centre what diseases were on offer in Paraguay, and what injections were required. It's hard to impress a British National Health doctor, but Paraguay did it for my GP. 'I say . . . malaria, dengue fever, yellow fever, blackwater fever, cholera, typhoid, jiggers, tropical sores, dysentery, plague, HIV, sleeping sickness, bilharzia . . . by golly, they've got the lot out there . . . it's a complete Royal Flush. Why are you going, if I might ask?'

I muttered something about work. 'Oh, and the llamas all have syphilis, due to the lonely herdsmen taking advantage of them in the *altiplano* . . .' Surely not llamas, in Paraguay? I queried faintly. 'Oh, sorry, my mistake, that's Peru, next paragraph down. Oh and meningitis, leprosy, river fever, Lhasa fever . . . you know I think it's easier to say what they haven't got in jolly old Paraguay,' he added jovially. 'Ebola – they haven't got that, it seems – yet.' I'd had to go three times to his surgery for various shots over a couple of weeks. 'Do please come back and see us again if . . . or I should say when you return,' the doc had said cheerily. 'The tropical medicine boys up in London like us to send up stool, blood and urine samples from people coming back from these sorts of places – you might pick up something really interesting, something new, even.' Carver Fever, I thought, a hitherto unknown infection, carried by mosquitoes, incurable, causing paralysis, catalepsy, raging insanity, multiple organ failure and agonizing, lingering death by multiple spasm, also known as the Black Twitching Plague, after its gruesome effects. First brought back to Europe from tropical South America by the late travel writer Robert Carver, who was its first known victim, and whose body had to be cremated in an isolation hospital to avoid contaminating southern England . . . I could be famous: dead, and famous. I said I would stagger in on crutches, somehow, so he could apply his leeches to my depleted carcass. I thanked him, finally, after the last jab session, with thinly disguised insincerity and turned to go. 'Oh, and I should take a plentiful supply of condoms – just in case any of those syphilitic llamas stray across the border . . . ha, ha, ha!' His laughter echoed tinnily round the surgery. I gave him a weak smile, but I felt perhaps the joke lacked a certain good taste, or just simple fellow-feeling. On my first evening's stroll in Asunción I was not particularly reassured to see a large sign with a vicious-looking mosquito on it in the Plaza Independencia, warning of dengue fever. '*No hay remedio*' ran the Goyaesque rubric underneath – there's no cure. Later, I was told that the dengue mosquito was slow and stupid and operated in Paraguay only by day, whereas the malarial mosquito was fast, intelligent and operated by night. The infectious dengue mosquito was male, the malarial female – make of that what you will. 'Women are just as good as men, only better,' observed D. H. Lawrence, who probably knew. The other Lawrence, T. E., contracted malaria while cycling in the south of France before the First War, while studying medieval castles. I had a great sack of anti-malarial and anti-every-other-damn-thing in my bags. If I had anything to say in the matter I was determined to avoid being immortalized in the medical history books.

The centre of old Asunción did have a certain faded elegance, reminiscent, especially after dark, of post-Baron Haussmann Paris, with tropical excrescences such as vultures perched on the telegraph wires, and impassive Indian women smoking coarse cheroots, squatting on the doorsteps. The park sported French 19th-century style wooden benches, white wooden slats held together by elaborate wrought iron, these boat-like contrivances designed for amatory ooh-la-la, even, perhaps, for complete copulatory performance, their arched backs swooning towards the grass. The palms rustled in the faint breeze, rats of impressive size scampering up and down the trunks with complete lack of *pudeur*, and groups of Indians in costume hunkered down for the night amidst the shrubbery, grouped around small, glowing fires on which they brewed their evening potations. By day, I later discovered, these impassive *indigenos* strolled about the town in loin cloths, amid the BMWs and Mercedes, proffering handicrafts, bows and arrows, and beadware, with very little evident enthusiasm or hope of a sale. These, I was told, were the Makká people, who had come in from the Chaco, the Paraguayan Outback that lay just across the river.

The old Post Office was the finest 19th-century stucco building I found, with a charming interior patio full of carefully tended tropical plants, and an elegant stone staircase up to the flat roof, where there was a café and an unrivalled view down across the square to the river beyond. Flags, of the Paraguayan variety, of all sizes, flapped energetically from many buildings in the strong evening wind that rose off the river, bringing the stink of the poor up into the centre of town. It was evident already that there were many poor, and they surrounded the city proper in their slums. A few of them slunk about furtively in the shadows, watched intently by armed police who carried shotguns, machine-guns and assault rifles, and wore six-shooters in black special-forces style low-slung holsters. I had been greeted jovially by a police officer as I walked about the square below the Post Office. He smiled elaborately and said that, with my permission, as I was evidently a foreigner, I would not mind if he gave me a few words of friendly advice. Under no circumstances was I to wander down the steps and into the *favela* – he used the Brazilian word for a shanty town – below us. The centre of Asunción was safe, he said, relatively safe even at night. The *favela* was not. I would be attacked, robbed and perhaps killed within minutes of going down there. It would be best if whenever I wandered around I kept an eye out for police and soldiers. If I could see police and soldiers I was probably all right – no one would attack me. If I couldn't, then I was not safe. There was a great deal of crime at the moment, he told me, due to the unsettled conditions in the country. Not only foreigners were at risk, ordinary Paraguayans were attacked every day, even here in Asunción. I asked if everyone had identity papers, even the poorest of the poor, even in the *favela*. Everyone had papers, he said, absolutely everyone. Not to have papers was a criminal offence in itself. He wished me a good evening, smiled again and then strolled away. His warning and the slight chill in the air had suggested I should now retire for the night. I made my way back to the hotel and shuttered the windows tight. There were many mosquitoes on the wall and I spent half an hour killing them before turning in. I couldn't really tell if these were the fast, intelligent variety or the slow, stupid ones. I rigged up my mosquito net, purchased in London, and crept under it. The bed was hard and uncomfortable. My room cost US$5 a night. I determined to move upmarket and out of the centre of town after the census was over.

Four

Du Côté de Chez Madame Lynch

Gabriella d'Estigarribia sat in the shade under a palm tree by the swimming pool and sipped her grapefruit juice delicately. She had a wide-brimmed straw hat on, her face in deep shadow, yet already the sun had caught the pale, fair skin of her face.

'Foreigners come to Paraguay, find they can do nothing with the people, become angry, then give up, eventually, and go away again in disgust,' she said evenly, not looking at me, but rather at the hummingbird which hovered like a tiny helicopter over the swimming pool.

'Why is it so hard to get things done, for foreigners?' I asked.

'Not just for foreigners, for everyone. Some say it is the mentality of the Guarani people, who used to be called "Indians" before they were converted to Catholicism by the Spanish. Then, by a sort of unexplained miracle they ceased to be Indians and became Paraguayans. People say the Guarani live entirely in the present – the past is forgotten, the future unimagined. Remembering things and making plans for the future are both of no interest to them. Promises are made, events planned, but nothing happens – inertia sets in. From the first the Europeans had to use authoritarian means – force, coercion – to get anything done. The Jesuits used to whip their converts on the famous, oh-so-civilized, we are told, Reductions, as well as the ordinary secular colonial overseers on the plantation.'

'That was a long time ago, surely. What about today, in the new post-Stroessner democracy?'

'His Colorado Party is still in power. He was displaced by an internal coup because he had grown old and flabby. He was arrested at his mistress's house. She was called Nata Legal – *nata* being "cream" in Spanish – that makes her Legal Cream in English, no? What better name for a mistress. He tried to call out the tanks but the only man with the keys for the ignition had gone off to the Chaco for the weekend – so no tanks. There was an artillery duel in Asunción – you can still see the pockmarks in the buildings from the shells – then he was gone, bundled off to Brazil where his stolen millions had been sent ahead. Now we have mounting chaos because no one is frightened any more. Corruption is universal. Everyone takes bribes if they can. Before, under Stroessner, you paid your 10% in bribes to the Party and then you were left alone. Under this so-called democracy you are constantly being made to pay up by everyone, and still nothing is done, because no one is forced to do it any more. You must have noticed the city is falling apart from neglect.'

In her thirties, married and with two small children, Gabriella came from an old Paraguayan family which had been in the country, on and off, since the Spanish Conquest. Her ancestors had come from the Basque provinces of Spain, as had so many of the other conquistadors. Like many of her Paraguyan ancestors, she had spent years abroad in exile, in her case in Miami, in Italy and in England, during the decades of political repression. We were sitting outside in the lush tropical garden of Madame Lynch's tropical *estancia*. Once this had been a cattle ranch in open country, belonging to the mistress of the dictator López, now it was a hotel, surrounded by a well-heeled suburb of Asunción, an hour's walk from the centre of town. You could get a bus or taxi down Avenida España, which made the journey much shorter, but the spate of robberies on public transport meant that many, including myself, preferred to walk. The Avenida España had well-armed police at frequent intervals, as well as motorized patrols during daylight hours, and most of the shops and

35

institutions on either side had highly visible private armed guards sitting outside in plastic chairs with pump-action shotguns or automatic rifles across their knees. At each petrol station there was an army patrol permanently stationed, two or three uniformed men with automatic rifles. This was the route to the airport from the centre of town. If there was a *coup d'état* or a revolution, this was the route the outgoing government would flee along: clearly they wanted to make sure there would be enough petrol available to get them to their planes. It was the petrol supply for Stroessner's tanks that had been under lock and key, I later learnt, when the crunch had come, not the ignition keys. Clearly, this government didn't intend to make the same mistake. Stroessner still gave maudlin interviews to journalists from time to time from his hideout in Brazil, where he bemoaned the fact that he was a much misundertood former dictator – but then they all say that, those that survive. An avowed fan of Adolf Hitler, his secret police, known as the Technical Service, were among the most feared in South America. Cutting up political opponents with chainsaws to a musical accompaniment with traditional Paraguayan harp music was a popular finale, the whole ghastly symphony played down the telephone for favoured clients. Like his local hero the Argentine dictator Juan Perón, Stroessner had a taste for young girls – very young, pre-pubescent. When a daring journalist had once asked Perón if it was true that he had a 13-year-old mistress, he replied, 'So what? I'm not superstitious.' His reputation among Argentines had soared after this was revealed, the ultra-young mistress being seen as a sign or both power and virility. The 13-year-old in question used to parade around Perón's apartment dressed in the dead Eva's clothes, to the slothful admiration of her ageing beau. Stroessner was reputed to favour the 8–10 age group. His talent scouts waylaid them outside school, from where they were taken to discreet villas to be enjoyed by the Father of his People. If they performed nicely they and their parents would be sent on a free holiday to Disneyland in Florida, the nearest Paraguayans can get to Heaven without actually dying first. Stroessner, the half-Bavarian, half-Indian dictator had sent a gunboat down the river for Perón, the mulatto dictator, when he had taken refuge in the Paraguayan Embassy, after his overthrow. Forced into exile, Perón had fascinated the young supremo by recounting his adventures and reminiscences. 'They used to worship my smile – all of them!' he cried. 'Now you can have my smile – I give it to you!' and here he had taken out his brilliant set of false teeth, and passed them across the table to the startled Stroessner. Perón had found Paraguay too dull, and he had to agree to abstain from political intriguing in Argentina, which was irksome, so after a short period of rustication up the river he had taken himself off to the Madrid of Generalissimo Franco, where he lived in exile with the mummified corpse of Eva Perón upstairs in the attic of his Madrid villa, surrounded by magicians and occult advisers. The mummifier, Pedro Ara, who had taken a year over his task, had used the 'ancient Spanish method' and had charged $50,000 for his work, a bill that was never paid. Throughout the last weeks of Eva's agonizing illness the embalmer had stood close by on guard in an antechamber, night and day, waiting in anticipation, for he had to start the process of mummification the instant she died 'to render the conservation more convincing and more durable'. Her viscera were removed entirely and preserving fluids were sent coursing through her entire circulatory system before rigor mortis set in. Some areas of her body were filled with wax and her skin was coated in a layer of hard wax. The complete process was slow, painstakingly slow. After the fall of Perón, the military mounted 'Operation Evasion' in which the body of Eva Perón was 'disappeared' to prevent her becoming the focus of a popular cult; for many people, particularly women and the poor, she has already become a saint.

The son of a First World War German officer, Lt-Col. Koenig was given charge of the body, and he showed it to a delegation of

Peronist CGT trades unionists to show that the military had not outraged her body. After this the mummy was hidden in various military barracks: but the people always found out where she was cached, and flowers, candles and votive offerings appeared as if by magic outside each new hiding place. For a long time Colonel Koenig refused to bury the mummy of Eva: some said he had fallen under her spell and used to sit up at nights talking to her as if to a lover, perhaps indeed having fallen in love with this masterwork of the embalmer's art. Eventually, under mysterious circumstances, the mummy was exhumed and smuggled out of the country to the Vatican by an Argentine priest, Father Rotger, aided by a posse of Italian priests well versed in the black arts of corpse vanishings. Finally, it seems, Koenig had managed to force himself to put to earth the mummy of Eva. 'I buried her standing because she was male,' he said later, and this vertical interment was confirmed, for when the mummy was examined in Rome the feet had been destroyed by the weight of the body forcing down on them. It was rumoured that even when buried, Eva had been consulted on various occult matters by the military, and burying her standing up made such consultations easier – the casket only had to be opened at the top, with a sort of cat-flap on hinges. Originally, Eva's mummy had been exhibited in a glass casket to her adoring public, her hands holding a rosary given her by the Pope; now her body vanished into limbo, finding its way by unknown means into Juan Perón's hands again in Madrid. After Eva's death, Juan Perón had made her brother Juancito fly to Switzerland and sign over her numbered accounts into his own, Perón's name; following this Juancito was conveniently killed in a car accident in Buenos Aires, and his skull ended up being used as a paperweight by Captain Grandi, a military official. Torture and bullfights had both been banned in Argentina in 1813, after the Spanish had been expelled. Perón reintroduced torture, including for women, especially to the genitals. His chief torturer was one Simon Wasserman, a Jewish police official. Like Stroessner, Perón was half-Indian. His mother was so dark that in the racially prejudiced Argentina of the era, she could not be presented in public. Perón had a sense of humour, however; when criticized for living with an actress – Eva was a famous star of the Argentine radio and cinema – he replied, 'Who do they expect me to sleep with – an actor?' He was just about to confiscate all the Catholic Church's property in Argentina, and turn the Cathedral in Buenos Aires into a social centre for trades unionists when he was overthrown. His antecedent – also of part-Indian descent – was Dr Francia, the first dictator of Paraguay after independence from Spain who successfully nationalized Church property, and said, 'If the Pope cares to come to Paraguay I shall do him no greater honour than to make him my personal confessor.' Dr Francia got away with it because he had eliminated all opposition from his rivals, and because Paraguay was so far away and so difficult to get to. Many people in Europe still do not know where the place is, including, presumably, the editors of the *Penguin History of Latin America*, who give the country a complete miss.

Stroessner observed all of Perón's antics and travails from up the river, and carried many of the murkier aspects of Peronism into practice himself in later years, particularly torture and the cult of the personality. There was even a 'Don Afredo Polka', the polka being the national dance, though nothing like a polka anyone in Europe has ever heard. Though the Paraguayans do not like you to say so, Paraguayan history sometimes seems to be a grotesque parody of what has already occurred down south. If the saga of Juan and Eva Perón reads to European eyes as a bizarre excursion into *Grand Guignol*, something from the pages of a magical realist novel by Gabriel García Márquez, it is worth noting that Márquez himself worked when a young man as a journalist on the Buenos Aires newspaper *Clarín* during the Perón years. To those who know South America at all, Márquez's fiction is closer to reality in that continent than many Europeans would credit.

The Paraguayan attitude to their neighbours the Argentines

was both complex and paradoxical. They professed to dislike and distrust them, but also, at some level, they admired and aped them. Their slang insult for them was 'pigskins', possibly because they were pink-skinned and hairy, like pigs; the Argentines responded by calling the Paraguayans 'redskins' and 'savages', but there were, of course, many intermarriages between the two peoples. Gabriella's mother had been an Argentine. '¡*Cuidado!*' she warned me, her voice rising. 'Be careful! ¡*Chantar!* You know this word? To boast, to brag, to bullshit, to bluff – all Argentines are the world's experts at *chantar*.'

I mentioned to her later that there was a possibility that an Argentine guide might be willing to take me into the interior in his jeep. 'He will cheat you,' she had said, though she didn't know him, and had heard nothing against him. To be an Argentine was enough. Not that she, nor anyone else I ever met had any enthusiasm for the Paraguayans, either. 'We overvalue foreigners, particularly Europeans,' Gabriella had told me. 'We Paraguayans do not trust each other. This is a land of false smiles and forced laughter. Many foreigners are taken in by this – the happy, smiling Paraguayan, true child of nature, and so on. Bullshit.' I had already noticed that everyone I spoke to had quite naturally disparaged the local climate, food, people and products. Nothing, it seemed, was as good as in Europe. Yet as an outsider this did not seem at all accurate to me. Few of the people I spoke to had actually been to Europe, and when I told them a few facts about the place they were alarmed, even horrified, and often even openly disbelieving.

The first, most obvious natural advantage Paraguay possessed was its mild sub-tropical climate, in which palms, bananas, oranges, lemons, limes, pineapples, sugar cane and hundreds of other exotic flowers, ferns and orchids flourished. The second was the great sense of space, and the complete absence of any sense of urgency or haste. The country was the size of Germany or California, and had very few people in it, mostly concentrated within a hundred kilometres of the capital; a third of the land area was still virgin forest, the rest agricultural or bush. Away from the towns you could stand on the top of a gentle hill – the country was very flat – and gaze around you 360 degrees and see nothing but forest and fields as far as the eye could see – no people, no houses, no roads. When I told Paraguayans that this was almost impossible in Europe, that we were densely packed, crammed in on top of one another, they were very surprised. When I told them also that in many places the government had the power to tell you what colour you could paint your front door, what type of windows you could or could not have in your house, what sort of tiles you could put on your roof, they were both amazed and indignant. 'That is tyranny!' they exclaimed. 'No Paraguayan would ever accept that. We may have a rotten political class, but they would never dare interfere with our private lives or property like that.' Many showed me by their expression that they were skeptical about what I told them of European restrictions and regulations – that you could not smoke in buses, trains or many restaurants, that the police photographed your car number plate and sent you a fine later if you went too fast, that the Customs in England could confiscate and crush your car if they felt you were bringing back goods from France they thought you might sell. 'Don Roberto, with courtesy and respect, of course, you must surely be mistaken – these things are impossible, inconceivable in a great continent of culture like Europe.' I told them that I lived in such a place of intense restrictions. It was called a Conservation Area, and any changes at all to the outside of my house – paint, door, windows, tiles – had to be approved by the local government council, in order to preserve the character of the area. 'How can you live like this? It is like being in a prison! No wonder so many poor Europeans come to Paraguay to live! We are free! We do what we want. Your house is not your own – it is the government's, evidently.' And moreover, I added, in Britain it was illegal for any private citizen to own a handgun. If you were caught with one you went to prison for three to five years. This was always the straw that broke the camel's back. I was obviously engaged in high-level *chantar*. Not to be able to own a pistol to protect your family from criminals? It was like saying to an Englishman that the ownership of handkerchiefs carried a three- to five-year gaol sentence, the two items being about as common as each other repectively in Paraguay and England.

After barely suppressed looks of complete disbelief someone would always ask, But why do people tolerate such restrictions – why do they not make a revolution? 'Because they – we are used to such government restrictions. The State is incredibly powerful in Europe, and it takes on more powers every year. The few that object sell up and leave quietly – they are welcome to go. For the rest they accept, they complain, they grumble – but they accept.' At this there would be shakings of heads and sighings of disapproval. 'Never in Paraguay – never in South America!' they always concluded. Indeed, the contrast between Europe and Paraguay could not be sharper. Paraguay was still in essence an 18th-century state, with a very small and almost completely powerless government. Life was dangerous, often violent, and there were many assaults and robberies, but there were very few constraints upon the individual's freedoms, including the freedom to starve, be unemployed, and live with no social security or health service. You could buy land, put up any sort of house, fly in and out of the country in your own plane, own firearms, pay no income taxes – and precious few other ones either. Private property was sacrosanct. To enter another's land without asking was to risk being shot as dead as a potential *malviviente*. Bureaucratic interference in people's lives was minimal. The state bureaucrats only turned up at the office once a month to collect their salaries. You could park, piss, smoke and drive where and how you wanted to.

The individual egotism and selfishness of the country could be gauged by its completely anarchic and manic driving on the roads. No one stopped for pedestrians or for any other reason either. If the police wanted to halt traffic they had to erect a barrier that would seriously damage vehicles if they drove into it. There were no safety nets to protect the old, the young or the infirm. The street children of Asunción had formed a Union, and they demonstrated frequently – on the streets, of course – for 'dignity and respect', and protested against a recent law which had sought to ban children under 14 from working. This edict caused great resentment, and thousands of children had protested that they were being denied the chance to support themselves. Like everything else, age in Third World countries and the West carried an entirely different freight of meanings. In Paraguay, as in Spain, the age of consent for sexual activity for girls was 12. In Paraguay, young ladies 'came out' on their fifteenth birthday – there were photographs in the local papers of these belles dressed up in white gowns and squired by their fathers at full dress Society balls. Life expectancy, so long we in the West are almost like Swift's Struldbruggs, and so short in the Third World, created quite different demands on people. In the West sexual activity among young people is discouraged for as long as possible, and seen by progressive middle-class adults as a bad thing, while in Paraguay it was encouraged and hastened in a land where a large family was one's only chance of survival in old age, and early, unexpected death was a frequent reality. To be a mother at 12 or 13, so shocking as to be seen as a social problem in the industrial West, was a simple reality of life in countries like Paraguay. In the moral panic that surrounds children's sexuality for many adults in England it is often forgotten that once England was itself a Third World country, where people bred early and died young. Shakespeare's Romeo was 14, one recalls, and Juliet 12 when their love affair took place. The Elizabethan audience had not been shocked. This had represented late-medieval reality.

*   *   *

Gabriella was the first Paraguayan I had met who had lived for an extended period in Europe, and who knew both cultures intimately. She had worked for the BBC World Service in London and her husband had worked in import-export. They had managed to save enough money to buy a small flat in a remote suburb of outer London. This, she told me, they rented out to a fellow South American. Like so many people from unstable economies with erratic currencies all over the world, a small stake in British real estate was a hedge against uncertainty at home. I asked Gabriella how she managed in Paraguay now that most of the local banks had collapsed. 'I only use my bank account in London,' she replied. 'I have never had an account here. I wouldn't trust any South American bank. When I want cash I put my UK plastic in the hole in the wall here, and draw out US dollars in cash.' This, I learnt, was quite common for middle-class South Americans in Uruguay, Paraguay, Argentina and Brazil. You had your bank account in Miami, in Dallas, in London, New York or the Cayman Islands; all your money you kept out of the local economy, because neither the currency nor the banks could be trusted. Those who had ignored this simple rule of financial security in Argentina and had trusted the government's one-peso-equals-one-dollar policy had lost their money when the government defaulted, devaluing the peso and freezing bank accounts.

The government had, in effect, stolen the people's money by reneging on their promise of parity. For the last two centuries South America had been a sink for capital. You could make money fast, but if you trusted the local banks or the local currencies you lost the lot, eventually. The ideal export product was cheap to make in South America and very expensive to sell for dollars or pounds abroad – hence the huge popularity of cocaine and marijuana as cash crops, and the fortunes made by processing and exporting these drugs in Paraguay and elsewhere. The whole country was dotted with illicit, hidden airstrips in remote places, where light aircraft – *avionettas* – landed and refuelled, carrying out drugs, contraband liquor and cigarettes, and carrying in guns, dollars and essential spare parts. These strips were constantly being discovered by the police, though very rarely were any planes intercepted. With extended fuel tanks fitted the standard light plane could reach Miami or Dallas – or private airstrips in the desert in Texas or Arizona – without having to land to refuel. The rich – and the criminal – all had private planes.

Since the arrival of the Spanish, and even before, South America had been a place of plunder. The great empires of the Aztecs and the Incas had been based, too, on military conquest and the exploitation of subject peoples; both of these tyrannies had practised extensive human sacrifice, the victims taken from subject and defeated peoples. This continent had long been a place where people imposed their will and seized what there was – gold, silver, slaves, sugar, cocaine; the products changed, but the economy of looting continued. It was normal and natural for South Americans to go into exile when things went wrong. The concept of life was still colonial, with strident nationalism in local politics, mirrored by a furtive, clandestine export of capital away from local risks – instability, revolution and chaos. When the time came to flee the exiles already had their money, their houses, their other lives in safe havens prepared abroad in safer places. Gabriella and her husband lived in Paraguay – but only just. Their capital, their property was in London. They rented in Asunción because it was not secure to own. Everything in Paraguay was very cheap to buy by US or European standards, and everything was up for sale. In the past, people had put their money into real estate because they didn't trust the local banks. Now they wanted to sell and go away again. Stroessner had been bad, but this pseudo-democracy where everyone was corrupt and everyone stole and no one was accountable was worse. You could buy houses, apartments in Asunción for half, for a third even of what people were asking, Gabriella told me. All the flights out to Miami and Dallas were booked up for months in advance, and the planes arrived all but empty. Gabriella and Hugo had shipped down some furniture from Miami when they came back. That could be sold quickly or shipped out again if things went wrong – Hugo had 'Italian papers' so they could always go to Italy, she told me. People in Paraguay talked of having 'papers', not of being a particular nationality. It was where you were allowed to live that counted. 'Life is easy in Paraguay, it is cheap and there are servants, but it could all go wrong very soon,' Gabriella told me. They had only been back a matter of months, and they were already thinking they might have to leave again. Almost unknown to the prosperous, secure peoples of the developed West, millions of the educated, the skilled, the able in the Third World live like this. In Sudan, in Albania, in Sierra Leone, Malaysia and Indonesia people watch nervously for the signs that some imminent collapse might be just round the corner. In Paraguay, the first casualty of any *coup d'état* would be the liberal media; there would be no place for a BBC reporter under a military dictator.

Before Stroessner came to power there had been a long, bitter civil war in Paraguay. As many as a third of the population had been killed – no one was sure how many had died. Lawlessness and banditry had been rife. Stroessner had taken over and enforced both peace and stability. Like Spain after the Civil War, the exhausted country had acquiesced. Yet with his peace came torture and institutionalized corruption, the eclipse of civic rights, and great injustice. As many as a third of the remaining population had fled abroad, mainly to Brazil and Argentina. Some had come back but many still stayed away. Paraguay was a risky place, but the safer countries they had fled to before, Brazil and Argentina were now themselves places of disorder, chaos and financial collapse. The press was full of massive banking scandals, directors who plundered their banks and then fled. In Argentina, the economic collapse had caused riots, kidnappings and massive unemployment. In a poll, 57% of young Argentines under 25 said they wished to leave the country as they had no faith in its future.

The world was divided into those countries everyone wanted to leave and those everyone wanted to get into. The latter group was very small, and mostly run by Anglo-Saxons or Scandinavians. Argentina, Paraguay and Brazil were all immensely rich – but then so was the Congo. There was no use in great mineral wealth, skilled and talented people, and bountiful natural resources if there was corruption, if everyone stole from everyone else. In such places your money, and in the end you and your family, were only safe somewhere else.

All over Asunción there were large, unfinished tower blocks, now rotting with decay. They had been overambitious for the scale of the city, clearly. Why had anyone ever put money into starting to build them? The price of entry into Paraguay during the *stronato* was investment in the local economy, Gabriella told me. The high-ups in the Colorado Party had owned construction companies which took the investors' money and ran up these partly completed structures, syphoning off most of the money into their bank accounts abroad, then simply abandoning them. Corruption under Stroessner became endemic and systematic. Even the very poorest had got into it. The '*hormigas*' as they were called, the ants, plied to and fro across the border with Brazil, smuggling goods to and fro by hand, in bags and cases, bribing the Customs each time. 'Contraband is the price of peace,' Stroessner said. Smuggling, bribery, corruption and illicit activities of all kinds became the bedrock of the economy. The country began to forget how to work. Once oranges, bananas, tropical fruit of all sorts had been grown commercially and exported to Brazil and Argentina. Now all these products were imported from Brazil, from Colombia. Under Stroessner everyone had been able to become a small-time *contrabandista*. One of the reasons for the complete absence of any coherent collectivist left opposition was the petit-bourgeois, small capitalist mentality that reached right down to street traders and Indians selling vegetables in the streets. There was no local car industry to protect in Paraguay, unlike Brazil and Argentina, so shiploads of second-hand cars came up the river, bought in job lots in the southern USA. And stolen cars poured across from Brazil, driven in from Sao Paulo, the Customs officials on both sides bribed. The contrast between the beggars on the streets, the mendicant cripples, the unmade roads, broken pavements and leaking water mains in Asunción, and the massed ranks of brand new BMWs and Mercedes was marked. The President and his wife were both alleged to drive cars stolen in Brazil – a local newspaper had exposed the story and printed photos of them getting out of the hot cars which had been hijacked from the streets of Sao Paulo. I mentioned J. K. Galbraith to Gabriella – she was a journalist after all – and suggested that his dictum of 'private affluence, public squalor' applied to contemporary Paraguay. She had heard of neither Galbraith nor his well-known equation. It was Gabriella, also, who denied that she knew the meaning of the word *'cacique'*, a term used all over the Hispanic world for a local political boss, but which came originally from a South American Indian derivation. I saw it printed in the local Asunción papers many times. The previous President of Paraguay, Carlos Wasmozy, was in gaol for four years, for having embezzled US$4 million – that was all they could find, anyway: a year for every million stolen. Getting corrupt officials into court at all was hard. *'Impunidad'* – impunity – was one of the problems. Bribery was so rife that a little well-spread money prevented much from coming into the open or, if it did come out, from anything being done to prosecute or convict. The ordinary policeman was paid US$100 a month – just $25 a week, the same as Gabriella paid her cleaning maid – and the police had not been paid for three months because the coffers of the State were empty, or so it was claimed. The prison guards had not been paid for a year. In the remote north of the country the press reported that these prison guards were being fed by the prisoners' families, who also brought food in for the inmates, who otherwise would have starved, there being no official funds to feed them. Under such circumstances corruption and bribery were inevitable. Wealthy prisoners who by bad luck found themselves in gaol soon managed to bribe their way out again: the papers frequently reported on such cases.

The question as to why no public servants had been paid for so long was easily answered: the government had run out of money, and if they simply printed more banknotes, as South American governments had in the past, they would fuel inflation and cut off the IMF and International banks as potential donors for further hard currency loans. 'You will have noticed how many of the waterpipes in the streets of Asunción are broken,' Gabriella had remarked. I had noticed. There were leaks everywhere, spilling out into the streets, flooding the pavements, a side effect of which was vigorous tree, shrub and weed growth beside the roads, among the cracked pavements, and even in the potholes of the lesser used streets. Asunción had been hacked out of sub-tropical jungle, and given half a chance the jungle would reclaim it again.

'The water company, State-owned, borrowed US$10 million for repairs from a US based international agency,' she continued. 'The construction company that got the contract was owned by the head of the water company's brother. A $10 million hole was dug in the ground, achieving nothing. No leaks were repaired. The hole was abandoned. *Obras inconcluidas* – "abandoned works" – should be the Paraguayan national motto. The $10 million disappeared abroad into offshore bank accounts. The water company officials have not been paid for more than a year. Now we have a large, useless hole, a $10 million debt, and a leaking water system. About a third of all the water is lost through leaks and broken pipes. Scientific tests have shown that the water is seriously contaminated – cholera and typhoid among other infections are in the system.' Before Stroessner there had been no piped water at all, just as there had been no airport, or paved, metalled roads. People had their own wells, or depended on water sellers who toured the capital with mule-drawn tanks. Now there were frequent electricity blackouts, and the petrol stations regularly ran out of fuel. Those who could afford them had emergency electricity generators. In spite of the fleets of stolen luxury cars, Asunción more closely resembled a decaying African city, falling apart after the European colonials left, than anywhere in Europe. Stroessner had attracted immigrants and capital because he accepted gangsters on the run, fraudsters, conmen, Nazi war criminals with stolen loot, and because he offered a stable, authoritarian government which built roads, created infrastructure, and limited corruption to himself and his cronies. Now he was gone what he built up was in no way maintained or replaced. Paraguayans had not paid for these things, foreigners had. They felt, like colonial peoples newly liberated, no debt to the past, no sense of possession. His successors were bent purely on looting the country and fleeing abroad with what wealth they could steal. According to a report in *Ultima Hora*, the only income the Paraguayan government now had was the monthly US$16 million from Brazil for hydroelectrical power Paraguay exported across the border. Without this sum the government would be completely bankrupt. Yet it was not enough to pay even the civil servants. There had been a plaintive letter published in the papers from Paraguay's ambassadors abroad. They, too, had not been paid for a year, and the rents on their embassies and residencies were in default. Unless money was forthcoming, embassies and residencies could soon be repossessed. This was all a minor nuisance for the few very rich in Paraguay, with their money abroad in offshore havens, their houses with tall walls built round them manned by armed guards, or sequestered on 200,000-hectare ranches. For the great majority of the country, it made life a grinding misery. Paraguay was potentially a very rich country, fertile and replete with mineral resources, yet so badly was it managed, and so feebly was it cultivated that it imported even basic foodstuffs. The supermarkets were full of goods brought in from Brazil, Argentina and Europe that could easily have been grown domestically.

'You cannot fire public servants in Paraguay,' Gabriella had told me. 'Once appointed, it is a job for life. Under Stroessner, the administration of the city of Asunción was carried out by 400 civil servants, who worked from 8.30am to lunchtime, then finished. They were all members of the Colorado Party. Although they worked slowly, and very easy hours, they did actually turn up and did actually work. Everything was kept in good repair, and new roads were laid, parks maintained and basic services ensured. Then, after Stroessner was ousted, the Radical Liberal Party managed to get into power in the Asunción local government. They could not fire the 400 Colorado Party civil servants, but they could hire 1,000 new civil servants – all Radical Liberal Party members. These are known as "*gnocchis*". There is a tradition in the River Plate countries, Uruguay, Paraguay and Argentina, that civil servants eat *gnocchi*, the Italian potato-based pasta, on pay day every month, usually the 29th of the month. It's an old tradition. In time, the civil servant who is purely a political appointee and merely turns up every month to collect his salary, became known as a *gnocchi*. This is how the political parties fund themselves – they reward their followers with civil service jobs when they are elected on the understanding that the party gets a kickback of between 50% and 90% of the placeman's salary. The *gnocchi* can have several jobs of this sort as all they have to do is turn up once a month to get the salary. Well, the Colorado civil servants naturally didn't turn up for work any more – they couldn't be fired, and Stroessner didn't frighten them now he was in exile. And the Radical Liberals didn't turn up because they were *gnocchi* and paying much of their salary back to the Party. So there was no civic administration and nothing got done and things started to fall apart. The disgusted citizens of Asunción voted out the Radical Liberals after this happened, and voted in a minor party who immediately appointed 1,000 of their own members on the same *gnocchi* principle. The local government now has 2,400 employees, none of whom turn up except to get their salaries. And none of them can be fired. As a result no maintenance work is done, no local taxes collected, and the infrastructure of the city is falling apart. And as there are no taxes collected, none of the civil servants have been paid for at least a year, sometimes longer.' The logic of all this, I had to admit, was inescapable.

A wave of nostalgia was now spreading for the 'good old days' of Stroessner when the firm hand had meant a degree of order and efficiency, and a level of corruption that now seemed positively moderate. *'Ya seria feliz y no sabia'* I had seen as a printed car rear-window sticker all over the city – 'then we were happy and we didn't know it'. Liberalization brought street crime, robberies, rapid inflation and a collapse of the infrastructure as well as the banks. Diphtheria, cholera, malaria, yellow fever, dengue and leprosy were all on the increase. There was no foreign exchange to import necessary drugs and medicines. Even the water supplies in the hospitals were polluted. 'Will you stay in Paraguay or go abroad again?' I asked Gabriella. She thought for a long time and gazed away from me into the middle distance. 'I don't know. We'd like to stay. It's much easier here than Europe. But if the chaos grows . . . I don't know.' 'Easier' meant cheaper, with servants, in a pleasant climate. 'Where would you live if you could?' I asked. 'Miami,' she replied without hesitation. 'It's a terrific city – culturally Hispanic but run by Anglo-Saxons, so everything runs properly. And so safe.'

Everything is relative. In England, Miami is a byword for violent crime, drugs, gangs and disorder. But from the perspective of Asunción it seemed as appealing as Switzerland. 'We need a government of honesty, austerity, and lack of corruption,' one Paraguayan had said to another in an *Ultima Hora* cartoon. 'That is to say, a foreign government,' his friend had replied. Gabriella gave me a list of useful contacts, people who would help give me an insight into the country – a radical priest, a German settler, a US drop-out living with a Paraguayan girl, and many others.

'Don't get too hopeful,' she cautioned me. 'You will be promised many things in Paraguay, and none of them will come to pass. There is much talk and almost no action. Everything that works here is run by foreigners – it has always been the case. This hotel is an island of German efficiency. If the Germans left Paraguay – and one in forty are of German descent – the country would go back to the jungle. And they are leaving, the foreigners, for Brazil, and Bolivia, those who can. The civil service wages bill consumes 87% of the government budget even when they have any money, which at present they don't. What the private sector doesn't provide simply doesn't get done. Government here equals a parasitic class which provides nothing.'

My own observations walking round Asunción confirmed the dereliction. In the municipal gardens there had been a man in rags sweeping leaves off the path with a cut palm branch. He wore no shoes and looked more like a tramp than a public servant. He took care not to disturb the beggars sleeping on the wooden slatted benches, on the grass, under the palm trees. There were very small children, from four upwards, who strolled about trying to sell chewing gum and sweets from cardboard trays. Lunatics from the local asylum wandered about aimlessly, cackling and grinning, dressed incongruously in old-fashioned evening dress – tailcoats, striped trousers, spats but no shoes – as a result of international charity clothing donations. The asylum had no money to feed the inmates, so they had been turned loose to wander the city and fend for themselves, scavenging rotting vegetables from the gutters, left by the Indian street sellers. They capered and loped about, these lunatics, distinctive in tailcoats stained by diarrhoea, adding a carnivalesque, grotesque note to the tropical dirt of the Central Business District. Neither the police nor anyone else paid the slightest bit of attention to them: like the vultures hunched on the telegraph wires, watching for a stray dog that had escaped attention, and the Makká Indians from the Chaco who drifted about in loincloths and painted cheeks, trying to sell bows and arrows, they were simply part of Asunción's dusty, stinking reality. In the air hung the smell of foetid, fermenting human excrement and urine; all these people were living, eating and eliminating in public, in a hot, humid tropical climate. They, like the street children and the beggars, slept in the parks. In daylight the streets were full of European-looking businessmen and their BMWs. At dusk these vanished to the suburbs, and the town centre became an ill-lit Indian-haunted place where *pistoleros* and whores roamed about and the police stayed mainly inside their fortified barracks. If the police had withdrawn completely the city would be given up to looting and uncontrolled violence: and the police had now not been paid for several months, and were extremely disgruntled. If the government could find no money to pay the police they would not suppress the next pro-Oviedo demonstration. And then there would be a revolution, democracy would be closed down, and a hard-line dictatorship set up again. Liberalization led to chaos and riot and so back to dictatorship again. It was like the ancient Greek city states, an endless swing between repression and licence.

All of this swirling, picturesque, smelly chaos was kept out of the Gran Hotel by high brick walls, 20 foot or more, and an armed guard at the entrance to the grounds with a machine-gun and stern glance who kept would-be intruders at bay. I had negotiated the room-rate down from US$100 a day to $40 a day, and thought I had done well. When I told Gabriella what I was paying she snorted, and went to harangue the middle-aged woman, once an ambassador's wife it was said, who managed the front reception. After a short altercation in Spanish, Gabriella informed me that as from today my room rate had been reduced from $40 to $30 a day, and when I went off into 'the interior' as the rest of the country was quite unironically referred to by the people of Asunción, the hotel would keep my room for me and all my luggage in it, ready for my return, at no charge to me. This was quite usual, Gabriella told me. 'There is almost no one staying here. They have dozens of rooms and almost no guests. They are lucky to have you.' The hotel was a pleasing old colonial affair in the Spanish style, with loggias and white stucco Tuscan columns, dark oxblood-red walls, roman tile roofs over verandahs. The windows had white-painted louvred shutters and the ceilings of the rooms were high, to keep the air cool. Each room opened out on to a courtyard garden planted with banana and citrus, bougainvillea and palms; ferns and bright orchids hung in baskets. The soil was dark red and the white-clad Indian gardeners moved about slowly, directing water, pruning, hoeing, weeding. When a guest passed them they stopped work, turned to face the passer-by and, smiling, said quietly, '*Buenos días, señor*'. This is how it must have been throughout much of Paraguay under Stroessner – calm, obsequious, well-ordered, the peons knowing their place. Now the Gran Hotel was an island of tranquillity in a sea of chaos and disorder. Behind the swimming pool lay a dusty tennis court, and beside this, shaded by trees, a tall metal cage which held two brightly coloured green parrots: at dusk these birds gave off terrible shrieks, as if heralding the end of the world. They were fed with cut-up fruits by the gardening staff – oranges, bananas, mangoes, and fresh leaves from tropical trees. They perched on one claw and slowly, delicately, nibbled at the fruit held in the other. There was also a large toucan in a separate cage on the other side of the swimming pool. This bird clambered up and down the wire, as if imprisoned in an adventure playground. He too lived on fruit provided twice a day, and was shy: if you looked at him, he avoided your gaze and trundled off, embarrassed, getting out of your eye line. Birds in cages always make me feel sad and depressed: not only do I feel sorry for the imprisoned birds, but it also reminds me of our own incarceration. I had felt oppressed and imprisoned in Europe, and now I felt oppressed and imprisoned in the gilded cage of this luxurious hotel and its grounds in Asunción. In Europe I could sit on a park bench in public, unnoticed and unthreatened – I was invisible. In Paraguay I felt unsafe in all public spaces. The eyes that searched me over were not friendly. It was noticeable that Paraguayans of European extraction spent as little time as possible in public spaces, passing through them in cars, usually, whereas the mestizo and Indian population, on foot, seated or sprawled on the ground, lived at ease in these spaces. My race, my pale skin made me an intruder.

Behind my room, in a small courtyard garden into which one could wander, was another prison, a small menagerie with hoopoes, cranes, two small monkeys in a cage, a couple of miniature deer of the muntjak type, and a large terrapin. As menageries go this was deluxe – leafy, calm, shady and private – but like the hotel, it was still a prison. The trees and shrubs in this small haven were dense and in deep shadow for much of the day. The birds and animals were so well hidden that you could be almost on top of them before you saw them. And everywhere, in the gardens, in the air, all around one, was Paraguay's spectacular birdlife – on the wing, perched in trees, darting between bushes, a rich burble of song. Like Manaos in the Brazilian Amazon region, Asunción was a small city in a clearing in the middle of the jungle. For thousands of miles in every direction there was nothing but largely empty countryside – empty that is of human activity. For the birds flying across Asunción, or attracted by the food, the several acres of gardens the hotel offered to them was just more native jungle as a convenient stop-over. Living in the depleted, overpopulated Northern Hemisphere where any signs of wildlife are rare and fugitive, I found the explosion of bird noise in Paraguay startling and sobering. It was evidence of what we had lost by our overbreeding. Perhaps Europe had been like this in the Middle Ages. It was a real pleasure just to sit in a cane chair outside my room looking at and listening to the birds. The only thing I can compare it to is being inside a tropical aviary at a zoo. Tiny hummingbirds smaller than the first joint on my thumb, rainbow coloured with iridescent green the dominant shade, hovered and darted by a hibiscus plant, long thin beaks moving inside the flowers to search for drops of water or nectar. I would sit for timeless periods, completely enraptured by the sight, the wings of this tiny dynamo revolving thousands of times every second, so fast all one saw was a blur, whirling beside the tiny body. The birds seemed completely indifferent to the ghost-clad gardeners who shuffled slowly to and fro, or to the few guests, who like me, sat outside in the shade drinking in this tranquil atmosphere. Overpopulation, pollution, the depleted environment are realities of our era; to come to somewhere like Paraguay was to realize just how much had been lost.

I walked back with Gabriella to her house, which was less than ten minutes away on foot: it was a small, neat semi-detached building with a thin strip of garden in front and a larger one behind. Workmen were engaged in some maintenance at the front. The whole neighbourhood was tidy and prosperous-looking, with well-kept gardens, lush shrubbery, and clean streets. It reminded me of middle-class parts of Los Angeles. I asked Gabriella which suburb of London it most resembled, as she knew both cities well. 'Kensington,' she replied immediately. 'It is where the embassies are and where the wealthy live.' I asked her what her house would be worth. 'Normally US$60,000, but because so many people are trying to sell, you could get a place like this for $40,000 – even for $30,000. People are only paying about half the asking price at the moment.' To put this in perspective, Gabriella was paying her maid $25 a week: 'and my mother thinks I am paying her too much – she only pays $15.' High unemployment, low wages, few people, inexpensive land and property, high crime and insecurity, imminent risk of political violence and revolution – it was a familiar Third World equation.

Gabriella invited me in to meet her husband Hugo, and their two small children. Hugo told me he had invested some money in a cigar-making concern, a factory dating back to the turn of the century. 'Paraguayan tobacco is good – not as good as Cuban, but close. We use Javan leaf for the wrappers, the rest is all local product.' How much did the local cigars cost? I asked. I had seen none on sale anywhere. 'That is because they are too expensive for most Paraguayans to buy now,' he replied. 'About US$2 each.' Cigarettes cost US$7 a carton of 200 even in my local supermarket. I assumed the smuggled items, or false brands were even cheaper. Paraguayan men were ferocious smokers. The local brands I had seen advertised promised exotic pleasures. There was 'Boots' (not, alas, 'Old Boots') featuring a US style cowboy. There was 'Palermo' (a wealthy suburb of Buenos Aires, as well as a city in Sicily). The slogan for Palermo was *Paraguayo y con orgullo*' – 'Paraguayan and with pride'. The poster showed a racing car, and a racing driver, fag in hand. Then there was 'Derby Club' a contentious blend, much copied, imitated, falsified and smuggled, a favourite of the contrabanders trade, according to press reports. Truck-loads of 'Derby Club' were frequently discovered crossing the Brazilian border, without the required tax stamps on them. There was also 'York' and 'US Mild'. In the local whisky line I particularly liked 'Olde Monke' and 'Gran Cancellor'. Close inspection of the labels of the locally manufactured whiskies indicated that they had been made from a base of sugar cane – in fact were really rum dressed up as whisky. The local rum, called *caña*, was a working-class peasant tipple with macho associations. Alcoholism among the peasants and Indians was a serious problem; drunken all-male rum sessions often ended in knife fights and death, 80% of all killings in Paraguay were caused by *armas blancas* – knives or machetes.

Hugo was a fan of Paraguayan *dolce far niente*. 'You cannot imagine how pleasant it is, Robert, for a man just to lie back in a hammock in the garden with a cigar all afternoon, just looking up at the clouds passing in the sky.' While your wife and the maid do all the work, I thought, but did not say. The work ethic appeared to have scant appeal to Paraguayan men. All across the city they were sitting, sprawling, lounging or completely prone, in a state somewhere between sleep and coma. What little work was being done seemed to be entirely by women, who looked as if they monopolized about 95% of all available energy – men slumped, women bustled. Hugo invited me to visit his cigar factory. 'You can buy the cigars at the special reduced employees price,' he told me. Like most other promises I was made in Paraguay this invitation came to nothing. Despite several requests neither the visit nor the cigars materialized. Did they exist? Was the whole thing a fantasy? Perhaps he just did spend all his days in a hammock, gazing up at the sky. More concretely, Gabriella cooked macaroni cheese for supper, which I shared with them, along with a bottle of Argentine red wine called 'Borgoña', which tasted nothing like Burgundy. 'Believe no one in Paraguay,' Gabriella had told me, 'believe nothing you cannot see or touch – this is a land of make-believe and fantasy – of *chantar.*'

I walked back to the Gran Hotel through the warm, velvety, shadow-strewn tropical night, the scents of the flowers and shrubs rising from the gardens around me along my way. Above hung the Southern Cross, that constellation which reaffirms that one is truly in the Southern Hemisphere. The petrol station at the crossroads at Avenida España was still open, and a lone soldier, the night shift, stood on duty, rifle at the ready, guarding the pumps. I turned off down a side lane, and walked a hundred yards away from the main road, the wine and the soft air having relaxed me. It was a mistake. The lane became dark, the surface under my feet was pitted and potholed. From a group sitting under a clump of trees a hundred yards further on, a man rose and lurched towards me. I was coming from the light of the main road and would be silhouetted clearly. He started to shout incoherently, angrily, at me, stumbling as he tried to run towards me. Out of the shadows I saw he had a machete, which he waved at me from above his head.

I turned abruptly, and made a fast trot back the way I had come, back towards the main road, and the petrol station with the lone soldier. I could hear the drunk behind me yelling and shouting at me now in incomprehensible Guarani. The lights of the main road grew nearer. I put on speed. I was sweating now, from the heat of the night and from fear. I was running. I could hear the man behind me, still coming on after me. If I slipped and fell, I would be done for. I ran really fast, faster than I had run for years. I got a sharp stitch in my side. I gasped for breath. Still I could hear the drunk lumbering behind me, breathing hard. The petrol station came in sight, well-lit, the soldier standing at ease, leaning on his rifle. I turned. The man was behind me, in shadow: he had stopped. He had seen the soldier, too. To chase a man at night in the streets of Asunción, waving a machete, was an invitation to be shot dead by anyone in uniform. The drunk mouthed angrily at me, but in silence, waving his weapon over his head, but he didn't come on any further. Now would be the time to shoot him, I thought, if I had a gun. But then, of course, the soldier would shoot me. The drunk took a swig of rum from the bottle which he still held in his other hand, swallowed, and then spat at me silently, in disgust. I turned back and ran on, more slowly. In a moment I was under the arc of light by the petrol station forecourt, a recent model BMW being filled up by the uniformed attendant, a European-looking man in an expensive suit sitting at the wheel. I paused, slowing to a walk, and caught my breath. I turned to see what my pursuer was up to. He had completely vanished, swallowed up in the shadows behind me, invisible. I walked slowly back to the Gran Hotel now, keeping in light the whole way, my chest heaving. The margin between safety and danger in Asunción was just a few yards.

In spite of the tight-meshed flyscreen covering the windows of my room, some insects always managed to get inside. Tonight was no exception. On my pillow was a magnificent golden and black bug, crawling slowly about, lost on the great white pasture of cotton. I put this intruder in a matchbox carefully, so as not to damage it, and ejected it into the night. I felt a humanist European completely out of place in the teeming South American interior.

Breakfast was a buffet served in the grand ballroom, its ceiling painted with frescos of tropical birds and foliage, 19th century in style and execution. Sicilian painters had been imported by Madame Lynch, I was told, to carry out this work. It would take a sophisticated, European sensibility like Eliza Lynch's to think of reproducing what was just outside the ballroom – tropical foliage and birds – inside the ballroom, on the ceiling. It was an artifice of nature present a few feet away outside: only to an émigré European's eyes would such a ceiling decoration seem exotic. Madame Lynch was the first person in the post-colonial era to see the immense possibilities of Paraguay. To Francisco Solano López, her lover and protector, she promoted the idea of the country as a place to improve, to embellish, to make chic and elegant. No one had conceived of Paraguay in this way before, it had simply been a colony to exploit. Under her influence all the imposing buildings, self-consciously imperial, were begun – the opera house based on La Scala, Milan, the copy of Les Invalides, the huge Presidential Palace, the tropical Gothic railway station. Most of them were never finished – she and López were people in a hurry, new people, on the rise, imitating that tornado of newness, Napoleon Bonaparte, patron saint of all pushy, power-hungry arrivistes who have decided to live by will power and naked force. Napoleon had proved you could do it all, come from nowhere – Corsica, to be precise – seize power with a whiff of grapeshot, eliminate your rivals, rule by sheer energy and dash, conjure an empire out of thin air, become a king maker and breaker, institute an aristocracy of merit and favour, these all new people who had more energy and more to lose than the old aristocracy of blood. And you could do it all in a few years, if you

61

drove people hard enough. Stucco was made for this style of rule. It looked like marble, or stone, or whatever you wanted to have it look like. And it went up so quickly – you just laid mudbricks or rubble walls, and then coated it and smoothed it down and painted it – presto! It looked just like ancient Rome. Peter the Great, another imperial arriviste, had used stucco to create his own fantasy of European civic grandeur, St Petersburg: take a dash of Venice, a draught of Amsterdam, add some London, and some Rome – and there you have it. In a few years, with enough slave labour and a few second-rate European architects – for who outside Russia has ever heard of Rastrelli, Hamilton or any other of Peter's experts – you had a brand new 'European' capital on the Gulf of Finland.

Against all the odds the adventurer Napoleon III had actually erected another ramshackle empire in France, a country that had completely lost its way after the revolution of 1789, which would try all and every system of government, one after the other, in case one might actually work for more than a few years. Solano López had been immensely impressed with the Second Empire in France, which he had seen for himself on his European Grand Tour: Madame Lynch was a product of its frenetic decadence, its squalid energy, its sense of nervous excess and self-conscious cultivation – the bombastic new opera houses, the Baron Haussmann-designed avenues in Paris, the braying brass bands and the opulent uniforms of army officers; and the Zouaves, that orientalist military fantasy in baggy pantaloons, floppy fezzes and curled-up slippers – a corps just made for Verdi opera, harking back to Napoleon I's Mamelukes from Egypt. All this López admired deeply and tried to imitate in Paraguay, where he could. If there were not enough men to enslave to build his new palace, well then, he would use child slave labour. To see what López and Lynch had in mind for Asunción it is only necessary to go to the spa town of Vichy, in France, for here Napoleon III, with his foreign architects, many of them English, created an eclectic, imperial yet Ruritanian pleasure-capital, small but with the flamboyance and grandeur of a capital city, right in the middle of nowhere, well away from cities such as Paris with revolutionary mobs. If López and Lynch had simply stuck to Paraguay, forgoing the dreams of conquering Uruguay, Brazil and Argentina, they would have created a complete mid-19th-century tropical-Gothic version of Vichy, and very extraordinary it would have been, too. Imperial overreach on a massive scale meant nothing was ever completed. What does remain – the Parisian-style parks, the ruinous stucco palazzi, the defunct railway station – are impressive enough: no Grand Tour ever bore such strange fruit, so far from anywhere. There are doubters, of course. Alwyn Brodsky, the American biographer of Eliza Lynch, among others, claims that the Gran Hotel was never Madame Lynch's country residence at all, that the whole story has been cooked up as a publicity stunt by the hotel's owners. Hard facts on which everyone can agree were always in short supply in Paraguay; more or less everything was up for debate. There were versions of events, narratives, claims, counter claims, refutations. The outsider became embroiled in these arguments, willy-nilly. What one person told you the next would vehemently deny. Reality was slippery.

Madame Lynch was the mistress and *éminence grise* to Mariscal Francisco Solano López, the third of Paraguay's dictators after his father Carlos Antonio López (*el fiscal* – the magistrate), and the founding father Dr Francia (*el supremo* – the supreme one). All of Paraguay's dictators had earned soubriquets: Solano López had been *el mariscal* (the Marshal) and Stroessner was *el rubio* (the blond). If Oviedo ever came to power he would inevitably be *el bonsai* – people called him that already – unless it was *el loco* which he was called, too. Beyond simple description no one could agree about anything Madame Lynch had done. For the Colorados she was a national heroine, whereas the Radical Liberals saw in her a manipulative exploiter who bled Paraguay white, along with Solano López, whom they viewed as a criminal lunatic. Both of these ambiguous historical figures had been co-opted by Stroessner and his regime, and the cult of their heroism promoted assiduously. Madame Lynch's remains had been brought back from Père Lachaise cemetery in Paris and buried in La Recoleta in Asunción. The man who had organized this transshipment, a Lebanese-Paraguayan, had profited from the occasion to import a large quantity of hashish in the coffin with the remains of *Madama*.

Often called 'Irish', Eliza Lynch claimed to have been born in County Cork of Ascendency, Protestant parentage, and educated in Paris. She was a woman of cultivation and taste, speaking French, Spanish and Guarani with fluency, and played the piano, sang and danced with distinction. She had attached herself to López in Paris when he had been Ambassador at large in Europe, arriving with a substantial entourage and ample funds, the first the independent Paraguay had sent across to Europe. López had made the Grand Tour through France, Italy, England and the Crimea, where he observed the war in progress. In France he collected Napoleonic uniforms for his army officers, and from England guns and steamships supplied by the London firm of Blyth Brothers, who were also to send out a stream of technicians to Paraguay which enabled López to build up his army, navy and arsenal quickly enough to take on the three other regional powers all at once, very nearly beating them. López and Lynch returned to Paraguay with a complete kit for DIY imperial splendour – Sèvres and Limoges china sets, a Pleyel piano, fabrics, sewing machines, books, pictures, manuals of etiquette and court ritual, ladies' maids and dancing masters, curtains, furniture and antimacassars. López actually went as far as to have a golden crown designed and sent out from France, but it was intercepted at Buenos Aires, and he never managed to have himself crowned Francisco I – even though he was referred to as such in some outlying provinces of Paraguay. Considered a great beauty, Eliza Lynch was the first modern career-blonde to arrive from Europe in South America with a mission, and a protector with enough money and political clout to make her ascent possible. Eva Perón, native-born South American, trod very much in the footsteps of Madame Lynch. Both of them were reputed to have been common whores working in brothels in their youth.

Madame Lynch created a sensation among the Guarani Indians, to whom she seemed an embodiment of the Virgin Mary. To the Creole elite of old Spanish blood she was an interloper, and a *putana* – a whore. They refused to recognize her, and eventually, when López got into his stride, were exterminated for their pains. López already had a wife and children established before he left for Europe and the new, big ideas he imbibed over there. *Madama*, as Lynch became known, was set up in style by López in Asunción, and formed her own alternative Court in her houses, which she decorated and furnished in the latest Parisian style. She was the cynosure of wit, elegance and art in a backward provincial capital that was nothing more than a village by a clearing in the jungle on the river. She came into her own when López senior died and Francisco Solano took over supreme power. López and Lynch turned the Pygmalion story upside down – Dr Higgins the rustic hayseed instructed by the sophisticated Parisienne Eliza Doolittle. Paraguay has always been, it would seem, a country of strong, capable women and weak, vain, indolent, incapable men. Whatever small quantity of sense Solano López may ever have had seems to have been provided by his mistress, though her detractors claim that it was her evil genius which spurred him on in his disastrous military and imperial ventures. The idea of becoming Emperor of Paraguay was not particularly absurd; there were in existence two new-minted empires – Brazil and France – as well as the older Russian, British, Austro-Hungarian and Turkish imperia. The fall of Napoleon III's empire saw the creation of a German empire to replace it. Nor was defeating Argentina, Uruguay and Brazil particularly ambitious. They were all weak, poorly led and disorganized. The problem was that Solano López was consumed with vanity and egotism, trusted no one, and set about killing off his family and anyone in Paraguay of any ability and competence. Had he done nothing, and let his generals, British technical experts and brave soldiers simply attack the enemy, there is little doubt he would have defeated them and become Emperor of southern South America.

What is not in doubt is that Madame Lynch introduced into Paraguay an element of courtly style, of elegance, of well-dressed chic which had never been seen before, and which among the upper classes, survives and flourishes to this day. Paraguay, under her aegis, became a place of masked balls, river-boat picnics with brass bands in attendance, elaborate full-dress evening dances, classical music concerts, theatrical and opera performances, and champagne suppers. Everything had to be shipped up the river, and before that across the Atlantic from France, but neither time nor distance was any hindrance to the dandies and belles of either the 18th or 19th centuries. The details of all the wine imported by Thomas Jefferson from Château Margaux to his estate in Virginia still exist today in the Bordeaux archives. The Madame Lynch belle-of-the ball legacy lives on vibrantly today, and one of the startling features which elevates Paraguay from, say, the Congo, which in other ways it closely resembles, is the old-fashioned chic and elegance of the rich in Asunción, who still dress in long white gowns, full evening dress, starched shirts and tailcoats, and attend high-society balls with bands, masters of ceremony, sprung ballroom floors and all the other appurtenances of courtly behaviour now more or less a memory in Europe. The Society pages of *Ultima Hora* revealed a social Asunción which looked like Paris before the First War – pearls, tiaras, wing-collars, black or white tie, patent leather shoes, full orchestras in uniform – all a thousand miles up the river and in the sub-tropical jungle. At the Gran Hotel I was witness to all this, for every weekend some celebration would be mounted in the ballroom: Strauss waltzes would echo from the Indian orchestra in dress uniform, and the belles of Asunción would trip the light fantastic while outside waiters in white-starched uniforms with cummerbunds would circulate with canapés and champagne on silver trays held high over their heads. The debutante balls of the season were all lovingly photographed and reported in the Society pages, everyone's name printed in full; it made light relief after the litanies of crime, corruption and bankruptcy on all the other pages.

Asunción's bizarre elite were really too much. In a city where so many were almost starving there were no less than four Tiffany's jewellery shops, and the company was doing so well that they could afford to take out full-page advertisements in the papers promoting their latest imported deluxe items from New York. Whether she had or had not lived in the old *estancia* that had become the Gran Hotel, all this was certainly the result of Eliza Lynch's meteoric passage through Paraguay. Without doubt she and López and their Court would have danced here, for it would have been one of the few ballrooms in the city of that time able to accommodate large parties. It was somehow very Paraguayan to have breakfast under an artificial, painted tropical sky, installed by émigré Sicilians, when outside through the open french windows real Paraguayan tropical birds sat in real tropical foliage, fed from time to time by indigenous Guarani servants. I was reminded of the old Chinese saying: 'Is Chuang-zu dreaming of the butterfly, or is the butterfly dreaming of Chuang-zu?'

Five

Paraguay, Champion of America

The census had not been a success, according to the press. Incomplete, notorious disorganization, several suburbs of Asunción left out completely the journalists all reported. Perhaps it had all been as inefficient under Stroessner, only then no one would have known, because in those days the press had been allowed to report nothing but peace, progress and order – the regime's apt motto, reflecting three much desired qualities in Paraguayan life, and notable mainly for their complete absence in the post-Stroessner polity. The students who had actually carried out the census with their clipboards and serious expressions, knocking on individual doors and demanding entrance, like latter-day emissaries of King Herod, had been paid 5,000 guaranis for their day's work, sometimes only 2,500 guaranis. A bus ticket in Asunción cost 1,300 guaranis. Everyone had been restricted to their place of residence all day long, forbidden to take to the streets, which was why I had received so many sidelong glances and felt so much discomfort when I was busy striding about the town taking photographs.

Now at last, it seemed, the country had won an international accolade. According to Transparency International, Paraguay was the third most corrupt country in the world, after Bangladesh and Nigeria, and the most corrupt in the Americas, ahead even of Haiti and Colombia. Less corrupt than Paraguay were Angola, Azerbaijan, Uganda, Cameroon and Kazakhstan, among others. The least corrupt countries were Finland, Denmark and New Zealand, in that order. Corruption in Paraguay was not individual or sporadic, it was institutional and endemic. Nothing could be done without bribes at every level, from the simple policeman manning a roadblock to a cabinet minister approving a government contract. Anyone in a position to milk money from the system did so. The country's economic plight was spelled out in its depressing list of negative statistics. There was a US$2,200 million external debt, the interest on which could not be paid, and a US$305,000 million budget deficit. Out of a total population of 6 million, 200,000 people were employed in the public sector, most of them unpaid for months or even years; 15.3% of the population was 'openly employed', 22% officially unemployed. There was an 8% illiteracy rate and 81% of the population had no health insurance. There was, of course, no government health service whatsoever; 33.7% of the population fell below the official poverty line of $25 a week and 16% (900,000) existed in extreme poverty, with no source of formal income at all. The most startling imbalance was the tiny proportion of public service workers – less than 3.3% of the population. In Welfare State Europe this figure stood at 45% or 50% of the population. But to employ so many people in the public services you had to tax people heavily – Europeans paid more than 50% of their incomes in direct taxes, pension levies and national insurance contributions, and then again on sales taxes, VAT and indirect taxes on such things as fuel, tobacco and alcohol. In Paraguay there was virtually no tax at all, which was what made it such a paradise for the rich. Huge tracts of Paraguay's real economy were illegal – smuggling, drug processing and export, arms trafficking, fake cigarette manufacture and sale, car theft, cattle rustling and extortion, money laundering and the government cheating on contracts. The government was simply bypassed by private enterprise – criminal and legal – and the administration was too feeble and corrupt to do anything about it. Paraguay was a classic Third World kleptocracy, bankrupt but enormously wealthy, all the money kept out of the country in hidden bank accounts in untraceable offshore havens. When Belgrade was being bombed by NATO and accused of alleged sanctions-busting during the Kosovo war, the then President of Serbia, Slobodan Milošević, commented that they really ought to be bombing the Cayman Islands, as that was where all the sanctions-busting was actually going on. Similarly, it would be futile trying to chase the missing billions in Paraguay as it was all hidden offshore.

The blame for the ruin of this rich and fertile country was laid squarely at the door of the Colorado Party by local historian Mida Rivarola.

The economic model invented by Stroessner turned a country that had been an exporter of agricultural products into an economy dominated by smuggling, crime and primitive State protectionism. When this model was exposed to more modern economies due to changes in the world it simply collapsed leaving poverty and corruption at every level.

Ultima Hora had produced a crime map of the country – drug smuggling, contraband, cattle rustling, piracy, marijuana cultivation, car theft, highway robbery, banditry, north, south, east and west, the whole of Paraguay was one large crime zone. Only bank robberies were in short supply, for most of the banks had closed, gone bust, or were defended by private security guards who looked like militiamen in flak jackets, armed with bazookas and heavy machine-guns. The streets of Asunción and other provincial cities were, from time to time, full of protesters complaining of all this. Mostly these demonstrations were peaceful, but they seemed to do no good: they belonged to the politics of theatre, the essentially futile statement in noisy collective form that people were unhappy with their lot, with the government, with the facts of Paraguayan life. No one had any answers or even any ideas except to borrow more money from the IMF, or to reimpose a dictatorship under Oviedo which, it was hoped, would at least limit the corruption to the Colonel and his cronies as in the days of Stroessner. The situation was almost beyond analysis, let alone solution. No one even talked of a Castroist, extreme socialist solution. For years young Paraguayans had been sent to Cuba to be trained as doctors. The Cubans hoped to induct them into revolutionary fervour: the opposite had been the result. They had all come back with horror stories of socialism in action. Even the bitterest critics of the Colorado regime admitted that Castroism was a dead loss and a cul de sac. There was no guerrilla movement like the FARC in Colombia, no potential President Chavez, a nativist anti-gringo rabble rouser, as in Venezuela. Paraguay was a pirate state, full of pirates, who complained only because the chief pirates were stealing all the booty, and they were getting little or none. The writer Jorge Luis Borges had wondered if his country's fate might have been better if Argentina had become a British colony after 1820, when the Spanish had been expelled and the River Plate region fell under the economic influence of the British Empire. This reflection was made during the years of the repressive military regime in which everything had gone to the bad. 'Colonies are so boring, though,' he had concluded. Better then, in South America, to be theatrically badly governed than boringly well governed.

The great unanswered question hanging over the whole Third World is still the one posed by Goethe: 'Injustice is preferable to disorder.' What the colonial world had thrust upon it by the European powers had been injustice and order, which in almost all cases had been replaced upon independence by injustice and disorder. Asked if he thought India would be better governed after the British had left, Gandhi replied, 'No, it will be worse governed.' That had been a brave as well as an accurate prediction. A refugee white South African academic, safe in London, had moralized to me that it was 'essential for Africans to make their own mistakes' and learn from them, that colonialism only mollycoddled people.

He, of course, did not have to suffer the effects of those mistakes, as he had fled, but he was happy to condemn the rest of the continent's population to the Idi Amins, the Robert Mugabes and the Mobutus, as an inevitable learning curve. With freedom had come disorder, and injustice in another form. A new, native ruling class had formed, corrupt, authoritarian, immune from Western liberal criticism, more oppressive in most cases than the old white supremacists. Most ex-European colonies were in a far worse state than they ever had been under direct colonial rule. The democracies imposed on them by the parting masters had all failed and been replaced by despotism, oligarchy or anarchy. In some cases, after years of fruitless civil wars and disorder, that quintessential postmodern phenomenon, the failed state, had emerged. Paraguay was not yet a failed state, not quite: but it was not far off one.

Walking round Asunción it was evident that the fabric of the city was collapsing: garbage was uncollected, streets and pavements lay broken and unrepaired, buildings were not just unpainted and peeling, but crumbling apart, showing cracks and bulges in the walls. The dead banks, great glass and concrete mausolea, lay silent and empty, front doors chained and padlocked outside, dust and emptiness within. Groups of Indians from the Chaco, or simply homeless, poor people had taken up residence on strips of cardboard in their doorways – shelter at least from the tropical downpours. The local markets had spilled out on to the pavements, and the streets were full of rotting vegetables and fruit. A whole tribe of people lived by scavenging from this bounty. All around the centre of the city vendors had set up shop on the pavements, selling cans of food, bottles of wine, packets of biscuits – all imported. The hotels in the centre of town were completely empty. I went inside to talk to the receptionists who were pretty, smiled a lot, and had time on their hands. They all told the same story: 'No one comes here now. Before, under Stroessner, there were tourists. Now nothing.' Cruise ships used to come up the river from Buenos Aires for winter breaks, duty-free shopping expeditions. Now Argentina was broke, and Brazil was in deep trouble, too; no boats with tourists came any more. Asunción had become too dangerous. Right in the centre of town knife-wielding robbers held up buses, one man with a blade at the throat of the driver, the other passing down the bus collecting the passengers' watches and wallets. On one such attack there had been an army major in uniform on board, a woman. She had had her face slashed. These attacks were happening all the time, every day, not at night in remote suburbs, but in the very centre in broad daylight. People were afraid to use the buses. Taxis were known to be used to kidnap people for ransom, or simply to rob and 'disappear' them. Many people walked, even long distances, rather than risk public transport, and I was one of them. The city was just about small enough to get around on foot. Everywhere, though, there was the same atmosphere of suspicion and mistrust. Each small shop had its assistant with a large automatic pistol. When they opened the cash box to get you your change their free hand would be on the pistol, finger curled round the trigger, in case you tried something. There were attempted robberies of these small stores every day, and shoot-outs leading to deaths. Every transaction, however small – a tube of toothpaste, a razor, a comb – involved a hand-written receipt with a carbon copy left in the receipt book: this was so the assistants could not steal from the till. The owners checked the takings against the carbon every evening and made sure the sums tallied. There were no smiles of welcome in any of the shops, rather wary caution or outright hostility.

That there had once been order and a degree of security was evident from the style of houses put up during the *stronato*. These were US-style villas or suburban bungalows with large windows and low fences, symbols of trust in the security the regime provided. Under Alfie a virgin could walk the streets of Asunción dressed in gold jewellery and risk no harm, people had told me, people who had opposed the old regime and hated the dictatorship. Then, everyone had been terrified of falling into the hands of the police. Now people had rights, but no duties. Improvised security precautions had been tacked on to these vulnerable homes of the Pax Stroessner era – iron grills on the doors and windows, razor wire on hastily erected high walls and steel fences, video security cameras and snuffling, whining guard dogs kept on short rations to make them hungry for burglar flesh. In all this I was again reminded of Los Angeles, with its neat notices in the gardens of dinky gingerbread cottages promising an armed response if you trod a step across the lawn.

The amenities of a capital city were absent in Asunción. There were no proper bookshops, only kiosks selling comics and religious kitsch. You could buy no foreign newspapers at all, anywhere. There were no coffee shops or bistros where you might relax in comfort and security. The park benches were filled with sleeping men, some of them police in uniform, and the parks themselves stank of human piss and shit and were full of rubbish. Concerts, recitals, theatrical peformances, art exhibitions were all absent; the few cinemas showed kung fu movies or sadistic pornography. There was one theatre show, I discovered, the English play *The Vagina Monologues*. It was a Buenos Aires production, and for macho Argentina the title had been redubbed *The Secrets of the Penis*. This was too daring for staid Asunción, and here it was running under the title *The Secrets of the Male*.

Although there were a few lurking stray dogs, with claw marks on their backs from unsuccessful vulture attacks, there were no stray cats at all – they were no match for the beady-eyed, telegraph-wire-perching birds of prey. A cat would only last a matter of minutes out of doors, I had been told; those that existed in Paraguay led cosseted, prison-like existences indoors, not unlike their owners. Small babies were never allowed out for the same reason – they would be snatched up from pram or cradle and torn apart and devoured in an instant. The man lost and waterless in the Chaco always saved the last bullet for himself, before the vultures tore his eyes out while he was still alive, but too far gone to defend himself. In the centre of town, by day, the police were about in force, lounging like the rest of the population, but kitted up in macho uniforms, with low-slung, black-holstered pistols. This fearsome image was assuaged to a great extent by the policemen's girlfriends, who also hung about with them, talking softly and weaving roses and other flowers into their caps and uniforms with one hand, while holding their beaux' hands with the other. These clumps of cops and lovers were particularly thick around the government buildings on the main plaza. One *coup d'état* had already been foiled and the Vice-President had been assassinated. No one knew who did it, so the authorities called in Scotland Yard, perhaps hoping that Sergeant Lestrade or Sherlock Holmes would be sent out to uncover the truth. From time to time passion would overcome the couples of policeman and lover, and they would detach themselves from the rest and make for a hot-bed hotel where you could hire a room by the hour. There was a constant traffic of heavily armed cops up and down the stairs of these establishments. As they hadn't been paid for so long I assumed they had a good credit rating. It was probably not a good idea to deny tick to a Paraguayan cop.

In the centre of town, on the main street, was a *ranchero's* outfitters; here you could kit yourself out completely with everything you needed to take on the Paraguayan *estancia* – leather chaps, saddles, bridles, lassos, boots, *bombacha* baggy trousers, saddle bags, revolver and rifle holsters, horseshoes, spurs and all manner of wide-brimmed cowboy hats. I spent ages in this shop, to the evident puzzlement of the assistants, fingering and peering at all these articles, which were laid out in piles on wooden shelves. The general ambience of the store was Tucson, Arizona, circa 1880. Unfortunately, I am large and Paraguayan *gauchos* are small, otherwise I would have equipped myself with one of almost everything. All the items were handmade and had a pleasingly rustic, archaic quality. If you wanted to set up a Wild West museum this would be the store to head for. Before Stroessner there had been few metalled roads, and Asunción was simply a cow-town; cowboys rode in from the Chaco, and tethered their horses at hitching rails in the capital. This shop must have dated from that era, but clearly still did enough business to stay alive, although I never saw anyone apart from myself and the staff in the place. Next door was the Café des Artistes. This had a vaguely Art Nouveau decor with marble top tables, red plush seating, a lot of mirrors, but no visible artistes, or indeed any clientele at all. The armoured, bullet-proof plate-glass windows and protective iron bars outside suggested that the absinthe-sipping decadents in floppy ties and Oscar Wilde-style velvet jackets had yet to come into their own in Asunción, or perhaps they'd all been gunned down in the civil war pre-Stroessner. It was always empty when I passed. Maybe all the artistes had left town or been shot up by the clientele of the cowboy joint next door. I liked the absurd juxtaposition of the two establishments, one pure 1880s, the other authentic 1890s, Arizona and Paris respectively: only in Asunción, surely, could you get a new set of spurs and a stetson with a rattlesnake skin swaggerband, then amble – or mosey, rather – next door for a few shots of Baudelaire, flowers of evil, and *la sorcière glauque*, as the *fin de siècle* crowd used to call the genuine sea-green wormwood absinthe, which, of course, though banned in France itself you can still buy in Paraguay. The waiters in the Café des Artistes were always asleep, heads on the bar, unless they'd been hitting the opium-laced *papier mais* cigarettes too hard, of course, and were actually on Cloud Nine.

All around the town stood tight-buttocked young men with rags hanging out of their back pockets, beckoning energetically to passing cars to come their way. In some cities of the world these might have been taken to be gay hookers, trolling for trade: in Asunción they were parking touts. They owned or rented a couple of parking bays on the street, informally, that is, from the police or the local *cacique*. These they deftly waved drivers into with their rags, promising to look after the car while the owner was away, in return for a few guarani notes. It was the smallest possible of all small businesses. And all across the city there were furtive men, furtively pissing. They pissed beside parked cars, in the parks behind trees or in the rubbery shrubbery, against walls, in the sandy soil, down the blocked drains, against car wheels, anywhere. '*¡No Pisar!*' read the signs impaled into the grass lawns outside the Pantheon of Heroes, but they pissed there too, in spite of the Honour guard in full-dress uniform with Mauser rifles and fixed bayonets. *Pisar* means 'step' in Spanish, not 'piss', so the signs really meant 'don't walk on the grass', but the synchronicity was too great. The reason for this great, national incontinence was the compulsive, endless drinking of yerba maté, once known as Jesuit tea, by most of the adult male population. Made from the cut-up leaves of the ilex tree, to which hot water is added, maté is a mild narcotic and is widely drunk throughout the southern cone, nowhere more so than Paraguay, where the majority of the crop is grown and harvested. The bitter, dark green leaves are put in a pot, cup or more usually a gourd known as a maté: hot water is poured on and the drink sucked up through a metal straw known as a *bombilla*. For a cold brew, ice or just cold water is added to the leaf, and the drink is then known as *tereré*. The drinking of maté is a bonding ritual for Paraguayan men: one man will brew up, slurp up a draught, add more water, and pass the gourd round to his mate, as it were. Each man follows suit – slurp, add water, pass on. As TB and other saliva-conducted diseases are rife, this isn't all that gets passed on, of course. Never mind, the macho Paraguayan male doesn't: police on duty drink it, beggars drink it, civil servants, businessmen, politicians, shopkeepers, truck drivers – every Paraguayan male is constantly drinking the stuff all day long. You saw thermos flasks for sale everywhere, usually brightly coloured and made in China, essential for the brewing process. Men carried the complete gear around with them, thermos on shoulder strap, packet of leaf maté, spoon, gourd and *bombilla*. People didn't go into cafés to drink it, they just made it up from their own kits wherever they happened to be – in offices or shops, on buses or in queues, squatting on the pavement or slumped in a park. The end result was a city full of men pissing all the time. In a shop selling religious icons I had noticed an almost life-size painted carving in wood of a Spanish friar, perhaps a Jesuit of yore, dressed in an old-fashioned ecclesiastical gown and a tonsure on his head. He had a straw in his mouth, and was sucking on what looked like a large, pear-shaped brown turd, but which in fact on closer inspection was a maté gourd. 'The reason *rioplatano* men are so useless is all down to maté drinking,' Alejandro Caradoc Evans told me one evening in the bar of the Gran Hotel, which was where he spent most of his waking hours. 'They are all mother-dependent, not properly weaned, and addicted to the tit. The maté habit enables them to suck in public, and collectively, like babies in a crèche. Also, the stuff is a poison, slowly rots your brain and drives you mad. It is as bad as cocaine, but not so fast and more insidious. Notice how you almost never see the women drinking it, though they do behind closed doors in Buenos Aires, I have to say.' Caradoc Evans was a Welsh Patagonian Argentinian, in his late twenties. He was cooling his heels in Asunción, rusticated for some unstated misdemeanour he had committed in Buenos Aires, where his family now lived. He had a complete contempt not just for Paraguay, but for the whole of South America. Like so many local critics, he had never actually left the continent, had never visited Europe, the place he dreamed of escaping to. He sat every day in the bar of the Gran Hotel, drinking beer and smoking cigarettes. He was allowed to run up a bar tab to a certain amount each day, and was allowed to eat in the hotel restaurant, but he had no cash. He was a prisoner of his family, under hotel arrest in Paraguay. He spoke perfect English and was dressed in a rather old-fashioned, officer-and-gentleman style, double-breasted blazer, club tie, light blue shirt, cavalry twill trousers and chelsea boots. He would not have looked out of place at a polo tournament somewhere near Cheltenham. His main aim, in so far as he had one, was to get a passport and go to Europe, and then never come back to South America again. 'Except to be buried. I don't mind them shipping my carcass home again. You may think this Third World dereliction is all very picturesque, but for those of us forced to live here it isn't. Have you read V. S. Naipaul on the return of Eva Perón?' I said I had. 'Well, it's a great pity he didn't come to Paraguay, isn't it? He could have out-Uganda'd his Uganda book here. This is the People's Republic of the Congo of the South American continent, Stroessner as Mobutu. There is still slavery in the interior and the Indians are still being exterminated by ranchers and loggers, just as they were under good old Alfie.' He spoke in fast, colloquial English most of the time, a language it was assumed most of the Guarani staff did not understand. 'You know they found another thirty *fantasmas*, don't you?' Alejandro continued. I asked him what *fantasmas* were. 'Well, when someone dies you don't report it, you just go on drawing that person's salary or pension – it means ghosts or phantoms. These thirty were army veterans, dating back to the Chaco War in the 1930s. God knows how long ago they died – decades, probably – still drawing their pay. One had a theoretical age of 120.' Alejandro's father had friends and business interests in Paraguay. 'Powerful friends, who keep an eye on me,' he added, with menace in his voice. 'You never grow up in these *rioplatano* countries, you are always a child and kept as a child.' It was evident that his clothes were expensive, but they were not well looked after and never seemed pressed. He looked rumpled and tousled as if he slept in his jacket and trousers. He was always well-shaved but often in need of a haircut. 'Once I get my passport I'm off for good – you won't see me for dust,' he concluded with some vehemence, swigging back his beer for emphasis. I had met Argentine émigrés like Alejandro in London, where they complained ceaselessly to anyone who would listen of the cold, the damp, the expense, the lack of servants, the frigidity of the women, the unfriendliness of the men, the smallness of the apartments, and the terrible food. When they finally went back to Buenos Aires, I had heard, they fell into a pine for London that sometimes lasted a lifetime, endlessly reminiscing in the Jockey Club or the tearooms of Harrods in BA about their years in paradise, now lost. Someone had once seen a somewhat flashy tweed suit advertised in a Paris gent's outfitters as '*Très chic – presque cad*'. No doubt whoever bought it was an Argentine anglomane.

Alejandro had been educated at an Argentine English-style Public School outside BA and his flawless English had cadences of the British upper classes of the 1950s. He said 'crawse' for 'cross', and his slang was dated, copied from the émigré masters, themselves products of the 1950s. This gave him the strange aura of being a contemporary of mine: he was young enough to be my son, almost my grandson – yet he spoke in much the way I had myself when I was about 12 or 13, before the 1960s really got going, and posh accents became a liability in swinging London.

'What exactly are you going to do when you get to Europe?' I asked him. I tried to imagine him among the pierced noses and glottal stops of the postmodern, multicultural, know-nothing estuary English.

'Live,' he replied with fervour. 'It's something you can't do outside Europe. It is all pretend here, in case you haven't noticed, pretend Europe, pretend USA. Everything that has been brought in from Europe has been misunderstood and misapplied. These ridiculous fake palazzi in the jungle put up by naked savages under the slave driver's whip. I mean Solano López's absurd fixation with Napoleon and imperial architecture – you know his grandfather, López's I mean – was a mulatto bootblack on the streets of Asunción, of negro and Guayaki descent. He had no Spanish or Guarani blood, which is why he had no compunction in slaughtering all the Spanish and Guarani Paraguayans. The Guayaki and the Guarani loathed each other from pre-Spanish days. You see, a *mestizo* has to prove himself by doing down the white Creole – just look at Juan Perón. Francia, the first dictator here, was another *mestizo*. He forbade whites from marrying other whites, by law. Remember, this was the early 19th century when whites ruled the whole "civilized" world, and certainly the whole of South America. The *mestizo* on the rise, typically, joins the army, dons a colourful, picturesque uniform of a style obsolete in Europe by some decades, preaches uplift for the Indians and downfall for the white elite, makes a *coup d'état*, bankrupts the economy, ruins the country, persecutes and tortures everyone, declares war on the world, particularly the Catholic Church and the USA, and finally goes down in a welter of blood and chaos.

'Francia avoided the latter because he was too paranoid and too mean to go to war. He just locked Paraguay in a prison for forty years instead – the anal retentive tyrant, the first truly modern totalitarian ruler, with secret police, torture chambers and the rest. Juan Perón in Argentina was the same type, a part-Indian whose mother was so dark she couldn't be acknowledged in public. It's part of the Argentine fantasy that there are no "natives" in the country, only aspirant Parisians and Londoners, though these are better dressed and sexier. In my grandfather's day, among the English of BA, they always spoke of "Johnny Sunday". Perón's first names were Juan Domingo, and it wasn't safe even to mention his proper name openly. When he was kicked out they found he had stolen US$500 million from the treasury alone. Solano López robbed the whole of Paraguay blind, stealing everything there was, including the jewels on the religious statues, replacing them with paste. Most of it got lost in his final retreat, but he did manage to transfer some of it out via Madame Lynch and the US and French consuls, through the Allied blockade, and so get it to Europe. His "heroic" death at Cêrro Corá was a mistake. He'd miscalculated. He was on his way to the Bolivian border and thought he was a full day ahead of his pursuers, which would have allowed him to get clean away. He would have ended up being fêted in Paris as a nationalist hero in exile, a sort of pre-Bokassa figure, complete with diamonds and crown.'

Alejandro lit another cigarette and motioned to the waiter for yet another beer. He had the most jaundiced view of Paraguay in particular and South America in general of anyone I had yet met in the country. In Europe, among expatriate South Americans, such views were more common; the exiles had left for a life abroad because they had such a low opinion of their homelands. It was interesting to listen to this abrasive and critical version of local history, to compare it with the bombastic nationalism of official Colorado propaganda which I got from other sources: you could always chose your national narrative in Paraguay.

'Had Stroessner and Perón met?' I asked.

'Oh, yes – when Perón was overthrown Alfie was just starting out as a Junior-Jim dictator. He sent one of those smart, black-hulled fascist-era Italian gunboats that are moored opposite the palace down the river to BA to collect Perón, who'd taken refuge in the Paraguayan Embassy. Perón was well on his way down the usual *mestizo* war-against-the-world track when the air force had enough of him and bombed him out of his own palace. I think the navy were involved, too. He'd opened hostilities against the Catholic Church – like Francia did here – and was about to close the cathedral in BA and turn it into a workers' playground. Every South American populist leader is potentially Tupac Amaru, the Inca noble who revolted against the Spanish in the 18th century. They want to bring down the house around them as they fall. Although they have absorbed all the French, Spanish and English customs, uniforms and ideologies, superficially at least, they remain spiritually Indian – that is, in revolt against the European way, while being besotted with the outward show of gringo style. It's the latino paradox. They love us and hate us, and end up hating themselves for having absorbed so much of us. The Brazilian literary movement of the 1920s and 1930s called the *antropofagos* had a saying that they "ate a Frenchman for breakfast every day". It was a reference to the Tupi-Guarani traditional cannibalism which the Europeans found so distressing when they arrived, on account of resurrection being made so complicated and difficult if people were eating each other all the time. I've never actually seen a direct prohibition on cannibalism in the Bible, mind you, have you? It's kind of subsumed in the love-your-neighbour guff, I guess. There's a strain in South American life that would like to undo the Conquest completely. It's much the same in Africa, which South America resembles far more than most Europeans realize. Bokassa, Idi Amin and Mobutu could all have been South Americans, easily – the uniforms, the mania, the corruption, torture and confusion. The cross-cultural derange-ment is there, you see, on both sides of the Atlantic. King Lear with a colour chip and a culture chip, one on each shoulder.'

It was Alejandro who advised me to make a pilgrimage to see the British Ambassador. I asked him why. It seemed such a curious mission to undertake.

'Because ambassadors have an unusually high profile in this country. Paraguay is right off the beaten track, the Gringo Trail, which you'll have heard of, does not pass through here, as it's too dangerous and not romantic enough, no native ruins and no McDonald's. So few foreigners of note ever come here – de Gaulle was the first head of state ever to do so, by the way – that the foreigner is wildly overglamorized, and certain ambassadors act almost as vice-regents, deferred to by the governments which are always lacking in self-confidence and savoir-faire, not to mention credibility. In particular the ambassadors of the USA, Great Britain and France exercise great influence and add lustre to the shabby local political scene. These are countries important to Paraguay. The country was so nearly snuffed out by the War of the Triple Alliance, that Paraguayans do not trust either Argentinians or Brazilians. Good, cordial relations with these three most power-ful states, who could stop any potential neighbour aggression, are very important here. You know that during the Falklands War, thousands of Paraguayans rang up the British Embassy offering to fight the Argentinians on the British side? What made it even richer was that the woman answering the Embassy switchboard was an Argentinian! ¡*Ole!* But seriously, if you ever found yourself in difficulties in Paraguay – and that is not hard to do at all – then knowing your Ambassador could prove very useful.'

But would the British Ambassador be in the slightest bit interested in seeing me, I queried. I couldn't really imagine him wasting his time on such a trivial matter.

'He'll be delighted. You will probably be the first respectable Brit passing through for quite some time. Usually, the only ones who come here are on the run from Scotland Yard. He will be sitting twiddling his thumbs up there behind the armed compound, and you will be good for a whole morning of diplo-chit-chat. He can put you in his monthly round-up to the FO – met and debriefed visiting British journalist and author Robert Carver who was *en mission* in Paraguay, a full and frank exchange of views ensued, etc. etc.'

I thought this was all highly unlikely, frankly, but I recognized good advice when I heard it.

'Get the old bat on the reception desk here to ring up the Embassy and make an appointment for you. Your status will rise 500% immediately inside the hotel, for a start, and word of it will spread through Asunción, which is a small and gossipy town, in the end. You will become respectable, in a word.'

I expressed the doubt that anyone in the city would find me of the slightest interest, respectable or not.

'Don't be too sure of that, Don Roberto. Every foreigner who arrives here is photographed at the airport when coming through immigration – you noticed the big mirror, which was a see-through one from behind? A file is opened on everyone by the secret police, just in case – where they stay, who they meet, what they say about Paraguay. The big paranoia at the moment is Colonel Oviedo's agents. A Brit would be a good disguise. Your profession, "journalist", is immediately of interest to the *pyragues* – the hairy feet, as the spooks are called in Guarani. Your suitcases will already have been searched, and the number and type of your cameras will have been noted. The hotels always have a tame *pyrague* to do such elementary first moves. Although local film developing is not up to international standards it would be a good idea to get at least two or three films processed and printed up here, and leave the results around in your room when you are out and about – snapshots of the national monuments, parks, palazzi and so forth. This will show you are not saving films with compromising shots – military installations, the air force planes at the runway, say – to smuggle out and develop in UK or Brazil, as you came from Sao Paulo, and are flying back via there. Oviedo is just across the border in Foz do Iguaçu, and it could be very convenient for him to use a visiting British journalist to take a few useful snaps for him. He'd pay very well, I'm sure. You could have been recruited in London. There are certainly Oviedistas there who have already been in negotiations with the UK government as to what stance the latter might have if and when their man seizes power here. As you have at least two different cameras, I can't help having noticed, one standard 35 mm, the other panorama, it would be a good idea to get at least one film from each developed, even if they can't do the panorama properly here. Just to show you are not hiding anything. This is how the secret service mind works, you see, suspicions about ordinary things like cameras, which most Paraguayans don't have and never use. Leave the cameras in your room, too, so they can be inspected. Notebooks, also. If you don't, they may assume you have something to hide, and your cameras may be stolen, just to see what's on the film inside. If you carry them with you all the time, this may mean you have to be attacked, possibly even killed, in order to get the films. Life is cheap here. It costs US$25 to bump someone off, I'm told – a policeman's wages for a week – when he gets them, which isn't often. It might also be a good idea to fax an editor in London, real or imaginary, a "colour" piece on Paraguayan wildlife, say – David Attenborough zoo quest sort of stuff – armadillos in the Chaco, pumas in the pampas, piranha in your soup, and so on. Say how much you are enjoying this peaceful, friendly country with its unspoiled, kindly people and charming, beautiful women. That is the sort of journalism they like, the *pyragues*, from foreigners. It will justify your existence here. Things not to mention are: 1) Oviedo and imminent, bloody *coups d'état*, which are called *golpes* in Spanish, by the way; 2) cocaine, *cocaleros* and drug smuggling; 3) Nazis and hidden Nazi gold; and 4) corruption and the crooked government – i.e. anything that is actually real. Keep all that until you get back to Europe. Alfie had an Interpol agent from France, a genuine Frenchman, mind you, not a local with Froggy papers, blown up inside his airplane as it was about to leave Asunción. It was on the runway, taxi-ing for take-off. Killed everyone on board, including the narco-cop, who had uncovered some embarrassing evidence of heroin smuggling among members of Alfie's government.'

I thought privately that this was all highly fanciful, and that Alejandro was more than a shade paranoid, though I said nothing out of politeness: in fact I took his whole spiel as alarmist, of the sort those in the know love to plant in the minds of the timid newcomer. As events progressed, however, I began, slowly and reluctantly, to come round to the idea that some, if not all, of what Alejandro suggested might have a grain of truth to it. His words echoed in my mind, right up until the last moment, when sweating and frankly terrified, I sat waiting on the tarmac in a crammed exit flight, waiting to see if we were in fact going to be blown up before we took off. Things fall apart, the centre cannot hold, as W. B. Yeats sagely observed: the questions no one can answer are: a) how fast are they falling apart, and will they take me with them when they finally explode? and; b) will the centre be able to mount one last horrendous act of violence before it falls apart and bumps thousands off including oneself? An old hippy on the island of Ibiza who had hitched right round South America, including Stroessner's Paraguay in the 1970s, had advised me laconically, 'It's very easy to get offed in Paraguay – *paranoiaguay,* as we used to call it.' How right he turned out to be, and how little things had changed in thirty years.

Six

An Ambassador is Uncovered

Finding the British Embassy was not easy. Once, it had been downtown, lodged in an upper floor of an office building. Terrorism and attacks on British diplomats in other parts of the world had meant a whole new secure complex had been built far out in a new suburb which hardly anyone in town knew how to find. It was not even registered in the phonebook, and it was so new the large-scale map of the city in the hotel foyer wall did not include the suburb. Eventually, after contacting Gabriella d'Estigarribia, who was up on these sorts of things, the hotel receptionist did manage to phone the Embassy, find out the address, and book in an appointment for me with His Excellency, whose diary seemed as empty as mine – any day at any hour of any day would be convenient, it seemed. I spoke to the Embassy secretary myself, after all the toing and froing had been got over: she had a brisk, efficient manner and spoke excellent English, yet was not herself English. I wondered if it was the same lady who had fielded all those calls from ardent Paraguayans volunteering to take a swipe at the Argies in the Falklands War. Plucky little Paraguay had a reputation for trying to get into other people's wars. Stroessner had volunteered to send troops to Vietnam, but Lyndon Johnson had turned him down; an unusual case of preferring someone to be outside the tent pissing in, than inside pissing out. A Paraguayan regiment or two, particularly of horseborne hussars, say, or lancers in 18th-century full-dress uniform, would have enlivened the bar scene in downtown Saigon, if nowhere else.

The Gran Hotel had a clutch of taxi drivers on call who were reputed to be reliable – that is they wouldn't rob and murder you, nor yet deliver you to kidnappers, or so it was piously hoped. On the appointed hour I took one of these safe-cabs out through quite light traffic through a part of Asunción I had never seen before. I was begining to wonder how much of Paraguay I was actually going to be able to see with such high levels of insecurity.

'Don't worry,' Alejandro had told me when I expressed this fear to him, '95% of the crime is concentrated in Asunción and a few border towns where the smugglers and arms traffickers hang out. The rest of the country is very quiet – except for drunken Indians with machetes, but those are a liability anywhere in the continent. My advice is to cary an automatic pistol and shoot at any Indian who threatens you. It's a well-known practice here. They tend to run off if you shoot at them. If they don't run off, you have to shoot them dead, of course, or they will slice you up with their machetes. Give the police $10 to get rid of the body, explain you are a personal chum of the British Ambassador, and Bob's your uncle. This is the wildest part of South America, you know. There's no point getting macheted for the price of a pistol, is there? Everyone who can afford one carries one, as you will have noticed – including yours truly.'

All this trigger-happy, shoot-'em-up macho stuff made me distinctly uneasy. Buying a pistol would certainly be no problem. Every supermarket seemed to sell them and the papers were full of adverts for the latest special offers on imported models. You bought a licence at your local police station. It cost US$5. You just showed your passport or driver's licence, so Alejandro told me. Even before I left for the interior, still in the comfortable womb of the Gran Hotel, I felt I was getting badly out of my depth. I had always avoided carrying firearms on such trips as these but could I afford to here? I asked myself.

The taxi ride to the Embassy took less time than I had been told. Outside a modern, white-painted concrete block with a garden in front and high metal railings stood a Paraguayan police-man on duty, sub-machine gun slung over his shoulder on one side, thermos for maté hot water on the other. There were con-crete lumps all along the front approach to the Embassy to stop potential suicide bombers from smashing a car through into the compound. This was not paranoia. In Buenos Aires, the Israeli Embassy had been bombed as well as a Jewish cultural centre, with heavy loss of life. The attack was believed to have been organized by Hizbollah, who it was thought had an active cell in Ciudad del Este in Paraguay on the border with Brazil. When my taxi attempted to get as close to the concrete lumps as he could, the policeman raised his sub-machine gun and warned my driver off angrily. The taxi stopped immediately and I got out, waving my British passport in the air and shouting '*Soy británico*' to the policeman in case he had mistaken me for a Middle-Eastern terrorist. This, the lady at the reception in the Gran Hotel had advised me, was the local form when approaching one's Embassy. It was easy to get shot in Paraguay for the wrong reason. A teenage daughter of the American Ambassador had been shot dead outside Alfie's palace during the *stronato*: the guard hadn't been told she was coming and she didn't understand his commands to halt. This cop registered that I was white, evidently a gringo, and perhaps taking cognizance of the red passport I held aloft, he waved me on and I walked inside a small metal booth, a kind of high-tech Tardis, the door of which shut behind me with a defini-tive click. I was in a decompression chamber, neither inside the Embassy, nor outside on the street. I was examined by a camera and asked who I was by a loudspeaker. After a pause in which my answers were weighed and found acceptable, the door in front of me opened. I stepped into a large anteroom which had a thick bulletproof window and a person sitting behind it, who took my passport through a thin letterbox, and examined it. This too being found satisfactory, a third metal door opened and I walked out of the Tardis on to a gravel drive, which was the Embassy forecourt, and so up some steps and in through a normal front door. In the entrance foyer, which was painted pale blue, there were chairs, a low table, and magazines praising the English country-side. I signed in, a cool, unsmiling young lady proffering the book and pen. Then, after a fifteen-minute wait I was ushered upstairs into the presence.

The Ambassador was a friendly old cove with a thinning thatch and silver-framed specs: he looked as if he was coming up for retirement, which turned out to be the case. Asunción would be his last posting. He was an old Asia hand, and had spent virtually his whole career in the Far East. He showed me to a seat by a coffee table, and we began to chat, as if by pre-arrangement, about living in *la France profonde*, this a subject we were both interested in, and one we had discovered in common within a few minutes of meeting. Having been based in Europe for the last 20 years, and having spent three of these actually living in France, I was in command of more up-to-date information than HE and I was gratified to see that he began to take notes. On balance, my considered recommendation was the Gers in Gascony, a region the Ambassador did not know personally but had heard good reports of before mine. Outside the Embassy, in full view of where I sat, hung the gold-starred EU flag, alongside its Union counterpart, justification for our euro-chat. Coffee, milky and in mugs, arrived with a plate of Nice biscuits: the British genius, at least in Public Service guise, did not extend to coffee making. This effort was clearly made from powder and probably imported from the UK, if not Eastern Europe or even China. The biscuits were soggy, and neither of us dunked them – they were damp enough already. Reluctantly, after a good hour of French real estate and lifestyle discussion, I dragged the conversation on to Paraguay. HE had a pre-prepared typed-out sheet of names and addresses of local politicos, with e-mail addresses and phone numbers to boot.

'What is the difference between the Colorados and the Liberales?' I asked.

HE shifted in his chair, raised his fingers together into a church steeple under his chin, and pondered. 'The Colorados are red . . .' he said after some thought, 'and the Liberales are blue . . .'

I waited for further elucidation, but none came. 'What are we doing in this part of the world, development, that sort of thing?' I continued.

HE looked through the church steeple and shifted in his seat again. 'Ah – well, now – I believe someone from Britain set up some sort of solar energy plant somewhere up near the Brazilian border a while back. If you go up there do please make some enquiries and see if anything came of it. I'd like to put it in one of my reports back to the CFO. It's the sort of thing they like to know about back home.'

I began to realize that Alejandro had been rather more accurate about Ambassadorial thinness of material than I had suspected. I then got HE on to Burma, about which he knew a great deal, having served there for many years, though the regime had not let him travel to see anything of the country. I recommended Shelby Tucker's books on the country to him, which he had not heard of, and in return he gave me a Spanish-language edition of Josefina Plá's book, *The British in Paraguay 1860–70* – now a rare edition, published in Asunción during the depths of the *stronato* and very hard to get hold of. I thanked him sincerely for this, a practical and most useful aid for me. I asked HE if he had read Roa Bastos's classic novel of Paraguay under the Dr Francia dictatorship, *I, the Supreme*, which also had as its subtext the dictatorship of Stroessner. Bastos was an exile during the *stronato*, in France and England, and his novel, which many experts on Hispanic literature rate more highly than García Márquez's *One Hundred Years of Solitude*, was banned in Paraguay during the dictator's rule. HE told me he had 'dipped into it'. Later, back in England, I was reading a volume of Spanish history which informed me that the Spanish Kings had signed all their official documents '*Yo, el Rey*' – thus '*Yo, el Supremo*', the manner of signing his official documents used by Francia, was a clear carry-over from the Spanish colonial period. I wondered if Black Rod in, say, the Nigerian or Zimbabwean Parliaments, still stood up and said 'Oyez, oyez, oyez' when Parliament was opened: I also wondered what 'Oyez' actually means – it sounds medieval French to me. (I was right. On returning to England I found it by chance in an original-language text of the *Chanson de Roland*. 'Oyez' means 'listen up'.)

It was time, after several hours, to leave. We exchanged cards. HE wrote his name with a pen on his card, and said, 'If you get into any sort of bother with the police or army, show them this, say you are a good friend of mine, and for them to ring us here to vouch for you, or else ring the President's office mentioning my name. Do this immediately if you are questioned by them, don't wait. Getting people out of gaol is much, much harder once they are inside. In a real emergency get in a cab and come straight here – I mean if security breaks down or anything, which I don't suppose it will for a moment. But we are on a sort of alert at present, though it hasn't yet got to advising British citizens to leave.'

I put his card carefully in my wallet, not realizing how prophetic his words would become, and how, covered in my own blood from a dramatic head wound, and in police hands, I would indeed do as he advised, hoping his card would work its magic.

The Embassy ordered one of their 'secure' taxis, and the police-man outside, now wreathed in smiles as I had both gone into and come out of my own Embassy, and so was obviously a good egg, offered me a slurp from his maté *bombilla*. I declined, but with smiles, and politely. The taxi journey back to the hotel was quick, the traffic having become even lighter. The lady at the reception desk, whom Alejandro had unkindly called 'that old bat' was also full of smiles for me as I collected my room key. 'Did you find the Embassy all right?' she asked. I replied that I had, that the Ambassador had been charming, that I had spent several hours in his private study with him discussing weighty matters, and that he had been most helpful. I showed her the Embassy printout of local politicos on headed notepaper and with my name inked in on it. Proof positive I hadn't invented the whole episode. She looked at this carefully, with great attention and approval. 'You are just the sort of passenger we like to have at this hotel,' she purred, handing me back the list with my room key. 'Passenger' was how, translating directly from the Spanish '*pasajero*', they rendered their guests into English on all the little notices stuck around the hotel, viz: 'Passengers will please refrain from allowing creatures into the swimming pool alone.' Creatures here was translated from '*criaturas*', and meant 'little children', which is I suppose where the US term 'critters' comes from, as in 'them darned little critters needs their asses whippin''. Passengers were also advised that the swimming pool area was not to be used to attempt to pick up girls: I only ever saw one girl by the pool, a chubby, very white Brazilian, who looked most disgruntled. I got the impression that she would have welcomed an attempt to pick her up, but none of the few of us available felt up to disobeying instructions, with such an unappealing potential prize.

I had to give Alejandro full marks for in-depth local knowledge. Everything he had predicted had come to pass. My status had indeed been enhanced by my little outing. I decided to retire to my room there to write a long, detailed fax to a London editor friend of mine, praising the local wildlife, waxing enthusiastic about a series of travel articles I hoped to write on the fascinating flora and fauna of this tropical paradise. The old trick of a hair from one's head stuck with saliva across the opening of a closed suitcase at the side is well known, but still effective. I had sealed all my cases and cameras before I had left that morning, and was not really surprised to find on my return to my room that every single hair had been displaced. A visit to the Embassy was a sure-fire opportunity to go through my effects without being disturbed. As Alejandro had predicted, someone was interested in what I was up to in Paraguay. I had, in fact, made no mention to anyone, nor made any notes about any of the sensitive subjects Alejandro had outlined, but I made a mental note now not to do so until I got out of the country.

II

PLOUGHING THE SEAS

'America is ungovernable. Those who serve the revolution are ploughing the seas.'

Simon Bolivar, 'The Liberator'

'Successful and fortunate crime is called virtue.'

Seneca

Seven

The Gigantic Province of the Indies

The central square in Asunción, now the Plaza de Independencia, forms the traditional defensive rectangle of the Spanish colonial city. Facing the river bank on one side, now the silted-up sandflat where the poor squatted in a plastic-sheet-and-corrugated-iron shantytown, it was formed by the cathedral, the old barracks and the administrative offices. What had once been the Plaza de Armas, the parade ground in the centre, was now a derelict park, around which vendors with cycle-driven or pushcart stalls sold fruit, ices, pies, juices, sweets and cigarettes. The cathedral was whitewashed and red-tile roofed, an old colonial structure, cool and dark inside; it would not have been out of place in a provincial Andalucian town. On the outside wall, facing the plaza, had been installed a large stone plaque, a carved tableau representing the coming of the Spanish conquistadors, and their meeting with the Guarani Indians. Presented to Paraguay by General Franco of Spain during the depths of the two dictatorships, one doubts if the Church had much say in whether or not this piece of lapid Hispanic propaganda was put up on the cathedral wall or not. Irala, the Spanish colonial *jefe* (chief), is pictured in heroic mode, his shirt open at the front and displaying a large crucifix on his chest; open-armed he is almost swooning in an embrace with the Guarani leader, who is depicted, like all the Indians in the tableau, with a hooked nose and decidedly Semitic features. Behind Irala hover monks with crucifixes and beatific smiles, and more noble-browed, handsome Aryan-looking Spanish conquistadors, all purveyors of Catholic faith and white European culture. The encounter between these groups, the foundation of modern Paraguay, is shown as a comradely, even saintly event, preordained by Heaven. There are no women in the tableau, of course, no sign of the riotous copulation which actually took place, when the sex-starved Europeans, including some Germans, and even an Englishman, encountered the Guarani maidens, who had been sent on ahead by the Indian warriors to blunt the fervour of the Christians' attack. And attack they had, in spite of Irala having been told by the Guarani that they had no desire to fight, that they regarded the Spanish as their friends and allies.

The Spanish had known about the Rio Plata, the River of Silver, since Cabot had discovered the Rivers Paraguay and Parana, which flowed into the Plate, while searching for that Renaissance hardy perennial, the westward passage to the Spice Islands. Christopher Columbus, pacing the sands of the island of Santa Maria in the new-found Azores, had remarked on the many large nuts of a completely unknown type which were washed ashore on the beaches facing the outer Atlantic, brought by the east-flowing currents from somewhere to the west. These must come, he reasoned, from westerly islands as yet unknown, close to Japan and Cathay. In fact, they came from the coast of Venezuela. It was Japan, Cathay and the Spice Islands Europeans wanted to reach, unencumbered by hostile Islamic powers which either would not trade at all, or which swallowed up all the profit for themselves. In a Europe still dependent on salted meat, with the animals killed in the autumn, preserved in brine and almost rotten by spring, spices were a vital necessity to make food palatable. They came from the East, overland, and were astronomically expensive. Anyone who could find a western sea route to the sources of supply, to buy directly from the growers, cutting out the chain of middlemen en route, would soon become very wealthy, as the Portuguese were to discover when they rounded the Cape of Good Hope and got to India via East Africa. Columbus went to his grave still believing his Caribbean discoveries were the fabled Islands of Happiness mentioned in Classical antiquity, and that they were close to Japan. The subsequent discoveries of the Aztec and Inca cultures in Mexico and Peru, both rich in silver and gold, gave Spain a more concrete reason for extending her rule over as much of South America as possible.

Since antiquity there had been a shortage of bullion in Europe; there was a permanent and chronic trade imbalance – spices and luxuries flowed into Europe from the East, gold and silver flowed from the West to pay for them. India and China were both sinks for precious metal: it never returned. Spain itself had first been of use to the powers of the eastern Mediterranean in pre-Classical times, as a source of silver and iron ore. Silver was almost more use than gold, for without it economies faltered and slowed. Before the introduction of paper money and letters of credit, transactions had to be made in silver or gold. The search for the Philosopher's Stone which would transmute base metal into silver or gold, was in reality an expression of frustration at the simple shortage of precious metals to make coin. Some gold flowed in from the mines of Mali in central Africa, but never enough. The hoards of silver which flooded into Europe from South America caused rapid inflation, but they supercharged those embryonic capitalist economies which were actually productive and net export traders, particularly the Netherlands and England. Inca and Aztec treasure flowed into Seville, but did not stay there: it moved to Amsterdam, Bruges and London, where bankers, many of them Jewish or Protestant, were busy inventing the modern world economy. To pay for her interminable wars in Italy and the Low Countries, Spain looted South America: it did her no good at all. Silver still flowed East never to return, via London and Amsterdam – Chinese porcelain, silk, rhubarb (for constipation, a chronic European condition due to poor diet), tea, nutmeg, pepper, and saffron all flowed back. The silver arrived in Spain via a long and insecure route from the slave-operated mines of

Peru and Bolivia down by pack mule to the Pacific coast; from there by ship to Panama, sent by mule again across the isthmus to the Caribbean coast; then by protected flotilla to Seville across the Atlantic. The whole process was complicated and dangerous. English, Dutch and French pirates and privateers learnt early on the immense profits to be had from seizing the bullion fleet on the high seas or the isthmus of Panama. If only a navigable river could be found on the Atlantic watershed of South America, which ran down the Andes and into the Plate, then ships could be sent directly to Spain with no transshipment or mule trains, by the much safer southern Atlantic route. And Cabot had found silver in Paraguay. The Guarani Indians he had met had shown him artefacts they had traded or stolen from the Incas on their expeditions across the Chaco. The Guarani valued the metal, and there was always the possibility that there were mines in the country, not mentioned by the Indians for fear of conquest and looting. This delusion lasted right through the colonial period in Paraguay; even the Jesuits, it was rumoured, with their agricultural, theocratic settlements of Christianized Indians known as *Reducciones*, were masters of great hidden silver mines, ruled by a secretive Jesuit King called *El Rey Blanco*, The White King. The Jesuits in Paraguay suffered the same fate as the Templars in medieval Europe: they were too successful, became too wealthy, too powerful, and excited the cupidity of the secular authorities.

Men share a marked tendency to believe what they want to believe. Irala set out trying to find a non-existent navigable river which rose in the Andes, and perhaps some non-existent silver mines into the bargain. He found neither, but he did settle Paraguay. At the place where Buenos Aires now stands, his men had been attacked by hostile Indians who resented his demands that they should feed his whole expedition. Several Spaniards were killed and then eaten, Irala thus supplying the Indians with food, rather than vice versa. The depleted party then moved upriver, avoiding what is now Argentina, and making for Guarani territory, where Cabot had been welcomed in a friendly fashion. The Paraguayan Guaranis, a branch of the Tupi-Guarani peoples, had spread down from the coasts of Guiana through Brazil: now they were in trouble. Southern Paraguay was as far as they were to penetrate. They found themselves, a semi-sedentary, relatively sophisticated farming culture, surrounded by hostile hunter-gatherer tribes which resented their intrusion, and the limits that their farming put on their hunting grounds. The Guaranis were attacked all the time, and were barely holding their own when the Spanish arrived. They had food surpluses, and women – both of which the Spanish needed. The Spanish had vastly superior firepower and better military technology than anything ever seen in the region before. The Guarani immediately realized the advantages of a strategic alliance. The Spanish insisted on an attack, a defeat, and a peace, to prove who was master and who was subject. But at the crucial moment in the attack the Guarani sent in their women, and the assault ended as an orgy. There was no more fighting. 'Every Spaniard has a harem of ten or twenty women. They do no work but lie in hammocks all day, fanned by their female companions, who also give them food to eat and maté to drink. Truly, we have found ourselves in the Paradise of Mahomet,' one conquistador wrote back to Spain.

Asunción was thus founded, and a Spanish colonial city grew up while Buenos Aires and Montevideo were both vacant building lots with wild Indians in situ. The hostile Indians of the Argentinian plains were all eventually killed by the Spanish; yet the Guarani still thrive and flourish, having long outlasted their Spanish overlords. Their language remains the official language of the country along with Spanish, and their own culture has survived to a degree undreamt of in most other South American countries. In Paraguay, there were always very few Spanish and very many Guarani. The latter ceased to be 'Indian' and became 'Paraguayan' when they were baptized as Roman Catholics and took Spanish names. Compared to Mexico or Peru, Paraguay attracted relatively few Spanish colonists, for it was soon discovered that there was no real gold or silver, apart from the trinkets from the Andes. Instead, rather a slow, sleepy tropical colony evolved, exporting hides and maté, wood and oranges, after European cattle and citrus fruit had been introduced.

Reared on the romances of Amadis of Gaul, the Spanish recognized in Paraguay an Arcadia, and the country became from the start a locus of fantasy, legend and of intellectual speculation. Perhaps the Guarani were a lost tribe of Jews, which would explain their apparently Semitic features? The Spanish took the Old World with them in their minds when they settled South America: the temples of the Aztecs and Incas were referred to by the conquistadors as *mesquitas* – that is mosques; and Indians were regularly called *moros* – that is Moors. Spain had just finished fighting a 700-year war of liberation against the occupying North African Berber-Arab Moors, and this struggle had entered deeply into their souls. Everyone not a pagan, a heretic, a schismatic or a Catholic, they tended to see as a Moor – and an enemy. There was nothing racial in this: Guarani who became Christian Catholics became, in the eyes of the Spanish, full human beings – though this did not stop them from being employed as semi-serf labour, but then so were Christian Spaniards in Spain itself. The recent fashion for multiculturalism in Europe has seen a romanticization of Moorish Spain. In reality it was a slave-state. The fortifications, the palaces, the marvels of Moorish Granada were all built by Christian slaves, captured either by Barbary pirates, or in the wars with Christian Spanish kingdoms. Moorish agricultural settlements were worked by Christian slaves. To be captured by the Moors was to be enslaved. The Christians, likewise, used Moorish slaves – *Quien tiene moros, tiene oro* went the saying (Who owns Moors, owns gold). The Jews were expelled from Spain at the same time as the Moors by Ferdinand and Isabella because they had played such a large part in the trading of Christian slaves, as well as their being viewed by some Spanish Catholics as infidels and Christ-killers.

Spanish colonial Paraguay was at first very large and mostly unexplored. It was known to the Spanish as 'The Gigantic Province of the Indies', and comprised of everything south of Brazil and Peru, that is to say much of present Bolivia, and all Argentina, Uruguay and modern-day Paraguay itself.

The Spanish who settled South America had to grapple with a whole array of complex intellectual problems. Firstly, who were all these peoples, previously quite unknown, that they had discovered? Were they fully human or not, with souls to be saved or damned, or something quite other? If they were men, and it was established early on by the Papacy that they were, why was there no mention of them in the Bible or the chronicles of Classical antiquity? The medieval mind was largely bound by the confines of biblical and classical knowledge. St Paul had not sent an Epistle to the Aztecs, and these peoples did not appear to be descended from the sons of Noah. Protestant and Catholic Europe still based all its orthodox secular knowledge on Greek and Roman philosophy and law, in particular the twin pillars of Plato and Aristotle, who were duly edited and annotated by scholars from ancient Alexandria to modern Padua, thus providing the explanatory mechanisms of the Renaissance world. It was Plato, in the *Timaeos*, who came to the aid of the puzzled scholars and theologians: evidently, the peoples of South America had come from the lost continent of Atlantis, which island had originally been populated by all the peoples of the Bible, whites, Semites and sons of Ham. It was no surprise, it was argued, to find these 'lost' peoples in South America: they had clearly crossed over from the now sunken Atlantis to the American islands and mainland, and there settled, bred, and forgot their origins. A concise and elegant exposition of this thesis is outlined by Agustin de Zarate in his introduction to *The Discovery and Conquest of Peru*. Zarate ends his short argument, before starting to describe Peru itself, by quoting Seneca: 'the age will come, in the ripeness of time, when Ocean will loosen the chain of things and bare new worlds to the stones. Then a huge country will be revealed and Thule will no longer be the last of lands.' The intriguing question remains, however: where did Seneca, a Roman from Spain, get this startlingly prophetic vision of the discovery of the Americas?

Persistent rumours and unorthodox traditions hold that the Carthaginians, the Tartessians who preceded them in southern Spain and Portugal, as well as the Basques of Galicia, and the Minoans of ancient Crete, all knew about the Americas centuries, perhaps millennia before Columbus. The Basques were said to have fished the Grand Banks off Newfoundland for cod for centuries, but kept it a trade secret. Silver was a motivating draw for the Phoenicians, Tartessians and Carthaginians – they certainly all traded as far as Cornwall for tin, and down the coast of Africa at least as far as Senegal. A cache of Carthaginian coins was found in a cave in the Canary Isles. Persistent stories of sunken Carthaginian trading vessels in South American waters exist, but as yet there is little hard scientific evidence which would convince the skeptic. It is claimed a tablet with Minoan writing was found in a centuries-old North American Indian chief's burial site. Seneca's vision, though, was enough to convince the medieval intellectual that the old adage 'there's nothing new under the sun' still held good. The Americas, in their guise as the colony of Atlantis, or perhaps the Islands of the Hesperides where the golden apples in Greek mythology came from, had clearly been known to 'the divine Plato', as Zarate calls him, and this fitted into the cosmological orthodoxy accepted by all devout Catholics and many devout Protestants. It is an indication of the pagan Plato's immense and unquestioned prestige in the late medieval Christian world that Zarate could, with impunity, call him 'divine' in a book which had to be passed by the Inquisition, and in an intellectual climate where Judaizing New Christians suspected of holding to Hebrew rituals in Spain were regularly burnt at the stake. The paganism of ancient Greece and Rome was no longer the threat to the Church it had been a millennium before: it had become an ornament to art and completely internalized in the Christian intellectual world view.

Others were not convinced by this convenient Atlantis explanation: they recognized that the discovery of the Americas was probably the most important event which had occurred since the fall of the Roman Empire. Holy Writ and Classical philosophy, twin pillars of all intellectual and moral life in Europe for 1,500 years, were both pessimistic in their essence. According to Christian theology, man was a fallen being, originally created stainless and perfect by God, but who by disobedience had sinned, and so known Evil: this world was a vale of woes which led straight to Hell, unless by the intervention of Christ's mercy, by which grace was extended to the miserable sinner. Patient abnegation and repentance, good works, faith, hope and charity were prescribed along with prayer, fasting and mortification of the flesh for a wicked mankind, eternally mired in Original Sin. Progress – that modern idea underpinning all notions of improvement – was simply impossible in this climate.

It was little better in Classical antiquity: according to Hesiod's *Theogony* man suffered from the Law of Inexorable Decline. In the beginning men had lived in a Golden Age, then a Silver, then Bronze, then Iron. A decline in morals, wisdom and behaviour had resulted in the lamentable falling off of humanity that everyone deplored – and man was getting worse, not better. The late medieval and early Renaissance mind was convinced that things had become so bad that the world would shortly end, destroyed for its sinfulness. The discovery of America coincided with the fall to the Turks of Constantinople, Europe's last physical link with the late Graeco-Roman world. Although frequently overstated, the movement of Greek scholars westward, the rediscovery of lost or half-forgotten Classical texts, the rise in intellectual independence in the Italian city states, and the questioning of medieval certainties by both theologians bent on reform and secularists and proto-scientists intent on either old knowledge lost or new knowledge discovered, led to a new Humanism – man at the centre of the Universe, fit subject for study, not merely moral condemnation. As Georgio de Santillana comments:

> The Renaissance looks like an explosion. Between 1450 and 1500 America is discovered, together with the Pacific and South Atlantic oceans; the world is circumnavigated, its real size understood, the Copernican theory denies the common idea of a well-ordered universe with the earth at its centre; the Reformation breaks out in Europe, and 20 million volumes come off the presses to replace handwriting. All this together, and even separately, would have taxed any capacity for adjustment.
>
> (*The Age of Adventure – the Renaissance Philosophers*)

It quickly became apparent to thoughtful men that the new lands and peoples dicovered so quickly had been completely unknown to the Greeks and Romans, as well as the Biblical Prophets – and even, though it was not wise to mention it aloud, to Jesus or any of his Disciples. It was a whole new hemisphere which Renaissance man had to grapple with on his own, with no help from the past at all. Moses and Joshua offered no more guidance than Plato or Aristotle. The Aztecs were not Moors and their temples were not mosques: European or Asiatic precedents were of no use in America. Modern man had to make of the New World what he could, on his own. Existential loneliness begins with Columbus's discoveries. These vast new regions, which made Europe seem like a collection of villages, how was the European to understand them?

This dangerous and invigorating realization spread fast through all areas of human endeavour – geography, linguistics, mapmaking, shipbuilding, animal husbandry, agriculture, botany, international politics, medicine, trade, governance, colonization, industry and literature. Nothing could ever be the same again.

New things arrived in Europe with startling rapidity – maize and tobacco, turkeys and parakeets, Indians themselves, and a host of other new plants, animals and clothes: the medieval schoolmen could never put the New World back in its bottle again. Optimism, that preternatural modern sin, raised its attractive, its seductive, its inflammatory head. A large new idea grew: reformed, remade, morally improved societies of men could be made in these new worlds, away from the sins and cruelties of the old.

The ancient world and Christendom had both devised Utopias and Arcadias before, but they lacked a plausible geographical locus: now there was America and Oceania. From now onwards writers wishing to satirize or ennoble mankind had a vast geographical territory in which to do so, one that existed in time and space, but about which Europeans still knew very little and from which new miracles appeared every year. Samuel Taylor Coleridge dreamt of founding his Pantisocracy on the banks of the Susquehanna River in North America; Voltaire sent Candide to Paraguay, and after escaping from the Jesuits, his hero made his way to an Andean country where gold and silver have no value and are used merely for kitchen utensils, and large jewels are employed by children as playthings, but where man is virtuous, kind, and lives in harmony with nature and his fellow man. Swift places his Yahoos on an island off Western Australia. A belief grew up that if man was subject to Original Sin in Europe and the Old World, this was not necessarily the case in the Americas.

The myth of the Noble Savage, though dating back at least from Roman times, gained new impetus with the discovery of simpler, more equal communities of men in the Americas and Oceania, many of which held property in common, did not recognize the ownership of land, and denied kingship. Why, then, should Spain and Portugal be allowed to dominate such vast lands, men argued, particularly in the Protestant North. Dr John Dee, Welsh magus, alchemist, member of Sir Walter Raleigh's 'School of Night', and necromancer at Queen Elizabeth I's Court, was the first man to coin the term 'British Empire' to describe a theoretical but possible future settlement in North America to rival the Spanish and Portuguese empires. Raleigh envisaged a native Guianese-English alliance against the Spanish, and brought back from his first expedition to Guiana many fruits, plants and medicines new to Northern Europe, including, possibly quinine, a remedy for malaria, then a common illness throughout England. America offered anything you cared to imagine. Skeptics had laughed at Raleigh's traveller's tale of oysters plucked from trees, but the mangrove swamps of Guiana at low tide offered just such a reality. America was a great escape route out of the mental and moral shackles of Old Europe: the past could be shrugged off – no tithes, no bishops, no kings, instead wonders aplenty – and hope. Ordinary men and women wondered if they might not find freedom of conscience and freedom of worship in the Americas.

Intellectuals hypothesized that new, rationally based, perfect societies could be devised and implemented, to prove beacons to the world. What was impossible in Europe could become a reality in the New World. American exceptionalism is not unique to the USA: the whole of the Americas were bathed in a sympathetic philosophical light, emitting hope, and a geographical centre for a Utopian future. The Bible and Classical antiquity could not be right or wrong about the Americas, they were useless authorities on the subject. Old World pessimism could be abandoned. America offered optimism, the future, man redeemed, a new society born. Why should European Kings or prelates have any authority over these new worlds? What had the Pope to do with the Americas? European restrictions were imposed on the new colonies, but they were easily evaded. Jews, Moors, New Christians, lawyers and all fiction were banned from entering the King of Spain's New World possessions: they all entered anyway, and a new hybrid Euro-American society began to form.

Cotton Mather wished to see the City on the Hill established in North America, a New England, Protestant, reformed Light unto the Nations, man spiritually reborn – but a humanity from which the native American was largely excluded. Whether as Noble Savage or cruel savage, the North-American Indian himself was not included in the European visionary future or the Utopian musings. The redemption of mankind meant the redemption of white European man. Within a few years of the first English settlements in North America, Indians were already being displaced or killed. In Paraguay the situation was quite different. There were no mines for the Guarani to be forced to work in as in Mexico or Peru, and the Spanish colonists had no desire to till their lands. The Guarani greatly outnumbered the Spanish, and interbred with them from the start. They laboured in semi-serfdom for their masters under the quasi-feudal *encomienda* system, but they were certainly better off than the natives of Peru, Mexico or North America. And it was in Paraguay that the Jesuits, spearhead of the Counter-Reformation, created an entirely new social order based around the interests, as perceived by the Catholic Church, of the Guarani themselves, deliberately to protect them from exploitation by Spanish Creole and Portuguese-Brazilian slave trader alike. The *Reducciones* of the Jesuits in Old Paraguay, now Brazil, Paraguay and Argentina, were the first and most successful examples of social engineering on a mass scale: too successful for their own good, for they were abruptly halted and liquidated, being too dangerous to the secular interests they challenged. Like Cotton Mather, and later in Paraguay, William Lane, leader of the Australian Utopian communists, the Jesuits intended to use America as an experimental springboard, a try-out for a Paradise without Serpents, a new social order which would be applicable universally.

Eight

MAMBFAK

The reality of modern-day life in Paraguay is indeed far from the hopeful dreams of European idealists who planned the salvation of mankind away from Old World corruption and temptations. 'A Paraguay without corruption would be like a Switzerland without snow, a France without wine, a Germany without Mercedes-Benz – it is our national activity par excellence,' opined the editorial writer in *Ultima Hora*, the country's most outspoken newspaper. In order to get one's car registered for the following year, the paper reported, it was necessary to queue all night, over several 24-hour periods, and pay bribes to the officials concerned of 50–100,000 guaranis. More than half the cars on the road were not registered at all: the owners preferred to pay small bribes to the police every time they were stopped at impromptu roadblocks. Those drivers with correct registration papers still had to pay the police bribes for imaginary offences – scratched mirrors, worn windscreen wipers and so on – so there was little advantage in being legal. A complete collapse of all State services was being widely predicted in the newspapers. A government could run on empty for only so long. Carlos Marti, journalist with *Ultima Hora*, complained of the '*permanencia de show de denuncias de corrupción sin sanción alguna*' (the permanent parade of denunciations for bribery without any resulting punishments). 'Other than a social explosion or a collapse of the State all we can hope for is more of the same,' he concluded. Carlos Sanchez wrote to the paper from the provincial town of Itagua complaining that when his car was stolen and recovered, the police in Encarnación made all sorts of problems and difficulties, although he had every piece of correct paperwork. What they wanted, they hinted none too subtly, were *incentivos* (incentives) or *propinas* (bribes) to permit him to get his own car back again. 'We must realize corruption is in our blood – so much so that we don't realize it . . .'

Three prison guards were being held in gaol and another under house arrest in Tacumbu, after the escape of three prisoners there. 'I am more than sure that there was complicity in the escape,' said the *Fiscal* (magistrate) Juan de Rosas Avalos to the Director of Tacumbu prison, Teodor Silva. The guards, too, had not been paid for more than a year: they were living on a 'tax' of the food prisoners' families brought in for them. Naturally, the prisons could provide no food for the inmates, as the administration had no money. From the interior there were reports from the police of large-scale sales of non-existent lands to banks, foreigners or insurance companies, and the gangsters responsible had threatened to murder the Head of the Public Land Registry Office if he did not assent to the issue of bogus titles for these imaginary pieces of real estate. Once issued, the fraudulent title deeds were used to give to the banks as collateral for loans: the money then left the country for the Cayman Islands and other offshore banking havens. You could trust nothing in Paraguay, not the water, the police, the banks or even the land title deeds. The currency, the guarani, was useless outside the country's borders, and suffered from constant inflation against the US dollar and all other hard currencies. A curiosity of the few banks still in business was not only that the rate of the dollar and the euro were displayed, but also for the 'old' pre-euro currencies of Europe – the Italian lira, the French franc, the German mark, the Dutch guilder. I asked a bank official why this was. 'We don't actually believe in the euro, frankly. We think it will go under, and the old currencies come back. We know for certain that the Italians and the Germans have emergency plans to reintroduce their own currencies, if things get bad enough, alongside the euro at first. We can't afford to be caught out.' I said that every time these rumours surfaced the Germans and Italians denied them strenuously. The official smiled at my *naïveté*. 'In that case, it will certainly happen, but when no one expects it to.' Paraguayan skepticism and mistrust extended far beyond their own borders: the world was a gigantic con and they were determined not to be had. Europeans may have waxed optimistic about Paraguay, but Paraguayans were the greatest cynics in the world – about themselves and everyone else.

One of the collapsed banks under investigation was the Banco Oriental, which had made unsecured loans of 4,307 million guaranis to the local financier Chang Nan Long, and also to directors of another local bank under investigation, the Banco Wai Hing Chan. The money had vanished and the bank had closed its doors. The former Minister of the Interior, Walter Bower, pictured in the press toting an assault rifle while briefing his moustachioed, uniformed and, presumably unpaid, policemen, was found to be in possession of two farms in Missiones Province, with a total of 8,000 hectares, or 20,000 acres, which he could not account for ever having purchased. A full-scale investigation of his allegedly illegal activities was promised, but no one seriously believed anything would happen. An opinion poll conducted by *Ultima Hora* revealed that 99% of those taking part believed that Paraguayan justice was corrupt. The Association of Judicial Magistrates took umbrage at this, and put a full-page advertisement in the paper, protesting against 'tendentious publications which militate against the administration of justice and discredit the image of magistrates'. They did not, however, deny that Paraguayan justice was deeply, almost universally, corrupt. In another case an estimated US$35 million in missing stamp duty and VAT since 1998 was claimed by the commercial tax authorities against 12 tobacco companies, which had simply evaded the duties, it was claimed. Fraudulent import and export bills were alleged to have been used to defraud both clients and the authorities of VAT. More than 70% of all businesses were alleged to use such false accounting practices. Haresh Jamdus Chandrani, Sunil Jamdas and Muskan Kamles, called *Los Hindues* in the press, were suspected of running an illegal arms business from Ciudad del Este, formerly Ciudad Stroessner, and were accused of money laundering, falsification of documents and criminal association. It was claimed that they had transferred US$130–140 million in a single day. They were under arrest and being investigated. Two light Cessna planes were caught flying between 400 and 500 kilos of marijuana (*la hierba maldita* – the accursed weed – as it was known locally, or else *macoña*) from Paraguay into Brazil, coming across from Capitán Bredos into Minos Gerais Province. The pilot of one plane, Carlos Diaz Canpuzano, was a Paraguayan. The dope was going to be sold in Belo Horizonte. The second Cessna, piloted by a Bolivian called Eduardo Marciel Dantas, known as *Ghagino*, had arms on board as well as drugs – FAL rifles, made exclusively for the Parguayan army by INBEL (*Industria Belica Brasiliera*), plus semi-automatic pistols. These were destined to be sold to the drug gangs in the *favelas* of Rio. Both planes were caught at a clandestine airstrip in the rural zone of Pimate. It was well-known that Paraguyan armed forces had long been involved in the illegal export of drugs and weapons to neighbouring countries. Paraguay had a venerable tradition of gun-running, going back at least to the Spanish Civil War, when old First War equipment was sold by the Paraguayans to both sides: they had bought it cheaply after the Armistice in 1918 and sold it dear in 1936 – for gold or dollars only. In a cartoon in the press one Parguayan was saying to another: 'It says that in the census the indigenous people [the Indians] are now part of society.' His friend replies, 'Of honest society or corrupt society?' So pervasive was the criminality that it was hard to tell them apart.

The 'new parliament' building, still a skeletal, unfinished ruin of reinforced concrete surrounded by abandoned, rickety bamboo scaffolding, had been funded by Taiwan, and the contractors, it was alleged, had stolen the money and then gone out of business. Asunción was full of such incomplete ruins. The most spectacular was a life-size replica of the White House in Washington, which, roofless and in decay, was being built by Stroessner's son Freddie, who had simply helped himself to money from the Treasury to construct his fantasy. He was aiming to live in it when it was finished, but his cocaine habit got the better of him and he died in his early twenties. The building was inhabited now by goats, and Indians, silent figures who squatted over iron pots on small fires in front by the weed-choked lawn, where they cooked their food.

Paraguay's bizarre relationship with Taiwan was frankly that of a client state. Paraguay had a seat at the UN and Taiwan did not. Every time a Paraguayan diplomat got up to speak at the UN he launched into a long list of Taiwan's complaints and grievances, otherwise unheard in the chamber, always ending with the demand that Taiwan should be given a seat at the UN. For this service Taiwan was alleged to pay out millions, perhaps even billions of dollars in aid, kickbacks, and sweeteners to Paraguay. When Winston Churchill had visited Mark Twain, the great American humorist wrote in a copy of one of his books: 'To do good is noble: to teach others to do good is nobler still – and no trouble.' That credo would stand as a fair description of Paraguay's advocacy for Taiwan. 'The Taiwanese pay well over a million dollars a word every time the Paraguayan Ambassador at the UN mentions them,' a senior EU diplomat told me in confidence. 'It is very good money for very old rope.'

Unsurprisingly, Paraguay had its own special word for corruption, theft, and graft – they called it *mau*. Stolen cars were *mau*, smuggled cigarettes and false documents, dope and guns were all *mau*; illicitly gained farms, bogus title deeds, rustled cattle – these too were all *mau*. This was, in fact, the land of *mau*. No one I asked was quite sure where the word came from. It was not Guarani, as I had first assumed. Some said it originated in the

1960s when Chairman Mao had been much in the news, others from the Mau-Mau in Kenya in the 1950s. In a newspaper the President was caricatured as a little green extra-terrestrial driving a flying saucer which bore the number plate 'Mau 1'; he was waving gaily, with a cheeky grin on his face. In *Ultima Hora* the cartoonists always had the last word: 'It appears from Transparency International that Paraguay has galloping inflation,' said one man. 'Galloping? I would call it Turbo-diesel,' replies his wife. The press in Paraguay – in particular *Ultima Hora* – was a real surprise: concise, witty, satirical, full of facts and figures, tables of international comparisons, with very sharp cartoons and penetrating open analysis of the country's faults. I had expected timidity or the sort of flatulent, empty rhetoric that exemplifies so much peninsular Spanish journalism, long on polysyllabic pomposity but short on realism, concrete facts and figures. *Ultima Hora* was a revelation: they exposed all the warts and named all the names, including senior generals and politicos. The newspaper *ABC Color* had been the most daring during the Stroessner era, but it had been closed down eventually, and when it reopened after the dictator had gone, it was never the same again.

With so much fraud, evasion, fakery, theft and deceit in Paraguay it was not surprising that the level of fantasy extended into almost every reach of life. Sometimes the telephones worked, often they did not. Sometimes there was running water from the taps, at other times there was none. Sometimes there were waves of kidnappings and hostage-takings, robberies on the buses and car-jackings on the highways, then a lull seemed to follow. There were no apparent reasons for any of this. There was ample food in the supermarkets, much of it imported from abroad – for those who had money to buy. Long conversations on the phone to arrange elaborately detailed meetings took place, but these always ended without a result. In Argentina, it was said, when two people agreed to meet, only one of them turned up: in Paraguay, neither of them made it. I had a long list of contacts, and enjoyed many fascinating conversations with people in English, Spanish and French, but all of these fantasy plans for meetings, outings, trips to the interior, stays on ranches, excursions into the rainforest, always ended the same way – with me waiting in vain at the meeting place, the contacts never turning up. In Africa, in foreign aid circles, this syndrome is known as MAMBFAK, or Many Appointments Are Made But Few Are Kept. At first I became annoyed at these no-shows, fumed and got all cross and European; then I drifted with the flow, absorbed the tropical atmosphere and simply laughed. 'They also serve who stand and wait,' observed John Milton, and, of course, not getting the result you want is a vital part of the travelling experience – humility grows with being stood up so often. You realize how utterly unimportant you and your mission really are. I saw a lot of Asunción on foot, trudging about, in the sticky afternoon heat, picking my way through the market women who squatted in front of their piles of vegetables on the pavements, past the cops in their black shades and low-slung pistols in big macho holsters. With my plastic supermarket shopping bag and my sunglasses, sleeves rolled up, straw hat on my head, cheap cheroot in my mouth, sweating and unshaven, I blended in, anonymous in the multiracial crowds, the only way for a travel writer to be surely. When Shirley Conran first met Bruce Chatwin at a book launch, she asked him the best way to see a country. 'By boot,' he replied. 'I thought he was from the North and had said "by boat",' she commented. He was right – foot is best. Shelby Tucker, who lives in leafy Oxford and footed it through Burma, suggested I walk through Paraguay. Given the time and a less fraught political climate it would be a good plan, but now not even the buses and taxis were safe, the interior was virtually unpoliced, and everyone was armed. I don't think I'd even have got out of the suburbs alive.

The dominant mood on the streets of the capital was extreme suspicion of everyone else. In all the shops I entered, however small, the owner stiffened with visible apprehension. Perhaps I was a robber? Some had iron grills across the counter and your purchase was thrust back at you through a little slot, wordlessly. The supermarkets had armed guards at the exits with assault rifles, just in case you thought of legging it with your trolley. This practice was to have terrible, tragic consequences later, after I left the country. Trying to make sense of this confusing social malaise wasn't easy, but help was on hand. The Faculty of Philosophy at the Catholic University of Asunción was offering a course in the thought of Karl Marx, given by a professor from Uruguay called Javier Caballero Merlo, who it was promised, had been educated in Europe with '*Bourdieu, Braudrillard [sic], Touraine, Saramango y otros intelectuales descados*'. The course lasted 30 hours, and was conveniently taught between 10 and 12 on Saturday mornings. You could nip in for a bit of Marx straight from Europe, fount of all knowledge, squeezed between buying some cocaine for the weekend, bribing the cops to release your wife's stolen car, and dropping a load of *mau* Derby Club cigarettes to some *camaradas* downtown. Perhaps only in South America could a Catholic University be offering courses in Karl Marx's thought.

After Fidel Castro was convicted and imprisoned for his failed attack on the Moncada barracks in Batista's Cuba, the Minister of the Interior had come to visit him in gaol to congratulate him on his speech in the dock. Dressed in a toga, as if an ancient Roman, Castro – a qualified and practising lawyer – had spoken in his own defence for six hours without a break, citing St Thomas Aquinas, Jefferson, Plato, Thomas More, Rousseau, Thomas Paine, Washington, Aristotle, Hegel and Schopenhauer, among many others. There had been frequent interruptions as the assembled court broke into frenzied applause at his high-flown, philosophically abstruse rhetoric, applause which came unstintingly from the judge and the prosecution, as well as the defence. It was a bravura performance, and even the censored press praised his 'eloquent latinity'. After Castro finally kicked Batista out, at a noisy politburo meeting at which all his ministers had been smoking cigars, talking loudly, and drinking rum, Castro ended the proceedings by shouting out, 'If there is anyone here who is an economist, wait behind and see me.' The ministers all filed out, leaving only Che Guevara. 'Che, you amaze me,' said Castro, 'I knew you were a physician but I had no idea you were an economist as well.' 'Oh!' said Che in surprise, 'I thought you said a communist. I don't know anything about economics.' 'Well, never mind, I need someone to manage the Central Bank of Cuba – you'll do just as well as anyone else – take the post will you, like a good comrade.' So he did. And that is why to this day, the banknotes of the Cuban State are all signed by Che Guevara, first governor of the revolutionary bank. The truth in South America is often so bizarre as to be all but incredible. When I got back to England and I told hardened travel writer friends about what I had experienced in Paraguay, many of them thought I was romancing. I took to carrying about with me a little wallet of press clippings actually showing the police in white gloves lighting candles to their patron saint, the President as an extra-terrestrial, the outlandish names . . .

If weekend Marxism didn't suit, more mundane needs could be satisfied in Asunción at the Cupido Sexy Shop – *Lencería Italiana y Sexy Accesorios Eróticos*, they promised. What would *Italiana* involve? I wondered. With spaghetti, perhaps, or gelato? Paraguay could also boast some of its own cultural leaders. There was Olga Blinder, German-Paraguayan painter, the first modernist to give an exhibition in 1950 – her name was often in the arts news. Somehow I felt Blinder to be a highly appropriate name for a Paraguayan painter. There was also Jacobo Rauskin, a poet; and sporting a fine moustache, the man of letters and statesman, Julio César Franco. My top journalist, who always came up with excellent investigative stories, was Erwing Rommel, who wrote for *Ultima Hora*, my favourite local paper. Many of its journalists had been in exile during the *stronato* and had returned to report upon the baroque criminality of the post-Stroessner Paraguay.

The air of unreality in Asunción was heightened by the exuberant names of Paraguayans themselves. What could you do with a country where Maria Mercedes Bougermini rubbed shoulders with José Raúl Torres Kirmser, where Wilson Ferreira hobnobbed with Juan Angel Dellabedova. Even Ian Fleming, who had invented Miss Moneypenny and Pussy Galore, would have had doubts about calling one of his female characters 'Dellabedova', surely? César Augusto Caiz, Olga Ninfa Talavera, José Domingo Adorno Mazacote, Maria J. Bogardo de Shubeiu, Desidero Arzamendia López, Nicandor Duarte Frutes, Bianca Mafalde Benitez Rivas, and Ramón Anibal Scapini were all genuine Paraguayan names I plucked from the newspapers and noted down in my journal. Asunción was probably the last city in the world that still had an Avenida Generalíssimo Francisco Franco, named in honour of the late Spanish *caudillo*.

Much English usage had crept into Paraguayan Spanish – *el pullover* was what you put on if the nights grew chilly; *el baby shower* was what your friends invited you to in celebration of their infant's christening; *el google* was Paraguay's favourite search engine; and *Willy, el can sniffer,* was the Drug Squad's prize pooch on the trail of all that cocaine and *hierba maldita*, carried down from Bolivia by the human 'mules' on the trans-Chaco buses. *El Shop* was where you bought sweets and cigarettes at the petrol station forecourt, and *el shopping* was a mall, complete with armed guards in baseball hats and sub-machine guns at either end to stop *el getaway* after *el robbery armado*. 'Baby' Emilio Cubas was a Presidential hopeful for the next election, and graffiti reading *Baby por el Presidente* in bright Colorado red paint adorned many Asunción walls. A curiosity of political posters was that many of them were hand-painted rather than printed: this was because printing them was more expensive than getting peons to hand-render them.

The local political scene came in for much abuse in the press – '*de hacer politiquería bufonesca*' (to make political buffoonery)

121

was *Cuarto Oscuro*'s comment. In the same paper was a comforting report that 'diphtheria was under control in the countryside, after a massive vaccination', but they did complain that '*los pacientes indigenos tienden a inventar medicamentos*' – the Indian patients had a tendency to make up their own remedies. '*Este es un hermoso país para evocarlo a la distancia*' (this is a charming country to think about from a long way away) claimed *Cuarto Oscuro*. In my journal I wrote 'living in Paraguay is like being trapped inside an unedited first draft of a novel by Gabriel García Márquez – not an entirely enjoyable sensation'.

The plague of kidnappings was thought to have come over from Argentina, where it was rife. There the sequestrators had perfected their techniques. Also, they had police and army in uniform, who slowed you down to check your papers at roadblocks, then robbed you, shot you, stole your car, or kidnapped you for ransom. In Colombia, world leader in kidnapping, the bandits checked your credit rating on each of your cards, this by mobile phone, then took cash withdrawals on the spot, with their own machines, to the maximum, demanding your chip and pin number – or your life. One person was kidnapped every 30 minutes in Colombia: it was known as 'miraculous fishing', after Jesus's instruction to his Disciples to become 'fishers of men'. It was a business in South America, like drug smuggling or gun-running, organized on professional lines, closely protected and profited from by high members of the government. In Argentina they had invented a new version called 'express kidnapping' – it worked like this: young, attractive student types with clipboards approached prosperous, middle-aged men about to go into the cinema for an afternoon or early evening showing. There was, the student interviewers claimed, a $5,000 lottery prize in return for two minutes of their time spent giving consumer-choice information. Everyone who took part got a ticket for the grand prize. What kind of whisky did they prefer, which cigarettes, what make of car did they favour, these were the sort of questions asked.

They also gave their names, addresses and phone numbers, so they could be contacted if they won. When the interviewees were safely in the cinema, the 'kidnappers' went by taxi to the address given and phoned the family from downstairs. They gave a description of the person 'held', and demanded an instant ransom, on the spot, or the victim would be killed. The sum demanded was always small, US$100, a sum almost all middle-class Argentines could raise immediately. Most families paid up, in the local bar or pizzeria, five minutes' walk from their apartment. It only worked, this scam, if the victim had no mobile phone, and so could not be contacted. Naturally 'Do you own a mobile phone?' was one of the first questions asked of the victim by the interviewers. Though sometimes the victims admitted that though they had a mobile phone, they always turned it off when they did not want their wife or girlfriend to know what they were up to.

'This scam would not work in Paraguay because the sort of people whose family could raise $100 do not go to the cinema, but stay at home and watch them on DVDs or videos. And very few middle-class people today could actually get $100 immediately – they are deeply in debt as it is. What would happen here is that the family would agree to pay the ransom, meet the contact in the bar, and then five toughs would jump the money-collector and threaten to cut his throat if he didn't authorize the victim's release immediately,' Juan-Carlos Arturo Macnamara told me, as we shared cold beer and a plate of toasted ham and cheese sandwiches at the Lido bar. Mac, as he asked me to call him, was in his early forties, but looked older, grey and lined, balding, paunchy, with an intermittent tic in his left eyelid. He gazed around anxiously, flicking his eyes to and fro, as if searching someone out whom he knew. He wore casual clothes, blue jeans and a red t-shirt. 'To confuse everyone,' he explained. 'Colorado above the waist, Liberal below.' He was a descendant of Australians from the breakaway Utopian community of Cosme, where the leader 'Billy' Lane, originally a journalist from Bristol, England, had taken the true believers, leaving the soft-left capitalist-roaders behind in Nueva Australia: these latter had allowed their children, for example, to own their own toys, rather than holding them all in common, and the women had been allowed to cook individual meals for their husbands, rather than eating collectively, as the charter of the colony demanded. Mac was one of the few people I had contacted whom I had actually managed to catch up with – and it wasn't easy because he was out of Asunción so much, looking after his business interests, import-export, which kept him in the north-east of the country much of the time, near – and over – the Brazilian border.

'The difference between smuggling and legitimate trade is an interesting one,' he remarked. 'In modern, developed countries, the businessmen pay the government taxes and VAT in return for protection, infrastructure and social and health security. Smugglers in these countries are those who evade the taxes but take advantage of what the government provides. In underdeveloped or collapsed States, the government can neither provide the protection, nor the services, nor even collect the taxes themselves. Instead, businessmen are forced to pay individuals and groups – local police, Customs officers, mafias and politicians who will at least allow them to continue in business, even if they provide no infrastructure or services. Who, then, is a smuggler in such cases? It would be absurd and unbusinesslike to pay twice, particularly for no services rendered, to an incompetent State which cannot even collect its own revenues. Thus, ordinary businesses simply bypass the State and make individual deals with officials and criminals. Personally, I would love to have an efficient, honest, trustworthy government to which I could pay taxes in return for services rendered – honest police and Customs officials, a good health service, roads, schools, etc. It would simplify my life a great deal and also, in the long run, would probably be less stressful. I might make less money, but it would all be simpler and easier, safer and less time consuming. Unfortunately, that has never been and never looks like being even a remote possibility in Paraguay. To pay the government any taxes would be just to add to the corruption – all tax money is siphoned off and stolen inside the bureaucracy. Nothing at all has been repaired or replaced since Alfie was kicked out – and much of what he did – the roads, the dams, the airport, for example, were really excuses for his cronies to rip off millions on the construction contracts.'

I asked Mac what the relationship had been between Colonel Oviedo, now in exile in Brazil, and the imprisoned ex-President Raúl Cubas of Paraguay.

'Well, Cubas is under house arrest, on the *estancia* of his brother Capitán Cubas in the Chaco, a place called El Trebol. That's the way with the political class, they never actually put each other in common gaols, always house arrest. Oviedo ordered the army to shoot some young demonstrators, which they did, killing a lot of them – the numbers are disputed, but it counts as "magnicide" as there were so many. Cubas allowed Oviedo to escape from prison and get across the border, so it's claimed; Oviedo may have had some sensitive material on Cubas that helped this process along. If Oviedo makes a comeback and succeeds in a *golpe*, Cubas could well end up as his Vice-President, which is probably why he hasn't taken an *avionetta* from the Chaco to Brazil himself. That is all the public is aware of – there may be convoluted ins and outs which insiders know, but we don't.'

It occurred to me, reflecting on what Mac had told me, that Paraguay was perhaps the last 18th-century state still surviving in the modern world, closer to the Poland of King Stanislaus Augustus Poniatowski than any contemporary 21st-century regime. In pre-partition Poland there had been an immensely rich and powerful landowning aristocracy which controlled all the land and disposed of the peasantry like chattels; they had been quarrelsome, argumentative, constantly forming and re-forming into rival factions, making any sort of stable government impossible.

They obeyed no laws, paid no taxes, aped the fashions of France and Western Europe, importing whole dinner services of Sèvres porcelain in oxcarts. Under them the peasantry had toiled for a pittance. Corrupt, inefficient, proud, in thrall to foreign ideas, sandwiched between three much larger states which had designs on its independence – Russia, Austria and Prussia – Poland had been a byword for folly, waste and aristocratic pride. The monarch had always been weak and almost powerless. Contemporary Paraguay resembled old Poland to a marked degree – vast plains with endless herds of cattle, huge estates, regiments of cavalry, hussars and lancers, the cult of the Virgin Mary, a sense of being cut off from the mainstream of European life and ideas. I had never been in a country that was quite so anarchic, so old-fashioned as Paraguay.

I asked Mac what he made of Stanley Guillermo the President of Union Industria's claim that 70% of all taxes were evaded, and if they could be collected there would be US$500 million to spend.

'Hmm, interesting. He assumes 30% of the taxes are being collected – that would be US$214 million, am I right? So where is this fabulous sum then? The government is broke, or so they assure us. If they had US$214 million per annum they could pay the police and a few other people as well. I don't believe any tax at all is collected – collected that is and spent on public services or salaries. It's all filtered off and stolen by politicians and bureaucrats and salted away in the Cayman Islands. There is a kind of fantasy in Paraguay that even educated people subscribe to, and it is always preceded by the word "If". If there was no corruption, if the justice system was honest, if there was no smuggling, if Paraguay could become clean, honest, hard-working, efficient, etc. etc. It comes from the Roman Catholic heritage, I think. If mankind were not sinful, if Jesus would extend his grace, if the Virgin Mary would intercede. All of these things lie in the realms of fantasy and wish fulfilment. They are like wanting Father

Christmas to exist, the fairies to come back to inhabit the end of the garden. The "if" game in Paraguay simply makes people feel better for a minute or two, nothing more. All these fatuous statements the good and the great make in the press, they could never become reality here. The facts are different, but unattractive, and so people try to "if" them away. Stanley doesn't mention the 30% of taxes he assumes are collected. Why not? Why didn't the journalist interviewing him query this? Fantasies and *fantasmas*. Take the railways. The last train jumped the tracks two years ago or more. It ran once a week to Aregua, 25 kilometres away, hardly the Pacific Express, eh? It was a steam train built in the north of England in 1865. But the Ministry of Railways still employs 25,000 people. Why? Can't be sacked. What do they do? Well, eat, drink, get married, collect their salaries every month – or try to anyway, for sure. The railway station? It's a museum – literally. Go and have a look. Full of 19th-century British gear – clocks, ticket punchers, cast-iron seats for waiting rooms, all shipped out in kit form. Some of the old carriages have been kept with loving care – look for the frosted glass with the initials of Ferrovia de Paraguay engraved on them – real craftsmanship. Imagine shipping all that up the river in the 1860s – heroic! But it started to run down when the British left. It was the same in Argentina when Perón nationalized the trains. Did you know that in Brazil 80% of the civil service budget goes on paying the pensions of retired civil servants? One thing Alfie managed to do was keep down the numbers of the civil servants. Everyone in South America – the poor that is – dreams of a safe job with the government, a meal ticket for life. In Italy it's called a *poltrona* – an armchair. Jorge Batlle in Uruguay turned a prosperous country into a ruin simply by expanding the public service until it embraced the whole country. No one actually produced anything at all any more, but simply sat in an office and shuffled paper. We are on the same road here, but there is a long way to go yet. Imagine! We actually import bananas and oranges, pineapples and mangoes now! All tropical produce we could grow ourselves. And England imports coal, gas and oil, I understand, yes? Everyone complains here about the price rises – 26% on public transport, 10% on dairy products, 10% on breadstuffs, and that diesel and petrol prices keep on going up every week. What no one seems to understand is that all these things are now imported and paid for with dollars – the public transport buses are US-made as well as the diesel that runs them. Even water needs machinery, pumps, filters and so on, that have to be imported. And the fall of the guarani in value against the dollar exactly mirrors the rise in prices. No one grasps this. If we produced more for ourselves, we would save money and keep prices down. With a proper train network using modern steam trains made in China, burning local timber of which there are endless forests, and cars and trucks run on ethanol alcohol distilled from sugar cane which we grow here – and which the Brazilians have used since the 1970s – we would be completely self-sufficient in transport. Not Paraguay, though, never. There is a complete lack of realism, of politico-economic literacy here, among all the classes. "If only we could get another loan from the IMF!" How often have you heard that cry, in the press or from a politico. Sure – give the alcoholic another bottle of *caña* – it's what he knows and after a quick guzzle oblivion follows. We can't possibly service the debt we already have, and all the loans are stolen or wasted and just embed us deeper in the mire. The trouble is people have swallowed the get-rich-quick fantasy economy of smuggling and tax evasion. Including me, because you'd be mad not to, given the absurd protectionist economies surrounding Paraguay on all sides. Imagine one state in the USA – say Wisconsin – could grow top quality marijuana and cocaine, and all the rest banned them. Well, the Wisconsin guys would make their livelihood smuggling dope to the rest, wouldn't they? That's what we do to Brazil, Argentina and Uruguay. We import Scotch, cigarettes, diesel – you name it – and smuggle it over to them for a profit. Plus all the dope, guns and other nasties, of course.'

What then, did he think the future held for Paraguay? He thought for a moment and lit another cheroot. Outside, I observed that across the road, by the front of the mock-Les Invalides, the honour guard were taking down the Paraguayan flag. They had, I noticed, changed into summer uniforms, neat white ducks with gold braid: this must mean that spring had officially arrived. Paraguay, although subtropical in the south and tropical in the north, still subscribed to the illusion, like Argentina, that it was a European country with four official seasons which had official start and end dates. One 19th-century Argentinian politico, Sarmiento, who ended his days in Paraguay as an exile, had decreed when he was dictator that all the palm trees of Buenos Aires be uprooted and replaced with plane trees imported from France. These shed their leaves in autumn, making the city look more like Paris, thus furthering the illusion for *porteños* that on some level they were living in the Northern Hemisphere in a temperate country, rather than in the Southern Hemisphere in an almost subtropical city. Mac toyed with a fragment of toasted sandwich and furrowed his brow:

'The chaos will grow, capital will continue to leave the country, disorder will mount until there comes a point when the army and police step in and a strong man will take over. It may be Lino Oviedo, or it may be a general or colonel this side of the border. You may be sure they have already made their plans. Some opportunistic politicos, probably both Colorado and Liberal, will join a junta, possibly starting a new political party – how about National Renewal or the National Salvation Front or the Paraguayan Patriotic Party? Then a new *stronato* will start – the press will be muzzled, the democrats will flee or be imprisoned and tortured, the demonstrators shot down, and death squads will scythe through the urban criminals in Asunción. Or if things get really bad there might be another civil war, elements of the Colorados with a faction of the army fighting it out with the Liberals and another faction of the army, just as there was before Alfie seized power. If there was real chaos the Bolivians might move in and grab back the Chaco – they have never reconciled themselves to its loss. In any case, I want out.'

Mac had spoken this long and not very diplomatic speech in an undertone, and in fast English. His pessimism about the country's future was the main reason he bothered to see me. Although he spoke good English he had never been out of South America, and hardly out of Paraguay, just across the border into Brazil and Argentina. He was attracted to the idea of leaving, but lacked the self-confidence and knowledge. He plied me with questions about England, Europe, the USA and Australia, all places I had been to and he hadn't.

'I might be able to get Australian papers,' he mused, 'or at least a study visa or something similar. There's an Australian-Paraguayan Society and they've got good contacts down in the Embassy in BA. Some descendants of the Australian settlements here have gone back – and they've all stayed and not come back, so it can't be that bad. Mind you, I've seen some Australian films and the place seems very crude, with the people primitive and unsophisticated – no finesse at all. The trouble is, Paraguay is very easy to live in, really, in spite of all the chaos – perhaps, actually, because of it. No one really does what you would call work, as you'll have noticed. Ever seen a Paraguayan running, off a football pitch? I haven't. You can't really be forced to do anything much except at gunpoint, and there just aren't enough cops or military to enforce anything. Especially as ten bucks will get 99% of those in uniform to look the other way. Outside Asunción you never see a uniform except at the checkpoints and on the borders, where they can tax you for bribes. What would I do in Australia? I don't know anyone and where you don't know anyone you end up doing the crap jobs no one else wants to do – that's a universal law. Paraguay is actually very hard to leave. Many try, most fail – they come back. Europe is too cold and too crowded, the USA is a bum-job-only destination, the Argies despise us as Indios, and you can't get anywhere in Brazil without perfect Portuguese. A few rich Paraguayans lie on the beaches in Brazil and smoke dope and screw little black girls and think they're being heavily radical; but they get homesick and come back, usually. We think we are worse than anyone else – except for in sport and the army, and there we think we are tops. Without confidence you are lost before you even start.'

I remarked that I had noticed exactly the same characteristics in Australians in Australia. Behind the macho swagger, the nationalist brag, was both uncertainty and lack of confidence – except in sport and fighting – two activities which were unambiguous, about which no doubt existed as to winners and losers, and which required no complex, difficult or cultural achievements to excel in – the same sorts of activities prized in primitive African communities, in fact. I didn't think that either Mac or Alejandro Caradoc Evans would ever leave South America. Mac might move across the border into Argentina or Brazil if the situation in Paraguay became too fraught, but he would continue as a smuggler, and move back when things quietened down again. Smuggling would go on whatever regime was in control – it was like oil exports for Saudi Arabia, or tea for Sri Lanka. Mac was too old and too set in his ways. He reminded me of all the middle-aged men in the BBC I had known who talked of nothing but going off to start a new life in Provence or Andalucia: they never got further than the Tabard Arms in Chiswick. Nevertheless, I encouraged Mac and said I would help him if I could. He had contacts in Concepción and the north of the country, which could be useful if the river ferries started running again. They had broken down, had been taken out of service, and were awaiting spares which had to come from abroad. You could get up to Concepción by road, but bandit activity had increased making this an unsafe option. There were, of course, pirates on the river, too, but so far the Asunción-Concepción route had not been subject to any attacks – probably because it was so little used with no ferries operating.

*   *   *

The kidnapping of a tobacco import-export businessman's 17-year-old daughter, named Katina, in broad daylight from a main strect in Asunción, had shocked everyone. She had been on her way home from school when two men forced her into a white car and drove her away. At first the demand for ransom had been US$400,000. After the intervention of negotiators, including a representative of the Catholic Church who, somewhat curiously, often get involved as middlemen in such negotiations in South America, the ransom had been reduced to 320 million guaranis. Once this had been handed over, Katina had been returned unharmed the next day in Lambare, a town just outside Asunción, now virtually a suburb of the capital. One of the kidnappers had been heard to speak with an Argentine accent, it was claimed. Some theorized that it had to be a foreign operation, as it had been so slick and efficient – a Paraguayan-organized kidnap like this would have gone awry – the car keys would have been lost, the wrong girl snatched, the car run out of petrol, something of that sort. The national inferiority complex even extended to crime, it seemed. There was a celebration to welcome Katina back, given by her classmates and teachers, beaming priests hovering in the background, doubtless invaluable negotiators. When I asked people if they thought the priests would have taken a cut of the ransom for themselves, or for the Church, I got scandalized denials. Paraguayan assumptions of universal corruption excluded Mother Church. There were photographs of the celebrations in the papers. The police had not seemed to be involved at any stage at all – unless, as some cynics suggested, the police themselves had actually organized the kidnapping as a means of getting an advance on their as yet unpaid salaries. This had been known to happen before. The kidnapping of Katina and her release had been so fast that *Ultima Hora* had printed a special edition, the front page headlining the kidnap, and page two announcing its resolution, complete with dramatic eyewitness sketches of the snatch.

'The flag of Paraguay really ought to be the skull and cross-bones,' commented Mac, when we had finished discussing the case. His tone of voice indicated sorrow rather than either anger or moral outrage. 'We are a nation of pirates, run by pirates, for pirates. There was in fact a Pirate Club, a sort of disco-nightclub, with skull-and-crossbone flags hanging outside, but it went bust.' I had seen this place on my walks around town: it had indeed suffered a pirate's fate, boarded by the revenue cutter or a rival pirate ship, and put out of business. It was very definitely closed for good, with broken windows, a dirty, empty interior clearly visible, its front doors chained and padlocked. I had yet to see a bankrupt and closed-down gunshop, by contrast, or a tobacco store. 'In the mornings,' I had written in my journal, 'Paraguay appears amusing; at midday, depressing, and in the evenings, tragic.' Mac, too, was now looking at the white-uniformed soldiers folding up the flag across the road. 'If Oviedo could stand for President in the elections he would win by a landslide,' he observed in a low voice, so as not to be overheard. 'You know what Perón's supporters used to shout when he was in exile in Spain, when they wanted him to be allowed to return? "Ladrón o no, queremos Perón" – thief or not, we want Perón. If you are so poor as to have nothing worth stealing, what does a thief as President mean if he at least controls all the other thieves and achieves order?' It was Stroessner's claim – 'peace, order, progress'. And he had delivered at least the first two of those qualities, all rare in South America at any period.

'What you don't realize about Paraguay,' Alejandro Caradoc Evans had said to me one evening in the bar of the Gran Hotel, when the beer had been coursing through his veins, 'is that the people of this country are so lazy, stupid and corrupt. It's only the Germans, who are all basically Nazis, who keep things going at all here. The Nazis are the good guys in Paraguay! When you get back to Europe you can tell that to all your liberal chums. Oviedo is too stupid to be a Nazi himself, but he would at least put them back in power again.' Across the capital Oviedo's name was splattered in graffiti on the walls: '*Lino-Presidente*', '*Lino-hijo*' (*hijo de puta* – son of a whore), '*Lino a carcel*' – Lino to prison. He was seen as either a saviour-in-waiting who would restore the order and peace missing since Alfie had been expelled, or else as a neo-fascist who would institute a reign of terror. He was rumoured to be homosexual, and his nickname was 'the bonsai horseman', because he was a cavalry officer, and because he was vertically challenged. Japanese metaphors and Japanese style were widespread in Paraguay. There had been substantial Japanese immigration into the country, and it was by no means unusual to see formal Japanese gardens complete with pebble beds, miniature trees and waterfalls, outside suburban houses. Eclecticism of style was a characteristic of Asunción. At the British Shopping Centre – completely deserted when I went there – the old red telephone boxes had been installed; these did not function, of course, but were merely for decoration. The derelict, homeless element of the population found them convenient places to crap in, this not entirely unknown in their place of origin, either. More dramatically, the Californian-style bungalows exploded into life in the capital; sudden electric, hot Cuban splashes of colour – lime green, bright pink, sharp tangerine. There were reported to be mock-mock-Tudor villas and repro-French chateaux, though I hadn't seen any myself. In lakeside San Bernadino, a few dozen kilometres outside Asunción, German settlers had erected Alpine chalets and timber Bavarian lodges, and I did once see, on the road back from the Brazilian border, a faithful copy of a Rhine castle standing beside a river, complete with turrets, though the clump of banana trees around the base rather spoilt the illusion. If you were into fantasy, Paraguay always had something to offer, even if it wasn't quite what you expected, much less wanted.

Paula had died suddenly, aged 40, of a heart attack, leaving a desolate husband and two small children. 'You must come to the funeral,' Gabriella d'Estigarribia said to me, after she had told me the news. Paula had been a good friend of hers. 'It will be interesting for you. You will see how we treat death in Paraguay.' I had not known either Paula or her family, but Gabriella said this did not matter. I was round at her house, trying to get her to explain to me some of the more complicated aspects of everyday life in the country: I was having a hard time getting any money. I had brought American Express US dollar travellers cheques, but no one was willing to change them for me. There was an AMEX bureau, but it only sold traveller's cheques, not redeemed them. There was a bureau called 'Paraguay Express' but they neither bought nor sold any traveller's cheques. I asked the clerk what they did do. He shrugged and smiled. Maybe he was waiting to be told. The Gran Hotel had told me they would accept travellers cheques, but at a rate 20% lower than cash – an unattractive proposition. No one wanted anything to do with credit cards either, at any price. As the rest of the world was moving in the direction of the cashless society, Paraguay trusted only cash, it seemed. What was the reason? I asked Gabriella. She didn't know, but rang round all the banks for me – those that were still open for business that is. All but one declined to cash traveller's cheques. 'Very curious,' commented Gabriella. 'I had no idea there was this problem – I only use my UK cash card. I put the plastic in the hole in the wall and draw out US dollars, and my London account is debited. So I never come into contact with the local banking system.' What was the problem, I asked. 'They say that the cheques have to be flown back to the USA before they get the cash. This can take weeks. In the interim the rate against the guarani can go up radically, and they can lose a lot of money. But there is one bank that will change them in the centre of town. We can go there en route to the funeral.'

Gabriella drove with abandon, like everyone else. Pedestrians had to be good sprinters in Asunción. The sun was hot and bright, and the crowds passed in a blur as we drove fast towards the centre: it all looked much less threatening from the front passenger seat. In the Americas there are two classes – those with cars and those without. I had realized this first when I had been in Los Angeles. Anyone there without a car was a third-class citizen. I had lived for years in London without a car, and when I did have one frequently I didn't use it for months. Though in Europe we complain about our public transport, it is, in fact, very good – so good that if you live in a large city it is easy to do without a car. My local MP, Sir George Young, a minister in the Thatcher government, cycled all over his constituency. When we had had problems with some Irish travellers squatting on waste land at the end of our road, he had cycled round and walked his bike down to the end of the road, to talk to the caravan folk, his bicycle clips still round his ankles. I found this civilized and humane. I often told this to friends in Los Angeles. 'Guy must've been fuckin' crazy,' they had replied. 'Coulda been blown away by one a' them low-life mothers.' But they weren't low lifes, I replied, just poor people who had no homes, and so had to live in caravans. 'Trailer trash,' they riposted, 'bogtrotting white trash.' They were exactly the sort of people who had been forced by poverty to emigrate to the USA a hundred years ago, I replied. How did they know their own ancestors were not just such poor people? At this they shifted restlessly and changed the subject.

The response would not be different in Asunción. The American view of poverty was harsh and uncompromising. Middle-class Americans simply didn't see the poor. It was no different in South America than the States. You could get no discussion going about poverty or the poor. It was a subject no one with money found the slightest bit interesting. The poor could simply live or die – no one cared about them. To be a pedestrian was to be poor, and so risk being run over every time they tried to cross the roads. No one in a car gave a damn about them. When I commented on the legions of poor people living in the streets – the cripples, beggars, street kids, lunatics in evening dress – I was assumed to be some sort of bleeding-heart socialist. Fifty years of redistributive taxation in Europe and high state employment and the welfare system had ironed out the gross visible disparities between very rich and very poor. Of course, Mayfair and the Gorbals were still very different, but they represented extremes. David Cameron, the Tory leader, and Boris Johnson, shadow Tory minister, both cycled through London every day to get to Parliament. Such an idea would be completely impossible in either Washington or Asunción.

After a week in LA I had known I could never live in the USA: you could walk, because I did walk, but it was difficult. There was nowhere to sit down, no parks, no teashops, no cafés, often no pavements. One good definition of a Western European is someone who expects to be able to walk around cities, with the afore-mentioned amenities in ample profusion. Asunción was better than LA, but it still failed the test as a civilized city: Madame Lynch had insisted on parks laid out in the Parisian style, complete with benches, but the sense of danger and dereliction that hung over these places made them unappealing. Asunción could never have grown into a Parisian city for the same reason that the Jesuit *Reducciones* could never have replaced the serf-labour *encomienda*. Both were alien ideas imposed by force of will on an unreceptive environment. Once the will was removed, the idea failed and faded away. *Madama*'s parks were still there, but instead of elegant ladies and gentlemen strolling to take the air, they were al fresco doss-houses and shitting-places. Nevertheless, though derelict, the parks did at least offer some respite from the urban ugliness in Asunción. 'What will happen when the gasoline runs out and cars can run no more?' I asked people in LA. 'We'll drink the water from our swimming pools and eat each other,' they replied, not entirely unseriously.

Gabriella simply didn't see Asunción's poverty. She drove from her house to the shops, to the bank, to her friends' houses, and back. She never used buses or walked, except in short hops in safe suburbs, such as from her house to the Gran Hotel. She had no idea what the central business district was like, as seen from on foot, because she had never been there as a pedestrian. I couldn't imagine living somewhere I could not walk freely, anywhere I wanted. You couldn't do that in Asunción any more than you could in LA. Civilization is an intangible concept, but being able to walk the streets in reasonable safety in daylight is surely one of the crucial indicators.

Gabriella was having some work done to the front of her house. The labourers – all short, dark, Indian-looking men – were laying tiles in concrete along her front path. When I arrived I made to walk towards the front door, through the garden gate, but they stopped me with sudden shouts and gestures; this was not because I was going to walk on their still fluid path, but because they didn't know who I was. Gabriella's invitation to the funeral had been made over the phone, and I had walked round to meet her. She hadn't told the peons I was coming, clearly. I explained I was a friend of the *señora*, but I was made to wait outside the gate while one of them informed the maid of my arrival. Eventually, after at least five minutes' wait, during which the workmen stood looking at me in a hostile fashion, Gabriella appeared, and I was allowed past the peons and inside the house. Dropping by, that very English custom, was unknown in Paraguay. Poor communication, too, was a local factor: no one bothered to tell the lower orders what had been planned.

Hugo was in a hammock, in the back garden, his usual post. I was more than ever convinced the cigar factory did not actually exist. Each time I visited he was always at home, usually asleep in the garden. Gabriella had hinted that London had not been easy for Hugo because his import-export venture had not worked out. I suspected that Gabriella had always earned whatever money the family enjoyed. Gabriella was glad to get out of the house as it was also her office. She had a spare bedroom kitted up with an ancient computer, a fax machine, telephone, e-mail connection –

Paraguay had broadband. What with hubby, the kids, the maid, the peons banging and singing outside, it wasn't the quiet haven a journalist might desire. I was an excuse, as was the funeral of Paula, for an outing. Paraguay was still a place were respectable middle-class ladies were expected to stay at home and look after the family. I suspected Gabriella missed the great freedoms and challenges of her London or Miami life. She was full of complaints about the macho attitudes of the Paraguayan men towards women in professional jobs. I had praised *Ultima Hora* as a surprisingly good paper. She had wrinkled up her nose and frowned. 'The editor is very full of himself. Arrogant, macho. He pretends never to remember who I am when we meet.' I mentioned I thought of meeting him, for an interview. She was frankly hostile to this. 'You won't get anything from him. He's an opinionated know-nothing. I can get you far more information.' I realized that I should not have mentioned *Ultima Hora* to her at all, but simply made my own arrangements. As soon as you mentioned one Paraguayan to another they immediately tried to convince you they were useless, became jealous almost. Gabriella was putting herself out to be helpful to me. She had already hinted that her normal fee for this sort of thing was US$100 a day. I made a mental note not to mention Paraguayans to each other – it was counter-productive. I suspected Gabriella had tried to get work at *Ultima Hora* and had been rebuffed by the editor, hence her hostility.

The funeral parlour was a strange, modern wedding-cake decoration neo-Palladian building on Avenida España. I had noticed it before and wondered vaguely what its function was, for it had no signs outside that might give one a clue. P. J. O'Rourke, the US author, had been in Asunción, and had written of the city that it was 'like a tropical Leningrad – a very relaxed tropical Leningrad'. I had been puzzled by this comment when I had read it in England: I could make no sense of it at all. Now I was here it was evident what he meant – it was the plethora of peeling, faded, neo-classical stucco mansions common to both cities. The Italianate villas off Avenida España, buried, choked under luxuriant untended gardens full of palms, bougainvillea, bananas, tropical shrubbery and flowers, were huge: the gates and railings were pitted with rust and streaked red with peeling oxidized metal flakes. Many had sagging balconies of wrought iron on the first floor, with faded pale green louvred shutters, these often hanging off their hinges. The ochre-painted walls had been bleached by decades of brazen sun. These magnificent follies were for the most part locked up and abandoned, though a few had become Embassies. Their dereliction was deeply attractive to me: the cracked, weed-infested paths leading to porticoed, balustraded steps and antique wrought-iron-protected double front doors deep in shade. They had a *fin de siècle* charm which worked its magic: if I had been forced to stay in Paraguay I would have tried to get hold of one of these monstrosities. Once, evidently, these had been the villas of the wealthy, before the rich had moved away to other suburbs more modern, or else left the country. This frankly classical European style had long been superseded by the Californian ranch look. Nature always won in the end, though, and nowhere more so than in the tropics. The gardens of these *palazzi* were turning back into riotous jungle, roots reaching out under the walls and forcing up the pavement outside. Leave a garden or a building for a decade in the tropics and it looks as if it was abandoned half a century ago. If you wanted to shoot a low-budget movie of a Gabriel García Márquez novel, one of these buildings would do you just fine. You could cast it from any of Asunción's parks, too.

Inside, the funeral parlour was bright, well-lit and antiseptic modern. There was no trace of any religious symbolism. I had expected bleeding hearts of Jesus, weeping Saints, dolorous statues of the Virgin Mary – none of that, just plain pastel modern functionalism. The body of the deceased lay in an open coffin in an inner chamber. People were making their way to and from the antechamber to pay their last respects. The mourners were middle-aged, middle-class Paraguayans, friends and relatives of *la difunta* – the defunct one, as they say in Spanish. There was much more Guarani being spoken than Spanish. I was introduced to the widower, to whom I offered my condolences. There was no priest, no pastor, no prayers; it was all apparently quite secular. No staff in serious suits were visible either. I had never seen a place like this before: it struck me as very strange, like an H. G. Wells vision of death in a future society some centuries ahead. There was no sign of either mourning, nor of a wake, a celebration. I met an elderly man of Uruguayan and Scottish origins, and we talked with Gabriella about the political situation and the economic crisis, which were the only topics of conversation in the capital. 'The government will simply print more guarani notes to pay salaries and so fuel inflation,' Gabriella said. 'Then they will get no hard currency loan from the IMF,' I suggested. 'I believe nothing – *nada de nada* – nothing at all,' commented the Uruguayan-Scot. Like everyone else I had met, he disassociated himself from the country in which he lived and worked. He had been born here, worked here all his life, yet as soon as you introduced yourself he told you he was 'really' a Uruguayan of Scottish descent. I wondered if when I said I was English, people thought I meant 'of English descent'. I think my poor Spanish may have convinced them I really was from *el viejo mundo* as the papers called Europe – 'the old world'. In Paraguay your nationality was where your ancestors had come from. 'Paraguayan' was code for 'Indian'. To be Paraguayan was not a statement of nationality, it was a predicament, it meant you had nowhere else to go. Those with 'papers' – Italian, Spanish, German – could get out and go elsewhere. There had been a rush on the Italian Embassy. Thousands of people whose grandparents had emigrated from Italy at the turn of the 19th century when Italy was poor and South America rich, were now trying to get Italian passports and return to claim the generous EU-funded social security payments.

The Embassy was not being co-operative. 'Go back to Italy, get all the papers, and then come back and apply,' they advised. There were millions of South Americans of Italian origin – Italy didn't want them back again.

Italy was now a place of wealth and security compared to South America. The miracle that 50 years of peace in Europe had wrought was a continent which imported the hopeful poor rather than exported them. All this had been achieved by redistributive taxation, subsidies from the richer North to the poorer South, and the creation of a vast, almost wholly unproductive public service sector, without which there would have been mass unemployment. This was paid for by high taxation. Countries like Paraguay still ran pre-World War I European-style economies, with very rich, very poor, and a small middle class. How long could the post-war European 'social model' last? Every year capital left the EU and very little entered it; businesses closed, factories relocated to cheaper countries; budgets shrank, tax avoidance grew, unemployment rose. High wages and taxes meant that an underclass of immigrants from the Third World formed to carry out work Europeans no longer thought it worth their while doing.

Outside the Gare du Nord in Paris I had seen an immigrant from black Africa roasting corn cobs over a small fire in a supermarket trolley, and then offering them for sale – a small business more suited to Mali or Chad than a modern European capital. There was a huge cash economy in Europe which was neither taxed nor regulated. The critics of the Welfare State system predicted an end like Batlle's Uruguay – a grossly inflated state sector which taxed the private sector into emigration, leading to complete economic collapse. When the tax base fell below a certain point the state either had to inflate its currency by printing more money, which chased ever-disappearing goods in an upward spiral of price inflation, or else cease to pay its public service employees and cut public services. The current exemplar of this meltdown was Mugabe's Zimbabwe, where starvation and hyper-inflation had followed the destruction of the productive white-run private sector, in particular agriculture. Paraguay was already on this road. Only its tiny public sector provided hope – that and the refusal of the capital-owning classes to be taxed. You could create new jobs in the state bureaucracy in Paraguay, but there was simply no way of paying for them. If the businesses in Paraguay could ever be taxed effectively, then a vast bureaucracy would be the result, because this is what the poor would vote for, but tax evasion was so ingrained in Paraguay that even draconian compulsion could do nothing. Virtually everyone could be bribed for a few dollars, and most of the real money was overseas already.

It had become apparent to me after only a few weeks in Paraguay that Miami was the real capital of the country, as well as of many other South American countries. People went to Miami for dentists and doctors, schooling and training, to buy what they needed and arrange the importation of everything from plant machinery to furniture. All the hi-tech goods that kept the creaky infrastructure from complete collapse – computers, cash registers, tractors, hospital equipment, mobile phones, petrol pumps, heavy trucks – all these and more came up the river, shipped down from Miami. There was virtually nothing in Paraguay that emanated from Europe except luxury foods, and cars which had originally been exported to the USA and were now re-exported to Paraguay. The US publication *Harper's Magazine*, a left-liberal monthly with long, serious articles on social and cultural matters, had posed the question to its readers: 'Is the USA an empire?' Naively, the response had been an overwhelming 'No'. You only had to come to somewhere like Asunción to see the imperial outreach of the USA's commercial and political grip. The US Embassy – positioned cutely on 1776 Avenida España – was vast; US military bases in the Chaco sent great cargo planes and jet fighters all over the world; and US narcotics police operated exactly as if they were in Texas or California. Every day, ships ploughed up the river bringing in goods from *el norte* as the US is universally known in South America.

There was even a University of el Norte in Asunción, with guards in baseball caps armed with pump-action shotguns to deter the kidnappers from trying to grab the well-heeled students from the campus. There was an 'Italian' restaurant within walking distance of the Gran Hotel: I went there one evening. It had booths, like a US eatery, and the pasta dishes came in plastic trays, packed in Miami, bland as only US restaurant food can be. Only a US citizen could be blind enough not to notice his country's imperial presence everywhere; he simply took it for granted. There was bafflement in the USA when a group of French farmers burnt out a McDonald's fast food outlet in the south of France. The local farmer who led the group became a folk hero in France. In the US, McDonald's was just a cheap eatery for the poor, it had no symbolic resonance. An article in a French paper by a well-known intellectual had lumped together Disneyland, McDo's (as the French call it) and Harry Potter as 'US cultural imperialism'. Though Harry Potter, his author and *mise-en-scène* were English, it was all American to the French, because it was in English and not French.

'Is England part of London, or London part of England?' a Paraguayan priest had asked a British traveller in the 19th century. Before one smiles, it is worth wondering how many people in Britain or the USA even know where Paraguay is, let alone the name of its capital. Prior to coming to South America, an Australian university lecturer from Adelaide had asked me where I was going for my next book. 'Paraguay,' I told him. He curled his lip with contempt. 'Bit bloody unoriginal, isn't it? That bloke Bruce Chetwind [*sic*] wrote a book about it already.' I pointed out that that was Patagonia, in southern Argentina. He waved this correction away with one arm. 'All a bit bloody exotic if you ask me.' That was the view of an educated Australian. After I left Australia, I went to live in Italy, and several cultured Italians had been surprised to learn that there actually were universities in Australia. 'Somehow, I thought it was all desert and sheep farms,' one said to me. 'I suppose I assumed the few Australians capable of education went to England or America to study at university there.' I had actually taught at an Australian university for three years. The professor and head of the department, with whom I had eventually fallen out, said when I left, 'You'll never work again in a proper job, because I'll give you a bad reference.' When I returned to Europe no one ever even asked me what I had done in Australia, let alone asked for any references: no one cared – I could have spent the whole of my stay on the beach as far as they were concerned. Australia simply wasn't a real place for Europeans, just a holiday destination. The wife of the mayor of Darwin, on her first visit to Europe, wondered why no one in Rome knew who her husband was: she said she thought it showed 'ignorance'. She also commented on how 'run-down and shabby' the Colosseum looked – 'pity they couldn't even give it a lick of paint' had been her view when asked, back home. It was impossible to communicate to Paraguyans that 99% of Europeans had never heard of their country, or knew where it was.

I was driven to La Recoleta cemetery where the body of Paula was to be buried by another lady, a friend of Gabriella. I had a feeling there might have been a bit of matchmaking going on. It was very warm and bright outside, the midday sun at its zenith. The tropical greens of the gardens formed a blur with flashing highlights raking across as we passed. My driver's car was old, but well kept, a small European economy model. For all their US dependence, middle-class Paraguayans have European tastes; they dressed like Italians in the early 1960s, smart, conservative good taste. You still saw young ladies in their twenties, in pastel twinsets, pearls and sensible shoes, the sort of clothes my mother had worn circa 1961. They often had permed hair, neat hats and wore gloves. Sometimes I had the feeling I had wandered into a tropical Italian-influenced 1960s neo-realist film, perhaps made by Nestor

Almendros in late-Batista Cuba. Only the big US gas-guzzling Yank-tanks were missing. In Paraguay the middle classes were neat, smart and subdued; the poor were dirty, scruffy, raucous and drunk when they could afford it. The hypocrisies of Europe, where the poor pretended they were wealthy with flashy designer clothes and fading BMWs, and the rich dressed down to disguise themselves, were quite absent. I had known a rich Argentine lady who ran an art gallery in South Kensington as a hobby, while her husband was doing a stint in a London bank. I had been to dinner with them in their rented flat near Victoria Station; they had brought their cook and maid over with them from BA, along with their furniture and oil paintings. The serving maid wore a black uniform with a white pinafore; she was about 18 years old. She chatted happily to her mistress in *porteño* Spanish as she served the dinner, while her husband talked to me about politics. The lady of the *casa* was dressed up to the nines in smart clothes and jewels: she was about 25 and still childless. We could have been in Paraguay, I now realized, except that here the maid would be Guarani, instead of third generation Galician. It was Disraeli who observed that 'colonies do not cease to be colonies merely because they become independent'. He was thinking of the USA in the 19th century, but it applied to Paraguay as well. The sense of déjà-vu, of old Europe preserved in aspic was sometimes so acute that I had to remind myself it was the first decade of the 21st century, not some time in the 1950s. I asked Alejandro if there was still duelling in Paraguay and Argentina. He thought about this hard: 'Well, among civilians, almost certainly not – I've never heard of it. But in the army, it probably still goes on here and there – and in Chile, too.' I had suspected this might be the case – you only had to look at their formal dress uniforms, dripping with swords and gold lace.

There had been an article in the Asunción press stating that 'bio-diesel was a reality in Paraguay'. Someone was mixing vegetable oil and alcohol in a 10–1 ratio and selling it from his garage to diesel users. It was vastly cheaper than imported diesel fuel, but this was one man with a few cans in a small garage, not an industrial enterprise. Paraguay had virtually free electricity from the huge Itapá hydro plant, yet there wasn't a single electric car in the whole country. The sun shone virtually every day of the year, yet there was no solar powered hot water – whatever the British Ambassador claimed. Paraguay was run as a colony still, run on imported ideas and technology created in the USA or Europe for quite other conditions. Paraguayans were incapable of seeing things might be done otherwise. When I asked about electric cars or solar power I got shrugs. When these things were made in the USA or Europe and exported up the river to Asunción, then Paraguayans would start using them. Being a colonial means not having to think for yourself, just imitating what has been evolved in other places. It is part of the great tedium of colonial life – no one is thinking, merely repeating what has been worked out elsewhere. Paraguay was run almost as badly as it is possible to imagine a country being run. Given a small amount of capital almost anything might be produced here. It was potentially immensely wealthy. In reality it survived on raising soya beans and cattle, and the ubiquitous smuggling. 'It has to be very easy, or Paraguayans lose interest immediately,' Mac had observed about the national temperament.

La Recoleta was an ornate Latin cemetery in the Spanish manner, with family vaults above ground which resembled small rococo temples or *palazzi*, each of which was padlocked and chained. There was, of course, a La Recoleta in Buenos Aires, similarly set out, but grander and more pretentious. These vaults were little houses for the dead, grouped as families in death as in life. The coffins were slid into place in wall niches, joining the other dead ancestors. My chauffeuse and I joined the procession which snaked through the walkways between these sarcophagi, following the pallbearers who carried Paula's coffin. I was expecting to see a priest at this stage, with incense, Latin, prayers.

There was nothing of the sort. It was an entirely secular funeral and rather impressive for so being. Paula had left one family house and taken up residence in another, that of her ancestors. This suggested to me that Guarani religious culture had survived in Paraguay despite the ostensible conversion of the country to Spanish Catholicism. There was nothing here of the intense religiosity, the death-obsessed ceremonies and iconography I was familiar with in the Iberian funerary tradition. We all filed silently past the vault into which the coffin bearing Paula had been placed. It was very hot and there was a dense, oppressive throng of people, as many as 200. No one spoke. How many people in Europe have 200 mourners at their funeral, I wondered grimly? I had never been to a funeral with more than four mourners: often I was on my own in the chapel with the priest. Clearly, behind the chaos in Paraguay an unatomized, strong family life persisted. It was heartening.

One of the least attractive aspects of modern Western culture is its intense selfishness. Travel writers from 'advanced' countries almost always go to Third World countries, because in these places people still live largely out of doors and talk to one another and to strangers without inhibitions. Travel books set in Europe or America always have the author spending a great deal of time alone, in hotel rooms and restaurants, and there are very few conversations with the locals. Every time I return to England from a 'poor' country I remark immediately on how alone and how unhappy the people look. The poorer the country, the more frequent the smiles on people's faces; the richer the country, the more evident spiritual misery – the USA being, with Scandinavia, the human high watermark in sheer spiritual wretchedness, with Britain not far behind. The only friend I made in Los Angeles was a 17-year-old boy called Fidel from the Congo: he was the nightwatchman at the boarding house in which I stayed. We spoke French together, and complained about LA and its hostile people. 'As soon as I get some money together I'm going back to the

Congo,' he told me. 'This place is death.' I couldn't have put it better myself. Perhaps now in Europe only a few peasants in the remoter regions of Greece, Italy and Portugal have any sort of organic social life which demonstrates the collective expression of joy and celebration, sadness and tragedy. These qualities, like extreme poverty, have been excised by the Welfare State, bureaucratic employment, and the cult of selfhood above all social ties and obligations. If you want to see unhappiness, boredom and frustration you have only to look at northern European tourists trying to 'enjoy themselves' in Mediterranean or tropical resorts – they are pictures of frustration and misery. To get blind drunk and to fight one another is almost always the end result. They have paid a fortune to 'come on holiday', but once there they do not know what to do: they find themselves as ugly aliens, barbarians in a balmy, long-civilized locale. Work, the slave-state, regimentation, the brutal ugliness of the northern European workers-barracks is all they know, drugs and alcohol their only means of temporary escape. The immense popularity of travel books in places like England, almost always set in Mediterranean, tropical or Asiatic countries, indicates the depth of the malaise. In a recent poll, 47% of British people said they would like to leave the country altogether, for ever. A Cuban refugee I knew married an Englishman, and exchanged extreme poverty and political repression for democratic freedom and bourgeois comfort in Winchester. She hated it. 'No one laughs, no one smiles, no one enjoys themselves, no one has friends or lovers – it's a nothing life, crammed full of goods and insincerity.' She left her husband after a year and returned to poverty and political repression in Cuba.

That there is something desperately wrong with modern Western life has been acknowledged since the critiques of D. H. Lawrence and others in the early part of the 20th century: quite what it is has been more elusive to pin down. Lawrence the novelist elided into Lawrence the travel writer and moral critic of

Western civilization. And there is a tendency for travel writers to become foreign-residence writers: they leave the places they come from, and set up in the places they used to visit. William Dalrymple, for example, now lives in New Delhi as well as London. After walking to Constantinople, Patrick Leigh Fermor built a house in the Peloponnese. There are whole shelves in WH Smith devoted to the genre I had dubbed 'How Green Was My Olive Oil' – the I-bought-a-Ligurian-farmhouse-for-a-song-and-lived-happily-ever-after books. In a world where few now believe in Heaven, the Mediterranean farmhouse has come to be its secular equivalent for millions of northern Europeans. When the Roman Empire was buckling under barbarian assault, one group of Germanic attackers said to the Romans: 'Let us in to settle in your lands, or we will invade and destroy you.' The Romans let them in and settled them on some land: modern second-residence tourism works on much the same principle.

Paraguay itself had once been an exotic tourist destination. Books were written about spending a few months up the river in the northern winter, enjoying the tropical heat and languid pace of life. From being a place of hope and romance, of escape and optimism, Paraguay had descended into that lowest category of contemporary countries – those that do not have their own guidebook for travellers. Graham Greene and Norman Lewis had both visited the country during the depths of the *stronato*; the former had, somewhat unconvincingly, set part of *Travels with My Aunt* in Asunción. The latter had, as usual, found evidence of genocide among the Indians of the Chaco. Neither had been back to report on the post-dictatorship chaos. It is easy to condemn dictatorships when you live in Europe and have just dropped by on a visit: much harder to admit that post-dictatorship democracy often made conditions worse for ordinary people than before. Democracy is an unchallenged good in modern Europe and America – it is simply never questioned. Yet for millions democracy has brought them nothing but disorder, violence and insecurity. Iraq as well as Paraguay suffers this fate as I write. The truth is that the Anglo-American version of democracy has existed in very few countries and for a very short time. As late as 1944 there was not a single democracy in continental Europe except Switzerland and Sweden – fascism or communism ruled supreme. Most European post-1945 democracy is fake, an imitation of a successful model derived from elsewhere. Italian, Spanish, German and French politics are still basically authoritarian, corrupt and dictatorial: the instincts of European politicians are bureaucratic and elitist, secretive and non-consultative. The administration of the European Union itself resembles closely the workings of a non-democratic imperial power of the 19th century, the Austro-Hungarian Empire, for example – EU Commissioners are neither elected nor accountable.

The most celebrated horizontal resident of La Recoleta was probably Madame Eliza Lynch, one-time mistress of the mid-19th century dictator López. She had been plucked from obscurity in the 1960s by the Stroessner regime, and exhumed from Père Lachaise in Paris, when her lover and protector Mariscal Francisco Solano López had been elevated to a national hero, and had been reburied in the Paraguayan Pantheon of Heroes. Expiring on the battlefield fighting the Brazilians with the appropriately heroic words, 'I die with my country' on his lips, Solano López had been hastily buried by Madame Lynch herself, with her bare hands, to prevent wild beasts devouring his corpse, before she was escorted by the Brazilian army downriver, into exile in Europe. Some bones, allegedly those of the defunct Marshal, had been excavated at Cêrro Corá, and reinterred in the mock-Les Invalides in Asunción. López had been turned from arch-fiend and national villain into fallen martyr and stout defender of Paraguay by Stroessner. Madame Lynch had warned off the Brazilian officer who captured her with the words, 'Respect me – I am English,' which was 19th-century code for 'Lay a finger on me and I'll have the Royal Navy up your rivers belching fifty-pounders before you can say Jaicomo Robinson'. He took the hint: she and her surviving bastards, and their not insubstantial loot, were allowed out of the country scot-free: the Paraguayan tradition of claiming any nationality other than Paraguayan *in extremis* was clearly well developed even in the mid-19th century. Madame Lynch's exile was marred by lengthy and acrimonious litigation in Scotland over missing sums of money she claimed she had given to Dr Stewart, a mercenary in the employ of López, when he left Paraguay, to bank for her in Edinburgh. She accused him of stealing it. She was not successful. The new Paraguayan government claimed she and López had stolen the disputed money anyway, and they should have it back: they were also disappointed.

Proving who owned what and who had stolen or smuggled what in Paraguay has never been easy. Possession is eleven tenths of the law, especially if the loot has been squirrelled out of the country and hidden where no one can find it, which is always the case. Now plain Mrs Lynch again, *Madama* retired to Paris, which was shorn of its imperial upstart Napoleon III, though cleaner, better lit, and in possession of more fine new boulevards. Here she lived in quiet obscurity, fading from the public eye. Her critics claim that she returned to the brothel business, in which she had been engaged before she met the Marshal, this time as a madame rather than a whore. She was eventually buried in a pauper's grave in Père Lachaise. While living she had actually returned to Paraguay to try to reclaim some property she said was hers; she was given a heroine's reception at the quayside by the Guarani ladies of Asunción. Perhaps they saw her as a fellow victim of López or perhaps she had been genuinely popular. At any event, the new government immediately shipped her downriver again; all her property in Paraguay had been nationalized, as had López's.

If the Liberales ever managed to get back to government again I wondered what would happen to the bodies of López and Lynch. Dictators who fall out of favour are given short shrift in Paraguay.

Dr Francia, the first of the great crazed 19th-century dictators, who made stark naked Indians wear hatbrims by law, which they had to take off when they passed a soldier, and who had people shot for not saluting all public buildings, or for coming closer than ten yards to his sacred person, was thrown into the river for the alligators to eat after it was finally ascertained that *el Supremo*, as he called himself, had definitely become *el Difunto*, or the Defunct One. After independence from Spain, Francia locked Paraguay up tight for his whole reign, more than 30 years, allowing in no foreigners and allowing out no Paraguayans. Those foreigners who did drift in by accident were kept under house arrest, sometimes for years. Francia made it illegal for Spanish Paraguayans to marry each other, forcing them to wed negroes or Indians, and was the first to organize a secret police, instituting dungeons called the House of Truth where prisoners could neither stand nor lie down, and were chained up and left in the dark for decades on end. During his reign, Paraguay became known as the 'Tibet of South America', so difficult was it to get in or out. Thomas Carlyle, a proto-fascist who admired strong, brutal men in government, wrote an admiring essay on Dr Francia. Paraguay still has not recovered from Francia and Solano López, the two men who between them ruined the country completely: Francia laid the authoritarian base, demanding absolute obedience to his will, Solano López using that dictatorial system to wage war on the whole world, including his family, leading to complete disaster.

The Authentic Radical Liberal Party – an outfit suggesting that there might be an Inauthentic Radical Liberal Party about somewhere, possibly in a Tom Stoppard play – took power after Solano López was killed; but under Brazilian and Argentine occupation, Paraguay had lost its independence, and lay prostrate, bankrupt and with very few adult men left alive, so ruinous had the war been. The émigré Liberals had formed an armed Legion in Argentina, and had fought alongside the Brazilians and Argentinians, something the Colorados had never forgiven them for to this day – they still called them 'legionaries' as an insult. Once it was thought that as few as 10% of the pre-war adult population of Paraguay had survived: this is now thought too low, but the country had certainly been desolated. It was from this time onwards that Paraguayan women stepped in to do much of the work that before had been done by men.

The enthusiasm with which the Paraguayan government welcomed the New Australian and New German colonies, both Utopian experiments which eventually failed, is a sign of how keen they were to get new settlers to repopulate the country. There was – and indeed still is to this day – excellent fertile land, well-watered and capable of bearing good crops, simply going begging, uninhabited and uncultivated. But Paraguay was pretty well last on the list of desirable places to emigrate to in the 19th century. It still is today. Europeans need no visa to enter Paraguay – you just turn up and they give you three months automatically. If you want to stay, buy land, settle, work – no problems. There had been subsequent waves of immigrants, Italians in the late 19th century, Japanese in the 1920s and 1930s, Germans in the late 1940s and early 1950s, Koreans in the 1960s and 1970s. The ousting of Stroessner had stopped the flow. The last in, the Koreans, with the Taiwanese, were now leaving or planning to leave – their roots in the country were still shallow. I had found a little corner shop a few hundred yards from the Gran Hotel, where I used to go to buy biscuits and fruit juice, tins of sardines and milk. It was run by a Korean and his wife, whom I got to know after a few days. We used to chat in Spanish together. 'It was good here,' they both said to me. 'But now it's not good at all. If we could sell this shop we would go back to Korea. It is better back home now.' This was the story I heard from virtually all the immigrants I met. The papers were full of advertisements for apartments, houses, shops, farms for sale, all offered at half or less what they could have commanded a year ago. Those with capital had moved it abroad: those with no money could raise no

154

credit. Counter-intuitively, this was probably the right time to buy, if you had the money – and if you could bear the thought of living even part time in Paraguay. A friend of mine had bought a seafront restaurant in Portugal at the time of the revolution in the 1970s, when it looked as if the communists were going to take over. He had paid almost nothing for it. The owners simply wanted to get out and escape to Brazil. The communists had been foiled, and he had made a good investment, as it turned out. But Paraguay . . . ? You would have to be pretty desperate, though at one time, of course, the country had looked like a sure bet. All the English engineers, artificers, railwaymen and other experts López had signed up to run his steamships, trains and arsenals in the early 1860s thought they were on to a good thing. Immensely wealthy country, go-ahead young President, modern ideas, willing population – place only needs opening up and developing, you could read these Mr Jingle-like opinions in their journals and letters home. Yet it had ended in death, ruin and disaster for most of them. They were never paid, and the few that survived the war emerged broken, with their lives ruined and their nerves shattered. López was no respecter of persons and had been as willing to shoot and torture the English as anyone else. All the grand projects in Paraguay, which started with such high hopes – the Jesuit *Reducciones*, New Germany, New Australia, López's bid for industrial and imperial power – all ended in catastrophic failure. It all looked so easy in Paraguay, but the serpent in this particular paradise always undid these idealistic or ambitious plans. As a country it bred pessimism and skepticism, because nothing ever worked out well, except smuggling, criminality and deceit, which had always been well rewarded and usually escaped punishment.

The post-1945 Germans had played the same role for Stroessner as the English had for López – to provide these men's dictatorships with technical and managerial expertise they otherwise did not have. Ex-Nazis ran Stroessner's army and navy, Dr Mengele of Auschwitz was his personal physician, and German émigré capital and talent ran the banks, factories and *estancias*. But now Stroessner had gone, how many of the Germans and their children and grandchildren would stay? It was not particularly difficult to get out of Paraguay if you were determined. In the USA alone there were an estimated 11 million illegal immigrants, mostly from South America, including a Paraguayan contingent. In Los Angeles I had never seen a middle-class home which did not have latino 'help', as the euphemism for servants was there.

Nine

Piranha Soup

I was now planning to head off into the interior. Alejandro Cara-doc Evans was full of discouraging and unhelpful information. The gist of this was that if I thought Asunción was bad, just wait until I got outside into the rest of the country. I had met a complete lack of national pride in Paraguay – rather the reverse – everyone I spoke to had a low opinion of both place and people. I found myself in the odd position of actually defending the country to its own inhabitants. Wonderful climate, superb natural beauties, unspoilt landscapes, uncrowded, very affordable, superb birdlife, generally friendly and helpful people – but perhaps this last was stretching it a bit far. There were no smiles on anyone's face, and no one knew anything at all when you asked them. The boat service to Concepción upriver? The ticket office by the port was generally closed, but when open it proffered two men asleep on the counter in a deserted and ticketless office. I awoke them both, but neither of them knew anything. '*No se nada, no se nada, no se nada de nada*' might have been the national anthem of Paraguay, I had heard it so often – 'I know nothing, I know nothing, I know nothing about anything'. It was one principle Paraguayans of all political stripes agreed on, they knew nothing. There was the missing spare parts theory, the shortage of diesel possibility, the sunken vessel scenario; perhaps corrupt elements in the government had sold the boats? Or the pirates had captured them? Or the Brazilians had repossessed them way upriver for outstanding debts. All was possible. But there were no boats, and so no tickets. Soldiers, loafers, drinkers around the port were all willing to discuss these theories with me over draughts of maté, but boats or tickets there were none, whatever reason might in the end be correct.

Caradoc Evans was going downhill fast. He sat at the bar in the Gran Hotel, the ancient fan churning the sultry air above his head, his clothes ever more rumpled, glass of beer before him and cigarette in his mouth, as if preparing for a Dylan Thomas self-destruct competition. The barman was still letting him chalk up his drinks and cigarettes. He still had no money or passport. 'Look at this,' he indicated a newspaper clipping with one hand. 'You should watch out when you go up-country.' I read that vampire bats, some infected with rabies, were spreading out of the Amazon region of Brazil into neighbouring Paraguay, due to the cutting down of the rainforest. These bats were biting men, horses, cattle and jaguars while they slept. One fully grown bat could drain more than a pint of blood at a sitting and, if rabid, they infected their victim with incurable madness. 'And then there are the piranhas in all the rivers. They are here in Asunción even, which is why you see no one swimming,' Alejandro added, lighting a new cigarette from the butt of the last. On the terrace outside, through the open french windows, another reception was in full swing, with the ladies in long dresses and the men in black ties and dinner jackets. Cocktails and canapés were being served on silver trays by the hotel's waiters in full-dress uniform, with scarlet cummerbunds, black patent leather pump shoes, snowy white trousers and shirts with black tie. A delicious scent of tropical blossom wafted in through the doors. Faint strains of the hotel band came from beyond the swimming pool, playing a soft cha-cha. 'They attack in swarms,' continued Alejandro remorselessly, signalling the waiter for another beer. 'They actually jump right out of the water in a feeding frenzy. The cattle abattoirs all along the riverside discharge blood and guts straight into the river and the piranhas thrive as a result. There are million upon million of them. You may have noticed the locals here eat a piranha soup – a short food chain, eh? The fish eat the men and then the men eat the fish. If you dip so much as a finger in any of the rivers you risk having your arm stripped to the bone in seconds – they can leap almost a metre out of the water. Fall in and you'll be a skeleton in a matter of minutes.'

With a sinking heart I ordered another beer for myself and tried to look on the bright side. There was the excitement of going into a tropical South American jungle, a wild and untamed nature ... 'And then there is the *candirú* – you know about that don't you?' he asked. I admitted I didn't. 'It is a tiny, microscopic fish that is attracted by the urea excreted by larger fish through their gills. It swims in as the gills open, plunges its fangs into the larger fish's flesh and then sucks the blood – a sort of tiny marine vampire if you like. Then when replete, it withdraws its fangs and swims out through the gills again. The larger fish knows nothing of this. Like the vampire the *candirú* injects a powerful analgesic when its fangs go in so the victim feels nothing at all, like at the dentists, without even the pinprick. The trouble is that the *candirú* cannot tell the difference between the urea a fish excretes and that which a man, a horse, a cow or a jaguar excrete when urinating in or very near a river, stream or pool of water. So when an innocent cow, horse or man decides to take a piss while crossing water, the *candirú* swims up the stream of urine into the penis or the urethra, and lodges itself there, plunging its fangs in and sucking the blood. The only trouble is, it can't swim out again. So it dies and festers, and the animal – or man – dies too, in excruciating agony, very slowly, of internal gangrene and rot.'

Without any conscious thought I found my hands had suddenly gripped my groin in a protective spasm. 'Is there no cure?' I asked. My voice was unaccountably trembly, I remember thinking. 'Well, for men, you can have your penis amputated, if it's caught in time, before the gangrene spreads, but usually you are so far from a hospital that it's not really practical. Some people try a machete job on a tree stump with a bottle of rum as anaesthetic, but you usually die of shock and blood loss. The easiest way out is a bullet in the head. For women there's no hope at all.' Alejandro took a definitive swig of beer with some gusto and stubbed out his cigarette in the ashtray. I was going into the interior, of course, not him. He picked up a small metal tea strainer from the bar that the waiter used for filtering cocktails which had fruit in them. 'This is your best bet,' he advised, placing the strainer in front of himself strategically, like a codpiece. 'Line this with fine-mesh mosquito netting, and take no chances – piss through it. If the mesh is fine enough the *candirú* can't get through.' I suggested, somewhat faintly, that wouldn't it just be enough never to piss anywhere near water. 'Well, in theory, yes. But they are great jumpers, the *candirú*, they can leap up waterfalls, like salmon. They can leap right out of the water, yards even, on the sniff of a stream of urine. You might think you were miles away from water, but a small rivulet can be hidden a yard or so away, under the shrubbery. You whip your dick out for a quiet piss and the little bastard takes its chance and leaps up. You feel nothing, of course, but you're a goner. Why risk it? Take a tea strainer, better be safe than sorry.' I began to think that perhaps I had taken on too much when I had decided to come to Paraguay.

'Have you noticed there are stand-up urinals here in the hotel, on your way to your room?' Alejandro added. I said that I had. He lowered his voice and continued in a confidential tone. 'The *candirú* have got into the municipal water supply of Asunción from broken pipes which lead from the river. The filters are all full of holes. The *candirú* can swim up into the tanks and reservoirs. Many men, here in the city even, prefer to use a stand-up urinal rather than piss directly into a toilet bowl. A boy had a *candirú* swim up his urine stream from a toilet bowl in the city only this year – the *candirú* jumped, you see – he died in agony. They got him to hospital but there was nothing anyone could do.

I always piss through a tea strainer lined with mozzy net, or else in a stand-up urinal.' I suddenly became aware of a prickling, painful sensation in my genitals. 'Don't worry,' he added, seeing my alarm. 'If you had it you'd know all about it. And then, of course, there's the *amigo del culo* – the arse-pal . . .' I had had enough of South American wildlife by now. A sympathetic London editor had advised me before I left to make sure I 'hugged some wildlife' while I was in Paraguay. She had been thinking of David Attenborough and his zoo quest, and I do not imagine for a moment she had these micro-beasties in mind.

'I don't actually want to know about the *amigo del culo*,' I managed to get out with as much firmness as I could manage. My right hand, I noticed, had developed a distinct tremor. 'Well, this little feller is a jumper, too,' he continued, completely ignoring me. 'You are walking through the jungle and it jumps up and grips your skin, like so,' here he mimed a grip with his two hands formed into claws, and made a grimace, baring his teeth. 'It crawls up your leg and into the crack of your arse, and then right up into your *culo*, until it lodges itself inside your lower intestine, where it drinks your blood in the usual South American parasitic fashion, and lays its eggs, which eventually hatch out . . .'

'. . . and eat their way into your vital organs until you die by inches in screaming agony,' I interjected. He looked surprised. 'Oh, you know all about this parasite already then . . . ?'

'I guessed the ending, that's all. No cure possible of course?'

'That's right. Cheers.' He took a swig of beer, raising his glass to my health as he did so. Perhaps, I suddenly thought, I could change my travel arrangements, get a flight out – say tomorrow morning – and go straight to a Greek Island in the Aegean, book into a hotel with a sea view, and write the rest of my Paraguay book from there. No one would ever know. It was a tempting idea. 'No one in their right fucking mind goes into the interior, unless they have to,' added Alejandro with vehemence. 'It's why the whole country is so empty. Snakes, insects, jaguars, pumas, piranhas, pythons, vampire bats, malaria, dengue, yellow fever – and the food is terrible and there's never any beer. Apart from that you'll have a wonderful time, of course.'

Veronica of Sunny Vacaziones had the same message. She turned up her pert little nose and said, 'Snakes and insects, Indians and crazy people, I hate the interior, and the Chaco is the worst.' This might have seemed a poor sales pitch for a Paraguayan travel agency, but Sunny Vacaziones existed to send people out of Paraguay on holidays to exotic, pleasant places. There were posters of Florence and Venice, Rome and Paris, London and Florida on the walls of their office, but none at all of Paraguay. I was like someone wandering into a Thomson Holiday office in Stoke-on-Trent expecting them to help me tour the Black Country. Veronica could book me on a pilgrimage to Lourdes, a beach holiday in Rio, a walking tour of Machu Picchu, a ranch holiday in Arizona, but not a trip to the Chaco, the Jesuit *Reducciones* or the old colony at Nueva Australia. 'No tourists come here because it is so horrible,' she said to me very frankly. 'I want to go and live in Miami with my sister and her husband – is a *paradiso.*'

Getting into the Sunny Vacaziones office was not easy. Although based in the prosperous and relatively calm zone where the Gran Hotel was located, there was a large, electronically operated metal gate behind which an armed guard sat in a white plastic chair, at the top of a stone staircase. He cradled a sub-machine gun in his lap and wore a baseball cap and wrap-around dark glasses, like every other armed guard in the capital. If he liked the look of you when you pressed the buzzer he slipped off the safety catch of his Uzi and pressed his buzzer to open the gate, keeping his weapon trained on you as you climbed up the stone staircase and turned left into the office itself. While examining the posters of Rhodes and San Remo, one was uncomfortably aware that the guard still had his weapon trained on your back through the open door from outside. 'It is necessary,' said Veronica sadly, aware of my unease. 'There have been many robberies. Last year the girl who had my job was raped as well – we had no guard then. Now we have Alfredo.' Unlike post-war Germany, where all the Adolfs simply vanished into thin air, post-*stronato* Paraguay still had plenty of Alfies around. Veronica smiled and gave the guard a little wave over my shoulder. She was a pretty girl, well dressed with a nice figure. The poster of Rhodes looked particularly seductive – no piranha, no *candirú*, no *amigo del culo*, no vampire bats, no Paraguayans. There were no posters at all of anywhere in *el cono sur*, as Paraguay, Uruguay and Argentina were called, anywhere in the city. I explained to Veronica what I was looking for – a skilled, experienced, intrepid and knowledgeable local guide, trustworthy and honest, dependable and reliable, with whom I could entrust myself in my voyages into *el interior*. She nodded brightly. 'This person will not be Paraguayan. I do not think this person is existing, actually, ever in the history of South America. This would be a saint whose blood liquifies every year and to whom the peons light candles. If he was skilled and knowledgeable he would not be in Paraguay, but in *el norte*, working and earning many dollars. If he was intrepid and experienced he would be a politico or a bandit – or both. The only Paraguayan who would go into *el interior* would be stupid, ignorant and without any culture, and who you would not want to let into your bathroom. Unless he owned a big *estancia*, of course and was very rich and had an *avionetta* to go to Miami for *el shopping*.' At this thought she brightened up considerably. 'Yes, you could stay on a big *estancia*. This would be quite comfortable with electricity and hot showers. You could ride horses and have an *asado* – a roast meat feast from the barbecue. This is what foreigners used to do when they came to Paraguay in the time of Don Alfredo.' She didn't actually cross herself at this point, or genuflect, but clearly Alfie had another devout fan in Veronica. 'It would be very, very boring, but you would see *el interior*, and not become a dying tourist in the process, which would be so sad,' she concluded happily. I had to agree with the last sentiment.

In fact, I didn't disagree with this proposition at all: getting anything at all organized in Paraguay was so difficult that the promise even of a full-costume Boy Scout Jamboree would have excited my interest. I tried another tack. 'What about a foreigner then?' I asked. 'Are there any of these acting as guides to *el interior*?' There had been a Mennonite called Paula who had once arranged trips to the Chaco and the jungle, I had heard, but she had moved to Canada. I had visited her erstwhile travel agency, now covered by an elaborate metal grill, behind which sat the ubiquitous Paraguayan security guard who pointed his Colt .45 automatic at my stomach, and repeated the Paraguayan national anthem '*No se nada*, etc'. Many of the Mennonites were reported to be leaving the country. 'Is very dangerous now, Paraguay. Everybody leaving,' Veronica chipped in when I mentioned it. 'I prefer Miami.' This was evidently an *idée fixe* with her.

The Annual Day of the Police had arrived. The newspapers all published reverential supplements praising the – as yet still unpaid – defenders of the whole society. The force, clad in military uniforms of a greenish-khaki hue, peaked military hats, white blancoed ammunition pouches hanging from white straps and belts, rifles at the ready, looked on as the Paraguayan flag was raised over the tomb of the Unknown Policeman Gunned Down By Drug-Crazed *Cocaleros*, and a pudgy senior officer bent over to light a candle at the shrine of Santa Rosa of Lima, the force's patron saint. Flowers in brass vases and other small votive gifts stood at his feet. By decree of Monsignor Anibal Mena Parte, the Church's high dignitary responsible for allocating saints, Asunción's Finest had been under Santa Rosa's personal protection for the last 19 years. The force was, in *Ultima Hora*'s words, '*una institución que está al servicio de toda la comunidad*', though not, one supposes, at the service of the substantial criminal elements of the community. On the other hand, perhaps it was, that is if there were any parts of Paraguayan society which could be considered completely non-criminal. The police chief himself was currently under indictment for corruption, and there was considerable local speculation into what precisely the police would do if they were not paid their back-wages before the big Oviedista rally-cum-demonstration was staged in a few weeks' time.

Taking advantage of the Police's Saint's Day was Perfecta SAMI a local gun retailer which had three special offers for its customers, pictured in its advertisement in the supplement. There was the .38 calibre Rexia revolver, available in matt black or silver; the 15 shot semi-automatic rifle Marlin – a direct import from the USA, we were advised – the best-selling rifle in the world; and for the ladies, there was the C2 automatic pistol, calibre 6.35, designed for the handbag, available in matt black. Customers with e-mail could order directly from perfecta@supernet.com.py.

The Paraguayan police in dress uniform looked like soldiers from the 1950s, General Franco's Spanish Foreign Legion, perhaps. The actual army itself was more exotic. In a country where horses cost as little as US$45 each and conscript labour was free, the exuberant, baroque spirit of the country flowered into esoteric cavalry regiments – lancers, uhlans, hussars, sabre-wielding horsemen, all in the appropriate 18th or 19th-century dress uniforms, accoutred with lance and sabretache, carbine and shako, frogging, knee boots, spurs and pennons. If anyone was so foolish as to invade Paraguay, they would be met with cavalry charges which would put the Polish army of 1939 to shame. Was there another country in the world that still had regiments of lancers? Paraguayans assured me that both Argentina and Uruguay still had them, too. Before I left Sunny Vacaziones, Veronica had opened a drawer to give me her card – and of course there had been a perfectly formed lady's pearl-handled automatic nestling in between a packet of Virginia cigarettes and a pack of tampons – the essential trio for every smart young gal about town in Asunción, surely. There was always the chance that Alfredo might nod off, that the Uzi might jam, or *force majeure*, in the form of a bazooka-wielder might appear. Or, more prosaically, Veronica probably had to go home by bus, like everyone else.

On my way back to the hotel I bought a bottle of Argentine red wine and a packet of biscuits from the Korean corner shop. I intended to consume these on my own, in my room. Every time I went into the bar I was waylaid by Alejandro Caradoc Evans who was proving depressing company. Mac was due back from Ciudad del Este shortly and had promised he would phone me: I was hoping his contacts in the north-east would help me. I failed to avoid Alejandro, however: he was sitting in the foyer in front of the large stone fireplace, watching a programme on local TV about diphtheria and yellow fever in Paraguay, entertainment custom-made for him. Small, diseased children, pathetic in their hospital cots, gaped and drooled at the camera. There were no blankets, mattresses or sheets, let alone medicines in the hospital: it was simply somewhere to take people to die. Against my better judgement, Alejandro led me off to the bar, where, I knew, I was in for another diatribe of some sort. The papers were full of the current spate of false police; they had been robbing Brazilian tourists who had come across the border in the north-east to buy contraband. 'The police don't get paid here, so they pay themselves by robbing the public,' commented Alejandro, settling again on his favourite bar stool. I said I thought these were 'false police', not real ones. 'The difference is purely academic in this country. All the police here are false police. The police are bandits and the bandits pretend to be police. How does anyone know whether they are real police or false police robbing tourists? If they are real police they just make sure they are using cars with false number plates – it's not difficult.' I asked Alejandro how people could bear to live under conditions of such chaos and disorder. 'They don't live, they go through the motions. They pretend. It's all V. S. Naipaul stuff – mimic men. Argentina is a copy of a forgotten, now imagined, Europe, and Paraguay is a distorted copy of a copy, with local crazies thrown in on account of the Guarani who are culturally out to lunch, and historically several sandwiches short of a picnic.' I asked him, then, where his remarkable knowledge of colloquial English had come from. I had met *porteños* – people from Buenos Aires – in London, but they didn't have his grasp of the vernacular. 'Well, both my parents spoke the gringo lingo at home, it was their mother tongue, not Welsh, and we all spoke it at boarding school. My Spanish is fairly ropy, actually. There are more than a quarter of a million Argies of Brit descent, mostly in or around BA, and we are quite cliquey, intermarrying and so on. I mean we are Anglican, my family, not Methodist or Papist. We all spoke of "the Argies" as the other lot, behind closed doors.' Who had his family supported during the Falklands/Malvinas war? I asked. Had he served in the Argentine armed forces? He looked a bit embarrassed about this, and twiddled with his packet of cigarettes, avoiding my eyes. 'God no, weak heart, doctor's certificate, no chance of my getting mixed up with those psychopaths,' he said finally. And the Falklands? 'Borges called it two bald men fighting over a comb. Who knows – there may be vast reserves of oil down there. My parents found it convenient to drag themselves over to Montevideo in Uruguay for a few months – they've got a flat by the seaside over there. I happened to be down in Pat with relatives, just a nipper, you see, remember nothing about it all . . .' his voice trailed away, lost in ambiguity. So who did you all support? I insisted. 'It was a bloody nuisance, as far as my parents have told me – embarrassing, dangerous and a waste of everyone's time. Maybe the Paraguayans should have the islands, then they could start a high seas piracy fleet. They could rename them The Isabels. Only one person has really understood Paraguay. Know who that was?' I said I didn't. 'Joseph Conrad. His novel *Nostromo* was based directly on his researches into Paraguay during the dictatorship of Solano López and the War of the Triple Alliance. If you read Masterman's book *Seven Eventful Years in Paraguay* you will find all the characters there that Conrad adopted for *Nostromo*. Monygham was an English sculptor tortured by López – Conrad turns him into a doctor tortured by his fictional dictator. Mr Gould was the British consul in BA who came upriver to try to get the British out, Captain Fidanza was an Italian ship's captain whose vessel was confiscated by López. This Fidanza, the name Conrad used for his hero-anti-hero Nostromo, was shot by López. Costaguana – the coast of birdshit, in Spanish – is a pretty good name for Paraguay when you think of it, though as it happens there's neither a coast nor any birdshit here, as such.'

I knew about this. George Frederick Masterman had been one of the many British experts, or mercenaries, employed by Solano López in his efforts to modernize Paraguay sufficiently to take on Brazil and Argentina, and so become Emperor of Southern South America. Masterman had been Military Apothecary at the General Hospital in Asunción, and had known all the principal players on both sides in the disastrous war. Unlike most of them he had survived to tell the tale. His book 'a narrative of personal experience among the Paraguayans' was published in London in 1869 when he was safely back in Europe again. He describes the grotesque cruelties of López in deadpan style. The dictator had two large jaguars in cages at Humaita, to which he fed Brazilian prisoners – 'immense brutes' is how Masterman describes them. They became so sated with human flesh that after only a short while López had to go back to shooting his prisoners. The jaguars, the '*tigres*' of Paraguay, were no longer interested. López's preferred torture was splitting the fingers and their bones with mallet and chisel, as well as the infamous '*cepo uraguayo*', originally called the '*cepo boliviano*' as it was invented during the Bolivian War of Independence. This device, one of South America's contributions to the world's stock of torture methods, was exquisitely agonizing: the victim had a musket placed under his bent knees as he sat on the ground. This was attached to another musket resting on his neck. The two were fastened together by tight cords on either side: additional muskets could be added on top of the neck. The back is bent, the head thrust forward, and blood circulation is inhibited. Even an hour of this torture semi-cripples a man for days afterwards, and the pain is excruciating. Before López's victims were put in the *cepo uraguayo* they were generally staked out naked on the ground in full sun, tied to four orange trees, for the whole day, and given no water. More than a day in the *uruguayana* crippled a man for life. Conrad gives a graphic description of this torture in *Nostromo*, which he got straight from Masterman. López was accompanied by his personal torturers and interrogators wherever he went; the two worst were Roman Catholic priests, notionally chaplains in the Paraguayan army, in uniform, with small crucifixes grotesquely sewn on to their tunics. Prisoners were loaded with double irons, blacksmiths forging fetters so heavy the prisoners could scarcely walk. Apart from splitting fingers and toes with hammers, whips for back and buttocks, iron scourges and red hot pincers were also used on eyes, noses, genitals and the soft fleshy parts. López had his own brothers shot for treason, after months of torture, and carried his mother and sisters around in iron cages on carts, taking them out to have them whipped in public at regular intervals. Anyone who surrendered or lost a battle or retreated was a traitor, and was tortured first, then shot or fed to the jaguars. Suspicion, whim or bad temper were enough for López to condemn whole regiments to torture and execution.

While his armies were fighting the Brazilians and Argentinians, his prisons were bursting with those suspected of conspiracy, plots and treachery. As these victims were executed, more were arrested and tortured. The whole country was a charnel house, hundreds of thousands perished in agony and for nothing. Garrisons were decimated, officers executed on the merest whims, the foreign consuls imprisoned, tortured, beaten and finally shot. Until right at the end, at Cêrro Corá, no one dared take the obvious step and shoot López himself, thus ending the grotesque carnival of madness. Disease killed the great majority of Paraguayans during this insane war, after that López's executions, and in poor third came casualties on the battlefield at the hands of the enemy: no one knows how many died, although the overwhelming majority of the male population perished. Masterman blamed the Jesuits for having inculcated the Guarani population into a blind, unquestioning obedience to their superiors. Many contemporaries of López, including Captain Richard Burton, who visited the battlefields while the war was still going on, refused to believe López's cruelties. It was only after the war when the collected testimonies of the survivors emerged that the full horrors of his regime were exposed. Politics and ideology played a part in this process of denial. Brazil was an empire which still had slavery; Paraguay a republic which – nominally at least – had abolished slavery. The Brazilian army was led by European aristocrats. Thus, supporting Brazil against Paraguay was very difficult for 'progressive' opinion in the USA and Europe to countenance. López, advised by Madame Lynch, portrayed himself as the gallant republican defender of a small 'native state' which had abolished slavery, and was progressive, freedom-loving: many fell for this astute but completely misleading propaganda. Masterman also blamed Madame Lynch: it was she, he said, who placed the absurd notion of López becoming Emperor in his head, encouraging him to emulate Napoleon I and III of France. There is a passage in *Nostromo* where one of the Costaguanan officers, who is busy stealing Dr Monygham's pocket watch, unleashes a paean of praise for Bonapartism and the 'higher democracy' where the heroic imperial master spirit unites the nation and raises it to an empire through glorious acts of war and conquest. Conrad always had at the back of his mind – and often right at the front of it too – the partition and subjugation of his native Poland by the empires of Austria, Prussia and Russia in the 18th century. He was acutely sensitive to imperialist oppression. His own family had been deported to Russia from Poland and killed. The reason he himself became a naturalized British subject, rather than a French citizen, was that France had a treaty of extradition with Russia and England did not. Conrad, once safely a British citizen, frequently went back to Poland. He was, in fact, in 'enemy' Poland when the first war was declared, and only managed to get out and back to England with much difficulty. Costaguana is based on Paraguay, but it also stands in for tyrannized, oppressed Poland, and it is no coincidence that his anti-hero who betrays the nationalist revolution by stealing for himself the silver of the mine is an Italian from another European Catholic country with a long history of partition and colonial oppression by Austria and Spain, reunited by Garibaldi after a nationalist revolution and war of liberation such as Conrad dreamt of for his own Poland.

Francisco Solano López, dictator at war with his whole people, scourge and flail, paranoiac destructor-general, had already been imagined before Conrad, by the Marquis de Sade, that anti-Rousseau who had taken the Enlightenment idea of 'Nature' and 'natural' and painted them red in sadistic tooth and claw. From his prison cell in the Bastille, held under *lettre de cachet*, de Sade imagined the King of Batua in the Congo, whose whole reign was an endless series of massacres, persecutions, tortures and destructions of his own people. The reason? Because he enjoyed it. Sadism, de Sade's involuntary contribution to the lexicon of sexual abnormality, is just that – the enjoyment of torture, pain and death. De Sade points out that nature is cruel and the most natural men and women are the cruellest, because Nature is merely a vast impersonal engine of destruction. Justice, fairness, kindness and love are all simply illusions, pain, suffering and death are the supreme realities. William Blake, in his poem on the fall of the Bastille, refers to de Sade as 'a writer prophetic' and in this as many other things Blake was more right than he can have known. De Sade's dystopian vision preceded the discovery by Europeans of African kingdoms in the mid-19th century, such as that of the Buganda in East Africa, which operated on precise and exact Sadean principles. The Kabaka of Buganda, as John Hanning Speke revealed after his visit to the country, executed sometimes dozens, sometimes hundreds of victims every day, merely for his own amusement. His Court laughed with him at the sufferings of the victims. Solano López, like Ali Pasha of Jannina, is a true Sadean hero, who murdered and tortured for pure pleasure, and who destroyed almost his whole country before he was finally struck down himself, probably by one of his own soldiers, after being cornered by the Brazilians at Cêrro Corá as he was trying to escape to Bolivia in 1865.

William Blake's rhetorical question, asked in his poem 'Tyger', what 'could frame thy fearful symmetry' is the age-old question about the nature of cruelty and evil. If the world was created by an omnipotent Power of Good, then who or what made the tiger and the typhus bacillus, the rabid vampire bat, the *candirú*, the piranha, the *amigo del culo*, and the Paraguayan Technical Service – and why? Costaguana, like contemporary Paraguay, had been imagined by de Sade two centuries ago. The most visionary authors are often not the most comfortable to live with. The dystopian futures imagined by George Orwell and Aldous Huxley have not come to pass exactly, but neither could it be said that they have proved false visions. Elements taken directly from the works of de Sade, Orwell and Huxley can easily be found in everyday life all around the globe. López was one in a long line of destructive dictators who ruined their people in pursuit of a fantasy of power. The guns and swords, glittering uniforms and brass bands, warships and cannon all proved illusory and useless: death and oblivion awaited them all. Alexander of Macedon – 'that tumour of a man' as Seneca rightly called him – was the model for Hannibal and Caesar, Napoleon Bonaparte and Hitler, and all the rest from Bokassa to Mobutu. The proposition – a man of destiny coming from a poor, backward outstation could by boldness, dash, genius, force of will, gather a huge army and conquer the world. Yet all of these would-be conquerors were failures. Alexander died at 33, a drunkard no longer in control of his own army. He had won a series of battles, but like Napoleon and Hitler, had achieved nothing at all. Psychologists have a theory that gamblers do not play to win but to lose, to ruin themselves, and will play on until they have achieved this goal. López, like Hitler and Napoleon, was of that ilk. The war he started against Brazil, Uruguay and Argentina was pointless and unwinnable. He could have stopped at any time. The Allies offered him peace at every turn and finally, when he had lost completely, proposed that he retire to Europe with all his loot, stolen from the people of Paraguay. He refused, out of vanity and stupidity, and so died in a swamp as pointlessly as he had lived, shot to death by an unknown hand. Nothing of his imperial vision survived him except the absurd half-made buildings he started to put up.

Yet Paraguayans – or many of them at least – thought all this was glorious stuff, that López was a martyr and that they should call their wretched *mestizo* offspring Anibal, Napoleon, Julio César, Alejandro and so on, just in case the sympathetic magic might work again. All over the Latin world – in Spain, France, Italy and South America – populist heroes with despotic ambitions kept coming up to overthrow kingdoms, republics or democracies. The French still had no real idea of why Napoleon and all his Marshals were defeated by Wellington. 'Waterloo was a first-class battle won by a second-rate general' is a widespread French saying, quoted approvingly by Victor Hugo himself in *Les Misérables*. Yet what did that make Napoleon, to be defeated by a 'second-rate general'? All over the world there are Napoleonic clubs and societies, replete with bees, eagles, imperial baubles and bagatelles, but there are no fan clubs for the victor, the man who beat Napoleon and all his Marshals – 'Villain-ton' as the French so wittily called him after the occupation. In South America, to this day, Hitler and Mussolini are both widely admired; no one has even heard of Montgomery, Patton, or Eisenhower, the men who had defeated them. 'He will not be content to stay as he is, now he has done what he has done – he will change the regime,' Bonaparte observed of Wellington, when on St Helena. Wellington, of course, did no such thing. He was a loyalist and a constitutionalist. He took his seat in the House of Lords, eventually became a very ineffectual Prime Minister, and was finally removed from office, still entirely loyal to Crown, Parliament and the British Constitution, the last of which he thought simply 'could not be improved upon' when he was once asked. Napoleon was merely thinking what he himself would do had he been in Wellington's place, make a *coup d'état* and impose his own personal rule. Undersupplied, poorly equipped, never wholly trusted by Parliament, dependent upon sea power for his every musket, bullet and gram of powder, unable to call upon conscripts, saddled with a drunken, ill-disciplined and often quite uncontrollable army, Wellington had defeated Napoleon's Marshals one by one in Spain by slow, dogged persistence, and intelligent, unshowy mastery of the military arts, particularly those of victualling, supply and strategic retreat.

Like Solano López, Napoleon never bothered himself with where his supplies came from and, as in Egypt and Russia, simply abandoned armies he led to disaster because they could not be resupplied. He could always raise fresh ones in France with conscription. Vanity, egoism and self-conceit motivated both of them, as it does all dictators and military adventurers. None of them ever learnt because they were too vain, too arrogant and too proud: Bonaparte told his Marshals to live off the land, to steal from the peasants in the countries they occupied, to rob, pillage and loot. The peasants, ravaged and plundered beyond endurance, in return formed into guerrilla bands, murdered French soldiers, and helped the enemies of Bonaparte all they could. 'A night in Paris will replace all these,' Napoleon had said, indicating the thousands of French dead on one of his battlefields. He used up his troops profligately, throwing them away as all absolute military rulers have done, including López and Hitler. Napoleon never grasped the importance of sea power any more than did Hitler. With England uncrushed and uninvaded, the dictators were going to be ground down eventually by a coalition of allies supplied through the element they could not control, with superior supplies intelligently applied. Wellington, like Montgomery, hoarded supplies and men and munitions. He also paid for what he needed: when he invaded France, inn keepers and peasants were astounded actually to be paid for what his men consumed. Rommel lost in the desert for the same reason López did in Paraguay – he ran out of supplies. Montgomery and the Brazilians won because they were better equipped and used their forces to better effect. López was always going to lose the War of the Triple Alliance for, like Napoleon and Hitler, he had no idea what made a victorious army. Winning battles is nothing at all in war, unless you defeat the enemy. López had as much chance of defeating Brazil as Hitler did of defeating the USA.

'A fool and his money are easily parted' has its military equivalent with a dictator and his armies. In a democratic system, even a limited aristocratic democracy such as Georgian England, the generals were subject to political restraint and economic discipline. If they made serious errors or overstepped their authority they were removed and replaced. Under the dictatorship, pleasing the dictator is all that matters; courtiers, flatterers and time servers surrounded López, Hitler and Napoleon alike, feeding their illusions: at the end, when disaster loomed, these all jumped ship and abandoned their masters, whom they had only followed for self-advancement. There is also perhaps a religio-cultural element in this equation. Perón, Hitler, Napoleon and López had all grown out of a Roman Catholic society, born and brought up where women, mothers and nurses all spoiled, petted and pampered boys, making much of them, and not breaking their wills. The authoritarian macho attitude in Catholic culture has been traced directly back to child-rearing differences between Catholics and Protestants. Traditionally, in Protestant countries the male child, perceived as sinful and wicked, was slapped down, his ego tamed, trammelled and trained to obedience. He was made to subordinate himself to authority and hierarchy, forced to co-operate with his peers for the good of the group. In Catholic countries the male child was indulged, spoiled and encouraged to be unreasonable, autocratic and uncompromising, expecting to subordinate others to his will as an adult, basking always under the sun of the Queen of Heaven's approval – whether the Virgin, his mother or his nurses. All the modern team sports – football, cricket, rugby, baseball, basketball, tennis doubles, etc. – are the products of Protestant Anglo-Scottish-American culture. They have been taken up universally, and played with great success in many Latin countries, such as Brazil, Argentina and France. Yet the brilliance of Latin sport is that of individuals dominating the group – the racing driver, the airplane pilot, the outstanding prima donna footballer. It is the individualist, passionate, egotistical, selfish; Pelé or Maradona are the Napoleons of the football field. They succeed because they exceed and tower over their own team by sheer virtuosity. They win like this for a while, but it is always a flash in the pan. Their talent fades, their squad is relegated after time. Coaches in all Latin countries face the same problem – attempting to get their players to operate as a team rather than as competing individuals.

All the problems of places like Paraguay can be traced back to what the Spanish called '*Yo-ismo*' – 'Me-ism'. The individual always considers himself first, second and last, even when it is evidently counter-productive. The qualities Latins most admire in Anglo-Saxons are self-restraint, self-discipline, sang-froid, reliability and punctuality, in Argentina '*la hora inglesa*' – 'the English time' – was a synonym for being bang on time, something they themselves rarely ever were. Although these qualities were admired they were not widely emulated. Style, elegance, brio, bravura (even to the point of arrogance), vanity, egoism and selfishness, were the qualities that were widespread in Latin countries. Honesty or criminality had nothing to do with it, the successful thief was admired, the unsuccessful honest man was not. In England or the USA financial impropriety always led to commissions of inquiry, scandals and forced resignations, in Latin America never. The cry of the *descamisados* in Argentina – 'the shirtless ones', as the poor were called – *'Ladrón o no, queremos Perón'* ('thief or not, we want Perón') expressed the Latin-American reality. Perón was a successful thief, that was his popularity with the poor. So why not then falsify the receipts, pilfer the stores, put your brother in office and abstract millions from the state and transfer it abroad, abroad to a banking system run by Protestants who would not, it was assumed, steal it again? Everyone else was doing it. 'The wealth of the state is an Ocean – he who does not avail himself of it is a pig,' went the old Ottoman proverb. Spain, it should be recalled, was ruled and occupied by Moors and Arabs from North Africa for over 700 years, and the oriental way of doing things has deep Hispanic roots.

What looked like folly – the offering of endless loans to these bankrupt regimes by the largely Protestant-run, capitalist West – was in fact a policy of cynical cruelty. The debtor nations had to keep servicing their debts or they would get no more loans. 'Rich countries don't like to lend money to poor countries,' Hugo had complained to me, self-pity in his voice, when the topic of the stalled IMF loan to Paraguay had come up in conversation. In fact, the very opposite was true. The capitalist system battened on to the feckless poor, the permanently indebted, who were charged outrageous interest rates on each new loan, whether to individual spendthrift proletariat or bankrupt Third World governments. The rich West loved to lend to poor, profligate, corrupt countries. These were the only ones which would sign up for the disadvantageous terms, not quibble over the onerous conditions, and strap themselves to high repayment interest rates. Catch the USA or Switzerland borrowing from the IMF? Not likely. Capitalism in its loan-shark mode works best when you have hopelessly improvident borrowers sitting on countries full of rich natural resources which can be used to service debt. Paraguay was not in reality a 'poor' country – it was potentially very rich. If it were owned and run by the Swiss, or the Singaporeans, instead of the Paraguayans, it would be one of the two or three richest per capita countries in the world.

'Derby Club' cigarettes were made by Anglo-American Tobacco in Paraguay. It was alleged in the press that five times as many 'Derby Club' cigarettes were manufactured than were consumed here, yet there were no legal exports. So where did they go? That they were being smuggled into Brazil, Uruguay and Argentina was a reasonable supposition. Money could be made in Paraguay, and was being made, but it did not stay in the country, nor was it taxed there. Nor did the international loans stay in the country either – these went straight back abroad again into numbered accounts in tax havens in the West. Foreign aid had accurately been called a system whereby the poor in rich countries were taxed to send money to rich people in poor countries, who then sent it back to rich people in rich countries to look after for them. The ultimate beneficiaries of foreign aid were banks in the West, which got the money back again, and the interest as well. 'If you see a Swiss banker jump out of a fifth-storey window, jump after him – there will be 5% in it,' observed Voltaire, who lived at Verney, within easy reach of Swiss territory, to where he could flee if the King of France decided to arrest him. An updated version of this saying would probably increase the profit to 15% or more. The scandal of Swiss Bank money laundering, particularly of Nazi loot stolen in World War II has been amply chronicled: no one does anything about it because all governments find it useful to have such bolt-holes for their own dubious transactions.

In a sense, Paraguay, which was an extreme example of the traditional Third World kleptocracy, was still fighting the War of the Triple Alliance, though now through economic means.

Uruguay, Argentina and Brazil were the targets of Paraguayan smuggling, dope and gun-running, Customs evasion, brazen theft and armed robbery, just as they had been in the 1860s when Solano López was trying to conquer them by force of arms. You could buy anything you wanted in Paraguay, and cheaply. Argentina, Brazil and Uruguay had high tariffs and protectionist taxes to preserve their industries and so employ their working classes. Paraguay didn't. The rich in Paraguay wanted for nothing, except national infrastructure and a sense of security. The poor got closer to starvation every day in a land with ample water and thousands of acres of fertile land which no one could be bothered to cultivate, in which vast herds of cattle roamed which were rendered down into Oxo cubes or killed merely for their hides and tallow. With its small population and favourable climate Paraguay ought to have been immensely prosperous instead of bankrupt and on the edge of dissolution as a country.

After far too many beers with Alejandro, pondering on these and other matters, I staggered off to bed in the still, warm tropical night, fragrant with the scent of jasmine and rose.

Ten

Up River

Dawn was the best time. While it was still dark I would rise, the slight chill delightful on my skin, and go out on to the terrace to sit and breathe in the fresh, dew-laden air. The whole of the city was silent, the traffic stilled at last. The heat and noise of the day was a memory, that of the day to come hours away yet. From the damp, ochre soil in the courtyard garden still rose the night scents from plants and flowers. I sat on an old white-painted wicker chair, and sipped a glass of iced water. All the charm of the tropics – the lush fecundity of the vegetation, the sense of bursting, thrusting life seemed suspended for an instant in time, that no man's land between night and day which is the dawn. First faint traces of pink etched themselves in from the east over the dark mass of the roman tiled roof. Around me, if I kept still, the birds fluttered and twittered, a last bat lurching and looping away through the air, fleeing the approach of day. At my right, by my shoulder, a tiny hummingbird, smaller than my thumb, was just visible, thrusting its beak into the nest of petals in a hibiscus, sipping nectar or dew. Paraguay at this time truly was a paradise, and without any serpents – they were asleep or otherwise engaged. There was nothing here that brought to mind this century or the last. This is how Madame Lynch, Dr Francia, Irala, all the person-ages of history would have known the land, its pristine magic intact. At such a moment it was easy to see how people could have dreamt not of silver or gold, but of perfecting mankind in a Utopia amid a benign Nature. Everything was so perfect, so beautiful, so exactly right. The problem as ever was the human element. E. M. Cioran, the Roumanian philosopher, remarked on the tragedy of having been born after man arrived on the scene – and now so many, so pointlessly many of our dreadful species. The world had supported half a billion before the advent of carbon-fuel technology; now it suffered six billion, and rising remorselessly. After he became bored in Italy and before he engaged in the crusade for Greek independence, Lord Byron had built a schooner called the *Bolivar* and had thought seriously of sailing to South America to buy a province in Peru. This, surely, was the dream of tropical America that had seduced Europeans since the Conquest; it was not a dream, but alas it only lasted a few minutes every day. I always stayed as long as I could on the covered terrace, watching the first rays of the sun, pale and vapid, striking the large banana plant across the patio courtyard, its light spreading through the leaves like veins of energy. The chill departed from the air; it vibrated with warmth. The birds were visible now, hopping and fluttering, crying more loudly in the light. It is worth coming to South America for the birdlife alone. It was like an illustration from a French medieval Book of Hours, *Les Très Riches Heures du Duc de Berry*, trees, plants, bushes were alive with birds of all sorts. One simple truth about the Southern Hemisphere is that there is less land, more water, and far fewer people than in the Northern Hemisphere. The south is simply less ruined, less used up, less degraded by the constant crush and press of an overnumerous humanity. Chateaubriand's observation that 'forests precede civilizations, deserts succeed them' is amply evidenced in South America, where, in spite of all the threats, there is still more forest than anywhere else on Earth.

A sudden light flooded into the courtyard, parting the dark shapes, making clear the individual plants and trees, splashing them with violent tropical colours: I was in a painting newly made by Gauguin or the Douanier Rousseau. The dew was sucked up invisibly, and vanished from the coarse grass. Now it was day, and the chatter of the first gardeners could be heard beyond the far wall, where they collected their hoes and rakes. Then – and only then – when paradise was about to be invaded by the omnivorous biped, would I abandon my reverie and my vision of what I had come to South América to discover, and go back into my room to shower and prepare to face the difficulties of the day ahead, where I knew from experience I would achieve little or nothing. Paradise in Paraguay lasted about ten minutes every dawn – after that two-footed serpents were in the ascendant.

It was on one such morning when the patio was still grey with half-light and the birds still mute and invisible that an unwonted shape made its way purposefully and silently towards my room, muffled in shadows. As the mystery visitor approached me on silent feet he put up his finger to his lips to bid me to silence. It was Mac, now evidently back from the north-east. He beckoned that we should go into my room. He shut the door behind us, and still standing, spoke in a low urgent tone. 'It's happened at last, the shit has finally hit the fan. Lino Oviedo crossed the border from Brazil last night with a group of Army officer malcontents. He is marching – or rather driving – on Asunción as we speak. Two regiments in the north are said to have risen already in his support, and are moving south to join him with several tanks and armoured cars. The news has not yet got out here – he's been cutting telephone wires and blowing up mobile phone masts I hear, and imposing a blackout on his progress. I had a call from a contact in Brazil fifteen minutes ago with the news. I came straight here. You have to get out, and fast. When the news gets out here there will be complete panic – every plane, every boat and every car is going to be heading for the border. There will be a stampede to get out before the fighting reaches here. The government will have to make a stand here. This is where the fighting will be.' I felt a chill descend on my stomach. My mouth suddenly felt very dry. 'Oviedo hates journalists. He has threatened to round up all he can find and shoot them all on the spot – foreigners included. There's nothing in between him and Asunción that I know of. He'll be here tomorrow, short of a miracle, the day after at the latest if the tanks break down, which they may. Now is the time for you to get out while you can. Delay – any delay – will be fatal.'

I sat on the edge of the bed, a sense of hopelessness flooding over me. Trust my luck to time my visit for the long-awaited military coup attempt. The country would probably be in chaos for months if not years, travel in the interior impossible. There might be a long civil war of the sort that killed hundreds of thousands before Stroessner came to power. 'How do I get out?' I asked. 'Start packing and I'll tell you,' Mac replied. 'Take your money, your passport, one change of clothing, whatever medicines you have, a notebook and pens, your mosquito net – leave everything else here. You have to travel light. Just take a day pack. If all this blows over you can come back and collect the rest later. It will slow you up now though. And you need to move fast.' This made sense. I had already arranged with the Gran Hotel to leave my belongings in my room when I went into the bush, and I had paid my bill just the day before, so I owed them nothing.

In less than ten minutes the two of us were moving through the still silent, shadowed gardens towards the reception. Mac explained to the desk clerk that I was off to the interior for a while, and to keep my room just as it was until I returned. We got into Mac's four-wheel drive and moved slowly – unnaturally slowly, I felt – out of the front gate and into the streets of a still slumbering Asunción.

'There is a *lancha* leaving upriver for Concepción right now. The *capitán* is both a friend of mine and an employee. I have had to move all my own plans forward because of this. It won't be comfortable but it will only be for two days and a night, *mas o menos*, more or less. In Concepción you'll be met. I've warned them already. They knew you were coming anyway. It's a Liberal stronghold and the Libs may come out for Oviedo. At any rate, he won't go there because it's irrelevant. Lie low and see what happens. If you have to get out fast – if Oviedo starts a real bloodletting, there'll be boats going up to Brazil and Bolivia, or you can catch a truck across the north-east border to Brazil. My guys will take you. Don't expect to hear from me for a while. I have to go to ground.'

We turned down to the right off Avenida España, by the old Botanical Gardens, heading for the river. We were miles from the port zone downtown.

'What are you going to do?' I asked.

'I have several important consignments that I have to disperse before the mob goes out on a looting spree. Then I'll head into the Chaco – I've got friends there. If the worst comes to the worst I can head down into Argie-land until the dust settles.'

It grew light around us. On the grass under the trees lay the bodies of sleeping Indians, huddled together for warmth. We drove down a rutted, sandy track after the road petered out, almost to the river bank. Before we got out, Mac reached into the glove compartment and pulled out an old matt black automatic pistol, a .38 Colt. He put three full magazines of bullets in a checked cloth, wrapped the whole into a bundle with the pistol, and handed it to me. 'Don't use it unless you have to, but if you have to shoot a guy aim for his heart and empty the whole magazine. Up where you're going $20 should see you right with the cops afterwards. Stick a knife in the dead guy's right hand, say it was self-defence, he attacked you. And give half of these to the *capitán*.' He handed me another bundle; this contained coarse black local cheroots, which looked like bent and deformed twigs. They were tied together with a tricolour riband in a bow – the Paraguayan national colours of red, white and blue. 'What do I do with the other half?' I asked. 'You'll need them at night yourself to keep the mosquitoes at bay. Remember, don't put your hand or even finger anywhere near the water, the river is teeming with piranha.'

With a sinking heart I got out of the jeep and followed Mac down to the waterside. The river was still covered in a thick mist, and the placid surface looked an oily gunmetal grey. Our feet sank into the sand. There was no sign of any *lancha*. Perhaps it had already gone, I thought, and I could go back to my nice comfortable room, which seemed ever more inviting by the minute. Mac clapped his hands three times, slowly, not loudly. The sound carried in echoes across the water. From somewhere in the mist beyond we heard low voices, and the muffled splash of oars. Then, out of the gloom, a small tender nosed towards us. 'It is the *capitán*, Don Octavio,' Mac said to me in a low voice. We gripped the prow of the wooden rowing boat as it touched. Don Octavio was alone. He wore blue jeans, a t-shirt, with a trainer top over it. He was probably in his forties, with a thick black beard, flecked with grey, pale green eyes and European features. He might have been an Andalusian or a southern Italian, except for his slight frame, which suggested Indian blood. Mac introduced us, and then talked to the *capitán* in swift, quiet Jalapé. He took out a US$20 note from his wallet, gave it to Don Octavio, who folded it neatly, put it in his wallet, and bowed his thanks. Then Mac said slowly to me, in Castilian Spanish, which he and I knew Don Octavio would understand, 'Pay Don Octavio another US$20 when you get to Concepción, *de acuerdo*?' I signified in Spanish that I understood and agreed, and shook the *capitán*'s hand to seal the bargain. He neither smiled nor showed any emotion at all. His hand was as rough as sandpaper. 'Your food and maté is included, *caña* is extra, as are cigarettes and cigars. Give the *mozo* a dollar in guarani if he serves you well, with attention, respect and politeness, when you get to Concepción,' Mac added, still speaking in slow Castilian, so there would be no misunderstandings later. I wondered if the slowness was for my benefit or the *capitán*. Mac was a businessman and a smuggler: he knew all about making deals stick. Then he shook my hand and said to me in English: 'He's a trustworthy man. Show him your automatic, in conversation, naturally, unloaded, but refuse politely to sell it. He will certainly offer, but say it is mine, and a loan. In Concepción ask for Don Umberto of the Liberales, he knows you are coming. Don't sell him my gun either – he is sure to ask, as well. If you have to go into Brazil sell gun and ammunition before you cross the border, any *tienda* or shop will buy it. You should get at least $150, make sure the notes are not fakes. I have got your e-mail in Europe – we can settle up later. If things go badly I may have to visit you over there . . .' his voice trailed away, and he looked gloomy, hunched up all of a sudden, his fear of abroad come back.

'*Vamos*,' said the *capitán*, and got back into the rowing-boat. I shoved off the prow and jumped in after him. 'Good luck,' said Mac. 'And if you do fall overboard, or the *lancha* sinks, make a lot of noise and splashing, and head for the nearest shore. The piranhas don't like noise, or so I've heard. I shouldn't fall overboard if I were you though.' He stepped back, gave a short wave; then was swallowed up by the mist on the river bank, as the *capitán* rowed us out to the *lancha* which was anchored more or less in midstream. The mist was thinning by the time we reached the boat, which was a low, concrete barge with blunt bows and two large Johnson outboard motors clamped to the stern. I climbed up a short, rusted metal ladder and on to the deck, which was loaded with sacks of rice, produce of the USA, according to the labels, sacks of Argentine cement from Mendoza, and open-slatted wooden boxes full of plumbing fittings – taps, sinks, basins, pipes and so on, all clearly visible in their containers, though loosely wrapped in grey corrugated cardboard. The *capitán* followed me up the ladder, made fast the tender to the boat with rope, and beckoned me forward. '*Mirá*,' he said, with some pride in his voice. The barge had twin diesel inboard engines as well as the outboards. 'Tractor,' he added, indicating a well-known US brand name embossed on the engine casings. '*Muy bien, muy fuerte*,' I commented, with what I hoped was enthusiasm in my voice.

'*Muy fuerte*,' confirmed Don Octavio, and wiped the twin tractor engines with an oily rag. '*Venga*,' he indicated, and we made our way aft. There was a small cabin with a single wooden bed, table, chair, cupboard and hanging wardrobe, about the size of those on a cross-channel ferry, though made of unplaned wood with glassless windows covered with rusty wire mesh to keep insects out. '*Por usted solamente*,' the *capitán* indicated, showing me how the louvred shutters closed on the inside to give shade and privacy. There was a blanket, a pillow and a thin foam mattress covered with a floral-patterned coverlet of nylon that looked to me of Taiwanese provenance. I had a feeling US$40 was buying me the *capitán*'s cabin. '*¿Bueno?*' enquired Don Octavio. '*Perfecto*,' I replied, and splitting the bundle of cheroots in half, presented him with his quota, tying up both bundles with the tricolour riband, which I cut with my penknife. He took his with thanks. '*¿Tranquilo, tranquilo aquí, por usted, vale? ¿En cinco pequeños minutos un café y desayuno, vale?*' '*Vale*,' I replied, and sat on the bed. It was very hard.

The *capitán* went forward, and I closed the door and shut the louvred shutters. I looked at my watch. Half an hour before I had been sitting on the terrace outside my room at the hotel. Now I was in full flight from a convicted mass murderer who would have me shot if he could; someone I had never seen and sincerely hoped I never would see. I lay full length on the bed, using my day pack as an extra pillow. From forward I could hear the heavy tractor engines turning and misfiring. I had a diesel myself in England and I could hear that these were damp, probably from the mist on the river. Eventually, one of the engines caught and then the other: with a rattle the anchors came up, fore and aft. I could hear the light step of the *mozo* passing down beside my cabin in bare feet: the *capitán* wore shoes. The *lancha* trembled, and very slowly, we began to move off, upriver, towards Concepción. There was a faint movement of air through the shutters, bringing the scent of diesel fumes. I spread my sleeping bag underneath me and took a swig from the water bottle I had brought with me. I noticed my hands were trembling, and not through the movement of the boat. I shut my eyes, but graphic images of revolution and civil war jumped up before me. I had, I reflected, spent more than the last two weeks trying to get a boat to Concepción, with no success at all. Mac had organized the whole thing in an instant. But he was of the country, of course, and I was not. I could not lie still. I got up and opened the louvres to look outside. The mist had largely gone, and pale early morning light flecked the river. On the other bank, the Chaco side, stood low, indeterminate foliage, scrub you would call it, jungle being too dense, too impressive a term for such sparse, pale green tracery. Occasionally there were trees, spindly, leaning askew: tufts of marsh grass, weeds, rank vegetation rose up from the swampy low-lying shore on either side. Already we were outside Asunción. From time to time a one-storey house appeared, with a path leading down to the river where a boat would be moored by a wooden jetty, or else a canoe. We were moving very slowly in our *lancha*, our tiny wake hardly rocked these moored craft. I wanted to go out on deck now we had left the city behind, but I had a feeling that Don Octavio wanted me hidden away until at least after breakfast. I began to get hungry. After an hour and a half – a fairly average to short Paraguayan *'pequeños cinco minutos'* – the *mozo* knocked discreetly on the door of my cabin. I could see through the louvres that he was carrying an aluminium tray with food and drink on it. I opened the door and let him in. He put down the tray on the table and indicated a thermos flask. *'Por el maté,'* he said, and then indicated a smaller metal pot, *'el café'*. I thanked him, and he bowed slightly and backed out, closing the door behind him. On the tray was an orange and a pair of bananas, a carton of orange juice, two boiled eggs and a twist of salt in a newspaper screw, *chipá*, a packet of Argentine-made sweet biscuits, as well as the coffee, hot water for maté, and a small packet of Paraguayan-made leaf maté. There was no maté gourd or *bombilla*, but as no Paraguayan man ever moved from his house without these essentials, doubtless the *capitán* assumed I had these items already. And he was right, in fact I did. I had been haunting the antiquaries in the weeks I'd been in Asunción, and had already purchased two silver 19th-century *bombillas*, and two attractive gourds, one made out of a curious tropical hardwood and chased with decorative silver around the base and top. For once I actually felt like maté. It quenches the thirst and calms the soul. I made myself a gourdful and attacked the breakfast with gusto. Things could be worse, I reflected. The automatic pistol, unwrapped and lying on the wooden table, indicated as well that they might yet get much worse.

I lay down on the bed again after breakfast – the cabin was so small that sitting at the table or lying on the bed were the only two options. I finished off the coffee and sampled one of Mac's cheroots: they were surprisingly mild and aromatic. I hoped the mosquitoes would dislike their smoke. From time to time I tilted the slats of the shutters and peered outside. The sun was higher and the dull, grey-green river bank we passed had been replaced by yet more dull, grey-green river bank. The river itself appeared to be deserted. We had passed no one and no one had passed us. We were the only moving thing on that watery expanse surrounded by bush; our two diesels thumping tractorlike amidships the only sound in that vast realm of silence. Not for the first time I thought of Joseph Conrad; about moving by boat upriver from civilization and its ambiguities to a primal, primeval world, ancient, sparse of men, a journey back to an earlier epoch of human existence. If Mister Kurtz were to go back in time, to the early 20th century, Paraguay was a good place to do it. Somewhere off to my right, up a branch of the Paraguay River, a group of Germans had done just that in the late 19th century.

Led by Elizabeth Nietzsche, sister of the philosopher Friedrich, and her husband Dr Bernard Forster, a virulently anti-Semitic

German chauvinist, a colony had been set up called Nueva Germania in 1886. Germany was rotten, they felt, decadent with Jewish usury and corruption, capitalists and stockbrokers: here, in Nueva Germania, Lutheranism, vegetarianism and rabid Teutonic nationalism would redeem the race, set free the tormented German soul and create a beacon for blond, blue-eyed *herrenvolk* everywhere. Elizabeth hoped her brother might quit Germany to join them, but he was unenthusiastic, and hated her husband Forster's anti-Semitism. The 'purification and rebirth of the human race', as Forster grandiloquently declared, was the object of the colony. Seventy kilometres from Antequera, deep in the bush, the Paraguayan government granted the settlement land on which to found their new imperium. The colonists, shipped out from Germany, built a vast mansion, Forsterhof, of timber and thatch, where Dr Forster and Elizabeth were to live. Peasants from Saxony formed the basis of the colony; Jews were forbidden, though it was suspected that at least one had smuggled himself on board, in order to wreck the venture. 'We have found the next thing to Paradise on Earth,' Elizabeth wrote to her brother, though one girl died of fever coming upriver from Asunción. In the evenings, she wrote, after work the sturdy German colonists serenaded her and her husband with '*Deutschland, Deutschland Über Alles*'. Feudal virtue, simplicity, prelapsarian harmony was to be re-established in the tropical wilderness.

The fantasy of Paraguay as paradise had taken over: fruit would fall from the trees, the natives were friendly and obliging, and a railway planned to cross the Americas would conveniently pass through the colony. Settlers from Germany would throng in. In reality the crops failed, there were fevers and snakes, insects and wild animals: the colonists barely survived and were not amused to be made to stand to attention and salute when Forster passed on his white horse. Forty families had come out from Germany but more than a quarter of them left within the first two years. Forster fell into debt, could get no more settlers to come out; he spent increasingly long periods out of the colony, soaking up beer and *caña* at the Hotel del Lago, a German-run hostelry in the overwhelmingly German settlement of San Bernadino just a few kilometres from Asunción, where more practically minded Teutons had reproduced a Bavarian lakeside pleasure resort in the subtropics. In the end it all became too much for this dreamer who had once been an intimate of Wagner and his circle at Wahnfried; in 1890, Forster killed himself in his hotel room with a self-administered injection of morphine and strychnine. He was just 46. Elizabeth hushed up the scandal and the death certificate of her husband indicated that he had died of a nervous attack, which was, in a way, also true. The colony continued its decline and Elizabeth went back to Germany to latch on to her brother's writings, and her brother himself in his long mental illness, as self-appointed Keeper of the Flame. She supported the rise of the Nazis and became an admirer and intimate of Adolf Hitler, who attended her funeral. Earth from the Fatherland was sent out by Hitler in 1934 to be put on the grave of her husband, who was claimed by the Nazis as a prophetic forerunner of their creed.

Paraguay had the second oldest Nazi Party in the world, after Germany itself, founded just a few years after the original. By 1991, when the author Ben Macintyre visited Nueva Germania to research his excellent book *Forgotten Fatherland*, there were fewer than ten families left, with names such as Fischer, Schubert, Halke, Stern and Sweikhart. They lived in huts and scratched a living from a few vegetable patches, surrounded by the forest. Some of the colonists had volunteered to fight for the Nazis during the Second World War. In the 1950s, a stranger had come into their midst, a refugee from Germany: this was the notorious Dr Mengele of Auschwitz, 'The Angel of Death' who had performed such disgusting 'experiments' in the name of perverted science on Jews, gypsies, twins and other helpless victims. He had at one time been personal physician to Stroessner, and later moved to Brazil where he died. He lived under his own name in Paraguay, and became naturalized as a Paraguayan citizen: it seems he was a well-known figure in Asunción.

If I had been Paul Theroux, at this point in the journey I would have unpacked my folding Klepper canoe – or perhaps my Feathercraft – and paddled away up the branch in the river to visit the remains of Nueva Germania. However, rather more comfortably, I settled for a bottle of *caña* from the *mozo* (US$1.25) and lay on my bed smoking cheroots, counting the thumps of the tractor engines and thinking of Hugo ('You have no idea, Robert, how enjoyable it is just to lie back in the afternoon in a hammock and look at the sky and smoke a cigar . . .'). Perhaps at last I was beginning to start to do things the Paraguayan way.

All the fantasy colonial ventures in Paraguay tended to have the same trajectory – initial enthusiasm and idealism, the investment of large sums of money and energy, the unrealistic expectations and dreams of world-changing Utopian perfection, the dictatorial, impractical, hysterical leaders, the split, the departure of the faint-hearted, the sensible, and even more diehard fanatics, the disillusionment of the settlers, the death or departure of the broken-spirited leader, the slow decay and eventual abandonment of the project which sinks back into subsistence farming at the same level or lower than the Paraguayan peons around them. Eventually, the jungle comes back and reclaims the site, lianas and vines snaking over the abandoned and roofless buildings. The Jesuit *Reducciones*, Nueva Germania, Nueva Australia, Nueva Bordeos (New Bordeaux), the colony of 'the Lincolnshire farmers' – a group of English 'agriculturalists' who had in fact been the sweepings of the London slums – all these had conformed to the pattern. Now in the far north, I had read, were colonies of Moonies who had bought large tracts of land and were trying the same thing.

The only outside group that had thrived in Paraguay, in the inhospitable Chaco, were the Mennonites, low-German speaking Christian followers of an Amish-like pacifist sect who had been

motivated by religious zeal and wished only to continue a way of
life they had developed in Russia over hundreds of years. Rather
than try to remould human nature in experimental form they
had merely sought to preserve what they evolved without state
interference. They demanded to school their own children, keep
out the corrupt world beyond, and not be subject to conscription
for military service. Russia, Canada and Mexico had all promised
these things, but always reneged: the modern state insisted on
interfering in citizens' lives, most notably in education and military service. The Mennonites had moved from Russia to Canada
and Paraguay, but now they were unhappy and were moving again
– to Bolivia, I had been told. Perhaps a litmus paper of the state
which interfered least in its citizens' life was where the Mennonites
were moving to at any one time. Was there anywhere on Earth, I
wondered, where you could get right away from the power of the
state? Only, perhaps, on very small and obscure islands in the
Pacific to which you could only get by private yacht, and on which
no one lived. Even the Antarctic and Amazon basin were staked
out, owned, colonized, regulated. You can, however, purchase a
passport for a country which does not exist: it is very useful for
leaving at hotels, hire car offices and so forth, where identification
is needed. Many people who have this passport have claimed that
it is also possible to cross some borders with it. The last refuge
of true individualists who wish to escape state control is the
ocean-going yacht: there are still vast tracts of the Southern Ocean
which are unpoliced, unvisited and unregulated. The nomad, as
ever, is able to evade what the settled must suffer – police, armies,
taxes, other people's rules, regimentation – in a word, the slavery
of mass society. The Mennonites' problem was that they simply
wished to avoid the post-Renaissance nation state, a desire incom-
patible with the all-embracing octopus of the bureaucratic society
whose *raison d'être* is regimentation and standardization. The
hardest thing in the modern world seemed to be simply to be left
alone to get on with one's life: the most expensive and desirable

real estate in the world were islands with no one on them. Paraguay offered a degree of autonomy, but also chaos and lawlessness. Perhaps if you got far enough into the jungle you might escape, but I rather doubt it.

I had expected that we would be calling in at various riverside settlements to collect cargo or passengers en route, but we did not. Don Octavio steamed ahead, slowly but steadily. From time to time he would leave the engines and come to see me in the cabin; eventually, when he judged we were far enough from Asunción, I was invited out to perch on a cement sack and admire the diesels again, thump-thumping away. He had seen Mac's automatic, which I left on the table deliberately: he had, as predicted, offered to buy it, but had not been offended when I refused. It emerged in conversation that Don Octavio did not want me to be seen by any riverine Paraguayan eyes. When we were approaching a small settlement I was ushered back into the cabin by the *mozo*, who would close the shutters for me. It was evident that to carry passengers some sort of permit or authorization was required that Don Octavio did not have. In all Hispanic countries people live in fear of the *denuncia*: fines, prison, aggravation, beating, forced bribes can all result from being denounced. And not just in Hispanic countries: a friend of mine in the Gers in France had bought a farmhouse, and on the first day of occupation was denounced by five people before lunchtime for painting her shutters without notifying the *mairie*. There were five houses in her hamlet, so every single household had denounced her. During the German occupation of France, the Nazis had had to operate a complete government department just to deal with the huge volume of letters from men and women denouncing each other to the enemy.

So for much of the time I sat in the little cabin and looked out of the window at the river, and the infrequent collections of mud and timber huts with thatch or rusted corrugated iron roofs. More than ever I felt I was travelling up a branch of the Congo. Usually there were no people to be seen, no smoke from cooking fires, not even a dog or pig scratching nearby. Very occasionally I would spot a woman gutting a fish beside a hut, or an Indian sitting in a canoe close to the shore, fishing. The only life generally, though, were a few scratching fowls, clucking in the dust. Once a settlement was well past, the *mozo* would come back and open the door, and I could make my way back to where Don Octavio nursed the diesels. '*Pyragues, policía – muy malo, muy, muy malo,*' he remarked to me, once, grimacing. *Pyragues* were the secret police. Could there really be police or, even less likely, secret police right out here, in the middle of nowhere?

More important, I felt, was the parlous state of the engines. The diesels were constantly giving trouble – misfiring, overheating, running irregularly. It would be too much to expect that they had been properly marinized. Sometimes one, or both, would stop completely, and we would start to move backwards with the current, drifting downriver again, until the *mozo* moved aft and started one of the Johnson outboards. He only ever used one, and then at very low revs: petrol was expensive and the outboards used a lot of fuel. Don Octavio would then dive into the engine compartment and start to tinker. We lost time when this happened, for the *lancha* reduced speed appreciably. Oily, covered in sweat, the *capitán* would eventually emerge, and the diesels would cough reluctantly into life again.

Lunch was cold rice, grilled river fish caught by the *mozo*, with chili sauce, followed by flan, or crème caramel from a plastic container, and another orange, followed by more excellent coffee, doubtless from Brazil. '*¿Te gusta más caña, señor?*' the *mozo* asked me after lunch. He had an opened bottle of Tricolor brand rum and three glasses. I said I did, and he balanced the three glasses on a sack of cement. The rum was sweet and strong. We drank three glasses each, then I retired to my cabin for a siesta. I rigged up the mosquito net and crawled under it. There were as yet no signs of mosquitoes but I wanted to be sure. I lit another cheroot and let the dull pounding of the engines relax me towards sleep. The cheroot tasted mild and nutty after the rum and coffee. I stubbed it out, after a while, and turning on my side, closed my eyes. I slept for several hours. When I awoke the sun was declining to the west. My mouth tasted bad until I had a swig of water. I looked outside: nothing had changed except the light.

Thus we progressed upriver. There was a small latrine that dropped straight into the river in the stern, where, from time to time, I clambered to relieve myself, hoping all the *candirú* were asleep or otherwise engaged. At regular intervals the *mozo* came to replenish my thermos with hot water for maté. The two of them had their own maté, but this was a crew-only affair, and I was not invited to participate, for which I was grateful. Supper was more rice, this time with a large, tough beefsteak, mandioca, tomato sauce, followed by a banana and more coffee. There was a small portable icebox amidships which ran off electricity generated by the diesels, where the food was kept cold enough so that it did not start to rot, though the box was not cold enough to produce ice. I saw to my alarm that by dusk I had managed to drink, with a certain amount of help from the crew, well over a bottle and a half of rum. After supper, at which we finished the second bottle, the *mozo* appeared with a third. '¿*Otro, señor?*' he enquired, but more as a formality than anything else: already he had the top off and was pouring three glasses. None of us was drunk, but we had been drinking steadily all day. This, I assumed, was what all Paraguayan men who could afford it did, day in and day out: it was no wonder the country had a severe alcohol problem. When night fell I retired to my cabin and rerigged my mosquito net again, making sure no insects had managed to get inside. It grew cooler and the night air was pleasant. I had done nothing all day except lounge and eat and sleep, but I felt tired and went to sleep easily, and slept well – perhaps it was all the rum.

In the morning Don Octavio said to me after breakfast, '*Hoy – Concepción*,' today we would arrive in Concepción. And we did make it that day, though very late in the afternoon, due to more engine breakdowns. I was led to my cabin and escorted inside by the *mozo* as we approached. '*Mucha policía – muy malo,*' he explained. '*Tranquilo, tranquilo aquí, señor.*' If I had been spotted on the approach I suspect Don Octavio would have been forced to pay out some *propinas* or *incentivos*. We passed under a large bridge crossing the river and slowly made our way to the dockside of Concepción. Low, decrepit buildings in crumbling, dirty stucco, rotting and leprous, lined the waterfront. Rows of wooden carts, on old car and truck axles and wheels with rubber tyres, stood by the dock, with small, exhausted-looking horses and mules between their shafts. One or two battered pick-up trucks waited nearby, the drivers asleep, slumped over the steering wheels, or in the back on piles of sacks. The main street led off the port, pitted and holed like a country track. Rusted tin roofs and looping telephone wires moved off towards the horizon. There was a concrete war memorial by the wharf, and along the river bank were moored ancient cargo steamers, apparently deserted. I grew to know this vista well, for I had to sit in the cabin, peering out of the shutters, for hour upon hour, while the *capitán* disembarked to sort out whatever paperwork needed to be dealt with. The *mozo* lay on a sack of rice and dozed. I finished the rum, my hot water for maté, and my cold water. Eventually, finally, well after dark, Don Octavio returned, and we moved off again, up-river, into more permanent – and more private – moorings. '*Cinco pequeños minutos, solamente, Don Roberto,*' the *capitán* promised me, but I knew what that meant, and the *mozo* prepared more food, rice, spam from a tin, chili sauce, *chipá* – and beer – Don Octavio had bought three cans in Concepción. It was Brazilian, and tasted quite different to the usual Paraguayan brew.

We ate, and then the *mozo* made more coffee. Don Octavio had a mobile phone and made several hushed calls in Jalapé, in which my name featured. But nothing happened. I went back to my cabin and prepared for another night on board. But after several hours, just as I was about to turn in and go to sleep, a black, closed hansom cab drawn by a skinny horse appeared to glide out of the gloom on the Concepción side of the river. Don Octavio had a low conversation with an invisible driver, lost in shadows, and then came to get me. '*Don Umberto y los amigos de su amigo,*' he said, meaning Mac. I repacked my meagre belongings, wrapped the automatic in its cloth again and made my way forward. I gave the *mozo* two dollars instead of one, which he took without comment or thanks. When I thanked him he said, '*A sus ordones siempre, muy mio señor,*' and gave a half-bow. I had paid Don Octavio his twenty dollars earlier, when the *mozo* had been aft, so as to retain decorum. He had folded it carefully and put it in his wallet along with the note Mac had given him in Asunción. The *capitán* helped me off the boat and on to the shore. He shook my hand and said, '*Vaya con Dios.*' I thanked him again, turned, and climbed up into the hansom cab. '*Bienvenido a Concepción, señor,*' said a voice from the driver's seat. Even before I had stowed my day pack and sat down we had bounced away at a cracking pace. We clipped along over cobbles, and I clung on to a leather strap which hung from the side. The glass windows rattled against the wood. There was straw on the floor for muddy shoes. I had never been in a hansom cab before, but the whole experience was entirely familiar to me from the tales of Sherlock Holmes. My grandfather Cecil Flower had been sent to Malvern College in the 1890s and had been met by a hansom cab at the station. His father had given him a gold sovereign, but in his nervousness he had dropped it in the straw, and had to scrabble about trying to find it: he never did, and cried bitter tears at his loss.

The blinds were pulled down, so I could not look out and no one could look in. They were fixed in place and I could not open them. It was now pitch black, the tropical night having fallen with its usual suddenness. I wondered if the revolution had arrived in Concepción, if the Oviedistas were in control. After the traffic and noise of Asunción, the calm of Concepción seemed unnatural.

Only a few vehicles, drawn by oxen or horses, had passed us. A few minutes' drive later, it seemed, we stopped, and the driver got down and opened the door for me. I got out. In front of me stood a crumbling Italianate stucco palazzo from the early part of the 20th century, completely enveloped in an overgrown garden of palm trees, rampant bougainvillea, orange trees, limes, and bananas, all visible under a pale moon. '*El Hotel Suizo, señor,*' said the driver, indicating a rusting metal gate, which indeed bore that legend on a faded brass plate; '*con electricidad y agua corriente*' it also boasted – with electricity and running water. If Asunción had suggested the 1950s and the ambience of Graham Greene, in Concepción I had stepped right back into the world of Joseph Conrad. '*¿Cuanto?*' I asked, fumbling for my wallet. '*Todo reglado, señor*' – already paid for. I tipped him half a dollar anyway. '*Vengo por usted mañana por las nueve y media, señor – ¿bueno?*' '*Bueno,*' I replied – 9.30 in the morning would be fine. I made my way down the path through the garden towards the hotel with the driver's soft '*Buenas noches, señor*' echoing in my ears. I realized I hadn't actually seen his face, he had been in shadow the whole time. I wondered where I would be going to tomorrow at 9.30. To see Don Umberto, perhaps?

The double front doors opened to my hand soundlessly. The entrance hall lay strewn in shadows. A youth lay slumped forward, fast asleep on the mahogany reception counter. A low light flickered from a brass oil lamp by his side. Large, lumpish furniture, armchairs and sofas, padded with horsehair which was now coming unstuffed, lined the walls. There was wainscotting painted brown to resemble fumed oak, pot plant stands with palms in brass buckets, and framed pictures of the Swiss Lakes on the walls, sepia photographs from the 1890s. Everything spoke of the first decade of the 20th century. The telephone on the reception desk was brass, of the crank handle and blow variety, as seen in silent movies of the pre-1914 era. Behind the sleeping desk clerk were wooden pigeon holes on the wall, from which hung the hotel room keys. None was missing – the hotel was empty. I cleared my throat, and when the clerk looked up at me muzzily, I asked, 'Do you have a single room with a bathroom?' in Spanish. '*No, señor,*' he replied. I found this hard to believe. '*No hay baños, señor.*' No bathrooms. A single room, then? Wordlessly he took a key from behind him, and with the other grasped the oil lamp. I followed him, cloaked in darkness, up the creaking wooden staircase. Despite the brass plaque outside there seemed to be neither electricity nor running water at the Hotel Suizo. On the first floor, down a corridor, the clerk opened a room with his key. The room was huge and had six beds in it. A single, I queried. Only for you, señor, he promised. All the rooms had many beds, it signified nothing. There was a china bowl and jug for ablutions and a chamber pot for convenience. It was three dollars a night. I took it. Was there a restaurant for breakfast? No, there wasn't, but one could be found just down the street. After further interrogation I found the hotel could supply Coca-Cola, a bottle of *caña*, a bottle of mineral water, two types of chocolate snack bar, one called 'El Snob', with a picture of a pre-revolutionary French aristocrat in pink frills looking down his lorgnette snootily at one, and another called an 'Umlaut Bar', depicting a mean-looking Neanderthal, Bavarian-style youth with violent blond straw hair, dressed in lederhosen, gleefully blowing down a large alpenhorn which curled to his feet. Also at his feet were either several discarded, unwrapped Umlaut bars, or else a vagrant pod of respectable-sized human turds, whose previous owner appeared to have been fairly seriously, even painfully constipated. Unwrapped, the Umlaut bar did indeed bear a remarkable resemblance to human excrement. It was full of roughage, in which were nuts and caramel, whereas the El Snob had effeminately pink, decadent-looking crème sandwiched between pallid, wussy-looking wafers. Practising admirable lack of prejudice, I bought two of each, plus Coke, *caña* and mineral water. I had to descend to the hall again to sign in the register and collect the goodies, which the clerk removed from a large, antique wall safe, which now served as a larder-cum-tuck shop. The register was a bulky book covered in leather, and had a blunt-nibbed dip ink pen attached to a chain beside it, so it couldn't be stolen. The youth poured some of his stale maté into an inkwell to liquify the ink. I scratched my moniker on the lined paper, and added under the column marked 'occupation' – *capataz de cargadores*. Under 'coming from' I put 'Costaguana' and under 'going to' I wrote 'Provincia Oriental'. I looked to see if Nostromo himself, Mr Gould or Dr Monygham had signed in recently. There was no sign of them. The last guest had left over a month before. Water? I asked. *Mañana*. Breakfast? *Mañana*. Electricity? '*Unos pequeños cinco minutos, señor.*' I took a candle instead and clambered up to my bedroom, laden with rum and the fixings. The youth's head was down on the counter again before I even started up the stairs.

I threw open the windows and shutters. The night was warm and soft, refulgent with amiable tropical scents. I rigged up my mosquito net and lay down under it, drinking rum and Coke, eating my chocolate bars, made in South Korea, I noted, with the ingredients listed in both Spanish and Portuguese. Then I lit a cheroot and blew out the candle, leaving the window open as the room was so stuffy: this was a mistake, but I didn't realize because I was so tired. I put my glass down on the beside table, stubbed out my cheroot, and closed my eyes for a few moments. Several hours later, the room now quite cold, I awoke suddenly with an unnamed dread and an unnaturally fast-beating heart. The room was bathed in clear moonlight. Two large black slippers, outside the mosquito net, had attached themselves to my big toes. I gasped with horror, reached for my lighter and snapped it on. The creatures squeaked and gibbered in terror at the light, and flopped off my feet, fluttering their leathery wings with frantic attempts to get airborne, bloated as they were with my blood. I gave an appalled shriek and leapt out of the bed as if scalded. Vampire bats! I kicked and struck at them as they tried to get out of the still open window, then, suddenly, they were gone. I shut the window, scoured the room for more of their fellows, and then examined my big toes. Both bore their teethmarks, and welling gouts of blood. I felt sick and weak, and fell back on to the bed. I drank a glass of *caña* neat and then bathed each toe in rum as well, the alcohol not stinging at all – the anaesthetic still working no doubt. How long had they been there? How much blood had I lost? Were the bats rabid? Well, I would know the last soon enough. I examined the room for other *bichos* – malevolent wildlife – found a couple of mosquitoes, crushed them with my shoe, and then went back to bed under my net. The moonlight was so bright I had not even needed to light my candle. It took me more than an hour to get to sleep again.

The next thing I knew was that the youth from the desk below was knocking on my door, telling me that the cab was at the door waiting for me below. It was 9.45. The question of breakfast now became irrelevant. In ten minutes I was trotting through the rutted streets of Concepción, in the cab, the blinds still down. We stopped at another of the town's *fin de siècle* Italianate villas, this example of one storey only, with a colonnaded portico in front, the floor to which was covered in terracotta tiles. There was no sign as to what this mansion might house. I got out, and clapped my hands three times, loudly, this being etiquette in rural Paraguay to announce one's presence. The hansom cab clipped away behind me. After a long pause, in which two green lizards darted rapidly across the tiles under the portico, the front doors, these screened in elaborate wrought-iron work, behind which was frosted glass, were opened from inside. '*Bienvenido*,' a small, very old man croaked at me. He wore carpet slippers of tartan material, and had a thyroid goitre of impressive proportions hanging from the side of his throat. His voice sounded husky and conspiratorial. He ushered me inside, into a large salon devoid of furniture save for a huge desk and several hard, old-fashioned wooden chairs. He indicated that I be seated and left me alone for a quarter of an hour or so. He returned with a bright red enamel coffee pot, a cup and saucer, a bowl of sugar and an aluminium spoon, and another El Snob bar, evidently a Concepción speciality, plus a bunch of five small finger bananas. These were all very welcome. The coffee was superlative, rich and strong, evidently straight from Brazil. It was perhaps the best coffee I have ever drunk in my life. The old man – some sort of caretaker I assumed – returned once again with a bottle of mineral water, again from Brazil, and a thick glass tumbler. I was grateful for the water as already the day seemed hot. I had travelled north towards the equator, and Concepción felt more of a tropical city than had Asunción. In fact, I soon began to feel as if I had actually left Paraguay behind completely, had entered another country, which resembled provincial Brazil circa 1910.

I had brought my day pack with me, Mac's automatic wrapped in its checked cloth. I kept it within easy reach. I had no idea where I was or who I would be meeting. My big toes both hurt and were leaking blood into my socks. I wanted to bathe them in hot water and get to a pharmacy to see if they had any suggestions for bat bite ointment. A long, long pause ensued. Nothing happened for what seemed like hours. I ate and drank everything and smoked three cheroots, very slowly. Finally, the old man reappeared with another pot of coffee and more mineral water, but no more Snob bars or bananas. I put myself in a mood of complete Zen calm and abandoned myself to Fate.

Eventually, at 12.30, the door opened again, and one young man in jeans and a blue shirt, and one middle-aged fellow also wearing blue, with a greying beard came in and sat down in front of me by the table. They introduced themselves as friends of Don Mac, but neither of them was Don Umberto, who was, it seemed, either in Bolivia or Brazil, they were not quite sure which. Mac had asked them to look after me in Concepción, which they would, of course, do – not that a stranger needed looking after in Concepción, unlike that nest of vipers and sink of criminality, that gulf of Colorado wickedness and abyss of depravity, that Sodom of the South, in a word . . . Asunción. After the introductions were over and substantial cigars had been produced, flourished, felt, sniffed, rolled, and finally lit, I asked them the question that was uppermost on my mind. What news did they have of the revolution? Had Oviedo got to Asunción? Was there fighting? Had the army risen in his support? What was the news?

'We know nothing,' said the older man: his companion nodded his agreement. 'And what we do learn from those *cabrones* – the cuckolds in Asunción – we have learnt to mistrust. They drink in lies with their mothers' milk down there. Our TVs are tuned to Brazil. We trade with Brazil. The Brazilians are our friends and allies. The Colorados of the south have ignored us for 50 years. They give us no money, no guns, no infrastructure. Even the boats have stopped. You have seen the town, a little. It is a ruin, a catastrophe, a farce sunk up to its ears in catatonic mud. If Oviedo reimposes a military dictatorship, it is nothing to us. He will still give us nothing. And we shall ignore him,' concluded the older man amid a cloud of cigar smoke. I asked if they had any newspapers from Asunción, had heard any news on the radio? Surely the Brazilians must have announced that Oviedo had crossed the border? Surely the fall of Asunción would merit a mention on their news?

'There has been nothing said as yet. We know nothing and we believe nothing,' said the young man, with finality. '*Nada de nada,*' echoed the older man, like a tropical chorus from Aeschylus. They made maté, now, and we drank this, passing the gourd around, smoking our cigars meditatively. Above us, from the ceiling, a three-bladed fan had started to churn the air softly: the town's erratic electricity had come back on again. The shutters were closed and the room was pale grey with shadows, thin bars of light flickered on the far wall, cast from outside.

'Did you bring the guns?' the middle-aged man asked me, eventually, in a conversational tone.

'What guns?' I enquired.

'Don Mac said he might be able to get us some guns, proper guns, AK-47s, mortars, Uzis, heavy machine-guns – proper, serious guns, foreign guns from *el norte*,' commented the younger man hopefully. I regretted that, alas, I was forced to disappoint them. They looked downcast at this, and gave resigned shrugs. No guns at all, the younger man put in, not even a small consignment, a trifle, a mere bagatelle – just the odd machine-gun? I showed them Mac's loan apologetically, explaining why I could not sell it to them. They examined it with mild interest, and got out their own pistols to show me, which were worn and ancient revolvers kept in leather holsters inside the backs of their trouser waistbands.

'We need heavy weapons, which we cannot buy from Brazil with ease. Pistols we have in plenty. Also shotguns and hunting rifles. Machine-guns, mortars, semi-automatic assault rifles we do not have,' said the middle-aged man, feeling at their absence inflecting his voice. 'Tanks also would be nice. Tanks and armoured cars, with flame-throwers, napalm and grenade launchers,' chipped in the younger man dreamily. I had a feeling I knew what these weapons would be used for if ever they did get them – an assault on their enemies down in Asunción.

'Never mind – we have no money to pay for these things anyway. We are so poor in Concepción that it is ridiculous,' commented the older man, and both of them laughed, at the ridiculousness of their poverty. The maté gourd passed round again and we dropped the subject of weaponry, for a short while at least.

Eventually, they took me to a Korean restaurant where we had a large meal of pork, rice, beans, green vegetables, *chipá*, mandioca and Brazilian beer. Unlike Asunción, it seemed to me that here the foodstuffs were locally grown and produced. I paid for this lunch, for they had no money, their ridiculous poverty being the cause, but as the whole meal scarcely came to five US dollars,

I didn't mind at all. 'Come and see us again,' they choroused, as we left, 'many, many times – we can talk about guns.' They had a large illustrated mail-order catalogue from a gun dealer in Houston, Texas, printed bilingually in Spanish and English, and they had shown me this during lunch. Copiously illustrated, it was well-thumbed and grimy with use, like a masturbator's favourite porno-mag. 'Wonderful!' they would breathe 'Look – here – exquisite – the sheer elegance of the lines! No?'

'But you have no money,' I commented. 'This is our tragedy, actually, our poverty. So poor and so far from all these wonderful weapons,' they agreed, sighing deeply again, and then calling for more Brazilian beer, in cheerful voices, from the Korean proprietor.

Concepción was deep in siesta as I walked back to the Hotel Suizo, which was not at all far on foot, in spite of what I felt with my painful big toes – a mere 200 yards or so from the restaurant. The sense of orchestrated subterfuge which had surrounded my arrival seemed to have entirely dissipated now, and my two hosts waved *adios* to me loudly and happily outside the restaurant. I had no guns, was harmless; I was like them, ridiculous in my poverty as well, perhaps. Later, in the early evening, the bells rang out from the large, twin-domed cathedral, and crowds of people flocked into the church for the service. Until now I had not been aware of being in a Catholic country at all. The cathedral in Asunción had always been deserted and I had never heard church bells.

I stayed at the hotel for a week, nursing my toes, taking bat bite medicines I had bought at a Taiwanese pharmacy: all the medicines came from Singapore, Taiwan or Brazil. I tried to find out what was happening in Asunción, and attempted to get information on any boats that might be going upriver to Bolivia or Brazil. No one knew anything; there were no boats going north that anyone knew of, but I had heard that story before down south. The few TVs in shops and restaurants showed endless soap operas in Portuguese, broadcast from Brazil: there were no newspapers and the radios could provide no news at all. Concepción made Asunción look like a modern, European city. I tried to phone Mac by mobile and landline without success. I tried to fax, e-mail and phone the Gran Hotel to get news, then everyone I knew all over the world. I had no success. Concepción was right off the communications map. The landline phones hardly ever worked, even locally. The electricity was off most of the time. If you ever need to hide away somewhere where no one has a cat in hell's chance of finding you, try Concepción. There may have been police and army there, but I never saw any. There were no real shops, except ice-cream parlours, and nothing whatsoever to do. You couldn't buy a book in any language. There was an open market where goods smuggled in from Brazil were sold, as well as local fruit, vegetables and dubious-looking meat – much of it, I suspected, from animals caught in the Chaco. It was very dirty, like the rest of Concepción, and the people looked extremely badly dressed and poor. Rain sluiced down a good deal of the time, and there were bevies of indolent mosquitoes: I was taking anti-malaria pills every day. The roads filled with water, the potholes brimming over with mud and slop. The whole place stank of horse dung and urine. Men in broad-brimmed cowboy hats rode into town on horses, openly wearing revolvers in waistholsters, rifles cached in leather stocks by their saddles. There were very few European faces in the streets, and people stared at me, which they had not done in Asunción. I was not threatened, however, and felt reasonably safe by daylight. I carried Mac's automatic everywhere with me though, and loaded. I did not go out at night. I slept for much of the time, drank a lot of rum, and ate too many Umlaut bars, which on balance, I came to greatly prefer to El Snob bars: the former had raisins and bits of figs as well as nuts and caramel, I discovered, whereas the latter became cloyingly sweet after a while, and fragments stuck in between one's teeth. I smoked the rest of Mac's cheroots and bought a fresh bundle all for myself for a trifling sum of guaranis. Although there was no formal bathroom, the Hotel Suizo did, in fact, have an antiquated cold water shower at the back, which drained away into the garden; when the water was on, which was rarely, I could have a long cooling shower for 10 cents a time, in what I assumed was unfiltered river water which came brown from the showerhead: I only hoped that any stray *candirú* would be so disoriented as to miss my dick, and I made damn sure I never pissed even within sight of the shower. The lavatory was an ancient *alla turca* at which I squatted, housed in a small room at the end of my corridor. I hadn't remembered to bring the tea strainer, so again I just hoped for the best. Out of boredom I did visit Mac's pals several times again, but as each of these visits inevitably ended in my standing them both a meal and beer at the Korean restaurant, I rationed these excursions somewhat. I never found out what they did, if anything. 'We suffer our ridiculous poverty in absurd tranquillity,' the middle-aged man had said to me once, with much gravity, when I asked what they did. 'With a placid stoicism not altogether unworthy of ancient Rome,' added his younger sidekick. 'Seneca was, of course, a Spaniard, and therefore, in a certain sense, a Paraguayan as well,' commented the older man philosophically. 'He would have understood our plight.' 'Understood, sympathized – and probably supplied us with arms, too,' suggested the younger man. I didn't feel I had sufficient evidence to refute this proposition. I suspected they were Authentic Radical Liberal politicos, and if they were, this placid stoicism and poverty explained why the party had found itself in opposition for so long: they had all the vitality and energetic optimism of torpid tree sloths.

In the market I was offered young monkeys, small *yacarés*, or alligators, brightly coloured parakeets, a baby cat-like creature that looked like an ocelot: these, I was told, would make excellent pets – or I could eat them for lunch. I declined to buy any of them. I was evidently on the edge of what I had come to regard

as David Attenborough territory, where pink, sweaty white men
of a certain age, dressed in khaki shorts and desert boots, were
wont to crouch unconvincingly in tropical shrubbery, whispering
inanely into microphones, while their cameramen pestered innocent animals, which would much rather be left alone, all for the
entertainment of the gormless millions crouched in front of their
TV sets during the endless British winter: a modern, electronic
version of Elizabethan bear baiting, in fact. I've never seen a
wildlife TV programme where the infuriated beasts turned on
their tormentors and ripped them into small pieces, and then
devoured them alive, on camera, but such a justifiable spectacle
would be well worth watching, and represent real value for money
for the licence fee.

The afternoon siesta of my second day at the Hotel Suizo was
marred by discordant, childish singing from the garden, directly
outside my room. Infants of the female, pre-pubescent variety. I
expected them to stop after a while, but they did not. They sang
the same song, again and again. Eventually I made out the chorus,
'*Pequeño burro, pequeño burro*'. I was being serenaded with 'Little
donkey, little donkey' in Spanish. Eventually, I was forced to go
downstairs to wake the sleeping desk clerk. 'Who are these children and how can you make them go away?' I asked. He looked
at me reproachfully. 'These are the school choir of the Santa Elvira
del Rio Bravo Home for Incurable Lepers,' he said. 'They have
heard of your culture and interest in the fine arts of Concepción,
and so have come to make a performance for you.' Clearly, word
had spread, and I suspected my open-handed lunch-buying pro-
pensities had not passed unnoticed.

Lepers. I was being chugged by small, pathetic Paraguayan
leper girls, who would never grow up to have *novios* – boyfriends –
to marry, or have families of their own. Their voices rose and fell,
fell and rose outside, an endless wave of discordant misharmony.

'They receive religious instruction?' I demanded mildly.

'Leprous nuns and priests furnish them with the comforts of Holy Scripture,' intoned the desk clerk. 'They worship outside church, under the shade of palm trees, so as not to discompose the congregation from within.

'They wear shoes – all of them,' he added proudly. 'Gifts of the wealthy citizens.'

Most children in Paraguay did not, of course, wear shoes, because they could not afford them.

'Are they disfigured – with the lion head?' I whispered, *sotto voce*.

'Hideously, *señor*. Many have lost their fingers and toes already. They have to wear veils to prevent the horses from bolting in the streets, so eaten away are their little faces. Some have no noses . . .'

'*¡Basta, hombre!* Enough! How much is required for them to cease their singing, and never return here again while I am in residence?' This question, too, had evidently been asked before: the desk clerk answered immediately, without having to think, 'Five dollars, *señor*, in guaranis.' The price of a slap-up lunch with the boys in blue, the Authentic Radical Liberales. Cheap at the price. Normally I bargain, but you don't haggle with plucky little lepers sweating in the midday sun under the protection of their patron saint. I took the money from my wallet and handed it over. The clerk reached under the counter and pulled out a long cleft stick of the sort Boy Scouts used to carry messages: he thrust the guarani notes into the cleft of the stick and advanced to a side window, opened it a fraction, and slid the stick out, notes forward.

This little drama had obviously been played out many times before: the singing abruptly stopped. A rustling, and low sussuration of girlish conversation then took place as the notes were removed from the stick and counted. The clerk then withdrew the stick and placed it under the counter again: I peered over, looked underneath, and saw the cleft end, where the notes had been, now rested in a large soup bowl of disinfectant. If it was a con, this added a nice, detailed touch to convince the hardened skeptic.

'*Muchas gracias, excellentissimo señor mio*' came the chorus from outside. A rustling of feet on grass and a happy collective chatter faded away into the distance. I turned and made my way upstairs again. Then a thought struck me.

'What do they do with the money?' I asked.

'They will have candles lit to Santa Elvira in the cathedral – and then go to buy ice creams with the rest. The shops know how to disinfect the notes properly.'

On the eighth day there was a message for me at the foyer of the hotel. A friend of Don Mac called Luis Osvaldo Domenicanos would collect me that evening at 8pm with his truck. Where he was headed I cared not – he was going to take me out of Concepción, which I seemed to have been cooped up in for approaching half my life. I packed, washed my socks and a shirt, had a last, large meal at the Korean restaurant, where the owner had got to know me by now. 'Concepción no good,' he said to me gloomily. 'All *ladrones* or *cabrones*' – thieves or cuckolds. I had half a mind to ask him about the little leper girls of Santa Elvira, but didn't: there are some disillusionments that might be too hard to bear. I sat in the foyer from 6pm onwards for fear of missing my lift. I had prepared for the journey by buying a large Chinese-made thermos for hot water, and bought yet another bottle of Tricolor rum and two plastic cups. By 9.30 I was beginning to give up hope and was preparing to check into the hotel again, when a large truck, the rear portion of which was covered with a black tarpaulin, stopped outside and hooted three times, the motor equivalent of the three handclaps. I was out of the hotel and into the cab within 30 seconds. At last – at long last – I was to escape from Concepción. 'Where are we going?' I asked Luis, after we had introduced ourselves, shouting over the noise of the engine. 'Brazil,' he shouted back. So that was that. I assumed the Oviedo *golpe* was a fait accompli and that Mac had sent Luis to get me out, and move one of his 'consignments' across the border at the same time. More Zen calm flooded through me. I had no visa for Brazil. I was carrying an automatic that didn't belong to me without a licence; I knew no one in Brazil and spoke no Portuguese. I was almost certainly in a smuggler's truck loaded with God knows what contraband, probably including illicit drugs and guns. I had no idea where I was going or what I was going to do. My cameras, and all the rest of my possessions, were in a hotel room in a city I was now unlikely ever to see again, a city which was probably convulsed in rape, murder and arson as the licentious troops ran amok. 'If I had known, I would have been a locksmith,' said Albert Einstein: I seconded that emotion.

Eleven

Smuggler's Paradise

The night outside was pitch black and there was almost no traffic, which was doubtless why a *contrabandista*'s truck set off at 9.30pm. We were heading for the smuggler's border town of San Juan Caballero in the far north-east of the country, reputedly one of the most dangerous and lawless places in all Paraguay. This is where all those stories about *avionettas* laden with dope, illegal gun imports, and hidden landing strips emanated from: perhaps I might meet Erwing Rommel, my favourite local journalist. Conversation was not easy over the engine noise and the loud Brazilian samba music coming from the truck's cassette player. Occasionally we would stop for a piss and more maté: on one of these breaks, the engine turned off, Luis explained that he was going to leave me for a couple of hours (*'unos pequeños cinco minutos'*) at a trucker's stop just this side of the Brazilian border, while he went across the border with his cargo, and then come back to collect me again. My heart sank. 'Not back to Concepción?' I asked. No, he told me, the next stop would be Ciudad del Este, also a border town with Brazil further on down south. This was closer to Asunción and also to Sao Paulo. 'There will be news of what Oviedo is up to there, the *cabrón*, and we can phone Don Mac from there, probably, to learn if it is safe to go back to the capital or not. If not you can cross the border and there are fast, comfortable and safe buses from there straight to Sao Paulo. Or anywhere else in Brazil.' He pronounced it 'Bratheeow'. 'What's it like, Brazil?' I asked. I'd only seen the inside of Sao Paulo airport

213

after all. 'A paradise, truly. They have everything, and the women – god you have never seen such women – ah, the best in the world.'

The truck stop was nothing more than a tin shack in the jungle with a thatched roof. 'Two hours, maximum,' Luis promised, leaving me alone in this dismal hole. He churned away in his truck, which was now covered with red ochre mud that had splashed up from our journey, during which rain had fallen in thick sheets for several hours. Inside were wooden tables, plastic chairs, a single counter with very little on it. I ordered coffee, mineral water, *chipá* and a packet of coconut biscuits called 'Tuareg', which showed a group of Al Qaeda plotters in robes hunkered down in the desert under a tall coconut palm tree, this parachuted in from Tahiti no doubt, with tethered camels in the distance. They were quite tasty actually, the biscuits. Following the local custom, I laid my head down on the counter and slept, my day sack open between my crotch, hidden from view. The owner had been asleep in a hammock behind the counter when I arrived and he returned to this posture as soon as he'd served me. The place was illuminated by strip lighting which I assumed was powered either by solar panels or a generator. They took Brazilian money as well as Paraguayan, and you had to ask to have your change in one or the other, or the patron mixed it up indiscriminately. Were we actually in Paraguay, or Brazil? I asked him. He looked shifty, and avoided my eyes. '*Un poco de los dos,*' he replied, ambiguously – a bit of both. No man's land, Tom Tiddler's ground, off the map – a smuggler's paradise, and no Customs snakes within miles I'd bet. We weren't on a proper road, just a muddy track in the middle of nowhere. I was actually very glad I had Mac's automatic with me.

How long I slept I don't know, but when I awoke I was aware of a very old white man, turkey wattles hanging from his neck, gazing at me intently from the other side of the table. He had very blue eyes and a beaky nose which had been broken and reset.

I raised my head blearily, my hands still on my open day pack. '*Shalom*,' said the man, quietly: and raised a small silver automatic pistol, which he aimed right at my heart. He couldn't really miss – the muzzle was less than two feet from my chest. My own fingers tightened on Mac's automatic inside my day pack. I raised my head very slowly, and said in Spanish, 'Sorry, I don't speak Portuguese, I am English from England.'

He absorbed this slowly, and lowered his pistol. It was still pointing at me, though obliquely now, and with less menace. 'Not Israeli?' he asked, very softly. 'Not Jewish?'

'No, no, no, *señor* – English – from London. Christian – Protestant – a tourist,' I said, slowly and clearly. He blinked his eyes, which watered: and put the gun down on the table. His finger was still round the trigger, and the weapon was still vaguely pointing in my direction. It was a small calibre weapon, probably only a .22. Still, it would kill me if he used it, without a doubt. If I was going to shoot him, now was probably the best time. But I didn't. Which was a good thing, for over the old man's shoulder I saw the patron of the roadhouse rise from his hammock, flick the safety catch off a shotgun, which he pointed at the middle of the old man's back. '*¡Ho viejo!*' he called out, and launched into a long tirade in *Portignol*, that mixture of Portuguese and Spanish that is spoken along the borders of Brazil. The old man half turned and, as he had been told, raised his hands, leaving the pistol on the table. I grabbed it quickly, and darted down to the ground in case the patron decided to blast the old boy anyway.

'*¡Tranquilo, hombre!*' the patron called out to me, and I kicked the old man's gun across the floor to the far wall, where he could see it. Still covering the ancient hold-up artist, the patron walked across, and picked up the pistol by the wall. I was on the floor, under the table, still holding Mac's pistol in my day pack. The *viejo* might have another pistol hidden away. I was hyper-tense and felt as if the hairs on the back of my neck were all on end. My heart pounded and I wanted a piss dreadfully.

'He is an old fool, *señor*,' the patron said to me, putting back the safety catch on his shotgun. 'He's not right in the head. He thinks the Israeli secret police are after him.' The old man turned and looked at the pair of us vacantly, his hands still high. My heart was pumping away, and an old tic in my right eyelid, which had not troubled me for years, was throbbing away. I was surely drenched in adrenalin coursing through my veins. I got up from the floor, sat down on my chair again, and put the day pack on my knees, invisible under the table. I still held the pistol, my finger on the trigger: I was obviously in a madhouse. The patron was giving the old man a bollocking in Portuguese now, wagging his finger, and pointing at me. The gist of it was, I think, that he mustn't come in here annoying the clientele with his gun and silly suspicions. Something like that.

'Well, he could be Jewish,' said the old man defensively, motioning towards me.

'I don't care if he's a ring-tailed baboon, an albino tapir or a golden-arsed macaque. Don't come in here again, ever. I'm sick of you, Don Gustavo – understand me?'

'What about my pistol?' said the man querulously, lowering his hands now, and shuffling uncomfortably, as if he might have crapped his pants, which in fact he might well have done. I know I nearly had. I realized that although I spoke no Portuguese at all I had understood exactly what they had been saying, *más o menos*. Amazing. Berlitz would be fascinated: learn a language instantaneously – just get held up at gunpoint by a senile old Nazi in a smuggler's roadhouse in the forests of the Paraguayan-Brazilian border. They could open a school up there, they could call it the Instant Terror Method.

'Send your son round for it tomorrow, now get out!' concluded the patron with a growl, and he indicated the exit in an unambiguous fashion with his shotgun.

The old man did as he was told, shuffling out with an old man's shuffle, looking behind at me, as if somehow it was my fault. He shut the door behind him, and after a few moments we heard an engine start up, and then a car drive slowly away.

'You can take your hand off your pistol now,' the patron said to me in Castilian Spanish. He went back to the bar and poured two glasses of *caña*. 'This is on the house,' he said. 'My sincere apologies.'

I drank the rum, holding the glass with shaking hands. Without asking he poured me another large shot. 'Who is he?' I asked, my throat very dry and hoarse.

'He's some old Nazi guy left over from the war. Lives hidden away in a *rancho* deep in the forest. He has a persecution complex, thinks the Jews want to kill him for something he did all those years ago in Europe somewhere. He comes in here like this with no warning when I'm asleep, and frightens the customers – most of them know him and know he's harmless, but as a stranger you obviously didn't.'

'I was within a few seconds of shooting him dead,' I commented neutrally.

'And you would have been quite justified in doing so, *señor*. You had done nothing to him, and he threatened you with a gun. However, he has friends, and it would have been a bad move for you and for me also, so I stopped it going further.'

'Is he really an old Nazi or a dreamer?'

'Who knows? It was so long ago. I think he has senile dementia, myself. Normally, his family don't allow him out alone, but occasionally he gives them the slip.'

I wanted to get out of this roadhouse right now, and out of this area of '*triangulación*', as it was called, the three borders of Paraguay, Brazil and Bolivia all being close and inviting contrabanders and criminals of all sorts. But I couldn't. I was stuck.

'Do you have a quiet place, a room at the back with a hammock where I can sleep?' I asked.

The patron nodded. 'Of course – one dollar fifty, or two dollars fifty with an Indian girl.'

'Just the room and the hammock, thank you.'

'And there's a cold water shower – the truck drivers use it.'

I followed him behind the counter. The room was very small, made of wooden planking with a mud floor. There was a bolt inside to keep people out, but no lock. There were no windows. 'Tell my friend where I am when he gets back,' I said, then closed the door, and bolted it. I took a long slug of water, sat in the hammock, and smoked three cheroots, one after the other. Thumpa-thumpa-thumpa went my heart. I rigged up the mosquito net and crawled under it. From outside I could hear a noisy dawn chorus of jungle birds starting up. I had missed a whole night's sleep. I felt drained, exhausted and my nerves jangled like cut piano wires. What the hell was I doing? I deserved to be killed, coming up here, into this region of the insane. Perhaps a fast, luxury bus straight to Sao Paulo was just what I needed. I felt sick: the rum had been a bad idea, also the cheroots. I lay back and swung clumsily, inadvertently, as one does in a hammock. It was cool, at least, dawn dampness creeping in through the slits in the wood. I wondered where the patron kept the Indian girls. In chains in a slave pit, no doubt. I knew I would never sleep, but I closed my eyes anyway. Perhaps this is better than Asunción in the throes of civil war, I tried to tell myself. As many as five million people may have been killed in the last civil war, before Stroessner came to power, I had read. Surely that couldn't be right? Was it a million in five years, or five million in five years? My brain was turning to fudge.

The next thing I knew was a faint, polite knock on the door. I jumped straight out of the hammock, fell on the floor, and grabbed Mac's pistol from my day pack.

'*No, no, señor, nada mal, seguro – tranquilo, tranquilo,*' came the voice of the patron, from the other side of the door, but well to the right, out of any direct line of fire. He had perhaps heard the safety catch of my automatic flick off, or else guessed, or heard my tumble to the ground. 'My' automatic, note. It was no longer Mac's, on loan, it was mine, and I jumped for it as a reflex.

'Your friend has arrived and has had a small sleep, and now wishes to continue his journey, if it pleases you, *señor*.' He was very polite and courteous, the patron. The wooden walls of the room wouldn't do much to stop any bullets, after all.

'*Unos pequeños cinco minutos*,' I replied, with some pleasure, getting up from the mud floor. I took a cold water shower, drank some more water, cleaned my teeth, scraped a razor over my chin, and then went out into the roadhouse, blinking in the sharp daylight. It was after midday. The place was empty, save for Luis, who was shaved, showered and wearing a fresh set of clothes, no longer a trucker, but a smart tourist type in colourful Brazilian shirt and smart slacks. He looked ready to take on Copacabana single-handed. We shook hands and I sat opposite him. He was eating fried eggs, ham, tomatoes, *chipá* and drinking coffee. I realized I was hungry and ordered the same.

'What news of Oviedo?' I asked.

'Nothing. There is nothing in any of the Brazilian papers, I looked. It means nothing, of course. We'll take back roads and tracks to Ciudad del Este – slower but safe.'

I didn't ask him how his business dealings had gone, and he didn't mention my contretemps with the old Nazi, if that's what he had been. Perhaps the patron hadn't even bothered to tell him. Up here these sorts of things might indeed be the small change of everyday life, mere bagatelles. My food arrived and I ate hungrily. The day was hot, I realized, and I was sweating mightily: that's what I told myself anyway. Better for the self-esteem than to admit I was in a steaming great blue funk. I was right out of my depth in all this. I'm a nicely brought up English middle-class travel writer, I pleaded to myself, get me the hell out of here! To Luis I mentioned nothing of my fears. *Cojones* for breakfast, as a side order, well-done, easy over.

We smoked a couple of Luis's Brazilian cigarettes, as a novelty for me, with more coffee. 'What do you think of them?' he asked. I thought they tasted disgusting, but I wasn't about to say so.

'Genuine or false?' I enquired.

'The cigarettes are genuine but the Brazilian tobacco tax seal on the top is false. It means they can be sold openly in kiosks and cigarette shops across there,' he indicated his thumb over his shoulder, meaning the border.

The light was very bright outside and hurt my eyes. My sunglasses were in Asunción, in the burnt-out ruins of the Gran Hotel, the waiters and reception staff all lying dead in pools of their own blood around the swimming pool, where they had run to hide from the rampaging soldiery, drunk on *caña* and slaughter. I looked around the parking lot, which was red earth pitted and tracked. No sign of Luis's truck, just a brand new luxury Mercedes-Benz with highly improbable Paraguayan number plates on. The car was covered in red mud, the number plates pristine. It was obvious the old, Brazilian number plates had just come off, probably in this very parking lot.

'Nice,' I commented.

'For Bolivia,' said Luis, 'the market is completely flooded in Asunción.' This meant we would be heading for Corumba, surely, across the border, and probably then on to Santa Cruz and Bogotá. Hey, hold on, wait a minute . . . my fuzzy brain was creaking slowly. This didn't make sense. Ciudad del Este was in the opposite direction . . .

'First Ciudad del Este, then Asunción if it's safe, then the Chaco route to Bolivia,' he explained.

'And if Asunción isn't safe . . . ?'

'Don Mac will know.'

I got in the front passenger seat. The car was very comfortable and smelt of expensive cigar smoke. Some luckless executive in Sao Paulo would at this very moment be filling out his insurance claim for theft. Luis drove slowly and cautiously. The car had to be kept in good shape, no dings or scratches. The air-conditioning purred softly and lush Brazilian music seeped from the stereo. The track was slick with greasy mud: it had been raining while I slept. We passed through dark green jungle on either side, occasional tracks leading off to where loggers had cut timber. It lay stacked in piles ready for collection. Although it wasn't raining we had to use the windscreen wipers all the time, with the squirter jets, to get the mud off the front glass. After a couple of hours we were completely covered in red goo. We stopped for a piss and some maté: before we left, Luis sluiced a whole bottle of mineral water down over the windscreen to clear it of mud. Twenty minutes later the heavens opened and washed us clean, but turned the track into a mudbath. We slid about hopelessly, the brakes useless. We were crawling in low gear, the wheels spinning up gouts of mud and water.

'I'm going to risk the highway,' said Luis after several hours of this. 'We'll be here until eternity otherwise.'

'Have you got the right papers?' I asked quietly, meaning for the car.

'Of course, Mac is a professional, not an amateur.' I shouldn't have doubted it. After 20 minutes more we emerged from the forest tracks on to a metalled road. The only traffic was slow-moving timber trucks, far apart, some of them hauling a trailer laden with logs as well. I was expecting roadblocks, police checks, army patrols: nothing, nothing at all. We made good time. We had no breakdowns, punctures or visitations from old Nazis. Luis refilled the car with diesel from a plastic jerrycan in the boot. 'I thought we'd be on forest tracks and nowhere near gas stations,' he explained. 'And anyway, they adulterate the diesel up here.'

'Who do?'

'They say it's the Chinese mafia who control the diesel trade up here, but I don't know. I've heard it clogs up the injectors, the stuff they sell.'

False cigarettes, so why not false diesel?

We made excellent time. There was one police roadblock

outside Ciudad del Este, but we passed with flying colours. It was pouring with rain again, now, and the town looked dismal, a low garish collection of tawdry shops and stores run by Lebanese, Syrians, Taiwanese, Indians and Koreans: 11,000 businesses had closed here in the last few years, I had read. The Arabs were leaving for Lebanon, Angola and Sao Paulo. The money had flown from Ciudad del Este which had been Ciudad Stroessner during the *stronato*, when it had been in its prime, a profitable smuggler's town.

We ate in a Lebanese restaurant with pictures of Baalbec, and cedars under snow on the mountains of the north on the walls. Felafel, humous, pitta bread, red wine, stuffed vine leaves – incongruous here, for me, right on the border with Brazil, in the middle of the South American jungle. Luis tried to phone Asunción, but the lines were down, we were told due to the storms. There was a pile of old newspapers in the restaurant, and I went through them slowly. In a week-old copy of *Ultima Hora* I found a lead article – Lino Oviedo and a hard core of dissident officers from the Paraguayan army had attempted to cross the border, but had been arrested by the Brazilian authorities before they even got anywhere near the crossing. Oviedo was being held under house arrest. The Brazilian police had discovered more than 20 mobile phones in his flat: he had been in direct communication with army officers all over Paraguay. The coup plot had been foiled. All was calm in the country. I checked through the more recent papers – nothing untoward had happened since the arrest, as far as Oviedo was concerned at least. In the north-east, where we had just come from, a group of 'false army' in stolen uniforms, had held up a taxi driver and robbed him of US$160,000. The paper didn't say what a taxi driver had been doing with that sort of money in his cab in the most dangerous smuggler's zone in the country. There was also a successful capture of a truckload of contraband cigarettes, imported from Brazil, with false Brazilian tobacco tax seals on. I showed this to Luis, who nodded and tapped his own packet, which was identical to those shown in the paper.

'*Si, si – lo mismo,*' he said, confirming the similarity.

There had also been an incident in the House of Deputies – the Parliament. There were graphic photographs to prove it. Four of the deputies had been engaged in a punch-up on the floor of the house, fists flying. The cartoonists, as ever, had the last word. 'The candidates are asking for another round,' commented one man. 'Of the election?' replied his friend. 'No, of the boxing match.'

There was absolutely no news in *Ultima Hora* from anywhere else in the world except Paraguay, but then with what went on inside the borders of the country you didn't really need any news from elsewhere. The drinking water in the national reservoir had been tested and found dangerously polluted, infected with many diseases. The water in the hospitals had also been tested and found to be infected with typhoid bacillus. I didn't actually care a damn. I was going to be able to go back home, as I now fondly thought of my little room at the Gran Hotel.

We stayed the night at a quiet motel outside Ciudad del Este run by Syrians and designed for Brazilian tourists coming across the border for a dirty weekend. For a supplement of US$5 you could watch the Playboy TV channel in your room, and for another US$15 they would fix you up with a local whore, in case you had forgotten to bring one with you from Brazil. The owners assumed we were Brazilian, and spoke to us in Portuguese, which I discovered, not to my surprise, that Luis spoke fluently and convincingly. There was a pancake house nearby where you could order waffles and maple syrup, and here we had breakfast the next day. It was still raining, and we heard on the Paraguayan radio news that sections of Highway 7 had collapsed. Heavy rains all over the east of the country, drought and Indians dying of thirst in the Chaco.

I had calmed down again after a good night's sleep. Shaved, showered and in a fresh shirt I felt human again.

223

The journey back to Asunción was uneventful, though there were four roadblocks manned by police: we had no problems and Luis paid them no bribes. He looked so smart, and in such an expensive car that they deferred to him visibly. He had taken the vehicle to a garage in Ciudad del Este and paid two boys to wash it down thoroughly with a hose, chamois leathers and buckets of soapy water. It gleamed silver now in the weak sun that broke through the clouds. It was a lovely car, and I left it at the Gran Hotel with a pang. I offered Luis some money for the diesel, but he waved me away with a smile. 'My pleasure, *señor!*' he said, and slid slowly away into the traffic. He was the slowest, most cautious driver I ever saw in Paraguay, which I suppose is one reason why Mac employed him to ferry very valuable contraband vehicles across the border.

My room was exactly as I had left it. I had been away ten days, or was it eleven? My brain was still fuzzy. I opened a bottle of tap water I had put in the fridge before I left. It stank of rotten eggs and I had to pour it down the lavatory and throw the bottle away.

I was able to catch up on the news from the back numbers of the papers the hotel kept. The storms had created problems with the *arroyos*, or watercourses, in the city. Normally these were clean, but since the rubbish had ceased to be collected people had been dumping their *basuras* in the *arroyos*. The flash floods had washed 'pestilential' torrents of this fermenting filth into the water system. '*Las propias autoridades comunales se sienten impotentes,*' the papers commented – the local authorities seemed powerless to deal with the problem. In the slum quarters people were drinking from these polluted sources of water: epidemics were predicted. At the other end of the social scale there had been a 'Mediterranean night' of fashion at a smart restaurant, '*con tops internacionales*'. 'Tops', I learnt, was the word for international top models. There were mouthwatering photographs in colour in the paper, and the sub-editor who wrote the captions was obviously drooling as well: Clara Baccini, a 'top' from Argentina, wore a skimpy G-string and red plastic top – '*una diosa total*' opined the paper (a total goddess) and who could disagree? Lara Bernasconi strutted her stuff in a blue miniskirt and white top, gaining rapturous praise as '*una rubia fatal*' – a fatal blonde. For the hippy element Ona Saez wore a long Earth Mother skirt, in the '*onda folk*' or folk wave. It was all in a good cause. The takings went to the Paraguayan Foundation for Diabetes (Fupadi), one of the world's less well-known charities. I wondered if ice cream and candles for the saint were included. More high life had been on offer at the '*Happy hour en el Centro Cultural Anglo-Paraguayo*'. The guests had enjoyed '*un agradable coctel*' – an agreeable cocktail – organized by the Anglo-Paraguayan Chamber of Commerce. Such well-known local Anglophiles as Joel Cano, Werner Baertschi and Juan Enrique Cabala had been in attendance, as well as notables from the British community, including my old chum the British Ambassador. Metro-fun and games.

Having been out of Asunción and seen Concepción and Ciudad del Este I now realized why 'everyone' stayed in the capital: there was nothing outside except bush and tiny cow-towns scarcely bigger than villages. It was as if in England, after London, the next range of civic entities were Shaftesbury, Tisbury and Sherborne. It made the phrase '*el interior*' seem realistic, not an exaggeration. There were two countries – Asunción and the rest.

III

FLOWERING CANNON

'*Kennst du das Land wo die Kannonen blühen?*'
'Do you know the Land where the Cannon flower?'

Erich Kästner

'There is no other "I" in the world.'

Don Quixote

Twelve

Rumble in the Jungle

'I have found a man who is willing to take you into the interior,' said Veronica from Sunny Vacaziones. 'I cannot guarantee for him – he is an Argentine, you see. He was in the army, the Special Forces. He is making adventure tourism in Paraguay now.' She paused and returned to her nails, which she was painting vampire-blood scarlet – very fetching. She sat at her swivel chair clad in a miniskirt, and flashed a smile at me, in between nails. 'If you decide to go with him you can make a report for us here. You can be Mister Experimental. You will be the first from us.' She gave a little laugh, not without a dash of *schadenfreude*: I would be going into the interior, not her. Alfie had traded in his Uzi for a pump-action shotgun and was sitting on his chair at the top of the stairs, as ever, waiting for someone to shoot. No luck as yet.

'What are his qualifications, apart from being an ex-Special Forces commando?' I enquired.

'He has a Japanese jeep. He has a team of experts he takes with him. He has a certificate in Tourism Studies from Asunción University. And a very big, professional-sized moustache – Don Bigote!' Veronica gave a sexy giggle, by which I assumed she quite fancied the proposed guide. I was trying to imagine what the questions in the Finals exams at the local Faculty of Tourism Studies would be like.

Question 1. If your client is shot, but not fatally, by a member
of the armed forces, at a roadblock, what do you do?

Question 2. How do you get an export licence for a client wishing to send four or more underage female Indian slaves back to his home country?

Question 3. In case of vampire bat bites in the interior, can you tell rabid from non-rabid bats? Illustrate, if necessary.

Question 4. In the middle of a remote swamp near the Bolivian border your client suddenly finds a *candirú* lodged up his penis: what do you do? No illustrations, please.

Question 5. A group of false army in uniform are engaged in a machine-gun battle with genuine police in plain clothes over a truckload of genuine cigarettes with false tax stamps being smuggled into Brazil in a truck stolen in Argentina but with genuine Paraguayan number plates. What do you do, why, and how quickly do you think you can do it?

Question 6. How can you administer anti-bubonic plague serum intravenously in the middle of a tropical storm, in a tent, with the patient in a hammock, without electricity for light? Show with diagrams your equipment and *fingerspitzengefühl* procedures.

Question 7. Your client insists on wearing Authentic Radical Liberale blue clothes and scarf at a Colorado Party National Day Rally where everyone else is wearing Party red. How do you incapacitate him without causing offence?

Question 8. During an Oviedista demonstration which becomes violent, your group is dispersed and lost in the crowd. Later, three of them are arrested by the police for alleged anti-government insults: none of them speaks Spanish or Guarani. They have been badly beaten, have lost consciousness, are losing blood rapidly, with many broken bones. How can you help?

Show useful bandage and tourniquet methods, if
relevant. Give unlisted phone numbers if required.
Question 9. A nervous client insists on an armed guard
with a bazooka joining the party to San Juan Caballero
on a 'Smuggler's Paradise Booze-Cruise Weekend'
expedition. The others say this will only attract bandits
and refuse to allow it: is compromise possible? Use your
negotiating powers.
Question 10. For self-defence against puma attacks in the
Chaco do you favour: a) sub-machine gun: b) pump-
action shotgun: c) running shoes with spikes? Give
evidence from past fatal and non-fatal attacks of this
sort.
Do not write on both sides of the paper at the same time.
Remember to answer all the questions. Students caught
cheating will have their private parts excised with a
machete by the Dean of the Faculty at a special,
televised event – tickets available for spectators, by
request. *Viva el sport.*

Doubtless the Tourism Faculty motto would be taken from the
dying words of Mariscal Solano López: '*Morir con mi patria*' – To
die with my country. Or perhaps '*Morir con los clientes*' – To die
with my clients.

A mere half-hour's wait after Veronica's phone call saw Marcello Warnes, Mr Adventure Tourism himself, bound up the steps
and into the office. He looked the part: lean and wiry, clad in
high boots, camouflage trousers, with flak waistcoat, and a broad-
brimmed hat: his moustache alone told you he meant business.
We shook hands warmly. 'He speaks English, too,' said Veronica
proudly. 'Birdwatching,' said Marcello, 'forest walks. No animals.'
This proved to be the extent of his English, in fact, but never
mind. You could tell he'd be a sound man in the jungle just by
looking at him.

A hitherto quite unsuspected figure, the *jefe* of Sunny Vacaziones, now horned in on the action, coming downstairs from a
hidden office to claim all the credit and whatever commission
might be going. We adjourned to the conference room, where
the *jefe* lit a pipe, Marcello chain-smoked cigarettes, I puffed a
cheroot, and Veronica was despatched to make coffee, she having
done all the work: macho South America, three hombres being
mucho hombre, cojones in the ascendant. It only needed a pack of
greasy cards and Clint Eastwood in a poncho and you could have
rolled the cameras on 'Paraguay Zoo Quest Impossible – the
Gambler's Tale'.

We thrashed out the details, which boiled down to US$35 a
day, all in, paid in advance, day by day, in US dollars, to Marcello,
and no dodgy ones, matey. As the minimum weekly wage was
US$30, often paid a year in arrears, if at all, this being what
police, teachers and government doctors earned, Marcello was on
to a good thing. And so was I, which made us all happy. Whatever
commission Marcello was going to have to pay to Mr Pipe Smoker
I didn't enquire. 'We will charge him nothing,' said Veronica to
me, afterwards, when Marcello was out of earshot: I wish I could
have believed that, I really do.

'You need clothes, boots, jungle gear,' Marcello told me, and
so off we drove in his Japanese jeep to the market to get me kitted
up. The number plate was marked TF in white lettering, unlike
Paraguayan plates which use Colorado red. TF stands for Tenerife,
in the Canary Islands. How had a jeep from the Canaries got to
Paraguay? Don't ask – I didn't. The vehicle was not Marcello's,
but another adventure guide's. Possibly the owner was indisposed,
in gaol, on the run or buried in a shallow grave outside San Pedro
Caballero. I genuinely didn't want to know: he might have been
wrapped up in a tarpaulin in the back as far as I cared, dead of
rabid vampire bat bites. Adventure tourism in Paraguay is not
for pussies or big girl's blouses, which is why I was completely
out of my depth. Never mind – with Marcello anything might be

possible. He had captured an anaconda in a lake, he told me, and had video footage to prove it, a-wrasslin' the critter in the mud. This was the kind of wildlife hugging London editors would die for: I wasn't actually going to try wrestling with an anaconda myself, but I'd be quite happy to photograph Marcello doing so, from a safe distance. What the hell, he was being paid US$35 a day, after all, which I suspect would buy you a whole heap of writhing anacondas the way the Paraguayan economy was going at present.

The market was quiet. Too quiet. We seemed to be the only shoppers. The stallkeepers positively fawned on us. *'Falta de plata,'* said Marcello – shortage of cash. He used a heavily accented *rioplatano* – River Plate Spanish, which I was unfamiliar with: *plata* (silver) for cash, *rico* (rich) for tasty food, and so on. He pronounced *'llama'* (call) as 'chama', and *'yanqui'* (US citizen) as 'chanqui'. In the back of the van were his two experts, both young Paraguayan lads, called Carlos and Hernando. Hernando stayed with the jeep to prevent vandalism, while the three of us scoured the market for my kit. All three of the adventure team wore quasi-military gear, and with the jeep we looked uncomfortably like my vision of a traditional South American death squad. It became evident that Marcello's idea of appropriate kit for me was paramilitary – camo trousers and jacket, army boots, cowboy hat. I gave in on the boots but resisted the camouflage gear, to which I have a deep-rooted civilian aversion. Marcello didn't insist. 'You need proper socks,' he claimed, and I compromised on these, buying a pair of long black efforts imported from Argentina, brand name 'MacGregor', *fabrica nacional*, worst luck. These proved to be a complete disaster: on the first outing they wore into ruinous holes, and when I took them off the dye had run all over my feet and legs, staining me with indelible dark purple, which I was still trying to scrub off months later in England: the Curse of the MacGregors. I could not convince my NHS doctor who treated my festering bat-bitten toes that the lurid, streaky discoloration was not part and parcel of the whole vampire experience. He even took some photos, saying he might give a paper on the subject at a medical conference in Glasgow dedicated to 'Bizarre Conditions I have Treated'. The boots were also an unqualified disaster. They were made of plastic, sweated like hell, and rubbed two enormous blisters on my heels in ten minutes in the jungle. Off they came, and back went the desert boots for the rest of the trip. None of the kit Marcello tried to get me to buy was necessary: he just wanted me to look the part, i.e. macho and South American and death squad-like.

Fashion follows power in authoritarian societies. Jewish prisoners in Belsen copied the kneeboots of the SS in blackened cardboard, because they were 'smart' according to Bruno Bettelheim. The Jewish Police in the Warsaw Ghetto tried to look as much like the Nazi German troops as possible: in the Ghetto Uprising they fought with rifles alongside the Germans, against their fellow Jews. In Paraguay, where the army had power and status, poor, marginal operators like Marcello and his crew copied army style: it helped them with police roadblocks, as a peaked hat and chauffeur's uniform helps professional drivers with the cops in England – men in uniform sticking together. I am resolutely non-uniform and anti-militarist, so I stuck to my civvies, which was actually worse. I looked like the German torturer from *la Technica*, and the cops all asked Marcello, 'Are you working for him?' meaning me, chief torturer, the beast staring out of the window, pretending the cops weren't there. Marcello said 'Yes', of course, and didn't even have to pay any bribes. They never dared ask me for my ID papers, either, though they insisted Marcello and his crew showed theirs. I was about the same age as the President of Paraguay, after all, and fleshy with obviously evil living, accoutred with a thick, grey torturer's moustache in a land where the Indians had no facial hair; I was white, European and wore blue clothes: probably a high up in the Radical Liberales, who were now maybe in alliance with the Oviedistas: Better leave him alone, they obviously thought. I had my own death squad, in semi-uniform, driving a foreign-registered jeep. Their eyes told it all – they were afraid of us. We were always waved on hastily, and sometimes saluted into the bargain.

There was a new piece of graffiti on the walls of Asunción, new to me anyway: LIBERALES + OVIEDISTAS = KILLER TEAM. Another read '*Tenemos dos tipos de politicos – los inca-paces, y los capaces de todo*' – we have two types of politicians – incapables and those capable of anything.

The plan was to head for a tract of tropical Brazilian rainforest far to the south-east of Paraguay, which was now National Park, and therefore notionally protected: here I might see birdlife, butter-flies – for which the rainforest is famous – and perhaps small animals. We would take tents and cooking gear. If this expedition was a success, more ambitious endeavours in the Chaco might be undertaken, weather permitting. Once the rains came in the west of the country, the Chaco turned from a dustbowl to a quagmire, and movement of any sort, even in a four-wheel drive would be more or less impossible. This first trip would just be for two nights and three days, to see how we got on. The Chaco expedition would be a major undertaking, requiring, Marcello claimed, two vehicles, and many of his team, perhaps half a dozen, to avoid getting bogged down in the mud which by then we would find everywhere. On one thing Marcello was adamant: he had to be paid his US$35 in advance, in cash. Without this he wouldn't budge. I suspected a dispiriting history of non-paying *clientes* lay behind this intransigence.

At 6.30am prompt he appeared at the hotel with his jeep, camping gear in the back, along with Carlos: for 35 bucks you only got one of his team. In the early morning light I counted out his first 35 dollars: he counted it too, with much satisfaction, and away we rolled out of the city and into the country, heading east. One of the few compensations for getting older is that one develops a sort of prophetic power about how events will pan out. I had noticed when shopping in the market that the needle on the fuel gauge of the jeep was almost touching empty. It was obvious from Marcello's general comportment that he was completely broke: the 35 dollars I had just given him was all the money he would have on him. The fuel needle was still touching empty when he collected me. Within half an hour it became apparent that he was desperately looking for a petrol station that was open at 7am. He found one, eventually, but, as I suspected, he had no guaranis to pay. No use looking at Carlos – he wouldn't have a bus fare on him. There was nowhere out here beyond the city to change the dollars I had just paid Marcello. I had foreseen all this, and brought 35 dollars' worth of guaranis, and a local paper giving the current exchange rates. My offer to change the money back was accepted with alacrity, and my dollar notes came back to me again; so we were able to fill up on fuel, and the two of them re-equip with a carton of cigarettes each. Both were chain-smokers. Maté they had in plenty, and Carlos was the *matero* in the back with the thermos of hot water: in fact this was his only role.

'*¿Te gusta un maté, Roberto?*' Marcello would cry out happily, and I would reply '*¿Cómo no?*' and Carlos would get weaving in the back.

So after a successful pit-stop we set off again, tanks full, Marcello in fine fettle and very cheerful. '*E noble,*' he said, referring to the jeep, and tapped it affectionately on the dashboard, as if indeed it was a noble, faithful steed. Suddenly, he became Don Quixote, the car Rosinante, and Carlos, Sancho Panza. I, well, I was a stray picaresque character whom they had come across in their wanderings, a foreign savant with a comical accent and outlandish notions. And this characterization as the man of La Mancha was not inaccurate: Marcello was a great romantic and a true adventurer. He had chosen to come to Paraguay from Argentina because it offered an exciting outdoor life in the tropics. He was the first person I had met in the country who didn't constantly run the place and people down, which was refreshing. I couldn't help feeling that in spite of the problems the country was extraordinary and the people basically decent. Marcello had travelled all over Brazil, Uruguay, Bolivia, Peru and Paraguay, as well as Argentina, so he had a subcontinental scale of comparison. He was also a realist as well as a romantic: he knew the price of everything and the conditions of the countries. He was the first person I could have a sensible conversation with about practical matters, without being engulfed in a tide of rhetoric. How much did horses cost? US$45 bought a good one; a cow was about US$20, though much cheaper in the depths of the Chaco. There was hardly any crime in the Chaco, he said, and the people were the best in Paraguay – honest and friendly, helpful and practical. He had a friend who had bought 20,000 hectares (50,000 acres) of land in the Chaco for US$11,000 – and he had paid too much for it at that price. He went there by motorbike. A Frenchwoman Marcello knew had a bigger rancho, in the more fertile north-east, this of 35,000 hectares (85,000 acres), which had a lake in it half the size of Lake Ypacaraí, on which San Bernadino was built. This lake had 30,000 caimans in it. She wanted to sell the property, if I was interested, for US$300,000. The price difference highlighted the fertile soils of the east with the barren, semi-arid wastes of the mineral-poor earth of the Chaco. I asked how the French-woman knew she had 30,000 caiman in her lake. Because she had an aerial photograph taken from a plane, had it blown up in sections, and then had them counted. Some Taiwanese were thinking of starting a handbag factory on the property, so they wanted to know how many there were, Marcello told me matter-of-factly. But of course.

Marcello much preferred the Chaco to anywhere else in Paraguay, though he also liked the deserts of southern Chile, and parts of Bolivia, too. He would have loved to own a property there with horses if he had any money, which, of course, he hadn't. US$11,000 – a sum many people in England could put on their credit card – was an impossible figure for Marcello. He had been to the furthest extremes of the Paraguayan Chaco, to the National Park which was half in Bolivia and half in Paraguay. The size of this last enclave of natural, unexplored wildlife was highlighted by the time it took the Paraguayan Park Ranger to drive round the outside of his half of it – a day and a half in optimum conditions on a dirt track. This would mean a circumference of three days' driving at least, for the whole park. The wildlife had learnt to move from side to side, exploiting the national boundaries of the two countries, in what ecologists have dubbed a 'sanctuary corridor': humans, too. This park was the last refuge in Paraguay of Indians uncontacted by Western culture: they were known as the Moros, and were part of the Ayoreo people. They knew whites, *mestizos* and tamed Indians existed, but made strenuous efforts to avoid them, for which they could only be congratulated, for contact with Western society meant slavery or death for forest Indians. The appalling abuses by fundamentalist Christian outfits such as the New Tribes Mission, exposed by Norman Lewis in *The Missionaries*, were still going on all over South America – slave trading under the guise of Christianization. To its credit the Catholic Church had spoken out many times against these abuses. I asked Marcello if he had seen any Moros. 'No one has seen them – only their arrows – but I have indeed seen those. We tried to enter the forest, an equipped party of us, with machetes to hack our way in. It was impossible. We travelled one kilometre in one day and were completely exhausted. The Moros fired on us with bows and arrows, but were invisible in the forest. We retreated.'

To drive from the Paraguayan side of the border to San Rafael, the first town on the Bolivian side, took about two and a half hours, to Santa Cruz, a proper town with an airport and flight connections to Bogotá and Miami, eight hours, or an hour and a half by Cessna light plane, which was how the ranchers travelled, he told me. They were oriented entirely towards Bolivia and Santa

Cruz, the ranchers, because it was nearer and more civilized than Asunción.

The Chaco was the site of another of Paraguay's insane wars, this time in the 1930s, with Bolivia, for possession of this barren semi-desert, which neither of them could really use. Reputedly, there was oil there worth fighting over, but none had ever been found. At great sacrifice and loss of life, not to mention the usual military heroism, Paraguay won this war, and so gained the Chaco, though no Paraguayan of Guarani origin ever went near if they could help it. The conscripts forced to guard the place in little *fortines* were said not to be given ammunition for their rifles, in case they shot their officers. Indians, Mennonites and those seeking large, open spaces, and magnificent wildlife did live there. David Attenborough's *Zoo Quest* had been filmed in the Chaco, and this was probably most people in England's vision of Paraguay. There was an air taxi you could get from your *rancho* to Santa Cruz – it cost US$110, Marcello told me – so you didn't even need your own plane. You just called them up on your radio, and over they popped to collect you. You could leave your *estancia* in the morning, see your dentist or gynaecologist in Miami late that afternoon, and be back home the next day, having done a little shopping. For large, bulky items such as bags of cement, timber baulks, iron joists, etc., for your buildings you hired a truck in Santa Cruz, which rumbled very slowly across on the dirt tracks, taking perhaps three days to get to you, the armed driver and guard sleeping on board, locked in to foil puma attacks. Some enterprising rucksack travellers came across on these trucks, but not many. This was the real pioneering life, but with modern comforts if you wanted them – solar energy, fridge-freezers, imported delicacies, swimming pools, and even exotic wildlife.

In Colombia, Peru and Bolivia it was a foible of the rich drug barons to import shiploads of wild animals from Africa for their ranches. Pablo Escaba of Medellin notoriety in Colombia had the best known of these, with not just lions, tigers, rhino, elephants, zebra, giraffe and all the rest, but also full-size concrete casts of various dinosaurs as well. There were one or two of these African-style dude ranches in the Paraguayan and Argentinian Chaco, Marcello told me, though he was vague as to exactly where they were. He had heard they were owned by Germans, which figured. The vast Chaco ranches were virtually small independent fiefdoms. No police or army ever went there, and the *gauchos* were all armed. Both the Nazi Party and the SS had bought such ranches before and during the Second War as potential bolt-holes, and transferred the ownership into the names of trustworthy Paraguayans or Argentinians of German descent and fascist sympathies. Particularly favoured were properties which straddled the borders, *estancias* with land in both Paraguay and Bolivia, or Paraguay and Argentina. Effectively these were immune from any sort of raid, and a perfect base for smuggling. It is on one such ranch that Martin Bormann, Hitler's deputy, was reputed to have lived for many years. To this day these are secretive, forbidden places, to which outsiders never go. Very easy to be disappeared in the Chaco. During the *stronato* the army used to take prisoners suspected of subversion up in planes and drop them over the Chaco: the wild beasts made short work of their broken bodies. The only commercial airline in existence in Paraguay was run by the army, though I had not heard of them throwing any passengers out, but you never know . . .

At one point, in Asunción, when I had become frustrated about not being able to get any transport to the interior, I had suggested to Gabriella that perhaps I should buy a couple of horses and set off riding round the country. 'You would not survive for more than a couple of hours. You would be run over by cars or trucks, or be shot,' she commented. I now asked Marcello if this sort of horseback trip would be possible. 'Nothing easier. You would ride from ranch to ranch, and be welcome everywhere, to stay the night, to eat and talk and sleep. You could travel for six months or a year right round Paraguay, Bolivia and Argentina doing this.' Urban Paraguay and rural Paraguay rarely met. Gabriella, I realized now, knew nothing about the interior and cared less, like most Asunceños. As with most Londoners or Parisians, she never left her suburban enclave. Asking her about the Chaco was like asking someone from Notting Hill about the Orkneys. Riding from *estancia* to *estancia* was how Cunninghame Graham and W. H. Hudson, the two best-known writers of rural South America in English, had travelled: but that had been more than 100 years ago. I wondered how much of Marcello's confidence in horseback travel was based on experience, and how much on an 'If only I could . . .' fantasy. If he had the money, the horses and was not saddled with a wife and son in the capital, there is no doubt this is the sort of trip he would have loved to take. His other great fantasy was going to the Orient, to Turkey, India, Malaya and China. As I had been to all these places and knew them well I was able to repay his information on Paraguay with stories and reminiscences of interest to him. Perhaps most outlandish though, and in some cases downright unbelievable to both Marcello and Carlos, were my descriptions of life in 'Socialist Europe', as they called it, meaning the European Union. 'Is it true that hospitals and medicine are free in England?' Marcello asked, echoing Mac. Was it really true that black African illegal immigrants were given rent-free flats, and money from the British government to live on? I was able to tell them even more fantastic things than that. British Customs officials didn't take *propinas* or *incentivos*, but instead seized and crushed in great machines British smugglers' cars coming from France or Belgium – part of the EU – if they had too much alcohol or tobacco on board. Cigarettes cost nearly US$10 a packet in England (30 cents in Paraguay) and a bottle of *caña* US$18 (US$1.20 in Paraguay). The government took about half of all your pay automatically before you got it. Cameras by the roadsides took photos of your car number plate and you were sent a fine through the post for speeding. The police, invisible in offices, watched the citizens as they walked through the towns via thousands of hidden cameras, ready to pounce. Government officials were employed at a salary of US$55,000 per annum to encourage people to eat five portions of fruit and vegetables a day. Unemployed single mothers got a government flat free and a sum of money to live on, plus more money for every child they produced. If you were wounded in a crime – a terrorist bomb, say – the government paid you compensation: if a hospital which treated you free made a mistake you could sue them and win millions of dollars compensation. Men who kissed girls who then complained to the police that they hadn't wanted to be kissed could be sent to gaol for sexual harassment. You could be fired from your job for making a sexist remark to a woman in the office.

Seen in the reflection of their astonished eyes, modern Britain seemed a combination of Kafka and Orwell, Aldous Huxley and Monty Python, which it must be said, it is, though few who live there choose to admit it, out of *amour propre* and simple blindness bred of insularity, and the slow accretion of restrictions and regulations over the decades.

After a few hours the two of them were reeling under this barrage of incredible information. 'You must have read about all this in the papers?' I demanded. 'Other tourists must have told you about Europe?' Marcello was wearing a natty pair of leather driving gloves with the fingers cut off, a present from a French client. 'We have read such things, but they appear to us as newspaper *chantar*. We cannot actually believe such things could really happen. It is like H. G. Wells, science fiction – cameras filming your car number plate, for example, police with spy cameras hidden in the streets. And other clients were not open and free with information, as you are, Roberto. They sit like so,' here Marcello crouched in a timid, rat-like hunch, so redolent of the gringo tourist out of his depth, 'and they say nothing.' I had lived for years in Australia, and had picked up free-and-easy colonial manners. I talked and asked questions boldly, as people did in

South America, too. 'You are not like a gringo at all,' a Mexican had told me in London, once. 'You don't even speak Spanish with a gringo accent, but like an Italian.' This was because I'd learnt Italian formally, at school, but had merely picked Spanish up haphazardly, and rather poorly, living in Spain.

There was no doubt that England and the EU were far more strange and exotic to Marcello and Carlos than what I told them of Turkey and India, which were, after all, Third World countries like Paraguay. Once out of the vicinity of Asunción, we might, in fact, have been in rural Java circa 1974, when I last travelled there. Slow-moving oxcarts, a very few Japanese pick-up trucks, dirt roads, tiny shacks by the road selling fruit and drinks and cigarettes, kids in bare feet, chickens scratching in the dirt, mud huts with thatched roofs, tropical heat and light.

We stopped after a couple of hours at a wooden, steep-pitch-roofed Bavarian chalet, run not by Germans, but by Paraguayans, who had simply liked the German style and copied it. It was a simple rustic café. Marcello had pointed to the pines planted all round German-owned *estancias* we passed. I told him the pine was a typically German tree, and that they probably made them feel more at home. He hadn't realized this, never having been to Germany. We had *chipá* and coffee, and sat out on wooden benches in the garden. There was a view, down across forests and bush. We had climbed up a little bit, and there was a vista. I asked if we could buy fruit, but we could not. I had, so far, not seen one of the orange trees for which Paraguay had once been famous. There is often one thing you say, something you tell people in foreign countries, that they flatly do not believe. Recently, in Australia, I had told friends that in England now, when you rang up your bank, say, or a large corporation with a query, you would often not be speaking to someone in England, but to an Indian in a call centre in Bangalore or Madras. All of these friends had been to Europe, to England, were educated people, but they just didn't believe this: they thought I was bullshitting them – that was their word for it. Nothing I could say would change their minds. Now, at this short coffee break, I told Marcello something I knew instantly he did not believe. We had been talking about fruit. 'In England,' I said, 'in the supermarkets, much of the fruit and vegetables are sold already packaged up, in plastic, sealed close. The packets have dates on them: when the date expires, the supermarket throws this food out, regardless of whether or not it is rotten. They reduce the price first, but if no one buys by the time the shop closes, it is all chucked away.' Marcello and Carlos both looked stunned at this. Shops throwing away food? Impossible!

'Why,' Marcello asked, 'if the fruit is sometimes still good? They could sell the good fruit.'

'The developed West works according to sets of rules, complex sets of rules devised by small committees of people. These rules are then carried out by junior staff who do not question them at all. That is not their job: they don't think, they just do what the rules tell them. If asked, they just parrot what they have been told. There need to be clear dates to show when produce should be replaced on shelves: so when the date expires, the food is thrown out, regardless. The shops could not have people going round guessing if food was OK or not. Bread, pastries, cakes, they all have these dates – out they go when the date expires.'

'But it is a form of madness,' said Marcello, still trying to grasp the idea of good food being thrown away by shops. I could see in his eyes he was trying to believe me, trying to work out a reason he could believe in. 'Surely poor people will come and take this food that is thrown away?' he hazarded.

'Sometimes, when it is thrown away into skips or dumpsters at the back of the supermarket, a group of people called "Free-gans" come and search through for food they can take away and eat. But often the thrown-away food is taken immediately to the rubbish tip and buried.'

Marcello and Carlos looked at each other and then looked

away into the middle distance: I could tell they thought I was bullshitting them. The conversation died.

The countryside was scantily peopled. After Villarrica, a small town with oxcarts and turn-of-the-century stucco houses painted in faint colourwash, we entered a zone, on small roads, tracks really, which was virtually unpopulated. From time to time, once every half an hour, say, we would pass a horseman in a cowboy hat, riding on a saddle made of a sheep's fleece, his stirrups worn very long. They always saluted us with a casual wave, these riders, as they cantered loosely along. We never passed any motor vehicles. I kept asking Marcello, 'Have we entered the National Park yet?' 'I don't think so,' he would reply. The term 'National Park' in European or North American terms implies a firm boundary with the outside land, park rangers in uniform, noticeboards with rules and regulations, information displays, camp and picnic sites, scenic views and panoramas, snack bars, restaurants and lavatory facilities – and hordes of tourists in cars. Not in Paraguay. It became evident as we advanced into virgin bush and then rainforest that 'National Park' was just a notion someone or other once had in Asunción: the land was exactly the same as the surrounding countryside; there were no signs, no rangers, no rules, no facilities – just the occasional squatter who had built a shack and was farming a hectare or so in a desultory fashion. There was no government presence at all. Much agricultural land had been abandoned, Marcello told me: much had not been farmed since the end of the War of the Triple Alliance, which had depopulated the country. A few people came in and squatted: no one bothered to move them off the land. There was no police or army presence, scarcely any human occupation. The difference between grazed land and bush was hard to tell. There were cattle here and there, then long stretches of bush, then more cattle, then a few scratched fields, the odd bitter orange tree – the fruit used to season meat, Marcello told me. I assumed the land must be infertile or lack water, but this wasn't the case. Could you grow avocados, lemons, sugar cane, pineapples and so forth? Yes, you could, Marcello replied, but no one bothered. Even on the cultivated land few crops were grown – a little mandioca, some bananas, tomatoes and peppers, maize for *chipá*, sweet potatoes, that was it.

The great plantations that the Jesuits had organized had fallen away completely. I thought of V. S. Naipaul's comment to Paul Theroux in Uganda in the 1960s, pointing out that the Africans never used the paved paths the Europeans had imposed on the land, but followed their own tracks or dirt roads: the European paved ways would disappear when the Europeans left, he remarked – they were not of the people or the country. The same had been the case with the Guarani; the great cathedrals, organs, violins, carved stone statuary, all the huge agricultural surpluses the Jesuits taught the Guarani to produce had all fallen away and vanished when the Jesuits had been expelled. Very little of what the Spanish had introduced to rural Paraguay had survived: cattle and horses, a few orange trees, open-air Roman Catholic chapels – Marcello crossed himself devoutly every time we passed the latter if they were on the right-hand side, but not those on the left – a curious omission, I thought. Asunción still had the ruins of a European imposed culture, falling apart daily, but the countryside had almost nothing left.

We passed a tree in impressive full yellow blossom. Among the monochrome grey-green of the rest of the foliage it stood out. 'What is that tree?' I demanded. There was a long and detailed discussion between Marcello and Carlos about this: eventually Marcello opined, not very confidently, that it might well be a *lapacho*. It was a *lapacho*, and I had asked this as a test question to see how much natural history they had learnt at Tourism College. Carlos also claimed to have a certificate in Tourism Studies. I knew it was a *lapacho* because *Ultima Hora* had done a recent supplement, featuring dozens of *lapachos* in blossom – a traditional symbol of the Paraguayan spring.

Once well and truly in the Brazilian rainforest proper, on authentically rugged dirt tracks, Marcello took us to a high point where we could see for miles – into Brazil itself in fact. The whole vista was a sea of green trees, not a house, road, pylon or any other indication of human habitation. I told Marcello that there were probably only two or three places in Western Europe where you could see so far with no sign of man, so crowded was the continent. 'I could never live in Europe,' he said with great seriousness. 'In South America we are free, we do what we want, no one interferes with our personal liberty. Our politicians are corrupt, the army and police oppressive, and we are poor – but we are free.'

'Free to be oppressed, to be unemployed, to starve, to let the rich pay no taxes, to die without medicine, hospitals, social security,' I added.

'But free, still, in a way Europe is not. The world you describe is a form of slavery, the slavery of the individual under a powerful bureaucratic state – a brutal master.'

I agreed with him, actually, but I thought – no, I was sure – I could not live in the Paraguayan form of exploitative freedom, the freedom of the rich to do as they liked to the poor. In Europe I was seen by many as excessively individualist, as a libertarian who disliked government regulations and controls: I realized in Paraguay that I was a child of the British Welfare State, and that Paraguayan anarchy shocked me. I had asked if Marcello and Carlos were going to be armed, before we left. 'No,' said Marcello, but he meant with guns. Both of them carried machetes and large knives. I had left Mac's automatic in the safe in my room at the hotel.

The high spot of the expedition, after driving through several flooded rivers and getting satisfactorily bogged in one of them, which involved much heaving and four-wheel-drive revving and splattered mud everywhere, was a modest waterfall in a glade by an abandoned Franciscan retreat. There were beautiful blue and white butterflies hovering and fluttering by the waterfall. It was here that my boots came off for ever, and I realized the disaster of the MacGregor socks. One of the things I had read about Paraguay was the well-worn traveller's tale of coming across abandoned orange groves, with the fruit lying at the base of the tree, free for anyone who wanted to pick it up. Oranges cost me 25 pence each in England. Yet here they were, all around the deserted Franciscan retreat, orange trees with fruit everywhere, on the branches and on the ground, rotting away. We helped ourselves: they were very sweet and juicy, with many large pips. The land all around was fertile and had been farmed: the Franciscan retreat was in good condition, with a watertight roof, yet the whole place had been abandoned. It was baffling. Here was a country with a poor, urban population which begged and stole, and fertile land was untilled and unoccupied. Stroessner had tried to deport the poor back on to the land, but it never worked: they made their way back into the cities again. The great urbanization of the world is an extraordinary phenomenon. In 1900, in France, 90% of the country's population lived and earned their living in the country; 100 years later, the figure was 90% of the population living in the cities, only 10% living in the country. 'Desertification' was the term French sociologists used for the abandonment of the countryside. On a smaller scale this drift was happening in Paraguay as well.

We camped nearby, Carlos and Marcello preparing a supper of pasta, tomato sauce, corned beef and maté – *gaucho* fare – on a small portable iron stove which was fired by wood. We sat around the fire afterwards and talked. It had been a good day, the best I'd had in Paraguay. The sheer emptiness of the countryside still surprised me. Marcello had no explanation.

Before leaving England I had asked an old Paraguay hand about the climate. 'Sometimes it's very hot, sometimes very cold, it depends,' he had told me. This was less than helpful. Being the tropics, in spring, I had not brought a thick jumper: I now realized this was a mistake. Instead of camo trousers and plastic boots, Marcello should have pointed out that it gets cold at night in the bush. As soon as the sun went down I began to shiver. I borrowed an extra t-shirt from Marcello but this wasn't enough. The sleeping bag was fairly useless. It was a cold night, close to freezing: I hardly slept. The other two shared a tent. I had one to myself. I was up before dawn, stamping and walking about to get the circulation going. There were no birds and no animals: I expect they had heard and seen us, and made good their escape.

The coffee and biscuits with yesterday's bread and some jam was our breakfast. Then came the problems. The jeep wouldn't start: we were in the middle of nowhere. I thought it was probably the damp, or else the battery was flat. Marcello fiddled with the motor for an hour, then two. Eventually, we tried push-starting it. After a long time the engine coughed sadly into action and we headed away. The most urgent task was now to find a garage – the nearest one turned out to be three hours' drive away, and Marcello didn't dare stop in case he couldn't get the jeep started again. Then, as it started to spit with rain, the windscreen wipers failed. This was not a vehicle that was ever going to make it to the Chaco and back, I had decided, so this trip had prevented a costly mistake. We made our way back on to the main Brazil-Asunción highway, just two lanes, grandly called an 'International Route' and found a small wayside garage with one bay in a tin shed. All along this highway were the remains of horrendous Third World car crashes – piles of mangled metal. Trucks rumbled along slowly, and pick-up trucks of ancient vintage slid about in the mud. The garage owner and his attendants dropped what they were doing and immediately fell to inspecting the Japanese jeep with foreign number plates, driven by, they assumed, a genuine Spaniard. Marcello corrected them, an Argentine, actually, but they were still fascinated: foreigners evidently never came to these tiny places. I kept in the background, and listened in to the conversation. The bonnet of the jeep was taken off and the windscreen wiper motor examined: it was defective and would need replacing. This meant a return to Asunción. The failure to start might be the alternator – the power in the battery was low – or it could be the battery itself. We spent at least an hour and a half at the garage, and the staff were as helpful and obliging as you could possibly want, albeit they could do nothing for us. They charged Marcello nothing, nor did he offer anything. The bonnet was screwed back on again, and we drove away, the battery starting us OK this time. It was obvious that the Guarani had a real feeling for machines and a light, dexterous touch with things mechanical. And they were so helpful and obliging. I thought of England and English garages – the rudeness and disobliging service, the slowness and poor workmanship, the vastly inflated bills: all these were a direct result of the acute shortage of skilled labour in Britain, and the century-old tradition of working-class bloody-mindedness, due to high wages and high demand. Even a lousy mechanic could quit and get a job anywhere the next day. Why bother being polite?

Marcello was now worried about the jeep, but we had another two days to go and he was not about to forgo his 70 dollars to come. So we made for a Scout Camp he knew, near the main road, where we could sleep in wooden huts, and where there were people who could push us in the morning if we got stuck. We cooked by oil lamp in the kitchens, and went to bed early. There was no electricity. They jeep did start in the morning, though slowly and sluggishly. We ambled back towards Asunción, stopping at San Bernadino, the German resort town on Lake Ypacaraí, where Marcello had caught the anaconda. The real estate in San Bernadino, a neat bourgeois town of well-kept gardens and pleasant villas, was the most expensive in Paraguay, Marcello thought. All was not well, however: the local robbers had been stealing the pumps from the swimming pools, and the local police patrol car was out of action as thieves had taken its wheels and tyres, leaving it up on bricks. There were photos in the paper. On the outskirts was a large imitation Arabian Nights palace, now abandoned: it had been a casino, a folly of the *stronato* years. If I was forced at pistol point to live in Paraguay I would probably choose San Bernadino. Or would I? We sat at the lakeside and had a fish and chip late lunch, Marcello's treat. We had seen no birds and no animals except a small peccary or tapir that had run away when Marcello and Carlos had tried to chase it, deep in the jungle.

There were pedalos moored by the shore, those two-person pedal-boats I remembered so well from my childhood days in Italy. Pedalos had been banned in the EU, I had read, because of 'safety concerns'. A steamer ploughed slowly across the lake from Aregua on the other side. As it approached, I was aware of a terrible sewer stench rising from the lake waters.

'The lake drains nowhere. And the settlers simply run their sewer pipes straight into the lake,' Marcello told me, matter-of-factly. Our fish and chips arrived. 'Is this local fish?' I asked, before touching mine. 'No, it is all imported from the USA – and the chips,' Marcello replied, tucking in. And it tasted bland enough to be true. Lake Cacapipi, I renamed the place silently. San Berna-dino, home to émigré Nazis and the cholera morbus – a winning combination surely? Most expensive real estate in the country, too. Up shit creek with Dr Mengele – great selling point, you'd have to agree. I'd love to hear a local real estate agent's pitch. 'God repairs at night all the damage that the Argentinians cause during the day' is a traditional *porteño* saying, to excuse their polluting ways: but, of course, He doesn't, never mind what the Paraguayans get up to. God, as they say, has retired, abandoned humanity, and is now working on a much less ambitious project.

The traffic was heavy as we approached Asunción in the early evening rush: cars, jeeps, motorbikes, trucks all jockeying madly for right of way, egos high, common sense way down low. Like competitors in a demented paraplegic Olympics, the city's cripples, on crutches or in wheelchairs, darted out in among the mayhem at the lights, begging for alms. 'Does this happen in

Europe?' asked Marcello, which showed that he suspected it might not. I had to think. 'In northern Europe, no. In Italy, in the south, possibly – in Naples, say. In Spain, maybe, in a few places, but maybe not even there any more either.'

A few months later, in Milan, on the way to the airport in a bus, I saw exactly the same thing: beggars in wheelchairs and on crutches at the lights. I asked the Italian guide on board why people gave alms. 'Because Italians are still Christians, at some level, and also because cripples are famous for being able to cast the Evil Eye, the *jettatore*. If they don't give, people fear they will be cursed.' He made the Evil Eye sign, at the ground, to avoid contamination, small finger and index finger extended, the others held down by the thumb.

I had told Gabriella d'Estigarribia that I was going into the interior with Marcello, and she had predicted all manner of disasters, none of which had come to pass: so I was pleased to be able to visit her and tell of my successful little expedition. I described Marcello and his merry men as a 'feudal equipage', citing Don Quixote and Sancho Panza, and giving a little demonstration of the whole maté ritual, with Carlos in the back as the *matero* – '*¿Te gusta un maté, Roberto?*' etc. This was a wild success: Gabriella burst into such peals of laughter that Hugo came in from his hammock in the garden to see what the fuss was about. 'Is so funny the way you say it! Say again for Hugo!', so I had to do the whole thing again, and he thought it was screamingly funny, too. This was the first time I had really entertained Paraguayans, and I wondered why. They made jokes about their politicians, but the narrative satirical tale on local themes with starring local characters was quite absent in their conversation. They were used to being entertained by Europe and the USA on TV and cinema, passively. The idea that people in Paraguay could be characters resembling Don Quixote or Sancho Panza was quite new to them; such a perspective evidently needed a foreigner to imagine and describe it. I never saw Paraguayans dramatize their own lives, their country or their culture. There was no fantasy, satire or ironic representation, except, of course, with regard to their politics. There were Paraguayan novelists and very good ones like Augusto Roa Bastos, but I had met no one who had ever read them. Entertainment was made elsewhere, by foreigners. I had tried to meet Bastos: he had returned to the country after decades in exile in Toulouse, France, where he had taught at the university, and London, where he had worked for the BBC. He was said to like sweet pastries and red wine, according to Gabriella, who claimed to know him, and was willing to effect a meeting. Like most other things planned in Paraguay this never happened. Two men I found asleep at their desks in the Ministry of Culture had differing stories: the first was that he had died, suddenly, in Boston, on a trip abroad, the second that he had returned to France for good – in any case a meeting was out of the question.

My growing familiarity with the Asunción street scene led me increasingly to be taken for a native of the place. Walking into town, bound for the Post Office one morning, I was accosted by a blond fellow with a beard driving a large, beaten-up American pick-up truck, with Argentine number plates. In the cab with him he had crammed an Earth Mother wife with pendulous breasts, and at least four straw-haired children, who gawped in authentic hayseed fashion, hicks from the sticks up in the big smoke for the first time. They looked like Okies on the way through the dust-bowl to California circa 1932, but I guessed they were probably Mennonites in from the Chaco. I was wrong: they were refugees from the mounting chaos in Argentina. There was no food left in the shops across much of the north-east of the country, where they had come from. The woman had a sister living in Asunción somewhere, married to a local, and they were looking for her house. They hoped I would know where it was. I knew why they had stopped by me: I was white, but looked as if I knew my way around, swinging my local supermarket plastic bag confidently. The street was full of Paraguayans who looked very small and dark beside the blond Argies. I didn't know where the sister's street was – it wasn't on the map I showed them. They were absolutely delighted to learn I was English and a visitor: it validated their decision to come to Paraguay – things must be OK if English tourists were here. The English still enjoy a certain esteem in Argentina in spite, or perhaps, in part, because of the Falklands-Malvinas contretemps.

The paterfamilias went on to say: 'Nothing here could be as bad as the catastrophe in Argentina.' He echoed Marcello who, when I had asked him, had replied 'Argentina has no future'. I suggested he ring the sister up from a service station nearby; an idea he took up.

I had no real faith in the Post Office. There were five impressive boxes marked '*Argentina*', '*Brasil*', '*Los Otros Países en America*', '*Europa*' and '*África, Asia, y Oceanía*' with slits in them for letters. I bought gaudily printed stamps from the counter, happy, chattering females tearing them off large sheets and shovelling my change back to me without breaking rhythm. I stuck these on my cards and letters and slipped them into the boxes thinking: 'This is a complete waste of time – none of them will ever get there.' I was wrong. Every single card and letter arrived. Other parts of the government might not be working, but the Post Office was in great shape. In the entrance hallway a woman had started a bit of free enterprise by renting a small booth and selling magazines, sweets and old postcards. I ended up buying all her stock of the latter: many were in black and white, dating back to the *stronato* and beyond. It was interesting to see the well-painted, prosperous streets in the 1950s, full of European men in double-breasted suits, and hats. I now knew these streets as tatty places of dereliction, full of Indians selling vegetables, the buildings rotting and unpainted.

I strolled downtown further, to López's wedding-cake palace, guarded by soldiers with guns and whistles. If you came too close they blew their whistles. If you ignored them, they shot you. They decided how near you could come. No one ignored those whistles, least of all me. Makká Indians hung around trying, as ever, to sell bows and arrows. No one was buying. According to Marcello, the tribesmen were actually hawking these items for Evangelical missionaries, who supplied them on tick. They procured these from yet another set of Indians in the Chaco, firmly under their control. This sounded like an urban myth to me, but in Paraguay you never knew, it might be true. Truth itself in this country was an elusive concept.

Moored at the river bank, at the end of the palace gardens, was the Paraguayan navy's one-time pride and joy – two elegant and deadly-looking black Italian gunboats from the fascist era, their lines redolent of Futurist chic, built in the naval dockyards at La Spezia, Italy, in the 1930s. Now these Mussolini-era antiques were floating museums, or so it was claimed. They looked to me as if they could be reactivated into service in five minutes flat. Everything was kept shipshape and Bristol-fashion. The guns on the fore and aft decks were freshly greased, the timber decks holystoned, and the diesel engines were being tested as I walked round on board. As a diesel engine owner myself I can vouch for the fact that they sounded in excellent shape. Paraguayan naval sailors in British style uniforms from between the wars – bell bottoms, flap-backed jackets, and round hats – moved about purposefully doing things nautical with coils of rope and shiny brass objects. There were triumphalist notices in Spanish and Guarani, boasting how, in their day, these vessels had been the most *puissant* on the Rivers Plate and Paraguay. Plucky little nautical Paraguay, 1,600 kilometres from the Atlantic, but still in there battling away. A heartbreakingly poignant girl of about three followed me about begging for money: her father, drunk in a hammock ashore, was urging her on with imprecations from a shack on the bankside *favela*. She was new to begging and wouldn't give up. I felt furious and outraged at what I knew this little waif's future fate would be: if I'd had Mac's automatic on me I would probably have gone over and shot her father. Eventually, she gave up, and went back to the shore. It was on these gunboats that a group of Chilean and Argentinian officers had been deeply shocked in the 1960s when their Paraguayan hosts had captured some guerrillas and paraded the men in front of them. They had been castrated with knives, on the decks of the boats, and their bloody genitals presented to the foreign guests as souvenirs: the guerrillas then had their throats cut and were thrown overboard for the alligators and piranhas to eat. At the time Che Guevara was trying to get a revolution going in neighbouring Bolivia, and Marxist guerrillas had entered Paraguay in an attempt to stir up the *campesinos*. Stroessner, knowing his people so well, had spread the rumour that the infiltrators were all carrying large quantities of gold on them. One or two corpses were left around, with gold coins on them, to add verisimilitude to the tale. The peasants gleefully hunted down their would-be saviours and tortured them to death, demanding to know where they had hidden the gold. That was the last time anyone tried to get a popular peasants' revolution going in Paraguay.

Dr Francia and Solano López both tortured their citizens to find out where they had hidden their gold, and the wise modern Paraguayan hid his instead in the Cayman Islands, where no one could get hold of it. Dr Francia, like the Emperor Seth in Evelyn Waugh's *Black Mischief*, actually went round Asunción himself, demolishing houses that didn't fit in with his newfangled grid system. He started to build a palace, a new cathedral, a theatre, an opera, a Customs house, a post office, and planned a vast block of government offices along the riverfront with an esplanade: none of these were ever finished, and they were abandoned after his death. He did manage, however, to demolish 99% of old colonial Asunción, as built by the Spanish. López completed the eradication, by exterminating the remaining descendants of the Spanish themselves.

When I got back to the Gran Hotel I found my pocket had been expertly picked somewhere en route. This didn't really matter, as I'd been warned by Mac always to carry a 'sacrificial' wallet with a large wad of local notes of low denomination padded out with a few dollars: this would suffice if I was mugged or held up on a bus. Three recent buses from the capital to Encarnación in the south-east, on the river border with Argentina on the Parana, had been held up by bandits and robbed. One man who protested had been shot dead: one of the buses had been hijacked as well, it being modern; it was thought to have been driven into Brazil to be sold, a reversal of the normal order of local auto thefts. I was going to have to take a bus to Encarnación if I wanted to see the Jesuit ruins nearby.

There is almost always at least one eccentric, if not downright insane, Pole involved in events in places such as Paraguay. I was pleased to discover there had been two involved in the War of the Triple Alliance. Lt-Colonel Robert Chodasiewicz, who had served in the Crimean War as a British Secret Service agent, found immortality in Paraguay by ascending 18 metres into the atmosphere in a hydrogen observation balloon at Tuyu-ti and Tucu-cue. Originally in the Argentine service, he had quit on account of not being paid – they owed him £300 – and taken up with the imperial Brazilian army instead, empires being in general more reliable paymasters than republics. The hydrogen and the balloon had been sent up the river by James Allen of New York – an early example of local dependence on US military technology. The Paraguayans had shot at the balloon, but ineffectually; instead they obscured their positions by burning damp grass. The second Pole was a refugee named Mirschkoffski, who was in the Paraguayan naval service. He built some torpedoes, had them strapped to a canoe, and set off to ram the blockading Brazilian ironclads.

However, he hadn't primed them, and they didn't explode. On board the torpedo-boat canoe himself, powered by Indian paddlers, he used the opportunity to desert to the Brazilians, who were known as '*macacos*', or monkeys to their enemies in Paraguay – or even more rudely as '*cambas*', or blacks, which the majority of the soldiers were. It is little known that 75% of all the black slaves transported across the Atlantic were landed in Brazil, leaving a mere 25% for the whole of the USA, Central America and the Caribbean. Yet how often do we ever hear from Anglo-Saxon academics about the iniquities of the Atlantic slave trade to Brazil? As for the slave trade of white Christians to the Barbary states in North Africa, that is rarely ever considered. Not only had Mirschkoffski the torpedo man not been paid by López, he had been in imminent danger of being shot by the dictator.

Captain Manlove, a Confederate officer from the Southern States of America, now a soldier of fortune, had passed through the Allied lines into López's camp with an original proposition. If López would be willing to issue him with letters of marque he would raise a fleet of Bolivian, Peruvian and Colombian warships, these as privateers flying the Paraguayan flag. Such vessels would then, according to international law, have been able to prey on all Brazilian and Argentine shipping in the Atlantic quite legally, taking such as prizes or sinking them. Manlove claimed to have access to two ironclad Monitors, ex-Civil War warships, in the USA, which would also join in for the prize money. This was an astute suggestion and had López taken it up he would likely have ended the war in his favour in a matter of months. He was too cautious, however, and suspected that Manlove was a Brazilian spy. He had him imprisoned and eventually shot. In the mid-19th century, mulatto rulers of 'native states' such as Paraguay was then seen by the European world, simply did not have white men shot: it wasn't done. It was seen as barbaric, and could lead to full-scale invasion and regime change – as happened to the Emperor Theodoric in Abyssinia by the British. In fact, at that time, apart from Haiti, Paraguay was the only country in the Americas ruled by what was then called 'a man of colour'. But all the shootings and tortures, imprisonment in irons and bombast and speechmaking were to no avail. By September 1867, López had lost over 100,000 men from his armies, 80% of these due to disease. According to the British diplomat Mr Gould's despatches to Lord Stanley at the Foreign Office in London, López had lost the war through poor hygiene and substandard diet for his troops. *'Espera hasta mañana'* was the motto of the country, wrote Mr Gould – wait until tomorrow. That, at least, had not changed in 150 years. I had been trying to get the Gran Hotel to repair the air-conditioning in my room: instead of cold air, it only blew hot. 'It must come from Villarrica,' I told the desk clerk, who smiled. Everything and everyone from Villarrica – a provincial town north of Asunción – was thought to be upside down, back to front, or topsy-turvy. There were always a thousand excuses, but the air-con was never repaired: it was still blowing hot on the day I left.

When I got back to my hotel room I was not at all surprised to see my things had been gone through once again, and one film had been removed from a camera and taken away, a replacement of the same type put in its place, but whoever had done this had wound on only ten frames instead of the fourteen I had taken: sloppy tradecraft, George Smiley would surely have observed.

Mac had returned from Argentina, and came round to collect his automatic. He always appeared at dawn, unannounced, when no one was around except the desk clerk, asleep in the front foyer. He wore rubber-soled suede boots, I noticed, and moved quite silently, like a cat on patrol. He was living on his nerves: he looked pasty and ill. I paid him back the US$20 he had given to Don Octavio for half my fare on the boat to Concepción as well as his pistol and ammunition. I asked him how Argentina had been. 'Worse than here, actually, if you can believe that. Food running out in the shops, no kerosene, electricity cuts for up to 20 hours a day, queues at petrol pumps. Don't think the Oviedistas have given up here, by the way. Lino is out of house arrest, and will try again. The Paraguayan government are trying everything to get the Brazilians to deport Oviedo to Europe. He, for his part, has said to the Brazilians that he will clamp down on the gun-running and dope and cigarette smuggling if he gets into power. That's an attractive proposition for them. He won't, of course, he'll just organize it all for his own benefit, but they don't know that yet. If the chaos gets worse they may let him across to have a go. He'd walk in over here. If I were you, if you want to see a bit more of the country, I'd make it snappy. I got an entry visa for Australia while I was down in BA. You never know. It's getting hairy.'

I had been trying for weeks to get Mac to go with me to Cosme, the breakaway Australian communist colony, or else Nueva Australia, now Nueva Londres, the first and original founder-colony, but he had been reluctant. There's nothing there, at Cosme, just a tiny village. As for the other place, he couldn't even bear to say it by name, so bitter were the antagonisms between the two groups to this day. 'My mob never has anything to do with those sell-outs. They all became rich *rancheros*, the Kennedys and so on.' If I was going to go to these places I realized I was probably going to have to go on my own, and do so pretty quickly. Democratic Paraguay looked as if it only had a very short time left before it collapsed into revolution and bloodshed.

Thirteen

The Book of Complaint
and Enticement

Once upon a time, the railway had snaked down across the southern part of the country, from Asunción to Encarnación. Across the Parana river from Encarnación lay Posadas, once Paraguayan, but Argentinian since the end of the War of the Triple Alliance. From Posadas there had been a train to Buenos Aires. From Bogotá, via Santa Cruz in Bolivia, the train ran to Corumba on the Brazilian border: the land between Asunción and Corumba was flat and easy to lay tracks on. In theory, with a minimum of effort and capital, a train link between Buenos Aires and Bogotá, via Asunción could have been made, with a branch leading off at the Brazilian side to Sao Paulo and Rio de Janeiro. This never happened, through local and national rivalries which led to wars, and the abandonment of southern South America as a place where sensible investors put their money. Sensible South Americans only ever invested outside their own continent from earliest times, like sensible Africans.

I did go to the San Francisco railway terminus in Asunción, one quiet Sunday morning, when few people were about. The ancient British steam trains with their tall black funnels sat where they had been abandoned on the rusting tracks outside the terminus, now surrounded by tropical vegetation and shanties. Indians had moved into them, living there as squatters. Inside the station itself I found the guardian of the train museum washing his motor car: it was parked on the railway track, in front of the exhibits. The steam trains and carriages in the station were kept Indian-free and in good condition. All of them had been manufactured in the north of England in the mid-19th century, as had all the wall clocks, ticket punches and wrought-iron benches which made up the museum. There was a marshalling yard down at Sapucai, south of Asunción, this a graveyard of abandoned, unrepaired trains and carriages: for almost a century this had been the place where the railway machinery had been put right and maintained, first by the British, then by Paraguayans. Now nothing was repaired, everything was left to rot. The Asunción train terminus was a palace, a secular cathedral with vaulting ceilings and wrought-iron buttresses, expressing the mid-19th-century confidence in progress and technology. It was a blend of French and English architectural styles, with a mansard roof and *oeil de boeuf* windows. All of this had come from outside Paraguay, brought in by foreigners who had designed and invented it: when the English and French left, the Paraguayans had simply let the whole enterprise decay and fall apart. One day, when the oil ran out or the spare parts no longer came up the river there would be a museum to the motor car. Toyotas and Mercedes would be lovingly kept and polished in garages, artefacts from a past era. With a few thousand labourers and a few hundred thousand dollars a complete railway network could easily be set up in Paraguay: the country was very flat and virtually empty. But it never would be; it wasn't in the culture to produce such things. As Dorothy Parker rightly observed, 'You can lead a whore to culture, but you can't make her think.'

The swindles of Paraguay – *estafas* – continued unabated: 78% of all the money that had been deposited in the local savings bank Fondos Mutuos Banaleman had been lost – stolen and transferred abroad by persons unknown. Would you have ever put your money in a Paraguayan bank called Banaleman, and if so which psychiatrist are you seeing? Multibanco had a new slogan: '*Cree en el factor humano. Multibanco también'* – You believe in the human factor. Multibanco likewise. Had they read Graham Greene's South American novel *The Human Factor*? I wondered. They were also getting into the culture game, sponsoring El Grupo Maximo Lugo in a stage presentation of *La Tempestad* by W. Shakespeare, for the benefit of the restoration works on the Municipal Theatre, which was derelict and in danger or falling down. What did Caliban and Prospero have to teach the Guarani, I wondered?

For the alphabetically challenged, in all local elections Presidential candidates had a sign as well as a name, as in India. Emilio 'Baby' Cubas chose an apple with a bite taken out of it, a star superimposed on top. The message was clear: vote for me and you'll get a bite of the starred apple, too. The apple, in Paraguay as in West Africa, was an exotic imported fruit, a luxury, like a mango or pineapple in Britain.

There had been a youth protest in Asunción, young, well-dressed middle-class kids with brooms sweeping the streets symbolically, to get rid of the corruption; *¡Paraguay limpia!* (Clean up Paraguay!), they had cried, and blown whistles and horns, making rough music against the governing classes. It was almost certainly the only time in their lives when they had held brooms in their hands. They might as well have stayed at home and demonstrated in front of their parents, since it was they who were stealing all the money. More than 20 Customs officials were under investigation for allegedly having taken millions of dollars in bribes: their vast mansions, built on the riverside, complete with huge motorboats on private jetties, were shown in newspaper photographs. There had been more than 2,000 *denuncias* of these *corruptos*, but no one had any confidence that they would be brought to book.

A readers' survey in *Ultima Hora* had indicated that 97% of those asked believed that the IMF loan being negotiated would not result in the creation of the 10,000 new jobs claimed by the government. Some put their faith in mysticism: a new graffito had gone up in bright pink paint on a crumbling, French-style 19th-century mansion. It read:

SHAMAN =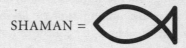

No one I asked had any idea what it meant. The mansion was in terminal decay and had a sign outside advertising it for sale. After the War of the Triple Alliance, Asunción had almost become a ghost town, with grass growing in the streets: I wondered if it could happen again.

In the centre of the business district, in the main shopping thoroughfare, the equivalent of Oxford Street in London, I saw a strange sight while walking back to the hotel. An open truck was parked by the side of the road, with several bags of cement inside; a group of workmen nearby were shovelling up the sandy soil under the pavement and resetting it with concrete slabs. There was a foreman in charge, armed with a shotgun, to stop anyone stealing either the cement or the truck. This was the first time I had ever seen any sort of repair work going on in all the months I had been in the country. I paused for a rest – the day was hot. I squatted on my heels in the shade of a building, leaned back on a wall, and discreetly watched the process unfolding. I had heard of the Potemkin village, but never the Potemkin sand-and-cement mix. But here it was: there was water, there were shovels, there was sand, there were men mixing up the muck, and then laying pavement slabs on top of the mix, but the bags of cement remained in the truck, unbroken and unviolated. I stayed there for almost an hour, taking my ease in the shade, drinking *terere* or cold maté like everyone else, waiting to see some cement, even a dribble, being added to the mix: it never was. The sidewalk was being dug up and relaid using just sand and water. The foreman had evidently indented for 20 or so bags of cement – there they were in the back of the truck. He would sell them later, and pocket the cash himself, giving the workmen a kickback to ensure their silence. The pavement would buckle again after the first tropical rainstorm, held down by nothing but dry river sand. There had been a long newspaper campaign to get this pavement relaid; it was so broken and pitted that people kept falling and twisting their ankles. Around the corner, in one of the private parking lots where the businessmen kept their BMWs and Mercedes, I saw one of the grimy lunatics from the defunct asylum, still in evening dress, taking his ease on the ground. He lay basking in full sun, his face wreathed in a beatific smile. He was lying outstretched on his side, sandwiched between two expensive black limousines. He had his flies open, and his erect, purple-headed penis stuck out prominently and was being slowly and rhythmically masturbated by his right hand. He was the only genuinely happy-looking Paraguayan I ever saw.

In the hospitals, I had read, many of the dialysis machines for kidney patients had been stolen. No one knew how or by whom. Friends and families of patients, too, were complaining that the hospital staff stole the watches, money, clothes and shoes of accident victims brought in unconscious from car crashes: when the survivors came round, or their relatives arrived to collect them, they found they had been stripped of everything; even their underwear had vanished. There were impromptu second-hand markets of stolen clothes – and everything else – on street corners all around the city. If you had enough patience you could track down and buy back your own stolen kit. The bedsheets, pillows and medical instruments in the public hospitals had all been stolen and sold long ago: some nurses and doctors had not been paid for almost a year. The cheaper doss-houses were all said to be equipped with stolen hospital gear, much of it unsterilized and laden with a lethal cocktail of germs and viruses. The rich flew to Miami when they were ill. There were even ambulance-

avionettas to whisk you there if it was an emergency. Local doctors advertised regularly in the papers – many had qualified in Roumania, Hungary, Nicaragua and even Haiti. I saw that none used ducks as their logos.

Illiteracy in Paraguay – *analfabetismo* – was a problem: 18% of the adult population couldn't read, according to *Ultima Hora*, as well as 39% of youths between 15 and 29. Clearly, you would need to be able to read to check you were actually stealing bags of cement, rather than bags of white sand or lime. It had been discovered that Idi Amin of Uganda had bought a plot of land in Asunción, thinking of it as a possible place to retire to: in the event he had chosen Jeddah in Saudi Arabia instead, where he was a pensioner of the Saudi royal family.

From the interior came news that in Nacunday, Naranjal and Santa Rita a scam involving the sale of yet more non-existent lands had emerged. Gangsters had threatened to murder the Titular de Los Registros Publicos – the Head of the Land Registry – if he refused to recognize these phantom properties. The amount of land involved was in the region of 63 million hectares, or 154 million acres. Three more 'mules' had been caught on a bus, loaded with 131 kilos of '*la hierba maldita*' – the damned weed, or marijuana. It was another red letter day for *el can Willy*, the famous sniffer dog, who had spotted the '*malvivientes*' or evil-livers.

In the hotel on my return a new notice had gone up in the foyer:

> Dear Passenger: The complaint and enticement book is in the Hotel Reception. For any complainted for alteration of the rates or service quality, please contact with. Secretaria Nacional de Turismo, Asunción.

I asked at reception to see this interesting-sounding book. The desk clerk denied it existed. I showed him the notice. He shrugged his shoulders, and said, '*Espera hasta mañana,*' or wait until tomorrow. I did. The notice had disappeared when I emerged for breakfast, never to return. 'You can observe a lot just by watching,' as the Californian sage Yogi Berra wisely remarked.

Recalling that angels are the powers hidden in the faculties and organs of men, as the Sufi Master Ibn El-Arabi had written in *The Bezels of Wisdom* in 1202, after a pilgrimage or haj to Mecca on which – despite being accused of heresy and worse in Egypt – he met certain Persian mages who had welcomed him into their fold, I decided to quit Asunción for a while, and risking the bandits on the road, take a bus and seek out the Jesuit ruins in the south.

Fourteen

Southern Exposure

The Hotel El Morocco had seen better days. Once it had been the
Hotel Gross-Deutschland, and before that the Hotel Adolf Hitler:
each name change and management transfer had seen a slide
from which one doubted the place would ever recover. The present
owner was a Paraguayan of German descent who evidently had a
penchant for small boys; they lay curled up like cats on sofas,
rugs and in the large, crumbling armchairs covered with brightly
coloured Moroccan throws that squatted like antique toads in the
halls and corridors. There were round brass trays on folding
wooden bases, brightly coloured tiles with geometrical patterns,
water pipes and copper jugs, elaborating the Moroccan theme. As
a single man of middle years, it was assumed by the management
that I might well share the predilections of the patron, and a
small, slim, jellaba-clad Paraguayan youth of about ten, with kohl
around his eyes, was sent in to turn down the sheets in my room,
and wiggle his bottom suggestively at me, hitching up his skirts
in an artful display of leg, while casting soulful glances at me over
his shoulder. Come bugger me, kind Sir, at your pleasure – and
mine, his wilting glances declared. I hadn't actually known this
was a pederast's palace until I had checked in, and by then I was
too tired to move elsewhere. I suppose it would be too obvious
to call the place Le Château de la Derrière, or The Crisco Manor
for Botty-Boys: I sent off young Abdul, or whoever he was, un-
requited, with his honour – if he still had any – unsullied by
me, and instead searched the room for hidden bats, vampire or

otherwise. My big toes were still suppurating and I wanted no more nasty suprises at night. I found none, though I did rake out a used condom from under the bed, which I flung from the window into the garden without examining it closely. The Hotel Embajador in Asunción, where I had spent my first couple of nights, had been a hot-bed hostelry, I had learnt later on, much frequented by police officers with their floozies. Now I found myself Morocco-bound in a Paedo Paradise. I examined the sheets gingerly: perhaps fortunately for my peace of mind the light was so poor I could see nothing.

The five-hour bus journey from Asunción to Encarnación had been uneventful, which was fortunate as eventfulness on this route consisted of being robbed and possibly shot. The bus companies had started sending their vehicles down with two armed guards on board, to discourage the bandits. We had a brace of these characters, armed with a pump-action shotgun and an AK-47 respectively. They were in their late teens, clad in the usual death squad attire of camo trousers and bulletproof waistcoat, with large cowboy hats perched on their noggins. They didn't look to me as if they had doctorates in philosophy, though I could, of course, have been wrong. However, they did have an ample supply of the *hierba maldita* with them, and wiled away the hours rolling and smoking enormous *porros*, or joints. They were soon so stoned that they fell asleep, and would have been fairly useless if we had been attacked.

Into the River Parana, with a bridge and ferries crossing over to the larger, more modern Argentine city of Posadas on the opposite bank, old Encarnación was sinking: the original town, with some pleasing colonial buildings, was decayed and subject to frequent flooding, due to a dam which had been built nearby. More modern buildings had been constructed on the heights above the river, which were not subject to inundation. Normally, Argentine tourists came across to buy duty-free electrical goods and multicoloured tat from the bazaar: now there was nobody about – *falta de plata*, the same old story. There were bright yellow horse-cabs in the streets, but no passengers. Encarnación was cleaner than Concepción, and less run-down – though no more prosperous, it seemed. The money, in all Third World countries, gravitates to the capital – and usually stays there. Paraguay was no exception.

It wasn't hard to discover the Hotel El Morocco's equivocal past as a Teutonic chauvinist outpost, because although overpainted by subsequent owners, one could quite easily read 'Hotel Gross-Deutschland' and 'Hotel Adolf Hitler' under more recent paint-work, evidence of the palimpsest that was modern Paraguayan history – pro-Nazi until the last possible moment and then some. The electricity was off, and there was a shortage of kerosene, so that the oil lamps were burning low, and we in the hotel were reduced to a few candles. We, because besides myself and the lugubrious owner, an elderly pederast with a droopy moustache, a paunch, and a drip on the end of his nose, there was actually another guest. This was a thrill – someone to talk to at last.

'You are, if I am not entirely mistaken, an Australian scholar, studying the Utopian communities of New Australia and Cosme,' he said to me, when I entered the hotel lounge after my day spent out at the ruins of the Jesuit missions, 30 kilometres or so from Encarnación. This was a pretty good guess, actually. His voice was deep and mellow, and had traces of both Oxford University and the American Deep South in it, but the core was educated West African. He sat in almost complete darkness, only the whites of his eyes showing, and his clerical collar underneath. The blackness of his face and hands was so profound that they blended invisibly into his black suit and shirt: he was a talking pair of eye-whites and matching ivory dog collar.

'And you are Dr Booker T. Wilberforce, originally from Monrovia, Liberia, but now resident in the Southern United States, where you teach at a college, and you are here researching the Jesuits,' I countered, sitting down opposite him, my eyes adjusting to the deep gloom of the lightless atmosphere. He gave a low, short laugh, and said, '*Touché*, Watson.'

'You have also studied at the University of Oxford, are married, and enjoy drinking beer,' I added. He laughed again. This wasn't so difficult, as he wore a gold wedding ring, and had a chrome wine-cooler in front of him with three bottles of Brahma beer in a pool of rapidly melting ice, from the kerosene-powered fridge. Another bottle, I could now see, sat in front of him with its cap off. It looked almost empty, or perhaps I imagined this. It was a matter of some interest to me as the proprietor had told me gloomily that Dr Wilberforce had the last four beers in the hotel. It was a hot evening and I was very thirsty. I knew his name because he had written it, with his degrees, in a fine copperplate hand in the hotel register, and had given his address as Smegma College, Georgia, USA, or something very close to that. So the only really daring guess of mine had been the Liberian origins, and the sojourn at Oxford University bit: a doddle this Sherlock Holmes and Watson stuff, when you get into the swing.

'You are not Australian, then, but an ironical Englishman,' he rumbled in his *basso profundo*. 'And I cannot quite guess what you are doing here, now. Perhaps researching the train, the old British train? It used to terminate here. There is still the station but no engines.'

'Jesuits – the ruins,' I said, eyeing the three beers, hoping he might offer me one.

'My post-graduate doctoral thesis, which I spent one year at Oxford researching, as you cleverly guessed, was a comparative study between the Jesuits' *Reducciones* of Paraguay and the post-Second World War Welfare State in Britain,' he remarked mildly.

'I imagine that made you very unpopular indeed among the left-leaning dons. I'm surprised they allowed it. The idea alone would be deeply repugnant to most British academics.'

'You are right. It was. They had no choice, since I was enrolled at a US college and was merely over there using their facilities for

271

my research. I was cold-shouldered. It confused them mightily. They take a pride in being hospitable to blacks from Africa, and they had to be cool to me because of the seeming right-wing slur on the political status quo in their country, still largely unchanged in spite of the short Thatcherite interregnum, which altered neither the corporatist basis of the economy nor the Statist, syndicalist system of education and social control,' explained Doc Wilberforce, eyeing the three remaining beers with evident relish.

'Did you like the beer in England?' I asked, desperately.

'I can't say I did. I found it warm, sticky and and oversweet. What do you think of the Paraguayan brews?' he replied, giving me my opening at last.

'At this moment, for me, any brew at all would be welcome as I am very tired and thirsty – but alas you have the last four beers in the hotel.'

Dr Wilberforce looked pained, and leaned forward. 'Really? How inconvenient . . .'

'Would you kindly allow me to buy a bottle, please,' I asked, as politely as I knew how.

'No, no – impossible – you shall have two as a gift. I have drunk one already, so we will have two each.' He moved with sudden catlike vigour, grasping a bottle by its neck, and nipping off the cap with an opener he had on the table in front of him. A satisfying gasp came from the top of the bottle, and pale foam was just visible, coursing down the sides.

'There's a very Christian offer, sir,' I ejaculated, 'and I shall be proud and pleased to accept. I would expect nothing less from so distinguished a "been-to".'

He chuckled again, and thrust the opened bottle across to me. 'You are well-informed, sir. There can be few English – or Australians – who know that particular expression. Not entirely accurate in my case, as it usually refers to one from West Africa who has not only "been-to" England or the States, but who has also returned, which I have not.'

I drank the beer with every effort not to appear greedy. It was nectar to my soul. Christianity, I decided, was a very wonderful religion. I doubted if even a Zoroastrian or a Parsi could have been more spiritually generous, let alone a Sufi master.

'Billy Lane, the New Australia prophet, was an enthusiast of the Jesuits, as their theocratic communism resembled his own mightily. Robert Bontine Cunninghame Graham, too, praised their work, for he was a radical Socialist. You will have read his book on the subject, *A Vanished Arcadia?* The title is indicative, bathed in retrospective romanticism. The Jesuits did not see their *Reducciones* as Arcadias at all, but as the forefront of the Counter-Reformation. They had two enemies: the Protestants, and the nationalist Catholic kings. The latter were more dangerous to them than the former, for these were jealous of the black-robes' power, and were intent on taking more and more independence from the Papacy. There were more Indians under Jesuit control in Paraguay than under secular Spanish rule. When the Fathers were at last given permission to train the Guarani with modern weapons – artillery as well as muskets and swords and pikes – they were a stronger military force than anything in the Americas. Another 20 years, another 10 years even, and they could have swept away the secular powers of the Spanish and Portuguese entirely. Imagine, a whole continent under the power of a militarized religious order, implacably opposed to modern capitalism, nationalist monarchy and the Reformation. The Jesuits in control of, what, a million, two million, three million armed and trained Indians, with artillery and muskets, holding the gold and silver mines of Peru, controlling the exports of sugar, tobacco, oranges, precious metals and stones – what chance would Spain and Portugal have had? And then the rest of Europe and North America . . .' His voice had taken on an incantatory tone, as if he were preaching to a small congregation.

'It doesn't sound much like Clem Attlee and Stafford Cripps to me, with their snoek and utility furniture, the East Africa ground nut scheme and the nationalization of coal, rail and steel,' I put in. More than half my first bottle of beer had gone already. I was going to have to do some post-war austerity rationing myself.

'Fabianism and the Webbs,' he continued. 'The intellectual elite had exactly the same aims as the Jesuits in Paraguay. To supplant the old property-owning classes, install a Platonic Guardian class of managers and intelligentsia, drawing all the productive forces of the economy into their hands, and providing an elite to dominate, control and exploit – the word is chosen with care – the British working classes for their own moral improvement. The British Labour Party, like Lenin's Vanguard, intended to be a self-perpetuating ruling elite; it was not intended that the Tories would ever be allowed to regain political or economic control, once they had been ousted. Even force was not ruled out to prevent this happening – it is explicit in the Webbs' own writings. The difference with the Jesuits lies in the fact that the British Socialists were as spectacularly incompetent in running a modern, complex industrial economy as the Fathers were effective in organizing a simple, agricultural one. The Tories were as useless an opposition as the secular Spanish were to the Jesuits in Paraguay. Labour defeated itself, eventually.

'The wealth generated by the Jesuits was immense. Objective Spanish historians have calculated that they had US$28,000,000 of capital when they were ejected and despoiled by the King of Spain in 1767, egged on by the secular white Creole elite who resented the economic power of the black-robes. This great wealth had been amassed in less than 100 years. The British Socialists, by contrast, were reverse Midases. Everything they touched withered and failed, ruining the economy and causing even worse food rationing than during the War. So the Tories returned, and the history of post-war Britain has been a see-saw of incompetence under the Welfare State Socialists, leading to economic collapse, at which the Tories are brought back in to balance the books and sort out the economy, so that the Socialists can come back again and ruin it again, essentially always doing the same things – increasing the non-productive sectors of the economy, raising taxes, and driving productive capital abroad. Every Labour government ends in a financial crisis.

'The dream of Gordon Brown is the same dream as the Webbs' – a Socialist Britain, with the means of production and distribution in government hands. They are managerial elitists who believe in governing by Soviet-style targets imposed by government and executed by a central bureaucracy; in essence, the way Attlee, Wilson, Callaghan and Blair ruled is exactly the same. Blair has had an easier ride because he did not restore the pro-syndicalist Trade Union legislation Mrs Thatcher got rid of which curbed wage inflation, and he has acquiesced in un-unionized legal and illegal immigration, which has further undermined collective wage bargaining. As you will know, under Mrs Thatcher, England – not Britain mind you, just England – accounted for 80% of all the external investment in the whole of the EU. Few as her reforms were, short as her time in power was, she made England the only attractive place in Europe for foreigners to invest in. A singular achievement, unmatched by any other Tory leader ever. Mrs Thatcher was, in effect, the St Teresa of Avila of modern Britain. An unpopular but immensely influential saint, hated by many but admired even by many of her enemies. Without her, Britain would be in a similar situation to Zimbabwe. Robert Mugabe has taken Leninism as far as it is possible to go. Lenin and Stalin didn't manage to reduce a whole nation to starvation, only some parts of it. Another singular achievement. The social and religious control the Jesuits managed to effect over their Indian charges was a direct result of the protection they were able to give them against their enemies, the Portuguese slave traders and the secular Spanish capitalists, both of whom wished to capture the *Reducciones* Indians as serfs or slaves. The Socialists in Britain failed either to control or provide for the British working class, which still votes them out when things get too bad. This is because the Socialist economic model cannot produce the goods and service people want, only those the ruling elite think the people ought to have – quite a different thing – and even then, as with the NHS, they cannot deliver.'

I could now see just why Dr Wilberforce's sojourn in Oxford would have been an uncomfortable one, for himself as well as his hosts.

'Surely, though, that is the long-term dream of all the Socialists in Europe – the EU hopes to achieve that by centralized control, eventually,' I chucked in.

'Go back a bit,' he countered. 'The Jesuits' economic model was successful because the Indians retained nothing from their labours except their food, and the settlements only received 10% of the gross profit from their economic activity – the Catholic Church in Rome retained 90%. The Socialists in charge of the EU project are rather a parasitic bureaucratic class who are forced to disburse subventions, subsidies and economic aid to powerful yet unproductive groups in the European states on quite irrational grounds. The vast bulk of EU tax revenue funds, for example, go to subsidize an inefficient and archaic agricultural system, because the French voter demands it. The Germans pay – they lost the war, after all – as a form of permanent reparations. The British pay, too, as the price of their entry into the market. All quite unlike the Jesuits in Paraguay, who received no subsidies, but rather massively subsidized the Church in Europe. The *Reducciones* were a more efficient form of colonial exploitation than any until the Russian Soviet exploitation of the Ukraine and Central Asia. The communists who ran the mines, farms and factories in Kazakhstan and Kirghizstan did not profit from their exploitation. The profits were remitted to Moscow. The first thing Dr Francia did when he came to power was expropriate from the Catholic Church in Paraguay – no more money was to be sent back to Rome – just as the first thing the Central Asians and Ukrainians did after the fall of the Soviet empire was to expel the

Russian apparatchiks, take over their enterprises, and send no more goods to Moscow.'

Dr Wilberforce spoke with both fluency and confidence, raising a solitary finger from time to time to illustrate a point. He had obviously studied the Jesuits and their operations from the broadest possible historical perpective. I was impressed. 'Why, if it was so efficient, did the Jesuit experiment fail, then?' I demanded. I was well into my last beer, and I could hear my bed calling for me.

'"How many regiments does the Pope have?" asked Stalin rhetorically, knowing he had none. Yet with the Jesuits and the militarized Guarani, the Pope had many. He did not know how to use them, though. The Papacy had been dependent upon Catholic European monarchs for so long that it could not imagine defying them. When the Kings of Spain and Portugal became alarmed at the growth in power of the Jesuit colonies in greater Paraguay, they put pressure on the Pope to acquiesce in expelling the Fathers. He should have refused – even to the point of abandoning the Papacy and Europe himself, and taking refuge with the Jesuits in Paraguay with his Curia. You are surprised, I see, yet this is what the King of Portugal did, when faced with Napoleon's invasion of his country – he took his Court to Brazil and ruled from there. The French could have done the same in 1940, ruling from Algiers, but Reynaud's mistress talked him out of it. Churchill flew to France expressly to persuade the French leader to take his whole Cabinet to North Africa and continue the fight from there. The Jesuits in South America were the last chance the Papacy ever had of throttling modern capitalism – and Protestantism. If the Pope had instructed the multiracial Jesuits who owed alliegance only to the Pope, to defy Spain and fight the secular arm, the Spanish colonial authorities, excommunicated and denied burial by the Pope, would have crumbled spiritually and militarily. An entirely different version of history was put down when the black-robes were sent back to Europe under the hatches of Spanish ships as prisoners. Did the Pope entirely trust the Jesuits? Did Hitler entirely trust Himmler and the SS? Probably not. Elite shock troops have a habit of revolting – look at the Janissaries in Ottoman Turkey. It is said that in China, when instructing the mandarins in Christianity, the Jesuits suppressed the Crucifixion. A Divinity who allowed Himself to be executed by foreign soldiers was not likely to appeal to the rulers of the Middle Kingdom.' The doctor of divinity in front of me chuckled softly. 'You have seen today the ruins of a world order that was aborted just as it was poised for world domination.'

The bus had taken me out to Trinidad, largest of the Jesuit *Reducciones* in Paraguay. We passed through a landscape of sugar cane and ploughed fields showing the ochre earth underneath. For the first time I saw the famous orange groves of Paraguay, and other fruit orchards, too. There were cattle grazing in neat fields and wooden barns with shingle roofs. We stopped in Colonia Hohenau: there was a Lutheran church and many pine trees. This is where Alfredo Stroessner was born, and where Dr Mengele, the torturer and sadist of Auschwitz found refuge, before he moved on to Brazil. I was not tempted to get down from the bus.

'It's just up the hill,' said the driver as he dropped me off near my destination. 'There's nothing to see – just ruins,' he added helpfully.

I walked up the hill in sharp sunlight. It was quiet, peaceful. On the brow of the hill, in a natural defensive position, stood a group of red stone buildings, massive still, built to last for ever, all that remains of a lost dream. There was a ticket office, tickets on the counter, but no one selling them; it was the siesta and I suspected a hammock was being occupied somewhere nearby. There was no one else visiting the ruins. I walked in undisturbed and wandered around.

Close to, the buildings, roofless and surrounded by old palm trees rustling in the breeze, seemed to be made of sandstone. All the Indians' houses surrounding the plaza were identical. There were the ruins of what had once been workshops, bakeries, prisons, granaries, asylums, armouries and the Fathers' houses. In the centre, around which all were grouped was the basilica, vast by comparison, large enough to accommodate 4,000 Indians as a congregation. The Jesuits had been expelled in 1768, and the settlement had been completely abandoned then: the roof of the church collapsed in 1800. Cunninghame Graham claimed he saw Indians in old mission-style clothes, saying prayers in Latin in the basilica in 1874, but this may just have been his romanticism at work. No money was used in the *Reducciones*, no secular Spanish or Portuguese settlers, not even the governors themselves – were allowed into Jesuit-controlled territory. It was the first ever state-within-a-state in Western history, self-financing, self-regulating, surplus-producing, excluding all outsiders, with its own effective system of armed defence. At the highest point of their development the *Reducciones* could put 20,000 trained Guarani soldiers into battle, officered by Jesuit priests. In the first Jesuit War against the Portuguese Brazilian slave traders, the invaders were soundly trounced by cannon and musket fire, and sent home after an abject defeat, a victory the Spanish in Asunción were at first delighted with, then began to have doubts about. European philosophers wrote about the Jesuit experiment in social engineering, as a later age would dub it. Montesquieu was a fan, and advised all Western states to adopt the Jesuit system: he saw in it the fulfilment of Plato's 'Republic', a polity governed by moral philosophers. Voltaire was openly mocking. In *Candide* Cacambo tells the eponymous hero: 'It is a wonderful system they have. There are thirty provinces in their kingdom and it is more than three hundred leagues across. The reverend fathers own the whole lot, and the people own nothing: that's what I call a masterpiece of reason and justice.'

The Indians were recruited directly from the forests and fields by the Fathers: being inside the missions made them safe from the Brazilian slave traders, the *bandierantes*, who were ravaging the land and taking people off after every raid – this was once permission had been given to arm and train the Indians, which was not for many years. During this earlier period, the Jesuits found they were conveniently gathering together natives for the slave traders to collect by force and take back to Brazil to be sold to labour on the plantations. The *Reducciones* Indians were subject to discipline: incest, bestiality, slaughtering livestock without permission and other crimes were punished with a whipping and imprisonment. The sinners had to kiss the sleeve of the Jesuit who had whipped them after their punishment.

The elaborate carvings on the basilica still visible were evidence of the high artistic levels to which the Guarani were trained by their mentors. All the musical instruments of Europe – harp and viol, harpsichord and organ, flute and drum – were reproduced in these settlements, and whole baroque operas and oratorios were staged with choirs of hundreds, in the middle of the jungle, at this very spot, at a time when there was not one opera house or choir anywhere outside Europe. At Trinidad there was a fully operating printing press, 100 years before Buenos Aires was to get one. Books, illuminated manuscripts, superb musical instruments, firearms, clothes, carvings, paintings, statues, all that the finest craftsmen of Italy, France or Spain could boast was produced here, a thousand miles up the river from the Atlantic. The scale and quality of the Jesuits' achievement was perhaps unparalleled in human history. There was no capital punishment. The Indians were protected from their enemies, Christianized, and civilized. At a time when everywhere else in the Americas the natives were being ruthlessly enslaved, murdered and tortured, these 30 settlements were a haven of relative security and sanctuary. And yet. No Guarani ever became a priest, never rose higher than a sacristan in the hierarchy. They were treated like children, unable to look after themselves. And when, suddenly, on the orders of the Pope, the Jesuits abandoned the Indians, the whole system collapsed immediately. It had been built on the sands of total dependence. The slave traders moved in and the Indians scattered back into the forests, many to be hunted down and captured.

Dr Wilberforce had sent a Parthian shot after me in the Hotel El Morocco when I went to bed. 'If the Socialists and the administrators, social workers and benefit grant officers suddenly abandoned the British lower class, whom at present they administer and sustain, what do you think would happen in your inner cities? If the dole stopped and the housing benefit ceased, and all the rest of it? What would happen, do you think the dependent classes could sustain themselves? There are no forests to run to in Britain any more. There would be anarchy, chaos and mass starvation. Perhaps a few thousand of the strongest would survive by cannibalism. Sleep well, and God preserve you, for your Socialists will soon not be able to, I rather fear.'

The Fathers had not taught their charges either Spanish or Portuguese – just enough Latin to pray. For the rest the communities used Guarani: dictionaries and a grammar were produced, another reason why in Paraguay alone in Latin America, the native language survives as an official tongue along with Spanish. It was smart for the rich white girls in Asunción to be able to sing traditional songs in Guarani, quite unlike places like Peru, where Quechua was the language only of the poor and oppressed.

The finest of the Mission churches was to have been at Jesus, ten kilometres or so from Trinidad. I started to walk, but a small truck soon stopped and gave me a lift. The driver was a Paraguayan of German descent, with grey eyes and brown hair. He owned a small farm nearby. He had a sick calf in the back of the truck, roped down, and was taking it to the vet. He was amused to learn I was English.

'We used to have tourists but now, they don't come any more for some reason. They say it's very dangerous up in the capital now, but down here we don't worry – *tranquilo, tranquilo.* There are Mennonites here, you know, as well as the Chaco – good farmers, very traditional, hard working. And Japanese, and

Koreans. *Poco de todos* – a little of everyone. This is the best part of Paraguay, the most fertile, the richest and the calmest. The further north you go the madder it becomes. I went up to San Juan Caballero once – never again. I was frightened out of my skin – bandits and cowboys! Have you been to Germany, then, on your travels?' I told him I had. He told me he hadn't. 'Pretty much like here, I should imagine – rich, well-ordered, calm.' 'Less sugar cane in the fields, and not so many orange trees,' I said. He laughed. 'The English always had a sense of humour, that's what I heard. Give my regards to the Queen!' he said, as he set me down, and waved me on my way.

There were a few wooden shacks and clumps of pine trees. Up on the top of a hill stood the incomplete cathedral, roofless, massive, framed by quebrachos and palms. This was to be the St Peter's of the Jesuit dominions, the largest religious building in the Americas. There was a Moorish-style arch through which you entered. The walls had never been completed, no roof had ever been installed; the cloisters had not been started, and the surrounding Indians' houses had not got beyond a rudimentary stage of construction. Here was a whole civilization that had suddenly stopped on that day in August 1768. I sat down in the shade and contemplated the scene. There was no one else around. A whole world had come to an end here, a worthwhile, civilized world. Individualists have problems with collectivist dreams of perfection. I could no more have lived in a Jesuit *Reducción* than I could have in a Soviet *kolkhoz*, but wishing the Jesuit project ill seemed like wishing the Old Age Pension or the National Health Service into oblivion in Britain. Given the alternatives available at the time the *Reducciones* were the most civilized option. But doomed. Could bureaucratic, uneconomic modern Europe survive any more than the *Reducciones*? In the end people, nations, cultures, have to earn their livings on their own, without subsidies and paternalism.

In Germany they had a word to describe the pointless, uneconomic, futile work of a people for the state – *Pyramidenbau* – pyramid-building. These ruins were *Pyramidenbau* of a sort, and more than half the populations of modern Europe worked for the state, too, producing their own little mountains and pyramids of paper. Travel gives you a new slant on your own world. The first thing I noticed when I got back to England was the thousands of government employees, in uniform and out, doing absolutely nothing at all, just sitting or standing, manning telephones, pushing paper, herding and cajoling, ordering, hectoring and advising. If the USA was an economy where people were selling hamburgers to each other, Britain seemed to be a state devoted to counselling itself into paralysis. I was trying to buy a slice of land from the local fire brigade for my garden. It took them three months to answer every letter I sent them. In the end, despite their endless prevarications and obfuscations, I bought the strip of land: the whole process took me five years struggling all the way. The previous owner of my house had actually died while negotiating the sale, which process had collapsed on his death, and had to be begun again from scratch by me. No wonder the books of Franz Kafka speak so directly to the post-war British.

I thought of the Jesuit *Reducciones* often – a lost paradise, a paternalist closed system, a theocratic state: but most of all I saw it as a precursor of the modern world, where the state, through its administration, herds the population, treating them as cattle, to be organized and milked, kept in good health and prevented from hurting themselves, beasts too stupid to look after themselves and too placid to revolt. The highest virtue in the modern European state is blind obedience to government direction: the loss of initiative, enterprise and sheer verve for living, never mind existential freedom, were the results we all lived with. Which was why travel writers went to the Third World, where this process was imperfect, partial and largely ineffective – and why the people back in the state-ordered prison camp at home envied them so much.

Fifteen

Du Côté de Chez
Voltaire Molesworth

I was going to get to sleep with Lolita Dellabedova. Let me put that another way. Señora Dolores 'Lolita' Dellabedova had invited me to stay with her on her *estancia*. For a fee, of course. After some prompting by Veronica of Sunny Vacaziones, who had been ringing round various *estancieros* to see if some hospitality for dollars could be arranged. It was going to cost me US$30 a day, plus about US$80 to have her *choffer* come and pick me up. Her *estancia* was in the east of the country, in fertile, rolling country, not the blistered wastes of the Chaco. This sounded fine to me. The *estancia* experience is a hardy perennial of the travel-writing genre. I had seen high-class fine-writing pieces dripping with nostalgia and silver-roundel spurs in Sunday broadsheets at home. There was always the old walnut grandfather clock ticking slowly on the wax-polished, aromatic terracotta-tiled hallway, brought out by an ancestor from Scotland in the 19th century. There was a paddock of full-blooded Arabian horses, which the writer rode with the style and aplomb of a Rotten Row *habitué*. The owners, sage and gracious, hair tinged with grey, hairy tweeds and golden labradors in attendance, offered old-time hospitality and vintage malt whisky in cut-glass tumblers. Deft, winsome maids in uniform, smiling shyly, turned down the sheets by candlelight. The *estancia* was ancient and feudal, with proud, devoted *gauchos* and *vaqueros*, whose families had been in the service of the family for centuries, prancing to and fro on thoroughbreds, in colourful costume, some of them even on horseback. The house itself was vast, antiquated and mellow, drenched in grapevines and bougainvillea. There was always an *asado*, an outdoor barbecue of roast meats, home-killed, and in the evenings the lilting, plangent twangle of the guitar and violin rent the soft, mote-laden air as the dusky Carmens and Conchitas in their spangled ankle-length dresses high-stepped it round the embers of the dying fire, and the watching *gauchos*, half-hidden in shadows and sombreros under the ancient *umbo* tree, furtively masturbated away their sexual frustrations into the red-and-white spotted handkerchiefs which normally they wore round their necks, or else sodomized each other with all the inbred skill of men born to ride in the saddle, gripping hold of their bumchums' leather chaps with horny hands, cracked with years of wielding a stockwhip at quasi-nudist fancy dress parties where the kinky *estancia* owners got their own jollies. Actually, I've invented the last bit, which the Sunday broadsheets would never in a million years publish on their travel pages, even if it were true, which it probably isn't. However, you get the picture: *estancias* were in, like tree hugging and wildlife cuddling, among those journalistic circles where the travel writers' reputation is made.

Nevertheless ... a possible Dellabedova suggested to me a possible leg-over. Was Señora Dolores, as she was properly called, a great beauty, I asked Veronica – a sultry siren of the South, a passionate embodiment of the gringos' fantasies about the Latin American female?

'Well, she has had her problems, the Señora,' Veronica replied in measured tones. 'Her husband is a naughty boy. He has many mistresses. And her son went to the bad – he became a cocaine addict. And her ovaries have been removed. So she is depressed, sometimes.'

I liked the 'sometimes': it showed precision.

'It would be good for her to have a paying guest at the Estancia

Agua Amarga. It might cheer her up a little bit,' she concluded, lighting a long, slim cigarette: no nonsense about not smoking in the workplace in Paraguay, everyone smoked everywhere, including doctors on their hospital rounds, dentists drilling your teeth, and priests hearing confessions. I'd seen one of the latter coming out of a confession booth with a curly Sherlock Holmes pipe on the go, clouds of smoke billowing up, as if from a chasuble.

Hmm. A visit to her *estancia* might indeed cheer her up, but would it depress the hell out of me? I wondered. The Bitter Water Ranch didn't sound a bundle of fun, somehow. If I wanted to write a feature for 'The Sunday Toff' that would have to be changed to the Sweet Water Ranch, I suspected, and the Señora's ovaries would have to remain a closed book. 'Mankind cannot bear too much reality,' as T. S. Eliot rightly observed, and above all in Sunday travel features.

'It is not certain, yet,' Veronica concluded. 'The Señora may be going to Miami to consult with her psychiatrist. He is orthodox Freudian – very strict.'

Buenos Aires is reputed to have the highest number of psychiatrists in the world, beating even New York. Why did Señora Dolores Sin Ovarias choose to go north rather than south, I asked.

'The orthodox Freudians in BA are not so orthodox, it seems,' Veronica replied evenly. 'The Señora found one analyst there who was living with a lady who was a Jungian, and to whom he was not married. Their children were very, very confused – primal confusion. So she doesn't like. Also she hate all Argentinians, basically, as artists of *chantar* – you know this word?' I said I did – to bluff, con or bullshit.

I contacted Marcello and suggested we go on another short excursion, one from which we could get back in case El Noble blew a gasket. He was all for it: business was bad. He was trying to get some money together to shoot some more wildlife movies for TV, but so far no luck. He had shown me some of his work already and asked me if I thought the BBC might be interested in buying it. On the small screen, with his long hair, greasy stetson, sinister moustache and goatee, Marcello looked as if he had just murdered the producer in a fit of dementia, and buried him in a nearby swamp, facedown, after conducting a Black Mass. I saw the famous grappling-with-an-anaconda-in-Lake-Cacapipi sequence, too. The anaconda was truly huge, and quite repulsive, writhing and twisting like a cornered New Labour Deputy Prime Minister caught with his extremities round a civil servant at an office party. Marcello wasn't so hot either, up to his boot-tops in liquid gunk, with that yucky lakewater full of you-know-what running down his hands, arms and body. There was typhoid in the lake and I wasn't at all suprised. I thought it would probably make the BBC wallahs feel rather ill: it did me. It also occurred to me that if a novelist invented a lake which had filled up over the years with human excrement, produced by émigré German Nazis who lived in luxury villas on the lake shore, his editor would probably accuse him of absurd, melodramatic overstatement and blindingly obvious symbolism.

The Virgin Mary enjoys the rank of field-marshal in the Paraguayan army. The many statues around the place showed her sorrowful and compassionate, as you'd expect, but also with her military medals pinned to her chest, and a broad, brightly coloured marshal's sash across her shoulder and down to her waist. No sword, though, alas – that would have been the *pièce de résistance*. The Lourdes of Paraguay, dedicated to excesses of Mariolatry, is Caacupé, where several centuries ago a miraculous statue of the Blessed Virgin was washed ashore after some floods, and the town has never looked back. A shrine, then a church, then a large St Peter's-like basilica were built: pilgrims from all over Paraguay made their way there to pray, beg for intercession, and stock up on religious kitsch, much of it doubtless smuggled into the country from Brazil. We bowled down Highway 2 from Asunción, Marcello at the wheel, Carlos in the back brewing up as ever.

'*¿Te gusta un maté, Roberto?*' cried Marcello gaily, lighting another cigarette from the butt of his last.

'*¿Cómo no?*' I roared back over the engine noise.

It was quite like old times. To our left a large group of young men in military uniform, but without weapons, were walking slowly in bare feet down the road. It was a tradition that after you ended your National Service in the army, you made your way on foot as a pilgrim to Caacupé to give thanks for surviving the psychopathic officer corps. The real keen-os did it in bare feet, even from the Chaco. Did they imbibe maté en route, I asked Marcello. He looked at me scandalized – certainly not! How about self-flagellation, then? He thought for a minute, then admitted there might be a bit of that. I wondered where they slept and what they ate and drank. I guessed they trusted to the kindness of strangers. We parked opposite the police station, as pilgrimage towns are notorious for car thefts – the villains can go straight to a church and get instant forgiveness, after all. The small town, quite dominated by the huge stucco basilica, was prosperous and orderly, smart villas in well-kept gardens. There was obviously *falta de plata* – lack of money – here too: the stalls of kitsch were loaded high, but there were no buyers. The basilica was empty, except for some pigeons; sunlight shafted in through high windows, bold streaks of light staining the walls. The people were all outside, at an open-air religious service being given by a rock band of truly Satanic quality. The lead singer, who caterwauled into a screeching mike, was a pastor of some sort. The style and presentation was US Evangelist, but it was a Catholic knock-off, or so Marcello informed me. The gringo Evangelists had made such inroads into the flocks of the faithful that the Catholic clergy had been forced to follow suit. Apparently only Catholics had to serve in the armed forces, Protestants and animist Indians being exempt.

All was not well in this bastion of Popery, however. The Bishop of Caacupé, Monseñor Claudio Gimenez, had threatened several of his '*fieles católicos*,' or faithful Catholics, with excommunication for producing '*desorientación y escandalos*'. He had decided to prohibit the activities of three *curanderos*, Valentin Santabria, and Rufino and Catalino Benitez, who had been soliciting bribes ('*limosnas*') from their clients for certain occult services not recognized by the magic-and-miracles section of Mother Church. They were *falsos*, in fact, without the correct tax stamps on, therefore contraband. Furthermore the Bishop forbade Ermuelinda Farina from '*realizar reuniones, celebraciones y oraciones de curación en nombre de la iglesia*', in other words from conducting freelance, unrecognized pirate services, claiming to be kosher Catholic but in fact being *falsos*. The Guarani genius for copying, imitation, faking, piracy and falsifying extended even into religious worship. The Bishop warned that if these characters persisted in their naughtiness, they would be excommunicated from the real, as it were, Catholic Church. In Spain, a renegade Catholic priest has broken away from the Church, built his own Vatican, and declared himself the Pope and the only true Catholic authority on all matters. If he set up shop in Paraguay he could have a rosy future, a false Pope being about the only thing the Paraguayans have not, yet, thought of, invented, or forged. I asked Marcello how much South American Catholicism was penetrated by *curandería*. 'A great deal, especially in Paraguay. You see the *campesinos* are not really Catholic at all. They revere the priests deeply – but as *curanderos*. All the women you see selling roots and herbs in Asunción will prepare you potions, spells and medicines as well. Some of them are very effective – I have tried them. The Indian – the true Indian, not the half-breed – is a *sabio*, a wise man.'

It was on this trip that Marcello told me one of his grandmothers had been a Quechua Indian. He was proud of this, in a quiet way, which was nice.

As we drove out of Caacupé I sprang my surprise on him.

'What, Australians – in Paraguay? No! I would have heard about them,' he exclaimed. I persisted, though. The settlement was only a few dozen kilometres from Caacupé. He stopped in at a little booth housing the Touring Club y Automobil de Paraguay by a service station. The man was asleep at the desk. Marcello woke him up and interrogated him. After ten minutes or so he came back to the jeep. 'These days it's called Nueva Londres,' he said. 'During the *stronato* they changed the name from Nueva Australia to Colonia Stroessner, after the dictator's father. Some idiot stood up in the Parliament and said: "Why should we honour these kangaroos when the Saviour of the Nation's Father is not honoured with a town named after him?" No one dared oppose him. After Stroessner was thrown out they changed it to Nueva Londres.' Marcello was intrigued. He was actually interested in Paraguay – the only person apart from me who was, it seemed. We rolled along on a good road through flat grazing country. The cows were often Herefords, big, fat and slow. When the Australian pioneers arrived here by oxcart in the 1890s from the railhead at Villarrica this had been jungle and virgin bush, thick with parrots and monkeys, jaguar and wild deer. The settlers had cleared the land, built their wattle-and-daub houses and tamed the land: now it was level fields that stretched on for ever, prime grazing territory. The little village was not noticeably Australian in style, being low villas with red tile roofs surrounded by well-tended gardens, though a line of ancient silky oaks, imported as seeds from Queensland and planted by the first fathers and mothers, cast their shade across the main street in a distinctly un-Paraguayan fashion.

We parked, and proceeded to stroll around. I asked a couple of children if there were any of the families of the original Australians still in residence. '*Si, si – Australianos – los Smeets . . .*' they choroused, and led me to the comfortable modern bungalow of Victor Smith and his now mainly Guarani clan. They were taking the air on their front verandah, and I introduced myself as someone 'from London and Australia' who had come to see Nueva Australia.

'Come in! Sit down! You are very welcome!' they cried, getting up from their recliners to examine me more closely. Marcello and

Carlos faded into the background now I had found some ethnic kith and kin: they'd wait for me in the jeep, they said. I was patted down into a recliner myself: the beaming Smith family clustered round me, and I was debriefed in Spanish. The soporific calm of rural Paraguay has to be experienced to be believed. Nothing happens very slowly for year after year out in the campo. Evidently, I was the most exciting thing that had happened to los Smiths for a long, long time. Coffee and a cake were brought, glasses of water as well, and my journey so far discussed and marvelled over.

'From London and Australia . . . all the way from London and Australia . . .' echoed Victor Smith, a blue-eyed gent in his late sixties, the head of the family and the only gringo. 'Where do your family come from originally in Australia?' I asked him in English. 'I really couldn't say . . . *no se nada de nada*,' he replied, fading away again into Spanish immediately. All his English had gone, he told me, his father had spoken it well, but not he himself. The family spoke Guarani now. He had been born in Paraguay, but his father and grandfather had both been born in England, somewhere, and his grandmother was an original communist from Australia. Today, he told me, Nueva Londres was overwhelmingly a Paraguayan village, which had just a few old families of Australian or British origin. Victor's father had been to England a few years before he died, and had brought back with him a right-hand-drive Mercedes-Benz. Victor's wife was Guarani, and their children spoke no English at all. Victor himself had been ill recently, had had a serious brain operation. He moved slowly and hesitantly. After I had drunk my coffee he insisted on taking me around the village himself in the family car, his son at the wheel. Whenever we saw someone he would indicate for his son to slow down, and he would say proudly to them, 'See, a visitor for me, all the way from London and Australia.' Clearly, I was something of a boost to the Smith status.

We parked by another modern bungalow with a pleasant garden, and I was ushered to the front door, which was rapped on by the son. '*El cura . . .*' said Victor, and he shuffled forward to do his piece about a visitor from et cetera et cetera when the door finally opened.

It was late siesta and Father Jim Feenhan, *el cura*, made a valiant attempt to show he wasn't too seriously irritated by our visit. We weren't exactly invited inside, but rather hovered, somewhere between being inside and out. Father Feenhan had been in Paraguay for 25 years, he told me, but came originally from near Dublin. He still had an Irish accent, and had not forgotten his English but spoke it fluently and well. I mentioned the original Australian settlement, and he remarked that the Kennedy family from the colony, now wealthy landowners with 13,000 hectares of prime grazing land, were parishioners of his. Father Feenhan kept scratching himself nervously, with his right hand, around behind him up in the small of his back; I think we had disturbed him from sleep, or perhaps he had just been confessing some local lepers and was trying to remember if he'd washed his hands afterwards or not. There was a faint figure of a Paraguayan female housekeeper lurking behind him in the shadows – her indoors, in fact. Graham Greene would have loved the whole set-up, and could have based a novel on just such an Irish Catholic priest exiled for 25 years in a remote parish in Paraguay, ministering to the half-breed descendants of a failed Anglo-Saxon communist Utopian settlement. He could have entitled it 'The World and the Flesh' or 'A Padre in Paradise'.

We were clearly not going to be invited inside formally, probably because I gave off invisible ancestral Protestant vibes, so I made an excuse and said goodbye politely, and our ever-so-slow tour of Nueva Londres by large Mercedes with steering wheel on the wrong side continued. At the end of the afternoon I could have run for Mayor. The whole village knew who I was and where I came from – London and Australia, in other words the far side of the moon. I doubted if many of these people had ever been as far as Asunción.

During our stately, six-mile-an-hour progress, I became aware of a large number of well-groomed horses being ridden down the main street by Paraguayans in full *gaucho* rig – high Spanish saddle with sheepskin undercloth on the horses, *bombachas*, boots, sombreros and colourful shirts and scarves on the men and women. What was going on? I asked Victor.

'Oh, it is just the Day of the Horse. Every year they have it, you know, people dress up and ride around in a ring.'

'Like a rodeo?' I asked. 'Yes, yes, that's it, a rodeo,' he replied in bored tones. I had chosen by hazard the one day of the year when something was actually going on in Nueva Londres. I persuaded Victor to take me down to the showground, which was guarded by a pistol-wearing fellow in full costume. We were let into the guests' enclosure after Victor had done his long explanation about where I came from. His son was sent away with the car, and Victor and I stood in the shade and watched the rodeo, or at least I watched it while Victor waylaid everyone he could see and told them about his visitor from . . .

In the middle of the showground, on a large four-wheeled trailer decked out with festive bunting a band in cowboy clothes and sombreros were playing amplified music, a cross between Mexican mariachi and country and western. The same tune went on and on and on, never seeming either to stop or get anywhere, musically speaking the electric equivalent of Victor Smith's conversation. What were they playing, I asked Victor? He thought for a moment. 'A polka, I think,' he suggested eventually. If that was a polka my name was Johann Sebastian Bach. Never mind, it was festive and noisy and it didn't seem to bother the horses.

In the arena were teams of horsemen and horsewomen, all clad in colourful costume, waiting in disciplined clusters. From time to time two of these teams would thunder across the ground towards each other, and a sort of mock battle or pseudo-polo match would take place, though with no ball, sticks or goals. The teams were wearing either Colorado red or Liberale blue neck scarves: the Colorados always won. The women's teams were much better than the men's. It was impossible to work out what the rules were or what was actually happening, but it was extremely typical of something or other, and was just the sort of thing people in Europe thought went on all the time in this part of South America, but never in fact did, except on one day of the year. It was a far cry from anything Australian – there were no violent drunks, foul-mouthed hoons, or swag-bellied larrikins, for a start – though we were on the same latitude as Rockhampton, and the countryside around us could just about have been a flat bit of Queensland. William Lane's nightmare had come true: Nueva Australia had just become another bit of Paraguay, albeit one with a sprinkling of ocker genes.

After a while, however, the still hot sun and the endless electric red-hot polka band began to drill deep into my skull, and I suggested it was time to wend our way back to find Marcello and Carlos. I took a photo of Victor Smith underneath the road sign which read 'Nueva Londres'. He was, I realized, slightly ga-ga, or else the brain operation had been more serious than anyone wanted to admit. Everyone he spoke to responded in that oh-yes-it's-the-village-simpleton-again way: they probably thought I was some cousin from Ajos, a few kilometres away.

'Come again,' he cried out as we parted. 'Come and stay for a long time. Paraguay is a perfect country – not too hot, not too cold – just right.' I thanked him for his hospitality and waved goodbye.

Marcello and Carlos were waiting patiently in the jeep. 'I like this place,' affirmed Marcello. 'Clean, modern – like Nueva Germania.' Apart from the silky oaks and the odd Anglo-Saxon surname there was nothing left to show this had once been a pioneer Australian colony, except the tell-tale blond and red-headed children, lanky and ungainly, who trailed around after Victor and me, giggling and whispering, but speaking no English.

*　　*　　*

On 11 October 1893, an official delegation from Asunción rode into this place, then merely a clearing in the jungle, where the New Australia colony had just erected a partially thatched hall, their first public building. Led by the colony's agent Alf Walker, the horsemen included Dr López, wearing a poncho, Minister in the Paraguayan government, the German secretary to the President, who spoke some English, the administrator for the local district of Ajos, a few other notables, and an officer and four soldiers of the Presidential Guard. A horn was sounded as they approached and the Australian colonists swarmed out to meet them, cheering. This was to be the day of the official flag-raising, the formal commencement of the settlement. After refreshments – non-alcoholic, for the colonists were strict teetotallers – the horn sounded again, and Dr López and the leader of the colony, William Lane, linked arms, advanced to the flagstaff and together hauled up the Paraguayan flag, as the soldiers fired a volley with their Winchester rifles. The Minister and Lane both made speeches, the latter expressing his gratitude to the Paraguayan government for their welcome and their generosity in granting land for their new settlement. The whole scene was witnessed by the four-year-old Voltaire Molesworth, son of James Molesworth who had purchased for the colonists' association the barque *Royal Tar* that had brought the 200 emigrants there present from Sydney to their new home. Years later, Voltaire Molesworth would recall that flag-raising with emotion, and the cheering Australian colonists saluting the '*Paz y Justicia*' on the flag. His own name, a strange combination of Continental European radical *philosophe* and solid Anglo-Saxon from the Shires, strikes the paradoxical keynote for the Utopian communists of Nueva Australia. This bizarre venture grew out of the embittered and radicalized Labor politics of Queensland in the 1890s. A sheepshearers strike turned violent after intimidatory picketing and the dynamiting of 'scab' labour transport which caused death and injury. The strike had been put down with armed force by the authorities and the ringleaders sent to gaol with hard labour for sedition. The time had now come, some radical Labor leaders said, for the ultimate strike, the permanent removal of labour from the bosses by emigration to another land, somewhere in which 'true mateship' could flourish and a communist reality could be built in a pure state, an agricultural co-operative commune in which capitalism was banned by the articles of association.

The undoubted leader and originator of this novel social experiment was the 32-year-old William Lane, a self-educated journalist and author, who had been born in Bristol, England, but who had sailed for the US aged 16 as an emigrant. He had married an American, and after 10 years in the US, had eventually found himself at the centre of radical communist politics in Australia, editing the *Worker*, and making inflammatory speeches wherever he could. His novel *The Workingman's Paradise* was a Utopian tract predicting a world to come when capitalism was defeated and communism made a reality. The model for his fictional hero Ned Hawkins, the idealized Queensland bushman, was Robert Louis Stevenson's cousin, David Russell Stevenson, who although from a landed Scottish background, had thrown in his lot with radical Labor in Queensland. Stevenson was a personal friend of Lane's and a political ally – and maybe more as well, at least on Lane's side. Stevenson was the Lothario of the Australian Labor movement, which had allies among radical and advanced Australian women, circles where feminism, communism and sexual emancipation made easy bedfellows, literally as well as metaphorically. He was tall, strong and immensely good looking, with great sexual charisma. He made many conquests, in Australia and in New Australia, where several women were said to have borne him children. He had a private income from his family in Scotland, which he used to spring treats on the children of the colony. He was an educated, cultivated man, an accomplished amateur actor, singer and raconteur, as well as being muscular, masculine and physically capable – a relatively rare combination of talents, particularly in British colonies, where male philistinism, lack of charm, and inarticulateness are the general norm as much today as they were 100 years ago. The Australian novelist Kathy Lette's description of Australian men as 'emotional bonsai' is cruel but accurate: by contrast, Stevenson was a positive Californian redwood.

Lane contributed £1,000 to the funds for the venture, others put in a minimum of £60 each. Some gave all they owned. More than 2,000 people came up with the money, and many more signed up for later emigration when the colony was established. Land was found by Alf Walker in Paraguay – the government there was eager to assist Anglo-Saxon immigration after the devastating losses of the War of the Triple Alliance. Forty square leagues, or 93,000 hectares of fine, well-watered fertile land were made over to the Australian Co-operative Settlement Association and the emigrants converged on Sydney to board the *Royal Tar*. No more radical communist community had been attempted since the Desert Fathers of the Early Church in Egypt. Everything was to be held in common, even cutlery and crockery, except worktools and personal clothes. There was to be no money, no wages, no savings and no capital. There was also to be no alcohol and no sexual intercourse with the natives. 'Our children must be white in order that they may take the lamp of progress from us and be able to keep it burning for the generation to come,' averred Lane. His prophecy of doom for Old Australia was that race war was inevitable now that the bosses had succeeded in importing Melanesian and Chinese workers who undercut the unionized Anglo-Saxons and Celts of British stock.

Brendan Behan, an old IRA man, observed that 'the first item on the agenda for discussion was always The Split'. No sooner do oppositional, revolutionary movements start to coalesce than they also begin to fissure, breaking apart into factions and conventicles of rival groupings. Lane's New Australia was no exception. Even before the first boatload of colonists had reached South America the party was divided into two disputing groups. 'The first revolt against Lane occurred on board,' reported James Molesworth. 'Lane had been given dictatorial powers until the settlement was constituted. He imposed restrictions ... we threatened to throw him overboard. The dispute was then amicably settled': some methods in Labour political circles never change, it seems. The problem, unsurprisingly, was over sex, and in particular David Russell Stevenson, known to the colonists as 'Dave', who now took on the role of Serpent in this proto-Paradise, apple of knowledge ready to hand.

As well as being a communist and a visionary intellectual William Lane was also a married man and father, a Puritan, and *au fond* a deeply respectable Victorian paterfamilias. He also had a club foot which had been operated on, but not mended. He had a pronounced limp, wore spectacles, was not physically robust, and was beginning to go bald: with hindsight one might suspect that he was sexually insecure – particularly about his own wife. Far from an advocate of free love or progressive feminism he believed strongly in 'the life marriage' and in women confining themselves to a purely domestic, supportive role. When he saw David Russell Stevenson canoodling in a lifeboat after dark with the only young single female on board without her parents – an 'advanced' Australian girl who was a qualified nurse – Lane was deeply shocked and forbade her on deck when the bachelors were taking the evening air. Clara Jones, a spirited 26-year-old, defied Lane publicly, tore his notice down from the mast in front of him, and danced on it before his eyes, an act of defiance to the patriarchy that would have warmed the cockles of the future Germaine Greer's heart. Lane was dumbfounded, and retreated to his cabin to sulk for several days. In his documentary novel *The Paraguayan Experiment* about New Australia, Michael Wilding suggests that Lane may himself have been subconsciously in love with 'Dave' Stevenson, and was jealous: there is a telling description of Ned Hawkins's lips being 'strangely girlish' in Lane's novel

The Workingman's Paradise, and the physical portrait of his hero Hawkins-Stevenson is decidedly homoerotic to a modern, post-Freudian reader.

Two factions now formed on board: the 'Royalists' loyal to 'King' Billy Lane, and the 'Rebels', later to be dubbed the 'liberty-and-*caña* mob' by the Lane-ites. These settlers were, after all, career agitators, revolutionaries and extreme radical communists who had spent their whole lives in revolt against the bosses, capitalism and the government. Opposition, sedition, revolt and protest, not to mention physical violence with fists, knives and even guns were their meat and drink, and had been all their lives. Many had been to gaol for their beliefs. Argument, disputation, ideological wrangling, faction-fighting, strike action and violent picketing were their daily bread. These were the sort of ultras whom Robespierre guillotined, Hitler had executed in the Night of the Long Knives, and Stalin shot or exiled to the gulag archipel-ago – the founding revolutionary fathers, the tough nuts and hard cases who are always devoured by their own creation when the revolution requires order and discipline in place of agitation and revolt. Government, order, discipline were not in the colonists' blood; revolt, rebellion and dissension were. The bosses of Aus-tralia were now far away: here, William Lane was the boss, the government, and the property-owning class all rolled into one. He had all the Association's money and all the power, which he would neither share nor delegate. As with all successful revol-utions, the revolutionaries found they had far less power after their leader had taken control than they had under the *ancien régime*. The Tsar was a far easier master than Lenin, Louis XVI than Robespierre, Weimar than Hitler. In the Second World War, the Japanese had no problems with their Allied prisoners. They allowed them to form into natural groups with natural leaders, then separated all the leaders and confined them in secure iso-lation camps. The leaders spent the whole war arguing among themselves, and the leaderless remainder rarely attempted any breakouts. Among Lane's followers were dynamiters who had blown up ships bringing in blackleg labour, men who would not hesitate to shoot at police or troopers if required: by removing these men from Australia Lane unwittingly paved the way for a non-violent transition from the revolutionary politics of class war to the parliamentary-based Labor Party which, using peaceful, Fabian tactics, succeeded in gaining a permanent place in Australia's democractic structures.

The settlers who volunteered for New Australia were self-selected – Lane had not chosen them or been able to weed out those he didn't like. Now, on board on the high seas, he found many of them to be petit-bourgeois city dwellers, artisans and shopkeepers, 'growlers' and dissidents, dissenters and malcontents: people, in fact, who disagreed with him and who would not accept his authority. He began to plot how he could get rid of them. Off the coast of South America he decided that the molasses they had brought with them might contain a small alcohol content, so over the side went the whole ship's supply, to curses and imprecations from the women and the Rebels. It was as if by his every high-handed action Lane was deliberately provoking a rebellion: and that, in fact, was his aim and his strategy – to provoke a final revolt and split so he could start anew with his own supporters.

Lane had the authority and the money; in theory no one should have kept back any private cash, but of course many of the women and even some of the men had. At Montevideo, after being at sea without a break for almost two months, Lane went ashore, but forbade anyone else to leave the ship. For the Rebels this was tyranny and they disobeyed, coming back late after their spree in a drunken condition. Knife and fist fights were now a regular occurrence between the two factions on board, and the drunken returnees were hailed with cries of 'Scab!' and 'Blackleg!' by those who had obeyed King Billy. In theory, Lane had authority; in practice he could do nothing about all this except sulk and plot expulsions and revenge when they got on to dry land in New Australia itself.

A crucial new recruit the settlers met in Montevideo was the young Englishman Arthur Tozer, who had been employed by Alf Walker to help him find land. Middle class, educated, serious and a good Spanish and Portuguese speaker, Tozer became Lane's right-hand man immediately, and a hero-worshipping Lane disciple who may himself have fallen in love with his hero. Tozer was armed with a Smith & Wesson revolver, had been involved in revolutionary activity in Buenos Aires, and decided to throw in his lot with the New Australians. He also became the Trotsky and Felix Dzerzhinsky combined to Lane's Lenin, the Enforcer of the colony, a one-man Red Army and OGPU-NKVD, armed and authoritarian, empowered by the Paraguayan authorities as Justice of the Peace and constantly on the lookout for backsliders. The whole enterprise now took on a resemblance to an almost caricatural degree to the early settlement of New South Wales as a convict penal colony: an English governor and his armed English aide-de-camp were in charge, with complete and arbitrary powers, even over matters of food, drink and clothing, of a group of politically malcontent working-class Celts and Anglo-Saxons, many with gaol sentences behind them, transported by ship across the ocean, in an attempt to settle and cultivate a new, strange land none of them knew anything about, the natives of which they completely ignored. The New Australians rather than the British authorities had paid for their own transportation this time round. 'Of course Australia is bound for glory – were not her people chosen by the finest Judges in England?' went the early 19th-century British jibe about convicts in Botany Bay. By a complex historical irony the New Australian colonists, in seeking liberty and true mateship had volunteered and paid for their own exile, and a form of absolute rule found nowhere outside Tsarist Russia or the Uganda of the Kabaka Mutesa.

Desertions began immediately: Lane did nothing. Rather he

seemed to be expecting them. 'The good ones, the true mates will stay – the dross will go,' he remarked. Those who left lost their stake in the colony. The central problem was Lane's inflexible authoritarianism and the ban on liquor. In a cynical and dismissive editorial, the Sydney *Bulletin* buried the colony with a derisive epitaph after its short and ignominious existence. 'The constitution of New Australia was based on the assumption that it is possible to create a community where every person is sober, moral, religious and full of holy yearning for self-sacrifice, and the collapse came about because there is no such community under heaven. Man will drink and gamble and prowl around the back doors of the dusky daughters of the land until the end of time.' William Lane's dream was, in fact, more suited to the 17th century of Oliver Cromwell's New Model Army than late 19th-century South America.

When they got to it, the land they had been granted was fine, the rivers clear and full of fish, the air clean and healthy. The Paraguayan government could not have been more helpful. Cattle were bought, crops planted, huts and shacks erected. New Australia was going to grow to be a colony of 50,000 people or more, idealists attracted from all over the world to build the pure communist society, that was Lane's vision. They would be a vanguard, a spearhead which would eventually convert the whole world to a better way of living. But in all matters there is the human element, and this was once again defective. Men shirked their labour and did not look after community property, which got broken, rusty and lost. Against all the rules *caña* was smuggled into the colony and the colonists made their way by night to Ajos where there were 40 women for every man. In the colony there was an overwhelming number of single men. Community tools were stolen and traded for rum. And every night the two factions, Royalists and Rebels, sat on logs opposite each other by the camp fire and argued until they were blue in the face. Lane expelled recalcitrants, and then expelled more; their friends and allies deserted the colony in disgust. In the end, Lane himself resigned as chairman and took his own core supporters, 60 or so of his favoured Queensland bushmen and shearers, and founded a rival colony called Cosme, 75 kilometres away. 'To save needless enquiries,' the prospectus for the second New Australia went, 'everybody should understand that Cosme is for English speaking Whites who accept the Life Marriage, The Colour Line and Tee-totalism among their principles, and who realize in their hearts that COMMUNISM IS RIGHT!' Not surprisingly recruitment was exceedingly slow. The Cosme land was not as good: there was malaria, flooding and poorer soils. It was out of the way and impossible to get to after heavy rains. Lane grew sick and nearly died: while he was recovering he, the strident teetotaller, became addicted to alcohol as a convalescent, supping up avidly the despised rum and wine. Yet more settlers fled this grim outpost of collectivist insanity in the serpent-ridden, mosquito-haunted depths of the deepest bush. Lane went to England, his ticket paid for by the Paraguayan government, to recruit more settlers. He all but completely failed in this, though he was accused of attempting to rape a married woman while her husband was away from home. 'The problem with the Labor movement,' Lane wrote in his later disillusionment, 'is the dirty tools you are forced to use.' It is unlikely he was referring to his own equipment here, but rather the Rebels who so obstinately refused to see sense and do what they were told. He arrived at the conclusion so many communist leaders come to, that the workers have betrayed the revolution. 'The people have failed, therefore they should be dis-solved, and a new one elected' as Brecht ironically observed. When the scheme had first been mooted the Sydney *Bulletin* predicted that 'there will be a few hundred people digging and fencing in a dreary, hopeless fashion out in the great loneliness, and living on woe and unsaleable vegetables and dreams of home. And meanwhile, the founder of the settlement will be foaming at the mouth and uttering poetry beneath a tree, and wildly asking the damp ferns, "What is life?"' Apart from the 'few hundred people' which proved a wildly optimistic estimate, this skeptical prophecy proved right in both essence and detail. Lane had increasingly taken to solitary walks in the *monte*, or long horse rides far away from the troublesome settlers: from leader of men he had become melancholy introvert, pessimistic, taciturn and dour, the genetic inheritance of his Puritan Scots mother in the ascendant over the fiery rabble-rousing of his booze-sodden Hibernian father.

However, after the secession of Lane, Tozer and their 60-odd stalwarts, New Australia started to pick up: the anti-alcohol and racist colour-bar rules were abandoned, and the land was eventually divided up into family holdings. These prospered, for many of the Australian settlers were able, experienced bushmen or craftsmen, often used to breaking new land and herding stock; and now they had an incentive to work hard – self-interest, self-improvement and profit – capitalism, in fact. Lane had, unwittingly, led his followers to a highly successful venue for exploitative capitalist endeavour and then abandoned them to their profits.

Another two-faction conflict arose at Cosme, and in despair Lane and his wife abandoned the second colony as well. Lane was sick of the Australian working class by now, and had turned increasingly to God, the prophet in ascendant over the communist. He developed into a deeply conservative Empire Loyalist, still faithful to his teetotalism and white supremacist views. He went to New Zealand, where he became a journalist again, under the by-line 'Tohunga', the Maori word for prophet, and eventually edited the *New Zealand Herald*. He died in 1917 aged 56. Tozer had abandoned him in disgust after the alleged attempted rape incident, but had stayed on in Paraguay, having a successful career as an administrator of the British-run railways. Cosme limped on much depleted, rum and native women now the norm, and Nueva Australia thrived as a capitalist cattle-herding venture. To this day there is bad blood between the descendants of the two settlements, and many of them will not talk to those of the rival camp. Without William Lane the idea of New Australia would never have been thought of, never attempted, and surely never carried through. He was a genuine visionary and idealist, but also a disastrous leader and an impractical intellectual. It was said of the 19th-century New England missionaries in Hawaii that 'they came to do good and they did very well indeed', becoming rich and powerful landowners. The same could be said of the remaining New Australians who followed the capitalist road after Lane left. Their descendants are part of the small landowning aristocracy of the country today. The jump from revolutionary agitator baying for communism to the plutocratic landowner, master of broad, well-watered acres is a short one. In the USA they talk of people going 'from Poland to polo' in one generation. In the Seychelles, the Creole French elite who still control the government and own much of the land are the descendants of the radical Jacobins the Directory shipped out as political exiles after the fall of Robespierre; they became rich and powerful very quickly. The economic drive behind the New Australia emigration was land hunger, not communism. The good land in Australia had all been taken. William Lane was a means to an end, not an end in himself.

The finances of the New Australia movement were always murky: forged signatures, vanishing trustees, absconding principals and empty safes found in abandoned offices marked the demise of the movement. Many of the investors lost all they had, though Lane himself seems to have been honest – he lost all he put in as well. The winners were the Rebels who drove Lane out: when the 93,000 hectares came to be divided up, they got it for themselves, like the dismemberers of the old Soviet Union, who 'privatized' a whole empire into their own Swiss bank accounts and formed the new ruling class in the capitalist successor state. The people who come out of the whole sorry saga best are the Paraguayan authorities who acted with generosity, intelligence, foresight and imagination. Under a better, more pragmatic leader than Lane the colony might well have attracted many thousands, even hundreds of thousands of landless people from Australia and England. But a more pragmatic leader would never have dreamt up the whole cockamamie project in the first place. An amusing film could be made of the New Australia saga, directed by Woody Allen, and starring John Cleese as William Lane. I wonder if George Orwell knew about New Australia. It almost makes *Animal Farm* redundant as a satire of communism. Lenin must surely have read about the experiment – petit-bourgeois romanticism would have been his evaluation. George Bernard Shaw knew about the colony, and sent the library there copies of his books. The *Manchester Guardian* wrote about them wistfully from time to time as 'arcadian idealists from the Forest of Arden', though they did not report that Lane called in the Paraguayan army to enforce his expulsions at gunpoint, or that Tozer patrolled around with his pistol sniffing the milk to see no *caña* had been smuggled in, and striking down with his fists Rebels who dared to challenge Lane's authority. Private property and the rights of individuals under the law remain the only guarantee that the William Lanes of this world do not metamorphose into the Lenins, the Trotskys and the Josef Stalins. The rise and fall of Nueva Australia should be examined by anyone who studies the communist movements of the 19th and 20th centuries: in microcosm it reproduces the whole catastrophe in which millions died for an impossible ideology.

On the way back, we stopped at a phone call centre: Marcello's mobile was out of action and he had urgent messages to impart. Carlos hung around outside with an embarrassed look, plucking up courage to ask me a question. He never addressed me directly, being too shy and diffident. Looking at the ground and scraping the dust with the toe of one boot, he finally asked in his thickly accented Spanish: 'Is there much *analfabetismo* in England?' This was a difficult one to answer, really, the illiteracy rate. 'Not so much really, no,' I replied mildly. 'There is a lot in Paraguay,' he responded, still looking at his toes. I wondered if he was one of them. Franz Kafka invented a Cinema for the Blind, and it would certainly not be beyond the powers of the Paraguayans to have created a university degree in Tourism for the *analfabeticos*. In many ways, given the conditions in the country, illiterate tour guides would probably be a plus.

Back at the Gran Hotel I noticed that in *Ultima Hora* the question of the day was, 'Do you believe that the government bureaucracy should be severely reduced?': 99% agreed, 1% disagreed. The police still hadn't been paid and were getting even more restive. A general strike was being planned by 60 trades unions. They intended to paralyse the whole country. Diesel prices, which had been increased, had just been reduced again, after a violent demonstration. After the War of Independence, Simon Bolivar observed, 'We have not had time to learn anything because we have been too busy learning.' That could be yet another national motto for Paraguay, where every attempt to bring in Paradise always imported the Serpents as well.

Sixteen

The Strange Case of the
Missing Pictures

All Asunción was talking about the daring theft of the collection of oil paintings from the National Gallery. There were many different theories but the facts were hardly in dispute. The thieves had rented a vacant shop on Calle Iturbe, formerly occupied by the Foundation of Piety, a charitable institution. The shop faced the side of the Gallery across Iturbe, a narrow side street running off the main road. Without anyone noticing them at work, the criminals had dug a tunnel down into the basement of their rented shop, under the road, and up into the cellars of the National Gallery. One weekend, when the place was closed to the public, they had removed every single painting through the tunnel, taking not just the pictures themselves but the frames as well. The '*caso cuadros*', or case of the frames, had the police baffled. There had been a '*testigo clave*', or key witness, one Raul Hernan Diaz: unfortunately he had been gunned down in the street, shot dead, it was assumed, to stop him singing like a canary. The police had no idea who had shot him, according to the *fiscal*, or investigating magistrate, Victor Hugo Alfieri.

One theory was that the robbery had been carried out by the government itself, to get collateral which was required by the IMF for the much discussed loan Paraguay was trying to arrange. Another theory held that these pictures, which formed the National Collection, had, in fact, been stolen over the years already, and copies had been substituted in their place, one by one, the forgers having been a team of experts imported specially for the job from Sicily, where they had been trained in a mafia art-forging academy. This theft was thus simply a cunning way of getting the insurance money, for now the worthless fakes had been stolen, the New York insurers would have to pay up as if for the 'real' ones, which had long ago been sold to collectors overseas. Another theory held that Oviedistas had carried out the raid, and that the paintings had been pre-bought by wealthy Argentinians and Brazilians from the catalogue: the funds would be used to buy weapons and suborn the army, paintings into magnicide. The most simple solution proposed was that the police had themselves carried out the heist, and that they had already communicated to the government that they would only get the pictures back when they had paid the police all their arrears of salary.

A plaintive note was struck by the Curator, who said that the fabric of the Gallery was now in danger, for the tunnel had seriously weakened the foundations. The building was a fine stucco mansion from the mid-19th century. There were, of course, no funds for the filling in of the tunnel or the repair of the foundations. The Curator expressed the view that the building would shortly fall down as a result of the damage, unless something urgent was done. This unleashed the further theory that the robbery was a blind – the paintings were worthless anyway – and the whole scam had been carried out deliberately to weaken the building so that it could be knocked down and the land sold for development. The real cynics claimed that the Gallery staff themselves had arranged the robbery – their salaries hadn't been paid for months either. The pictures had never actually been taken out through the tunnel, the staff had smuggled them away in a van: the digging was just a blind. You could see the tunnel, crudely filled in by the police, and the newspapers were full of photos of the inside of the underground passageway. There were also accusations in the press that President Macchi was implicated in the disappearance from public funds of 16 million dollars: his wife, it was alleged, had several unexplained foreign bank accounts. None of this could be proved or disproved, but no theory was too wild to gain some credence in the current atmosphere of cynicism and despair for the country's future. The President of Argentina was claiming, in the same papers, that Argentina was 'a good debtor country' because although it had defaulted with interest repayments on its loans it 'intended to pay them in the future'. In this part of South America, evidently, the intention to repay made you a creditworthy debtor.

I had discovered a rich vein of fascinating if useless junk in the antiquary shops in the old part of Asunción. These lay behind unprepossessing shopfronts and were always empty of people apart from their suspicious, hostile owners, who sat cradling their pistols waiting for someone to just try a robbery and thereby make their day. Paraguay had been looted of its gold, gems and jewellery by Marshal López and Madame Lynch, of its archives and libraries by the victorious Brazilians at the end of the Triple Alliance War: to this day all pre-1864 records of the country are held in Rio de Janeiro. As a result, everything in these shops dated from after the 1860s, and most of it from the 1920s onwards. There were vast, well-built wardrobes made of fine local hardwoods in a late 19th-century French style: no Argentine or Brazilian tourist would have wanted to ship such heavy items down the river with them. There were piles of broken, deformed and often limbless plaster angels, putti, friars and Madonnas from a period of greater piety than today. There were treadle sewing machines, dismal prints in cracked frames, and mounds of simple junk – broken dishes, ashtrays, forks, spoons, featureless lumps of metal, and so on. You could not have given this stuff away to a charity shop in the poorest part of Britain. There were also quite a few ancient guns – a French chassepot, a battered British Brown Bess musket and a Brazilian copy of a Winchester carbine were on offer. Inevitably, there were pistols and automatics galore in various stages of disrepair – Lugers, Webleys, Smith & Wessons among others. The best find was a Paraguayan officer's sword in scabbard, made in Germany, and engraved with '*Vencer o morir*' – Victory or Death, the army's motto. This was only US$50 and I was tempted to buy it, but the current paranoia about weapons and hijacking in the UK suggested I probably would not get it past the Customs. One shop led to another, the owners pointing out on my map – usually incorrectly – where their cousin's, brother's or uncle's shop was. The stock was similarly hopeless in all of these establishments. Because they thought I was German, I was always approached at some point or other with a whispered '*Kommen sie her, mein Herr . . .*' and led off into a secret lair where the Nazi memorabilia were kept. Signed photos of Adolf, sheets of mint stamps with his head on, SS daggers in sheaths, Luger pistols in wooden presentation cases, photos of Party rallies, it was all here, if you wanted it, which I certainly didn't.

I did find an attractive small oil painting of St Anthony of Padua, patron saint of hopeless causes. It had been executed in a painting factory in Peru in the 1920s, according to the owner of the shop. It wasn't old, certainly, for the canvas had machine-made printing on the back. I haggled the owner down from US$25 to US$20, which he didn't like, but accepted. I rolled it up in old newspaper and carried it away under my arm. Walking round the capital with an oil painting was probably not a good idea in view of the National Gallery robbery. I also managed to find a huge photo of Alfie Stroessner in dress uniform that had been hand-tinted in colour. I felt the US$10 asked was too much, and demanded why. The frame, came the answer. How much without the frame then? A much more reasonable 50 US cents was the reply. I also bought a large Alfie-era Paraguayan flag at the same time: it is the only national flag in the world, apparently, where the two sides are different from each other. 'Because we are a two-faced nation' was a common jokey Paraguayan explanation:

low self-esteem in this country extended even as far as the flag. What had happened to all the photos of Stroessner, I asked? They had been thrown in the wastebasket immediately he had been ousted, I was told. When in power his photo had been on display in every office and shop, hotel and business. So now I knew the cold market value of a time-expired South American dictator – 50 US cents.

I wasn't the only one in a spending mood. Miraculous to say, the police had at last been paid their wages. I actually saw a long line of them, each holding his pay cheque in his hand, waiting to get into one of the few banks still operating, looking forward to handling some cash at long last. The government had left this crucial move until the last possible moment: that afternoon and evening, the big Oviedista rally and demonstration was to take place outside the government buildings in the Plaza Independencia. No pay would have meant no police, and the government buildings might well have been stormed, occupied, and a revolution effected. Clutching my huge unframed picture of Alfie, wrapped loosely in a black plastic sack but clearly visible to anyone who peeked inside, and my outsize Paraguayan flag, I passed the cordon of soldiers and police who were frisking anyone who wanted to enter the Plaza Independencia. I was searched politely, but my equivocal souvenirs excited no comment from the policeman: perhaps these were just the sort of things one would take to an Oviedista rally. The demonstrators were overwhelmingly Guarani, *campesinos* and ordinary working-class Paraguayans. There were almost no white faces to be seen in the crowd, only on the dais where a rock band belted out songs about corruption, and politicos who had thrown in their lot with the Oviedistas making speeches about corruption in between the music. It was early and the police were still polite and good-humoured. They had been paid, and had obviously eaten a good lunch. But it was hot and they would now not eat or drink again until the demo was over: their tempers would inevitably fray as the hours went by. The crowd were drinking *caña* and beer, a carnival atmosphere in the ascendant. This wouldn't last either: they would get drunk, aggressive and violent – that was what happened when Paraguayans drank too much *caña*. The police had confiscated hundreds of small Paraguayan flags stuck on to small but stout hardwood sticks: these could easily be sharpened into daggers and dirks by the knives all the peasants carried in their pockets. Women moved around selling *chipá* and beer. There were small stalls with roasting kebabs and sausages. It was all good-natured, peaceful and non-threatening. But it wouldn't last. It would certainly end in tears and bloodshed.

I passed back through the lines of police and made my way to the Post Office, which overlooked the Plaza Independencia, climbing up on to the roof: sure enough there were army and police marksmen in uniform and combat helmets, armed with sniper rifles, lining the parapet, looking down on the crowd: here was potential magnicide in the making if I ever saw it. I made my way downstairs again quietly and went back to the Gran Hotel on foot, an hour's hot, dusty walk. I no longer trusted the buses at all – there were too many robberies and assaults on them every day now. The whole of the centre of Asunción was criss-crossed with roadblocks, police standing on corners with billy-clubs, and demonstrators still coming in from the countryside. I just knew it would all end badly. I could feel it in my bones. Either the Oviedistas would make a successful revolution that night, or they would be crushed with force. I was fairly certain it would be the latter.

Back in my room I had a shower, enjoyed a pot of Indian tea with lemon on the verandah outside, then drank half a bottle of wine, and ate a packet of Spanish olives, brand name Borges, packed and distributed by Medist Czech s.t.o. Revolucai 13, Praha, which I had bought in the supermarket en route back from town. They were nice olives, juicy and full-flavoured. I wondered if there was a brand of Czech plums called Kafka, packed and distributed by Frutaspana S.A., Avenida Libertad 12, Madrid 2. *¿Quien sabe?* I now regarded Paraguay as a sort of surreal parallel universe in which almost anything might be possible, the less probable the more likely.

I turned on the TV in the late evening to see how the demo had ended. Water-cannon spouting, furious police baton charges, terrified crowds milling to and fro, old ladies clubbed to the ground, ringleaders or mere unfortunates hauled away by the cops or kicked in the guts on the ground, clouds of tear gas wafting about, fear and loathing, screaming and shouting. Long experience had taught me that police tempers started to get frayed in about the time it took for a meal to be digested and hunger pangs to start up once again. There was no magnicide this time, however, and the snipers on the Post Office roof hadn't opened up. So, the Oviedista coup had been averted and order restored. Doubtless the police, now with cash in their pockets, had dined well in the evening after their brisk exercise. The next morning, *Ultima Hora* waxed indignant: '*Carne de canon*' was their headline – cannon fodder. If not magnicide this had been magnassault. Several of their photographers had been beaten up. Still, no one had been killed, which for a Paraguayan demo meant that it had all passed off relatively peacefully.

The same could not be said for the ever-increasing crime situation, especially around the bus terminus. Robberies, attacks and murders here were reaching epidemic proportions. I avoided this part of town unless I absolutely needed to go there. However, one day, while buying a ticket for Filadelfia in the Chaco, I saw a Chilean, a middle-aged man with a rucksack, shot dead by a young Paraguayan street kid. The Chilean had not even got down on to Paraguayan soil yet, was still on the bus descending the steps, when the street punk rushed up, shoved a pistol in front of him and demanded his money. The Chilean, obviously a foreigner from his clothes and facial features, brushed the kid away. Several shots followed and the man collapsed on the ground, his clothes covered in blood. He was very obviously dead. The punk ran away into the crowd. He was later arrested on a bus into which he'd run and hidden, so I read in the papers. I didn't know the dead man was a Chilean until I read that either. It was shocking and alarming to see someone gunned to death right in front of you, a few yards away. I got straight in a taxi and went back to the hotel and stayed there for three days. I didn't feel safe in Asunción any more. I didn't feel safe anywhere in Paraguay, in fact. I wanted to leave the country as soon as I could. I should, in fact, have followed that gut-feeling of mine and got out then. I would have saved myself a lot of grief if I had. I was asked when I came back from my trip to Albania if I would have gone had I known how dangerous it was. The answer was certainly that I would not have done. I now found myself in the same situation again – in a completely lawless country in the grip of a violent crime wave. I wished I hadn't come to Paraguay, and I wished I could leave immediately. I was right out of my depth, frankly. I was a travel writer, not a war correspondent.

In one of those dreadful epiphanies which thankfully come but rarely in one's life, I saw my doppelgänger the next morning as I crossed Avenida España to get my newspaper. My double was crossing in the other direction, a briefcase in his hands. He was obviously as appalled to see me as I was him. He was my exact double, but wearing a summer-weight Nazi-style light beige Afrika Corps-like army uniform, full colonel's crowns on his epaulettes, the ensemble complete with frogging and horrible dangling fascist dagger and Luger in leather holster. We did not break pace, but gazed sideways at each other in absolute horror. No wonder Paraguayans thought I was from *la technica*. In this parallel universe I almost certainly was.

Seventeen

Gran Chaco

There's a strange unoriginality about many South American place names and informal topographical soubriquets. The Matto Grosso region of the Amazon is called '*L'Inferno Verde*', or the Green Hell. The Pantanal region of lowland Bolivia and Brazil is called '*L'Inferno Verde*', or the Green Hell. And the Gran Chaco of Paraguay is called ... but you guessed it already of course. Why, that's what I want to know? St Petersburg is called the Paris of the north, but few, if any, call Paris the St Petersburg of the south. Edinburgh is similarly called the Athens of the north by a few wildly optimistic Scots, but few in their right mind would call Athens the Edinburgh of the south. Tom Stoppard got it just about right when he called Edinburgh the Reykjavik of the south. Travel writers perpetuate these myths. Norman Lewis, on safari with Don McCullin, lensman of the internationally sordid par excellence, in search of human rights abuses for the *Sunday Times* colour supplement in an era when the liberal bourgeoisie wanted its conscience outraged over morning coffee at the weekend, refers, of course, to the Chaco as ... the Green Hell. The trouble is it is neither green nor hellish, unless you are colourblind, or have never been anywhere more challenging than Hampstead Heath on a Friday night.

The Chaco is big, that one can admit, about 270,000 square miles, which is greater than Spain and Portugal combined, and more than three times the size of the United Kingdom. It has very few people in it – just 3% of the total population of Paraguay,

100,000 or so, of whom about 20,000 are Indians. It is very flat, rising at a rate of one inch per mile as it creeps towards the Andes. It is full of strange trees with spikes, armour, prickles and weird shapes that led Gerald Durrell to call it *The Drunken Forest*, also the title of his book about the place. Quebracho, palo santo and palo borracho are the best known trees along with algarrobo and indeterminate thorny scrub, which when dense enough to rip your flesh if you tangle with it is called *monte*, but not, alas, harbouring any pythons, though many other terrifically deadly snakes abound, including anacondas and rattlesnakes.

'The whole landscape did look as though nature had organised an enormous bottle party, inviting a weird mixture of the temperate, subtropical and tropical plants to it,' observed Gerald Durrell. In the Chaco there are also elegant, tall, rather superior-looking palm trees called caranday, which have an air of drooping, fashionable ennui about them, these the etiolated, anorexic fashion-models of the tree fraternity. There are also original and genuinely Paraguayan types of wildlife, combining the bizarre with the vicious, such as the owl which mimics the cries of its avian prey, then swoops and devours them when they come to investigate; *yacarés* or alligators which drag men and cattle underwater and drown them before devouring them; and long-legged maned wolves, assertiveness-trained pumas, upwardly-mobile anteaters, herds of swirling rheas, which are feather-duster-like ostriches, and of course familiar chums such as vampire bats, piranhas, blood-drinking killer-bees and malarial mosquitoes, without which dear old Paraguay would not be the country its aficionados come back to for their holidays year after year. There is, I was assured, a Ministry of Tourism in Asunción, but it is reputed to have been closed for as long as anyone can recall. A tourist in Paraguay as a concept is a bit like a Liberal Democrat prospective parliamentary candidate in a Taliban stronghold in southern Afghanistan – not a happy camper at all. There is also a fictional animal in the Chaco – at least I hope it is fictional – called the

Ow-Ow: this is a man-eating giant sheep, which chases its prey across the bush and up trees, follows them, drags them down to the ground and devours them. I haven't just made this up, honestly, I got it out of a travel book on Paraguay, so it must be true. It's called the Ow-Ow because that's the noise its victims make when they are being eaten alive. Personally, I think the *hierba maldita* has a lot to answer for in South America.

However, it must be reiterated that the Chaco is just not green at all, and it certainly does not look like anyone's vision of the infernal regions. Perhaps calling it the grey-brown-fatigued-looking-spindly-tree-and-dust-semi-desert-only-not-quite-but-almost didn't seem poetic enough for whoever dreamt up the *Inferno Verde* moniker. Maybe there was a whole department in the Spanish Colonial office in Seville given over to this sort of naming thing, viz:

Don Juan-Carlos López García, *Gran Jefe de Nomenclatura Imperial (Segunda Classe)*: (pointing at map of Paraguay) 'Look, *hombre*, here – this empty bit, there, west of the River Paraguay, up to the Andes. What do you think, eh?'

Pedro Domingo Luis Calderón, *el mozo inferior*: 'Hmm . . . says here [consults his notes] snakes, crocodiles, lions, tigers, swamps, palms, cannibal Indians who drink your blood, vampire bats, lungfish which live in mud, mosquitoes, jaguars . . .'

Don Juan-Carlos: 'How about . . . Sangre de Cristos Mountains? . . . Or Arizona?'

Pedro Domingo: 'No mountains, and not dry enough. Anyway both are already taken, as is, well, let me see on the list . . . California, already taken, Montana, that's gone, too, and Florida and Labrador. I see the Indians call it *charqui*, or *chaco*, this blank space, which is the Quechua for "good place for hunting".'

Don Juan-Carlos: 'Not exactly catchy, is it – charqui or
    chaco? Let's be frank, we're running out of place names,
    aren't we? New Granada – taken, New Carthage – gone;
    how about New Extremadura?'
Pedro Domingo: 'Are you taking the Michael, squire?
    That's where I come from, Extremadura.'
Don Juan-Carlos: 'Ooops, sorry, well how about . . .
    L'Inferno Verde?
Pedro Domingo: 'The Ports have already used that for the
    Amazon.'
Don Juan-Carlos: 'Yes, I know, but we haven't . . . have we?'
Pedro Domingo: 'Well, I suppose not.'
Don Juan-Carlos: 'Right that's it then, settled, done and
    dusted, matey – the Green Hell it is. Now this bit
    inland from Labrador, right up north by the icebergs,
    where there's sweet fuck-all, absolutely nothing – *aquí
    nada* – how about – Canada?'

It takes seven hours to get to Filadelfia by bus from Asunción,
and that's not counting the roadblocks with morose, exhausted-
looking soldiers who wave you down, clamber on board and
check your papers, and then after relieving the driver of some
local currency, wave you through angrily. You can understand
their point of view – you are going somewhere, they are staying
where they are. It is said the officers do not dare to issue ammunition to these conscripts, as in the past they have used their
bullets to shoot their superiors and flee into the bush. In 1979, I
was once stopped at a roadblock in the Egyptian desert between
Alexandria and Cairo, which was manned entirely by members
of the Egyptian Navy, each clad in World War II British uniforms,
complete with bell-bottom trousers and round white hats. They
were all completely stoned out of their minds on hashish, and
were handing enormous joints back and forth while giggling
uncontrollably. I asked the driver of the car, an old Egypt hand,

why the navy were being used. He thought for a while. 'Well –
ships of the desert, I suppose – it makes a kind of sense.' The same
kind of sense as having the Paraguayan army make roadblocks in
the middle of the Green Hell: doing it in central Asunción, where
all the crime was would be more to the point.

There is a lot of dust in the Chaco: it gets in everywhere,
through closed windows, into your socks, boots, hair, eyes, nose.
When it rains, apparently, the dust all turns to mud and the roads
become impassable. It hadn't rained for a long time. There were
some boggy, emerald green patches with reeds and scum on the
top, and these, after storms, turned into lagoons and swamps.
You could buy bits of the Chaco for a few cents a hectare, and
now I saw it for myself I wasn't surprised. There were cattle there,
with Paraguayan cowboys or *gauchos*, who raised one languid
hand in salute as we churned past them, showering up clouds of
dust. Some of the cows had humps and big horns: these were a
cross between Indian cattle from India and Herefords, or so I was
told, combining meat with drought resistance. They were called
Brahma, after the well-known local beer, which had a picture of
a cow on the label. I doubt if Mahatma Gandhi would have
approved. Most of these animals are turned into hamburgers or
stock cubes.

Eventually, if you go on long enough across the Chaco you get
to Bolivia. This can take about three days or even a week,
depending on pumas, bandits, the army, *cocaleros*, rustlers, punctures, getting bogged down, rainstorms, floods, vampires, etc. It
is said that no one who has ever done this journey ever repeats it
willingly. Filadelfia is about halfway and quite far enough for
anyone not either completely insane or a professional cocaine
smuggler. It is the capital of Fernheim, or 'Far-home', one of the
three Mennonite colonies which were granted a *priveligium* by
the Paraguayan government, as an inducement for them to settle
in this uncompromising region. This means no taxes, no military
services, their own schools, laws and administration – a state

within a state in fact, on the New Australia model. Mrs Thatcher once observed that the only free lunches are those on offer in mousetraps, and the gift of this Chaco land to the Mennonites certainly comes into this category. Firstly, the land was already occupied by Lengua and Toba Indians, sometimes called Guaicurus by the Guarani, which some say is derived from the name for a medicinal herb '*yerba del diabolo*'. Norman Lewis, ever keen to criticize the Guarani, claimed it meant 'rabid rats' in their language: like the Ow-Ow, everything is basically up for semantic grabs in the Chaco. Secondly, the whole of the Chaco was claimed by Bolivia, so the Paraguayan government were actually giving away something their neighbours didn't agree they owned. Pacifists and believers in adult baptism, the Mennonites were old-fashioned Anabaptists who had been driven from pillar to post since the 17th century in an attempt to keep their own faith and their children out of other people's schools and armies. Some of them managed to sneak out of the Soviet Union, that well-known paradise of tolerance, good sense and multiculturalism in the 1920s, and ended up in the Chaco. Others winged in from Canada and Mexico, both of whose governments ratted on their agreements to let them alone. In spite of all the odds these *plattdeutsch*-speakers in their old-fashioned clothes made a roaring success of their settlements. Filadelfia is not going to win any architecture competitions, but it does have a modern hospital, shops, a hotel, a co-operative, lots of ice-cream parlours, and is the centre of a thriving beef and dairy industry. It does not run to paved road, however, and dust is the central motif, along with gaggles of Indians squatting against corrugated-iron walls waiting for Mennonites to drive in and employ them on their farms. It could easily be a cow-town in the Northern Territory of Australia, except for the lack of drunkenness.

The main drag is called Hindenburg, on account of the German General and President having negotiated the Mennonites out of the Soviet Paradise in 1927: it's also called the Hauptstrasse, or

High Street. There are a few other streets on a grid, Trebol, Bender and Unruh, but all the action happens on the Hauptstrasse. This consists of Mennonites in pick-up trucks moving very slowly down the street, parking outside the co-op, and coming out with groceries, barbed wire or branding irons after an hour or so. The best thing to do in Filadelfia is drink milk shakes, eat yoghurt and lick ice creams. It is very hot and all the cows mean there is a plentiful supply of dairy products. Supposedly, you can buy beer and tobacco in Filadelfia, which is regarded as the fastest and most decadent of the Mennonite townships: maybe there is even a speakeasy there. I didn't find it, however. You can get a good meal at the Hotel Florida, with steaks and grills an obvious favour-ite, and their rooms are clean and air-conditioned. It was a great relief not to be taken for German, at long last – except by the Indians, who kept coming up to me and asking in German if I wanted any labourers for my *finca, mein Herr*. At least that's what I think they were offering – it could have been their wives or daughters, as I don't speak German, least of all 17th-century *plattdeutsch*. There must be some Guarani Paraguayans some-where in Filadelfia, I suppose, but I never saw or heard them. I had an introduction to a Japanese-Paraguayan general in the army, but no one had ever heard of him, and so I suppose he was in the other parallel reality. I might as well have left Paraguay and been in another country. I was very tired after the long dusty journey, and so was pleased to collapse into a bed with clean sheets at the Hotel Florida. There was even air-conditioning that worked and a private bathroom, though I was too exhausted to have the cold shower I really needed.

In the morning, after a luxurious shower and a copious break-fast in the hearty German manner, heavy on wursts and black bread, yoghurt and cheeses, with strong black coffee, I rambled around the village, chatting to the shop assistants, who spoke rather better English than Spanish. Times were hard in the Chaco, it seemed, as elsewhere in the country. Many of the settlers were leaving or thinking about leaving. The Paraguayan government was suspected of contemplating revoking the *privilegium*, as the Canadian and Mexican governments had done before them. Modern government is an immensely expensive activity. There is a constant demand for cash, for fresh taxes. The underclass everywhere – all with votes – demand jobs, housing, healthcare, schools, leisure facilities. The rich, even the prosperous are few, with few votes. To tax them, to confiscate legally their assets is always a temptation, often overwhelming. The Mennonites had arrived with nothing, and in under 80 years had turned a desert in a war zone into the most prosperous and orderly part of Paraguay. Naturally, the government in Asunción now cast envious eyes on this asset.

The Rebels had driven Billy Lane out of New Australia and inherited the rich 93,000 hectares of grazing land. If the Paraguayan government revoked the *privilegium*, the Mennonites, or most of them would leave the country. The government would then inherit their land. What they did not realize, any more than Mugabe's ZANU-PF Party had in Zimbabwe, was that merely replacing one set of efficient white farmers with a set of inefficient native farmers would achieve nothing except economic collapse. If Guarani farmers from the east of Paraguay could ever be induced to migrate to the Chaco, which I doubted they ever could, they would be able to do nothing except scratch a mere subsistence living, for that was all they did in the much better land they occupied already in the east. Indeed, there were thousands of hectares of excellent, well-watered, fertile land in the east completely uncultivated. Why would the Guarani bother with this highly marginal land in a drought zone? They wouldn't, of course. If the Mennonites left the Chaco it would go back to what it had been before – scrub desert with a few nomadic Indians hunting and gathering. However, this would not stop the Paraguayan government shooting itself in the foot, eventually, by revoking the *privilegium*.

Very few governments in the world observe the sage minimalist doctrine of leaving their citizens well alone to make money and become prosperous, and simply taxing consumption rather than income and savings. Politicians and civil servants do not understand how money is made, only how it is spent – by them. Even when billions start to pour, leak or flood out of an economy, legally or illegally, governments still go on raising taxes, hiring civil servants, increasing politicians' pay and perks, embarking on ludicrous and costly programmes of public spending. It takes about 20 years of persistent folly to ruin an economy completely, as the Zimbabwe case exemplifies. The result is always the same – a permanent capital and skills flight, astronomical unemployment, a siege economy, food rationing by price, a collapse in public services, hyper-inflation with mounting chaos and disorder, responded to by repression and state violence. Eventually, the government collapses. Paraguay was a little over halfway down this road, by my estimation. Only the complete inability of the government to collect taxes prevented the usual massive civil service overspend. Even in dictatorships government depends on at least passive consent. If the whole people withdraw their labour and export their capital, government becomes a hollow exercise: there is nothing and no one to govern. In the end, only the politicians and bureaucrats remain, defending their offices and houses from the irate mobs outside whom they have ruined with their extravagance and short-sighted stupidity. They keep on doing it, though, completely oblivious to the lessons of the past. For them the goose that lays the golden egg is only there to be starved to death.

If this happened in Paraguay, the Bolivians might well chance their luck and reinvade the Chaco. They had never reconciled themselves to its loss after the Chaco War of 1932–5. It was still marked as Bolivian territory on their national maps. At the time it was thought there might be oil under the ground, and it was alleged that two major oil companies were bankrolling both sides in the hope of concessions, but there now appears to be no oil there at all. It was another pointless, futile war, fought in harrowing conditions, a sort of desert version of the trench warfare of the First World War, complete with biplanes on strafing missions, Mills bomb-throwing soldiers, and machine-gun detachments. Instead of mud and cold the soldiers had suffered thirst and impossible heat. The Bolivians, most from the cold highlands, the rarified atmosphere of the *altiplano*, had suffered far worse in the desert conditions than the Paraguayans. The Bolivian Commander in Chief was a German soldier of fortune with the highly unfortunate name of Kundt, who put his faith in armoured cars and warplanes, but who was beaten by tough Guarani endurance and staying power. It was known as the '*guerra de sed*', the war of thirst: water had to be brought by the *trencito*, the little train whose track was laid to bring supplies out from eastern Paraguay, and by *choffers* who drove cars and buses to the front line with water for the soldiers. The supply situation got so bad that sometimes the Paraguayan air force was reduced to bombing its own troops with ice cubes. There were dogfights between ancient biplanes – the last the world was ever to witness – and mercenaries from all over the world flocked to fight on either side. The Bolivians were out of their element, and the Paraguayan tactic of outflanking their enemy, separating them from water, made mass surrenders inevitable: 21,000 Bolivian soldiers and 10,000 civilians were captured and put to work as prisoners in the fields and gardens of the east; many stayed on after the war. Immense booty was captured – 28,000 rifles, 2,300 machine-guns, US$10 million of ammunition. It was to set Paraguay up as a major arms exporter for years to come. Much of the equipment used by both sides in the Spanish Civil War was bought in Paraguay from these stocks.

All across the Chaco were little *fortines*, tiny entrenchments where the two sides had shot at each other, gasped for water, and died in large numbers. The only gains were on postage stamps, both sides printed exaggerated maps on their stamps, which claimed huge swathes of enemy territory. In all the war claimed 88,000 lives, 36,000 of them from Paraguay. Kundt's tanks and planes and flame-throwers all failed; he was fired and went back to Germany, having proved himself, in fact, a complete and utter Kundt. The mercenaries were not much use either. A group of *chantar* artists from down south calling themselves 'the Machete-men of Death' proved adept only at pillage, and were packed off back to Argentina. Alfie Stroessner made his reputation as a general in this war, which once again exhausted Paraguay, although in the end it was notionally the victor, in that it had seen off the Bolivian challenge and gained an extra 20,000 square miles of useless semi-desert it didn't know what to do with. Fear that Bolivians might one day come back kept the Paraguayan army chained to the Chaco, manning useless *fortines* and patrolling empty tracts in the middle of nowhere. The army had a sinister reputation for bullying, torture and worse out here. In a 10-year period 103 conscripts had met violent, unexplained deaths, almost certainly from their fellows. They army was also reputed to be deeply involved in gun-running, cocaine smuggling and manufacture, and marijuana growing. There was also said to be a secret US airbase deeply hidden in the desert somewhere, much of it underground. None of this was apparent from Filadelfia – the city of brotherly love, after all – but it was out there, with the Ow-Ow and the anacondas.

There was a stranger in the restaurant of the Hotel Florida at lunch. He was obviously no Mennonite. Dressed in faded blue jeans and embroidered jean jacket, he had shoulder-length blond-white hair, wore impressive cowboy boots and a stetson with a snakeskin dandyband and dangling shark's teeth at the front. Although seated, his immense height was evident in his crouched position and long legs sprawled out on either side of the table at which he was sitting eating a solitary lunch. With a beaky nose and light blue eyes, he looked like the actor Klaus Kinski's wilder younger brother. He was perhaps about 50, in a lean, well-preserved sort of way. Most curiously, he had slung over the back of his chair a particular type of straw basket on long thin strings which is only made and used on the island of Ibiza. He resembled, in fact, a late-1960s hippy from Ibiza who had taken a wrong turning at the Straits of Gibraltar. He looked up at me sharply as I came in. We were the only two people in the restaurant. I gaped at his bag, and pointed, saying involuntarily, 'Ibiza!' He looked as startled as I felt, and indicated the chair in front of him. We started speaking in Spanish, then switched to English. I had lived on the island on and off for 20 years or more, and we soon found we had friends in common. I ordered my lunch and we talked on, obsessively now, about the island and its past. 'You know, I had thought I didn't miss the place at all,' he said at one point, lighting a long black cheroot, in spite of the frowns of the waitress, 'but you've brought it all back to me.' I asked him where he had lived on the island. 'Oh, all over, but the best place was somewhere you would never have heard of, much less have been to.' Try me, I told him. 'A *finca*, on the north shore, at a place called Cap Blanc . . .' I didn't let him finish. 'On a long peninsula that sticks out into the sea, terraces all around with olives and almonds, descending down to the rocks below, the *finca* being the only house on the peninsula, that guards the entrance . . .' He gasped with astonishment: 'You know it!'

'I nearly bought it,' I replied, 'but I couldn't raise the money.' He thrust out a long thin muscular hand and pumped mine enthusiastically. 'Jurgen,' he said, introducing himself. 'And what are you doing in the Chaco?' 'Looking for land to buy, maybe an *estancia*. Europe is all washed up . . .' This was a cover story I had evolved after finding that the terms 'journalist' and 'author' brought with them suspicions of investigation of criminal activities, and therefore a degree of reticence and even hostility. 'You must come and visit my *finca*,' he used the Spanish terms in use in Ibiza, 'it's only an hour and a half away – well, two hours if there are headwinds.'

The use of 'headwinds' should have alerted me to the probability that this was two hours by plane, not road but it didn't since I was still in shock over meeting someone from Ibiza in the middle of the Chaco. An hour later, with my bags packed and bills paid, I found myself sitting beside him in his private *avionetta* on the way back to his ranch. He had been in Filadelfia to see the dentist, he told me – an old crown had fallen out. He hardly ever came in, maybe only twice a year. Like many in the western Chaco he was oriented towards Bolivia. He flew to Santa Cruz for preference. 'Much more sophisticated than anything in Paraguay, really quite a nice town actually, almost civilized. You can sit at pavement cafés under the palm trees and watch the giant sloths clambering about above you in among the foliage.' In reality in places like the Chaco the idea of nations and nationality is reduced to absurdity. Argentina, Paraguay and Bolivia all shared the Chaco and none of them really controlled it in any but the vaguest sense. People moved about at will, across borders, with no one to stop them. It was by chance that Jurgen had happened to find some land he liked and could afford in the Paraguayan Chaco rather than in either of the other two jurisdictions. He had nothing to do with Asunción or with the Guarani elements in the country, any more than the island people of St Kilda off the west coast of Scotland had with London and England in the 18th century.

The Chaco looked no better from a light plane than it did from a bus, although there was no dust to contend with. I had no idea which way we were heading. Very occasionally we would overfly an *estancia* with a silver corrugated-iron roof and perhaps an identifying number painted on top, this to give bush-pilots an idea where they were. There were also straggly cattle roaming about in search of food, tiny from our height. After two hours and twelve minutes we came in to land at a narrow strip with a single windsock which stood limp at the mast: there had been no headwind at all. If there had it would have been more like three hours. We must have been very near the Bolivian border. A Japanese Land Cruiser stood under an open-sided thatch-roofed sun-shelter, the windows all open. We drove a couple of hundred yards to the ranch house which shimmered white in the heat-haze. I could not help myself from laughing – it was a reproduction of an Ibicencan farmhouse, complete with flat roof, *porche* on the front, and single date-palm in front of it. There was a conical bread oven and *corrales* around for the animals. 'Too much!' I spluttered. 'You've built a complete Ibicencan *finca* reproduction – it's highly authentic.'

He smiled with evident pride at his creation. 'It's made of mud bricks rendered with sand and cement – well, earth and cement really. Come and look.'

It was cool and shady inside. The roof beams which would have been *sabina* or juniper in Ibiza were here *quebracho*, he told me. It was comfortably furnished with modern white fabrics, deep arm-chairs and long elegant sofas. There were ample bookcases, a good music system and Moroccan and Turkish carpets. 'What do you do for electricity?' I enquired. 'Solar,' he told me, 'with a generator as back-up.' He showed me round his *finca* with enthusiasm. Once indoors it was hard to believe one was not actually in Ibiza, so uncanny was the resemblance of his faithful copy to the original.

We had tea and then he showed me to my guest room for a late siesta. It was still very hot and I was glad to dive under my mosquito net and doze off for a couple of hours. When I emerged it was getting dark. A splashing drew me to the back of the *finca*, where Jurgen was swimming strongly in a large open-air pool, shaded by mature palm trees. 'Come on in, it will wake you up,' he cried. I needed no second invitation. I stripped off to my underpants and dived in – it was deliciously cool. Lights came on automatically as dusk fell. 'Timer switches, every modern convenience,' chuckled Jurgen, as he clambered out and shook himself like a dog. He did not bother with swimming trunks, I couldn't help noticing. He had a deep all-over body tan. 'What about water? You clearly must have plenty.'

'We dug a well, after a dowser roamed around for ages searching, and when we found water, plenty of it as you said, that's where I built the *finca*. There's a wind pump that raises it and a storage tank which feeds into the pool, the house and the vegetable tunnels,' he explained.

The rear had an area that was out of doors but also with thick metal mesh fly-screen all round it, so that mosquitoes, vampire bats and other *bichos* couldn't get in. We sat there and drank tea, and then cocktails, and talked on about Ibiza and our old friends there. Did he really miss it, I asked, or was this all enough? I was genuinely curious to know.

'I do and I don't. I miss the social life – there's none out here, really, though occasionally a few friends from Santa Cruz come and visit. The thing is, though, I felt crowded out in Germany – too many people. That's why I went to Ibiza, living in the most remote part of the island. Then mass tourism came and it all became impossible, so I moved to the desert in Almeria, down near Tabernas, on the mainland. Then tourism started down there, motorways, airports, huge developments on the coast, agribusiness inland. There's nowhere now in Western Europe that is genuinely peaceful, isolated and where you are left alone. Noise, people, development everywhere. I have many thousands of hectares here, which I bought for almost nothing. You can't drive a vehicle on to this property, not without a detailed map, which no one has except me. I can get on and off with my Land Cruiser, if I really want to, but it takes a hell of a long time. When the builders from Bolivia came in with the roof sheets, the cement, the water pump and all the furniture, I had to guide them in on dirt tracks, and then guide them out again. The army don't come here – it's too remote for them – so no one bothers me. My nearest neighbour is more than 50 kilometres away, over impassable terrain. I'm as away from the world as it's possible to get these days,' he said, refilling my glass as he spoke, evidently pleased at his self-willed isolation.

'What about an emergency?' I asked.

'I employ about 30 people on the *estancia* – *vaqueros*, general workers, cooks, cleaners and so on. I have some cattle, which frankly I'm not very interested in, but there are enough to sell the surplus every year, and pay everyone, and turn in a small profit, a few thousand dollars over expenditure. The *vaqueros* drive the cattle slowly to the abattoir – it takes them more than a week each way. The men can all operate the short-wave radio set. If I fall off a horse or get appendicitis, a flying doctor from Santa Cruz can be here within a couple of hours. If it's not so serious I can fly out and get treament. It's a lifestyle choice . . . you have to take the risk . . .'

What about the isolation, then, surely that must get to him after a while?

'Well, yes and no. I spent so much time in Europe trying to get into genuine wilderness and avoid people that frankly it became a bit of an obsession. I don't have to worry about that here. I go for long horse rides, and sometimes take the Land Cruiser out for a few days' safari in the wilder reaches of the *estancia* – the birdwatching is terrific. I put a bed in the back and sleep inside to avoid puma attacks. You know the British travel writer, Bruce Chatwin? Someone once described him as a clubbable loner – I like that English word "clubbable". But I don't think I am any more. Once I was, in Ibiza, in the early days when there were very few people and it was all fun.' He paused and thought for a moment. 'You get set in your ways out here.'

Did he ever go back to Europe, I asked.

'I used to go every year – friends and family. Then it became every two years. It's been five, now. I don't really enjoy it. Too many people all crammed in together and far too many rules and regulations. I find eastern Paraguay far too crowded. You come to the Chaco only when you are willing to sacrifice everything else for personal freedom and an absence of people. Do you think you are ready for the Chaco yet, yourself?'

I had to admit I didn't think I was. It was too extreme a solution. He laughed softly. 'Give it a couple of years yet. You'll move to rural Spain from England, then find that too crowded. Then you'll think back to this place – the nature, the peace, the wildlife, the heat, the great empty spaces – complete untamed nature just as it was thousands of years ago. Then you may just come back and buy a place here, or across the border in Bolivia. You are the type. I can see myself 20 years ago in you. Just don't leave it too late.'

'Disraeli once said, "a landed estate is a small kingdom",' I commented. Jurgen smiled with a smile of recognition. 'Very good. I shall remember that. Now, for dinner, I suppose you want to eat meat?'

'Well . . .'

'I am a vegetarian, but of course the peons all eat meat so it will be no problem, no problem at all,' he explained. I burst into an involuntary peal of laughter. 'Jurgen, you are too much really – a vegetarian cattle rancher in the remotest part of the Paraguayan Chaco . . .'

Jurgen looked a bit embarrassed, but did manage to give me a sheepish grin. 'It does sound a bit crazy, but I really came here for the peace and quiet, the nature, the absence of people – not the meat. I just don't like the stuff.' I asked him how he managed to grow his vegetables. 'Irrigated poly-tunnels, to prevent them being roasted under the sun. I grow citrus under shade from overhead arbours, and it all has to be fenced in to keep the animals from eating everything. We've got everything here though.' I told him I would be delighted to go vegetarian for my stay – I had eaten far too much meat in Paraguay already.

So we had a delicious supper of roast and steamed vegetables, with fresh fruit afterwards, and good Argentinian red wine which Jurgen imported directly from the grower down south in barrels. 'It's amazing what you can get in one of those *avionettas*,' he commented. 'There's a surprisingly large cargo section behind the seats.'

We were waited on by two shy, smiling Indian ladies in long white dresses who padded about silently in bare feet, and vanished as soon as we had been served. 'They don't see many strangers,' he added, by way of explanation for their timidity.

After dinner we sat outside again, drinking brandy and smoking cigars, watching the stars, very bright and seemingly very near, for we were far from any source of light pollution. 'Tomorrow we can go for a horse ride and see a bit of the *estancia*,' he promised.

A week passed as if it was a few hours. We rode out into the Chaco on large, powerful horses, imported from Argentina especially, for the local breed were not up to Jurgen's weight and size – he must have stood six foot four or five in his socks. We took it easy and meandered, avoiding *monte* and swampy bits alike, and not trying anything terribly heroic. Sightseeing on horseback really. Jurgen carried a GPS and a portable radio transmitter, in case of emergencies. 'It is surprisingly easy to get lost out here,' he observed mildly. He showed me how to operate the radio if something happened to him and he was incapacitated. 'You just press this button and it sends out an emergency signal – the *vaqueros* will come out by jeep and find us,' he explained. I asked what might happen. 'Well, a snake can spook a horse and throw you – you break an arm and your shoulder and can't remount. Or a puma sneaks up behind you and drags you off your horse, you shoot it, but again you can't remount. Or your horse gets bogged, breaks a leg and you are stuck. It can happen, you have to be very careful out here. One minute everything is fine, the next you are on the ground with a broken limb, many kilometres from help. No one would ever find you. The vultures and foxes would finish you within a day and a night. There'd be nothing left to find. This is real wilderness, not pretend.' It was strangely, eerily beautiful, with birds everywhere – storks, what looked like egrets, vultures, hawks, and many species I could not recognize.

We were armed with Winchester carbines, these in leather

buckets next to the saddles, revolvers on our hips, and Jurgen had a sawn-off shotgun across his back. 'It's not theatricals,' he explained, 'a bull in heat can attack you out of the *monte*, have to shoot it at short range with your pistol, or it will gore your horse and trample you. And the pumas are very bold indeed.' Of course, Jurgen did not take me to any difficult or remote parts of his ranch, nevertheless, we did go to a low-lying swamp, where a large number of *yacarés* or alligators were lying about like so many logs, and in the distance, after a long trot into the bush, we saw a far-away flock of rheas bowling across the landscape. The vampire bats were a real nuisance, he remarked, as far as the horses were concerned. He kept his own choice bloodstock indoors at night, in bat-proof stables. Until he had built these, he told me, his mounts were getting bitten on a regular basis and several had died as a result.

One afternoon, after my siesta, I descended to the pool a little earlier than usual, and Jurgen was still asleep upstairs. Out of simple curiosity, I wandered across to one of the poly-tunnels where the vegetables were grown, pulling back the door to peer inside. The whole tunnel was full of mature marijuana plants in large pots. I let the door swing back and hurriedly returned to the pool and dived in. I was energetically splashing about when Jurgen appeared and joined me a few minutes later. I said nothing about what I had seen. Jurgen was obviously a professional dope farmer. Witnesses to such places had a tendency to end up in shallow graves, and my welcome might have swiftly evaporated if he suspected I knew what he was up to. I was never entirely at ease after this discovery. Jurgen smoked a lot of dope himself, but privately. He would appear with the familiar red-eyed, slightly disconnected air of the zonked, and listen to rock music from the 1960s and early 1970s with great intensity. He was older than I had first thought, in his late fifties: he just looked younger because he was fit and bronzed.

After a week I told him it was time I was heading back. He

offered to take me to Santa Cruz, which was tempting, but I needed to get back to Asunción, in the opposite direction. He offered to fly me there, if I could wait another two days, he had to pick up a consignment from the airport – of what he didn't volunteer and I didn't ask. I gladly agreed – avoiding the seven-hour plus bus journey back from Filadelfia was a huge bonus. 'Let me give you a gasoline contribution,' I insisted, when we arrived on the tarmac back at the capital. 'I would have come anyway. It's been good to have some company. I really must get back to Ibiza for a trip next year, you've reawoken my appetite for the island life. Come again to visit me, and when you are ready to buy some land let me know. I can help you avoid the pitfalls.' We shook hands and I caught a taxi back to the Gran Hotel. It had been a risk him inviting me out to his dope farm, but I guess he just got carried away – or was more lonely than he let on. I had asked him several times how far we were from the Bolivian border, but he was always vague. I suspect he owned land on either side of the border, so that he could slip across into the other jurisdiction if the heat was on. I asked him about Ayoreo Indians. It was rumoured that there were still tribes uncontacted by Westerners in these remote regions. 'Certainly there are. I've seen their arrows. They fire at you from thick jungle if you come too near. But if you leave them alone they leave you alone – except for the odd cow being killed and eaten.'

I didn't tell Marcello Warnes that I'd been to the Chaco as I knew he was still hoping I might hire him and the ailing El Noble to take me. Instead, I suggested we go to Altos, which was just a few kilometres away. 'You'll like Altos,' a lady at the hotel had said to me. She didn't say why. Since Nueva Australia, Marcello was quite happy to go where I wanted without query – I was paying after all. We cruised around Altos asking various peons sitting in the dust in the shade where the Country Club was – this was the main attraction I had been sent to see. No one knew, so we

cruised on until we eventually stumbled on it by accident, up a
hill, on a bluff looking down over virgin bush and forest. You
had to pay a two dollar entry fee, which was refundable on your
first drink, we were told by the gateman. The grounds were neatly
planted with mainly northern European trees and shrubs. The
club itself was inside another planted park, at the end of a windy
track through a sort of nature reserve planted with pines and full
of cute wooden bridges over artificial mountain streams. There
were notices everywhere in German and Spanish telling you not
to walk on the plants. Marcello and Carlos were frankly puzzled.
I had brought them to yet another Paraguayan mystery. What did
it all mean? Marcello was my guide, but I was guiding him to
places he didn't know existed or understand.

'It's a club for Germans,' I said. 'This is the way they do nature
in Germany – neat paths of sand, little wooden bridges over
streams, pine trees, signs telling you not to walk on the plants.'
We strolled into the clubhouse itself, a Bavarian log cabin. The
doorman looked at Marcello and Carlos with no enthusiasm at
all, and at me interrogatively. 'Who are these?' was his unspoken
question. I gave him a curt nod and said '*Gruss*,' which will get
you out of a lot of sticky social situations with south Germans,
I've found. He '*Grussed*' me back and we stepped inside. They
weren't actually all dressed up in Waffen SS uniforms and singing
the Horst Wessel song, the clientele, but they might just as well
have been. There were tables full of overweight blond beasts
attacking steins of lager and outsized Wiener Schnitzels. There
was a Guarani harp orchestra in full local costume serenading the
eaters at the trough. This was the only time I heard the famous
Paraguayan harp music while I was in the country. At the bar a
line of hostile Teutonic faces, red and bloated, stared at us, evident
interlopers. 'Do you want a drink?' Marcello asked me. I felt like
Lawrence of Arabia in the 1962 David Lean film, when, after
capturing Aqaba, Lawrence turns up in a Cairo bar with his Arab
boys, asking for lemonade, faced with a line of outraged British

officers. 'Get the ruddy wogs out of here,' they cried, and I could tell that's what the bar-krauts were thinking, too.

'I think not,' I said, and headed back out of the door again, into the fresh air. If anywhere was ever a lair of Nazis that place was. It made me feel physically sick.

'What was it?' Marcello asked me, as we drove back to the capital. He was genuinely puzzled.

'A colonial-era German country club,' I replied, but of course in Paraguay it was still the colonial era.

The *estancia* stay with Señora Dellabedova was off, Veronica told me, when I rang her. She had gone to Miami for an indefinite period of time. She wanted to avoid the General Strike and the tractor sit-in which were shortly to bring the country to its knees, so the organizers hoped. The tractor-in was a Paraguayan wheeze whereby all the tractors in the country were driven into inconvenient places in towns at the same time, to block the traffic and cause paralysis. This was to protest against fuel hikes, as well as everything else. The Argentinian Finance Minister, one López Murphy, had said he was 'hopeful' that the IMF would lend his country money again, very soon, even before any repayments of interest had restarted. I wondered if having a Finance Minister called López Murphy was really such a good idea in South America, all things considered.

Eighteen

Sol y Sombra

I finally ran out of luck at 11.30am one Sunday morning. I was walking into town, had just passed through Plaza Uruguaya, turned off Calle Estigarribia and into Calle Iturbe – where the notorious art-thieves' tunnel was still visible, crudely filled in with earth. I had my smallest camera with me cupped in the palm my left hand. I carried no bag and was dressed as normal, in blue slacks, with a pale, nondescript shirt, no wristwatch, no rings, grubby desert boots on my feet, Mr Ordinary personified. I had taken a photograph of a closed bank façade while in Plaza Uruguaya, and in retrospect that was probably what attracted my attackers: it marked me out as a stranger – no Paraguayan would have ever taken such a photo. The camera was as small and discreet as such an item could be without arousing suspicion of being a 'spy camera'. I had used it successfully all over the Third World, including Albania. When covered by my hand it was virtually invisible. But someone had seen me use it.

Suddenly, from out of my right-field of vision, a small, dancing figure darted in front of me, waving a very large, old pistol at my head. He was a child, or at least a very small, dark, young teenager, somewhere between 12 and 15, I guessed. He danced about in front of me, whispering, and indicating that I hand over my camera. The pistol was moving all the time, deliberately, to avoid me striking at it, but it was always pointing at my head or torso. My attacker kept whispering, *'Dame, dame, dame'* – Give me, give me, give me.

Without thinking I veered sharply to the left, back towards the relative safety of Calle Estigarribia, the main, central artery of Asunción, the Oxford Street in London terms. I was only about ten paces from this major thoroughfare, which was crowded with cars and people. Then, from out of nowhere came another attacker, on my left, who pushed me sideways sharply. I stumbled and fell towards the ground, putting out my left hand with the camera in to break my fall. As I did so, the punk with the pistol in front of me brought his gun down with a sharp crack on the top my skull. Had I not been falling anyway, this blow would have done me serious damage, perhaps knocking me out, or cracking my skull. As it was, the barrel caught the front of my head and skidded off. I felt a gout of blood spurt out from my head and splash down my face. I was in trouble, big trouble. Fortunately for me, I had seen the Chilean tourist gunned down by just such a punk: I took the attack seriously now. '*¡Coño!*' this one hissed at me, still in a whisper. '*Dame, dame . . .*' The next move would be several bullets inside me, I knew. '*¡Si, si si!*' I shouted, and thrust my camera at him. It had taken the full weight of my fall, and I could feel it was damaged beyond use – he was welcome to it. He pocketed it without looking, his pistol still pointing at me. '*¡Otro! ¡Otro!*' he whispered – Another, another. I had a sacrificial wallet prepared, in my right pocket, secured to a belt loop of my trousers with a leather thong, this against a simple pickpocket. I had bought this cheap wallet in Athens in 1976 and carried it for well over a quarter of a century as a potential sacrifice, in case I was attacked. Now, at last, it proved its worth. '*¡Si, si, si!*' I shouted out. I was up on one knee now, getting the wallet out and handing it to him, still attached to my belt loop, which I knew made it look valuable. '*¡Coño!*' whispered the punk again, grabbing the wallet, which felt satisfactorily full. He wrenched it and the leather thong came away tearing off the belt loop. Satisfied with this, he and his sidekick now ran away down Calle Iturbe, in the direction of the *barrio* by the river. They were wearing flip-flops and couldn't run very fast. Now would be the time to gun them down if I'd still been carrying Mac's automatic: until they turned their backs on me a pistol would have been no earthly use at all. Now, though, they would have been an easy target, slow moving and still near. It was a good job Mac had got his pistol back, because if I'd had it then I might have used it, which would have been idiotic.

I was up off the ground immediately. I ran, crouching low, back into Calle Estigarribia. The whole attack had taken perhaps two minutes, maybe less, but in that time Iturbe and Estigarribia had completely emptied of cars and people, as had the nearer half of Plaza Uruguaya. In a street hold-up or shooting, everyone made themselves scarce for fear of further robberies, or a violent reaction from the armed police when they arrived.

I was pumping blood from my head wound. It was spurting out and running down my face, all over my shirt and down on to my trousers. The wound itself didn't hurt at all. My left hand hurt, where the palm carrying the camera had hit the tarmac of the road. I was alive and able to run and I kept running, weaving and dodging about, in case the thieves decided the sacrificial wallet was not the real one, and came back to finish me off. In a minute, maybe, I was back in Plaza Uruguaya, a large square with palm trees, planted gardens, the San Francisco railway station on the side nearest the river. I was aiming to get somewhere where there were people, maybe police, which would discourage a further attack. On this one day of all days there were no police about in the square. Usually the whole central district was crawling with them. Later, I learnt that this was because there was to be another big demo the next day, and many police had been given leave to rest up and prepare themselves for the confrontation on the morrow. A perfect time for muggers to strike, of course. I had no handkerchief or anything to stop the blood from my head. It just kept spurting out, made worse by my exertions in running as fast as I could to get as far as I was able from the scene of the attack.

I was now in the dead centre of the square. A Paraguayan woman who was chatting to a taxi driver gave me a look of absolute horror. '*¿Qué pasa, hombre?*' she gasped. I could tell from the shock on her face that I must look a mess. By now the whole of the front of my shirt was covered in blood, as were the top of my trousers. My face was streaked with blood and I could feel the stuff coming out of the open wound on my scalp. I held this closed as best I could with my left hand. I explained, rather breathlessly, *dos pistoleros* – a robbery . . . in Iturbe . . . my wallet and camera stolen . . . not shot but hit on the head. She led me over to a taxi, the unhappy driver following, and she sat me in the back seat. A newspaper was found and put under me to catch some of the drips, and I thrust a large wad of the stuff on my head wound to absorb the blood. The poor old taxi driver looked most distressed at what this was doing to his nice cab, but there wasn't much he could do about it. 'The hospital or the police station?' the Good Samaritan lady asked me. '*Policía,*' I said immediately, and off we drove, she beside me in the back, voicing her outrage that such attacks could take place in daylight Calle Iturbe – the equivalent to a side street off Oxford Street.

Why did I say police and not hospital? Because firstly I knew I was not seriously hurt. Head wounds look dramatic, with a lot of blood, but the fact that I had been able to run a hundred yards or so with no ill effects, was conscious and thinking quite clearly meant that all I had got was a superficial cut on my scalp. The blood was bright red, not dark red – no artery had been severed. Second, of course, was the notorious condition of Paraguayan hospitals, with no medicines, filthy water, viruses galore, and pilfering staff. I still had my passport, credit cards and travellers cheques hidden away in a money belt next to my skin: all that would vanish if I went to hospital. Most importantly, I had lived in Latin countries for long enough to know that if you can crawl and breathe, your first move after an attack is to go to the police and make a *denuncia*. Not to do so is to put yourself in the wrong, and perhaps be arrested and charged yourself.

The police station was only about five minutes away up the road. The poor old taxi driver got no fare, I fear, and wisely scooted off as soon as I clambered out, assisted by my helping angel. Up the concrete steps we went into the Seventh Precinct police station. It was obvious what we'd come about, as my bleeding head and bloodstained clothes told the whole story. The police station was having a quiet spell and we were shown straight away into an open-air courtyard which acted as a processing hall. The Paraguayan lady with me started to explain what had happened, and two policemen started to get out their handcuffs to put on her. '*Perdoneme, señores – no, no, no*' – I intervened, and explained that she had saved me, not that she was responsible for my attack. I shook her hand warmly, thanking her in Spanish, and shooed her out of the police station effusively. I was a white middle-aged European who had been attacked, she was a dark-skinned Paraguayan who had not been attacked: it would be all too easy for the police to chuck her in the cells. Wisely, she vanished down the stairs, and I turned to the two policemen and said, 'I wish to make a *denuncia* for armed attack and robbery in Calle Iturbe, Asunción, today, ten minutes ago, on me, a foreign journalist and friend of the British Ambassador.' I said this very calmly and politely, and called them '*ustedes*' and '*señores caballeros*'. Form, politeness, dignity and graciousness are highly valued in Spanish-speaking countries. As are *cojones*, *machismo* and what Hemingway, who knew Spain well, called 'grace under pressure'. You got nowhere becoming excited, shouting or weeping with Hispanic people – you lost their respect, that was all.

The two policemen indicated to a table and chair in the courtyard garden. Behind the table sat a desk sergeant in uniform. He was in shade, the complainant's or suspect's chair was in full sun. *Sol y sombra* – sun and shade. Not just the bullfight and the bullring, but all Hispanic life can be divided into these two absolutes. One sits in the shade, the other in the sun. Now, it was my turn to sit in the sun, who for virtually all my life had sat in the shade. I stood beside the chair and asked the sergeant very politely if I might sit down, with his permission. He gave it. In front of him sat a large, old-fashioned metal office typewriter, with three sheets of paper, carbon between them, already gripped in the roller. I repeated my desire to make a *denuncia*. 'Name?' said the sergeant, 'Age? Address? Profession?' He had taken in my head wound and bloodstained clothes, but said nothing about them. We carried on as if there was nothing amiss. I was still bleeding, though with less force now I was seated. The sun was behind me, hot on my neck and head. I managed to extract my passport from my money belt to supply him with number, date of issue and all the rest of it. I also extracted the British Ambassador's visiting card. There was a slight pause after the first page had been typed up and new paper was threaded into the machine.

'This is the personal card of His Excellency the British Ambassador,' I said in Spanish. 'He is a personal friend of His Excellency President Macchi. His Excellency the British Ambassador is a good personal friend of mine, and he asked me to present his card to any officer and *caballero* of the distinguished and honourable Paraguayan police, if the necessity should occur, asking that his office be informed immediately if I needed any assistance.' I don't really speak very good Spanish, but at some subconscious level I must have prepared this little speech in advance, for out it trotted with a life and fluency all of its own. The sergeant took the card from my bloodstained hand and looked at it closely. It had its desired effect. He handed it back to me carefully, and said, 'There's a cold water tap over there, you can go and wash your face.' He indicated off to the right of the courtyard with a slight inclination of his head. I put the card down between us on the table: it was still in play, not yet finished – maybe a trump, but maybe just a joker.

This concession of the water tap was a major advance, however. The sergeant had admitted my wound without my ever mentioning it, or asking for any favours concerning it. This showed that I had dignity and *cojones*, and that my honour as a man was still intact. These are vital matters in Latin countries and I knew it. '*Muchas gracias, señor,*' I said politely, and in no hurry strolled over to the concrete sink, and risking the water, splashed some over my face and rinsed off my hands. Blood was still coursing down my face – there was nothing I could do to stop it: the wound needed stitches. The newspaper wad had become soaked and I had discarded it. On my way back to the chair in the sun I noticed that against the far wall of the courtyard a man lay sprawled out on a concrete bench, as if in sleep, deep in the shade. I sat down again and we continued the *denuncia*. A subtle shift had taken place in the interview. The questions were no longer tinged with either aggression or hostility: they were neutral, and that was an advance, too.

We went through what had been stolen. I made light of it. I explained about the sacrificial wallet. There had been 100 dollars in local currency and a few low denomination US dollar bills. The camera would only have been worth perhaps US$150 at the most. It had been an amateur attack. In Colombia, where these things are carried out with professionalism, the muggers take their victims at pistol point to a secluded part of a park and force them to strip off completely, taking away all the clothes and shoes, for they know money and credit cards will be hidden away in them. I didn't tell this to the sergeant, of course, for reasons of national pride. As in Eastern Europe, in South America comparisons are always invidious.

After the second sheet of paper was completed, the sergeant said to me: 'You can move your chair into the shade, it will be more comfortable.' I thanked him, and did so. I was now no longer a suspect or a *coño*, but a real person. We continued with our question and answer session for perhaps another hour and a half. These things take their time and no one is in a hurry in Paraguay, except escaping muggers. From time to time in these leisurely proceedings I would be instructed to go and wash my face again at the tap, when the dripping or splashing of my blood on the table threatened to get on the sergeant's paperwork. The sprawled figure on the bench had not moved all this time: I realized after my second journey to the tap that he was, in fact, dead, was resting just where he had been laid down by whoever had brought him in. That would have been me, but for fate, chance and a lucky break. I had avoided death by the narrowest of margins. A gunshot in the centre of town would have attracted the police very quickly, which was why the punk with the gun had not shot me – that and robbing a dead or wounded man is harder than one who co-operates with you. And the punks hired the pistols and ammunition. If they used bullets they had to pay for them. A tap on the noggin cost nothing.

The British Ambassador's visiting card still sat on the table where I had left it. It was still a pregnant bit of kit, with a neat red thumb and fingerprint indented on it in my blood. The sergeant could still see it, was aware of it. It was a reminder that I was well connected, that it would not be in his interest to just have me thrown in the cells to await events, as could easily have happened. Great detail about the make of camera, age, cost, value, and the denominations of the banknotes was required by the sergeant. This might have been normal: it might also have been that the sergeant did not want me putting in any complaints afterwards that my *denuncia* had not been taken seriously. While this was going on the patrol cars had been out scouring the streets for pairs of young street punks, one of them in a blue shirt – for such was my description. Pairs of such suspects – always in plentiful supply – were dragged in off the streets and brought before me for possible identification. They all looked exactly the same. 'He lies like an eyewitness' is an old Russian saying, and now I understood the truth of this myself. I was the eyewitness and I could never have recognized my attackers. I wasn't even sure about the blue shirt, though I didn't tell the cops that. '*El golpe avisa*' as the Spanish say – the blow lets you know. I was certain that I didn't want to get involved in any year-long court cases against two-bit street kids whom I couldn't even identify properly. 'It's not them,' I told the police, time after time, after examining the suspects closely. They were led away and yet more hauled in. I had a hunch I was getting the deluxe, VIP police service. If I had identified two of the kids I had few doubts that confessions would soon be beaten out of them.

In the end, when we were done, and I had signed everything in triplicate, the sergeant said, 'What can we do for you now, *señor*?' This was the first time I'd been granted the honorific. I picked up the Ambassador's card and put it away carefully: it had worked its magic. 'I would be grateful for a lift back to the Gran Hotel, if you have a patrol car going in that direction, please,' I asked. I didn't feel up to walking, frankly. The sergeant nodded, and orders were given. I thanked him for his help and courtesy, and made my way in a dignified fashion down the steps again, an embodiment, I surely hoped, of grace under pressure: Papa Hemingway would have been proud of me. When Sigmund Freud was deported from Vienna after the *Anschluss* by the Nazis the Gestapo were very careful to act 'correctly' towards such a famous man. As he was about to leave, they asked him, politely, if he would write them a short testimonial, to prove he had not been mistreated. Wordlessly, he wrote on one of his visiting cards: 'I can recommend the Gestapo to anyone,' and signed it 'Sigmund Freud'. The Gestapo took this at face value, apparently, not understanding Freud's irony. The Paraguayan police have a poor reputation: however, I have to say, with no irony at all, they treated me with complete fairness and even-handedness. Some might claim that the offer of a glass of water, perhaps the attentions of a nurse or medical orderly, even an aspirin might have gilded the lily somewhat, but I would not be one of them. Without irony, I could certainly recommend Asunción's Finest to anyone who has been attacked, but I'd advise them to keep their cool and have an Ambassador's visiting card on hand, just in case.

The squad car outside was a modified pick-up truck. The back was full of fairly hard-looking cases in uniform, armed with an assortment of sawn-off shot guns, automatic rifles and the usual array of low-slung pistols in gunslinger holsters. This was a real death-squad vehicle and no mistake. Room was made for me in the front, squeezed in with three cops. 'Where to?' the driver asked. 'Gran Hotel, off Avenida España,' I said. The cops had just been told by radio to collect me and drop me off – they didn't know the details, so I was quizzed on what had happened. 'Calle Iturbe? That's outrageous,' commented the driver. 'Right in the centre of town in broad daylight.' One of the other cops asked me where I was from. 'London, England,' I said, as they would have heard of these. 'And can this happen in London?' asked the driver, with an aggressive tone. 'Yes, absolutely, it happens there every day, *señor*,' I replied calmly, and completely accurately. 'It can happen to anyone and in any capital city in the world.' All the cops in the front nodded sagely at this, and were pleased, too. They were evidently glad all this mayhem was not just afflicting them. The lads in the back were curious about whom they had picked up and why. The information was relayed back to them. '*¡Calle Iturbe . . . Iturbe!*' they all echoed. It was definitely a cheeky hit, of that they were all in accord.

Our arrival at the Gran Hotel caused a sensation. Ignoring the guard with the machine-gun at the gate, we swept in regardless, billowing up dust and high drama. A small offshoot of the Makká Indian tribe who sold bows and arrows around town had established themselves on the steps leading into the hotel whilst I had been away on my travels. From here they tried in a half-hearted fashion to sell craft artefacts to the hotel guests, and waved these in a desultory fashion at whoever left or arrived: doubtless they paid a percentage of their takings to the management for the privilege. They saw the cop car approaching them now up the drive at a rapid rate, laden with armed and angry-looking uniformed *hombres* in the back: the Indians jumped up as one with a yell, and vanished into the shrubbery, running as fast as they could. You don't mess with the Paraguayan police and they knew it. The armed guard at the gate had evidently radioed to the hotel that trouble was approaching. I could see inside through the large glass doors a fearful conclave of desk staff peering out at the death-squad vehicle, but very wisely not coming outside to see why it was here. I clambered out, thanked my driver sincerely and wished the whole patrol a '*Buenas tardes, señores caballeros*' and gave them a smart salute, standing to attention. They gave me a '*Buenas tardes a usted también, señor*' and saluted me back. I stood to attention as they drove away down the drive, then walked slowly inside the hotel. It was the least I could do for them.

This was, even for Asunción, a fairly spectacular arrival by any standards. I was ushered inside by the desk staff with cries and whispers of – '*¡Oh! ¡oh! ¡oh . . . señor! ¿Qué pasa, señor, qué pasa?*' I explained in brief. More 'Oh's from the gathering and an 'Ah!' from the senior desk manager, Señor Umberto. '*¿En Iturbe? – en el interior!*' he gasped. Iturbe is a town a long way away up-country as well as a street in the capital. I disabused him of his error. I was still bleeding, though much less fiercely now, just a trickle, but I knew I still looked a mess.

The general manager and owner, Señor Horst, until now an invisible figure to me, was summoned and appeared. He was all sympathy. I was aware that all around me horrified whispers were going on among the gathered staff, the maids, waiters and cleaners who had assembled to look at me. The Gran Hotel is the Dorchester, Savoy and Ritz of Asunción, the true *sanctum sanctorum* of rich, establishment Paraguay, all of this rolled into one: and now one of their sacred passengers, a foreigner to boot, had been attacked and robbed, in broad daylight, in the middle of town, on a Sunday morning. Galileo's deeply unwelcome news about the movement of the heavenly planets had caused no less a stir in Rome than this derangement in the natural order of things did at the Gran Hotel.

Had I been to the police to make my *denuncia*, Señor Horst now asked me urgently. I told him I had, that all the paperwork had been completed, and that I had to return there in two days to collect a copy of the *denuncia*, which would have by then been typed up, for my inevitable insurance claim. Señor Horst sighed a visible sigh of relief. 'I will send one of our best men with you when you go. It's always best to have a witness. We know people in the Seventh Precinct station.' Then he added softly, 'You did absolutely the right thing in going to them first of all. Now what do you need?' he asked, one hand on my arm in sympathy. 'A cup of Indian tea,' I replied, and this was brought forthwith.

'I would advise against going to any hospital,' said Señor Horst, for reasons he didn't need to spell out. 'We have a qualified nurse here who will look at your head.' The hotel had its own water wells and electricity generators, also, in case things got bad: in Paraguay you just never knew – there might be another revolution and chaos tomorrow – the wise were prepared. The 20-foot brick walls which completely surrounded the property were not there for decoration or effect.

So, while I sipped my lemon tea, a young female Paraguayan nurse disinfected my scalp wound with alcohol, put in half a dozen stitches with sterilized cotton thread, and sponged off the caked blood from my face and hair, a great deal of which had become matted and had to be cut off. The bleeding stopped: the wound started to sting, and I felt it for the first time. I began to get a headache, which did not leave me for several days. While doing this for me, she deplored the wave of violence washing over the capital. '*Necesita la mano dura*,' she said – a strong hand is needed – and she cut the air with the side of her free hand to reinforce the point. Oviedo evidently had another firm supporter in her. 'It never happened when Stroessner was in power,' she remarked several times. 'We need the firm hand back again.' All over Paraguay millions of people were thinking exactly the same.

Nineteen

El Día de la Virgen de la Merced

All over the country there were celebrations to mark the Day of the Virgin of Mercy. In the prisons, priests and even bishops in mitres gave the sacraments to prisoners: 31 convicts were confessed and another 30 baptized, *Ultima Hora* reported – not exactly a huge religious wave of enthusiasm given the many Paraguayans in chokey. There were, however, pages of photographs of these religious ceremonies among the pious cons. There were two missing, of course – the little bastards who had robbed and magnassaulted me.

There were complaints, too, from the priests about conditions in some of the schools in the poorest *barrios*. The children frequently came to classes without having had any breakfast because their parents were so poor: that or many of the dads had drunk the takings of last night's heist already, so no *chipá* for the nipper. Once, the teachers said, the state had provided dried crackers – *panini* – for the starving infants to take the edge off their hunger pangs before they settled down to studying the *stupor mundi* that had been the Paraguay of López and *Madama*. Now there was no money for such luxuries, for the state was broke. It was hardly surprising young kids became street robbers: if you are starving you will steal to eat. There was no suggestion by the priests or teachers that the Church should do anything to feed the starving children. In the photos the priests and bishops were all Europeans, white, and plump with good health and wholesome food. Providing for the poor was someone else's job, not theirs. The Church collected money from the poor, did not dish it out to them. The Virgin of Mercy gave spiritual succour, not nutritional. 'What must I do to be saved?' the Centurion asked Jesus. 'Give all you own to the poor and follow me,' replied the Master. The Centurion made an excuse and left, as indeed I would have done, and virtually everyone else over the last two millennia has. No text from the Gospels had ever been more ignored by those who over the years have claimed to call themselves Christians. 'Christianity cannot be said to have failed,' observed George Bernard Shaw, 'for it has never even been tried.' Jesus himself remarked that 'The poor will always be with you', a text quoted by conservatives at do-gooders to absolve themselves from any remedial action.

In the 1960s there used to be a saying that went 'a conservative is a liberal who has just been mugged by criminals, whereas a liberal is a conservative who has just been beaten up by the police'. I was a newly minted conservative: my sympathy for street kids and their hard lot was tempered by my recent attack. I was in OK shape, really. My head ached and I was jumpy and nervous, unable to sit still, or rest, or sleep well, and I had a marked aversion for going out on to the streets of Asunción, which made my presence in the country rather pointless. 'You are leaving because you've left already' is an old Spanish saying, and it was true – I now simply wanted to get out as soon as I could. Which was easier said than done. The planes were full up for months ahead: I wasn't the only one who had decided that out was healthier than in the way things were going. My second visit to the Seventh Precinct police station went without a hitch. Horst provided a calm and kindly member of the hotel staff, who drove me there, took me in, and stayed with me while I collected my copy of the *denuncia*, he a speaker of soothing words and emollient compliments. It was always better to go into a police station with someone they knew and trusted, to make sure you came out again, and were not thrown into the cells on suspicion of something or other. Once you were in a Paraguayan police cell it was by no means easy to get out again. We stopped at traffic lights on the way, and small boys crowded up to the window to beg for coins or sweets. My companion Luis, a kindly middle-aged man, smiled at them and joked, handed out boiled sweets in wrapped twists of cellophane which he kept on the dashboard: they would grow up into beggars, as that was what they were in training for already. 'Tomorrow's robbers and *pistoleros*,' I remarked to Luis as we moved away from the lights and he wound up the window. 'No! No!' he demurred, shocked at my cynicism. Well, I had been mugged, not him. 'All will be well when the United States lends us some more money – or the IMF,' Luis said happily. I said nothing: more begging – beggars on horseback and beggars on foot. 'Unteachable from infancy to the tomb – there is the first and main characteristic of mankind,' as Winston Churchill observed to Max Beaverbrook in 1928. Nothing would change in Paraguay, I now knew, any more than it would in any other Third World kleptocracy. There would be riots, rebellions, revolts, coups, military takeovers, dictators, magnicides, magnassaults, massacres, civil wars, torture and cruelty until the end of time or until a merciful set of large asteroids slapped into Earth and washed off the pond-life scuttling round on the surface, in particular the unpleasant race of killer apes which had gained temporary ascendancy, and of which I was a deeply reluctant member. Getting hit over the head with a pistol does not do anything for one's bumps of benignity, I had found. On the other hand, it had made me remarkably positive, upbeat and optimistic. I was still alive – others, millions of them, were dead. Minor problems were shrugged away, the great thing was still to be alive when I might just as easily have been lying in a mortuary with a pistol bullet in my head. The point of life, said Kafka, is that it stops. Mine had not – I was amazingly lucky. I felt flooded with sheer joy in life, in living.

Alejandro Caradoc Evans had vanished from his usual bar stool. I hadn't seen him for almost a week. I asked the bartender where he had got to. The man avoided my eyes and looked deeply embarrassed. He banged his wrists together at the pulse and held them together – the local sign for handcuffs and arrest. '¿*Policía*?' I asked *sotto voce*. He nodded and started polishing glasses, displacement activity. I didn't ask why: without any reason I knew it would not be a good idea.

I did manage to contact Mac on his mobile phone. I told him what had happened and that I was leaving. He thought I was doing the right thing. He said he was going to Chile for a while, to see how things panned out after the General Strike. 'There might be a revolution, or a military *golpe*. There could be a lot of bloodshed – it's why everyone with money is leaving.' Señora Estigarribia was adamant I shouldn't go. 'It means they will have won! You have to get out there again walking around, and taking the buses too – it's the only way.' I said nothing. She never walked in the centre of town, nor took buses. Nothing is easier to give than advice you don't have to take yourself. She didn't offer to come and see me before I left. She had been dropping heavy hints about her 'daily fee' for information again. Marcello Warnes was surprised and upset to hear of my attack, but not to learn I was leaving. He offered to take me to the airport. Luis had already been delegated to do this by Horst, so I absolved him with thanks, but it was nice that he made the offer. Marcello came round to see me at the hotel to say goodbye. I offered him a drink in the bar or tea or coffee on the terrace. He declined both, but sat on a chair by the deserted swimming pool, smoking a cigarette as ever.

'It is a great pity you are leaving,' he said. 'Very few European sages [he used the term '*sabios europeos*'] come to Paraguay, and they – you – could do us much good. You have read all the books on Paraguay and South America and know the world, the East, Europe, Asia. We do not have the books here, they are all in Europe. We do not know ourselves at all well. We learn from people like you who come here.'

As a reply I said '*El golpe avisa*' – the blow lets you know. He lit another cigarette. 'I will stay because I have nowhere else to go. Things will get worse but then they may get better. I have a wife and child here.' His son was called Rolf. I had seen him on Marcello's computer screen: he used the child's face as his back-drop. 'A Viking name,' I had remarked. It turned out he was obsessed with the Vikings, and believed, as many Paraguayans did, that the Vikings had sailed up the Paraguay River in search of timber. When I didn't laugh at this fancy he had taken me out one day to a cliff, a set of rocks which had etched on them what were claimed to be Viking runes. I had said to him, on the spur of the moment, 'Do you read the work of Robin Wood?' He had looked at me sharply and replied with fervour, 'I like this writer very, very much.' Robin Wood was a Paraguayan success story. Born to an unknown father, thought to be a high Paraguayan officer, and a blonde mother from the Australian Utopian com-munity at Nueva Australia, he had been brought up, by his mother only, in Buenos Aires and Asunción. After many struggles he had become a fantastically successful writer of what the Japanese call '*mangas*' and the French '*bandes dessinées*', that is to say serious if fantastic cartoons on historical, mythological and political sub-jects for adults. These are read all over the Hispanic and Latin world, though are unknown in Anglo-Saxon countries. Paul Ther-oux, flying to Argentina, was offered one of these 'comic books' as he called it by a trades unionist sitting next to him. Theroux, the ex-college professor, was disparaging: 'Grown-ups don't read comics' was his unspoken response. But that was his ignorance and ethnocentrism speaking. The work of Robin Wood repays close reading by anyone interested in the Latin American men-tality. His most potent creation is Monro, a tall, long-blond-haired outlaw who carries a Mauser automatic and smokes a long thin cheroot, and is somewhere in that moral hinterland between a Hemingway hero and a character from a Spaghetti Western – Clint Cantwell, or Across the River and Into the Restaurant, as

355

Cyril Connolly wittily put it in his send-up of Hem's style. Marcello himself was about 60% Monro in personal image. This blond giant was everything South American men fantasized about but were not. They were trapped inside lousy jobs or no jobs at all, hemmed in by family, oppressed and disempowered by an authoritarian and chaotic political world over which they had no purchase. Monro was free, effective, strong, powerful and ethical in a brutal, macho fashion. In a continent of short, dark, pudgy men he was tall, thin and blond, in a world where Jesus and the Virgin Mary were always blond blue-eyed gringos. Anne Whitehead in her excellent book on the Australian communists in Paraguay has a good chapter on Robin Wood. His cartoon strips were to be found in the Paraguayan and Argentinian papers every day, usually with pithy if simplistic political and moral content.

Marcello and I talked very frankly, more frankly than we ever had before, for now I was leaving and we would never meet again. I asked him why there was no leftist opposition in the country. 'It was crushed and wiped out in the long years of the *stronato*. And Cuba is an unattractive model – no one wants that sort of regimentation. Paraguayans are too individualistic, too anarchic and also too respectful to authority, paradoxically.' I asked him if he wanted to see the small zoo in the hotel gardens. He didn't. I had told him about it before. 'It is illegal,' he had commented. 'But not prohibited,' I had riposted. He agreed. There were laws but the rich and powerful ignored them. I asked him about the rich, the numbers. 'There are perhaps two hundred families who are very rich, then perhaps two thousand who are well off, comfortable, and then the rest are poor, owning more or less nothing or in debt.' He said this without bitterness. He was a man who lived in the margins, right on the edge of society, an adventurer and a romantic. He had warmed to me after all my tales of the East, of the Cathars in medieval Europe, of the Celts and their myths and legends. He asked me many questions and was interested in my point of view. '*¿El líder maximo de la iglesia en Inglaterra es la reina, no?*' he had asked me on one of our trips. It sounded strange to hear the Queen described as a '*líder maximo*' but it was true, she was head of the Church in England. I thought this showed a considerable depth of knowledge in Marcello. '*Cacique*' the word Señora Estigarribia had claimed not to know the meaning of was printed in *Ultima Hora* in almost every edition somewhere. How could a journalist not know it? Why had she pretended to me that she did not know what it meant? Paraguay and its people still baffled me.

'Will you come back?' Marcello asked. 'No,' I said, 'I shall never come back.' There was no use pretending. I was finished with Paraguay for ever now. He made no comment. I walked with him back to the mud-bespattered El Noble which was parked amid the Mercedes and BMWs. He had been to the Chaco over the weekend, he had told me. He loved the Chaco more than ever. We shook hands and said our goodbyes. I thanked him again for his help and wished him well. He nodded seriously, and started up the engine. 'Safe journey, then,' he said, and slid away down the drive and out of my life. He was the best person and the most sympathetic I had met in Paraguay, and I was sorry to see him depart.

Getting my plane ticket changed was not easy. I had to pay a forfeit of US$100 but that was nothing – it was getting on a flight to Sao Paulo that was the problem. I shamelessly played on the heartstrings of the Paraguayan lady in the travel agency booking office.

'I have been attacked in Asunción and robbed,' I said, bowing my head to show my elaborately stitched wound. 'My wife and children are waiting for me in England,' I lied, a half-sob creeping into my voice. 'They are anxious to see me. I telephone them every night. "Papy, Papy, when are you coming home to us, Papy?" they cry, my little ones. And my wife, she is not well, she is sick in fact. She needs me by her side . . .' All of this in my most pathetic-voiced Spanish. The lady melted, and jiggled and joggled at her computer. 'Asunción is a very dangerous place,' she said, concentrating on the screen. 'My wife will offer up prayers for your salvation,' I threw in. It sounds less corny in Spanish, somehow, and it was the Day of the Virgin of Mercy. In the end she bumped someone off a mid-afternoon flight in three days' time, and only charged me US$77 instead of 100. 'God will bless you for your kindness, *señora*,' I intoned with liturgical fervour. Feminists – and others – will not be surprised to learn that it was always the women in Paraguay who helped me out, and always the men who got me into hot water.

I went back to the hotel and packed, repacked, unpacked and packed again. I wanted to leave right now. I tried to read and couldn't concentrate, paced around the grounds, glanced at the newspapers, swam in the pool, ate long over-copious breakfasts, smoked and drank much too much. I looked at the animals in the small zoo with new eyes: I was in a little zoo now with them. I didn't go out. I didn't feel safe. Trujillo, the dictator of the Dominican Republic, who fed his enemies to the sharks down a blow-hole, was reputed to have a special torturer who was a dwarf. His *pièce de résistance* was to jump up and bite off the testicles of his victims with his teeth. I felt my balls had been bitten off, too. I had completely lost my nerve. I was also very angry and full of violent feelings – a not uncommon reaction after being attacked, or so I have read. I looked with complete suspicion on everyone now, and if anyone came too close to me, or did anything I interpreted as even vaguely threatening my head started to pound, my mouth went dry, my heartbeat raced and my veins flooded with adrenalin ready to fight or fly. Man is by origin a flight-or-fight predator, and these responses occur at the deepest primeval levels. I was a bear with a sore head all right. I was killing time, and time was slowly killing me, too.

Twenty

Endgame

The airport had an air of imminent, looming disaster about it – milling crowds loaded down with luggage, crying, fractious children, anxious womenfolk, shouting, pushing, angry men gesticulating and shoving. I wasn't the only person desperate to get out of Paraguay. Armoured cars stood parked in the sharp sunlight outside. Heavily weaponed police and army were everywhere. There were queues for everything, mobs rather, trying to get foreign currency, tickets, water, food. It took me over an hour to check in. I was convinced that I would not get on the flight. Luis had dropped me off earlier and I had given him a fistful of dollars in spite of his protestations. I was sure I would be bumped off the flight and be forced to get a taxi back to the Gran Hotel again. There might not even be a room for me. Ahead of the General Strike, hundreds of senior labour leaders and trades unionists had been pouring into Asunción: many had booked into the Gran Hotel on the principle that nothing is too good for the working class – and especially for their tribunes. Señor Horst had told me confidentially that he had given them 'special rates'. This might be good tactics if there were to be a revolution. I began working out how much it would cost me to get a taxi to the Brazilian border at Foz do Iguaçu: I was really desperate to leave.

In among the milling crowds wandered a solitary Indian child of perhaps six or seven, trying to sell bows and arrows to the waiting would-be passengers. If there was one item a departing – fleeing even – citizen of Paraguay was unlikely to want to buy just as he was making his exit surely a miniature Indian bow and arrow set was just about top of the list, along with perhaps a 19th-century hardwood wardrobe or a complete set of leather armchairs and sofas. The boy kept on circling and offering, circling and offering. I was in no mood for Indian boys or bows and arrows, and he got some heavy-voltage don't-mess-with-me-sunshine glances when he approached. I was ready with my bag to swipe him aside or club him to the ground if he looked like attacking me. Maybe his arrows were tipped with curare: I was willing to believe anything now in my paranoia. He gave me a look of open fear, the poor devil, and scuttled away out of range. I had joined the clan of gringos driven plumb *loco* by South America – a substantial fraternity.

I had a long and futile argument with the check-in staff, who insisted I put my grip in the hold. Sao Paulo was notorious for luggage thieves who ransacked bags in transit – all the guidebooks warned you not to check luggage through. I expostulated, argued, explained, cajoled all to no avail. My bag had to go in the hold. Cursing, I unpacked it and took out the silver *bombillas* and maté holders, camera and lenses, vital books and other things I didn't want to vanish, loading these into a small handgrip. Then I had to queue to go through passport control. A woman in a glass booth demanded US$12 as an exit tax – cheap at the price you might think – but the sign printed in front of her read quite clearly 'Exit Tax US$5' with another notice next to it reading 'Help Stamp Out Corruption – Do Not Offer Bribes'.

'It is five dollars,' I said. 'Look – it says so here.'

'It has gone up,' said the woman. 'It is now twelve dollars.' She showed me the receipt book which had printed on it 'US$5'. This had been crossed out in biro and 'US$12' written by hand next to it. Hardly the most sophisticated forgery project in the world, but simplicity in certain circumstances reaps dividends.

'This is an *estafa* – a swindle,' I said. 'I refuse to pay more than five dollars.'

'Then you can stay in Paraguay for the rest of your life, *señor*,' she said. The people behind me were becoming restive. If I lost my place in the queue I would miss my flight.

'Call the manager,' I demanded.

'I am the manager,' she replied with no irony.

'Call your superior,' I demanded. I was getting ready to strangle someone. My head was throbbing dangerously. I was about to reprise the Monty Python sketch about the dirty fork with me playing John Cleese, the manic chef with the war-wound. She rang a bell and a middle-aged man came over. He obviously knew what the problem was.

'The tax has gone up, *señor*, I assure you. It is not an *estafa*. It is now twelve dollars,' he said without even having the matter explained to him. I didn't believe him. On the other hand he was wearing a large automatic pistol in a waist holster, and also had a pair of handcuffs attached on the other side. Any argy-bargy and one could well end up arrested, beaten, in gaol and the whole cycle would start again. I bit down my anger and bile, paid over twelve dollars, and was given a receipt. As I moved forward into the transit lounge I could hear the man in the queue behind me start to argue, insisting he would only pay five dollars. It was a smart little scam – the immigration staff must be making hundreds, even thousands of dollars out of this swindle.

In Africa, when things got bad and meltdown happened, the soldiers roamed around the airports simply stealing the outgoing passengers' watches, wallets and jewels at rifle point. Kinshasa, Brazzaville, the Congo massacres – this mêlée at Asunción had all the stink of an imminent collapse about it. Twelve bucks was cheap – they could have demanded a hundred, two hundred – what could we do?

We had to get out. The guns Paraguayans always carried were packed away in their cargo luggage, so no one would shoot the scammers, as might well happen elsewhere. I wondered if there would be more taxes later on, at the door of the plane even.

¿Porque no? There was another little act in this farce to be played out, though. Customs. Or was it Security? Whichever it was, two slow-moving Paraguayan girls rummaged and sifted their pudgy little fingers through everyone's bags, supervised by an older man, who in true macho style did nothing but look on benignly. I was carrying my larger-than-life portrait of Alfie Stroessner partly hidden in a black rubbish sack. There had been no problem about me carrying this on board as hand-luggage – ex-dictators go gratis, evidently. The supervisor spotted Alfie's face, darted forward, and gently pulled out the portrait, holding it up. He hadn't been quite sure what it was, and his curiosity got the better of him. Now he looked shocked, startled, amazed. He held up Alfie for the searching girls to see – *'¡Mira! ¡Mira!'* he said – Look! Look! The girls just looked bored. They were too young to be impressed, Stroessner meant nothing to them. The supervisor, who was evidently a prize plonker, started waving the portrait around, telling everyone to look, look. It was a Bateman cartoon – the man who was caught exporting the portrait of the deposed dictator. The whole queue froze and stared first at Alfie, then at me – the gringo nutcase who was evidently still a *stronista*.

'¿Alemán?' asked the supervisor – 'German?' *'Inglés,'* I replied, taking the portrait back from him and reinterring it in the obscurity it deserved inside its plastic shroud. Perhaps I was actually exporting the last existing portrait of the dictator from Paraguay. I had searched high and low and this was the only one I had found.

We waited in humid tropical heat for the plane to arrive from Cordoba in Argentina. Most people had hand luggage vastly larger than the bag that the staff had insisted I check in. I realized now this was another scam. I was expected to offer them five or ten dollars as a *propina* to allow my bag on board with me. I kicked myself for my stupidity. In my mind I had already left this land of squeeze, graft and corruption, and so had not even thought of the obvious solution. There was nothing to eat or drink in the transit lounge, no kiosks, shops or bars. The lavatories were stinking and there was no water there, even. The seats looked as if the lepers had been at them, and possibly the vampire bats as well. We waited, and we waited, and we waited. Finally, two hours late, the plane came in. No one got off the flight, not one person.

The doors to freedom were unlocked, our boarding passes collected, and we surged out on to the tarmac to walk the hundred yards to the waiting plane, which shimmered in the heat, lines wavering and trembling in the air as if the machine might be a mirage. I put on a spurt. If anyone was going to be left behind it was not going to be this little cream-puff, as the Australians say in such circumstances. This was the worst airport scenario I had been involved in since the summer of 1967 when the Lufthansa plane taking me from Istanbul to Rome had been forced to land at Athens by Greek jet fighters to collect weeping and traumatized foreigners trapped in the *coup d'état* mounted by the Greek Colonels. We were the first plane in and the military were hysterical with tiredness, nerves and fear. The coup was by no means certain of success and if it failed many of the army could expect to be shot. We were herded off the plane, shunted at gunpoint into a waiting area, screams, shouts, plumes of smoke from fires all in evidence around us. When we were finally let back on the secret police came down the aisles checking our passports slowly to see there was no one there they wanted: these were the most frightening, evil men I had ever seen in my life. All of them were clearly torturers and murderers. The refugees were then herded on to the plane by men with rifles. We were way over capacity – people were standing crushed together in the aisles, you could not move. We flew like this all the way to Rome.

I got inside the Brazilian plane OK, one of the first aboard, and found a seat. I was now not going to move come what may. The people who had prevented me bringing all my luggage on board had in fact done me a huge favour. I had been able to move across the tarmac far faster than those laden with heavy bags.

There was a crush at the doors now, shouts and screams. The Brazilian cabin crew pushed the latecomers back, for we were soon full up, and swung the doors shut. There was hammering and cursing on the door from those left outside. There would not be another flight out for a week, and in that time the General Strike would take place. I was on the last flight to freedom. I sat and sweated. We weren't airborne yet. This was the time that (traditionally) the Paraguayan secret police blew up planes which had on board people they didn't like. I could well be one of them. My attack and robbery, it had already been discreetly suggested to me, might not have been a complete accident.

Several jeeps loaded with armed military swung across the tarmac towards the plane and started chasing the unsuccessful passengers who had failed to get on board, harrying and chivvying them back to the terminal. There were dozens of these poor devils. Our flight was full up to the gills; there wasn't a single spare seat.

We sat and waited. The cabin crew obviously knew what sort of flight this was. Once the doors were firmly locked the stewards started down the aisles handing out bottles of mineral water, ice, plastic cups, whisky and rum. The litre bottles of liquor were plonked down between the passengers to help themselves: they – we – were not slow to get stuck in. There is no nonsense about not smoking on South American airlines, and everybody including me had lit up, cheroots, cigars, pipes – and the *hierba maldita*, unless my nostrils were playing me false – were all blasting away as if lung cancer had never been heard of.

'Things are bad in Paraguay, too, then?' enquired my neighbour, helping me to a tumblerful of Scotch whisky, from a bottle undoubtedly *mau*. He was a businessman who lived in Cordoba, he told me, but was moving to Bahia in Brazil because the situation in Argentina was so chaotic. We swapped horror stories about our respective cities. There was very little food in the shops, he told me, fuel shortages, power outages, false police, kidnappings, the banks all closed, no money, hyper-inflation, the whole meltdown South American nightmare. I told him a few choice tidbits, morsels from everyday Paraguayan life: he was impressed, I could tell. Meanwhile, the Scotch spread through me like some miraculous ichor, life blood from a far-off, wondrous planet. 'If the worst comes to the worst, I have Italian papers,' he confided 'I can always go over there.' 'I have British papers, so I can too,' I added. We toasted our sagacity in being so well-prepared with yet more Scotch. I was pleased to note my Spanish had definitely improved after the last few months. I was much more fluent.

Eventually, we taxied for take-off, revved up, and then – up, up – we were away, the grey-green river glinting below us, the jungle and chaco all around the city like a ring of dark glowing emerald. The whole plane burst into applause and cheers, clapping and whooping as we took off. '¡Bravo! ¡Bravo!' rang out the voices. A holiday atmosphere now gripped the flight. I let out a huge sigh of relief, the tension draining from me like air from a punctured balloon. I was out, away, free, gone – *chin-chin, mau-mau* – *adios and vaya con Dios Paraguay* . . . I had escaped.

I drank well over half a bottle of Scotch on that short flight to Sao Paulo, and I was one of the more conservative imbibers on the plane: happiness in such circumstances is an ice-cold Scotch, believe you me. At Sao Paulo there were the same impossibly slim and elegant Brazilian black men strolling to and fro in the airport, and serving in the duty-free shop, where any currency was acceptable – apart from all those from South America, of course. I bought a very large box of cheroots and two litres of Scotch whisky: I was a convert to a new religion, it seemed – Scotch on ice.

The three-hour wait for the London flight was a dream. I found an English-language newspaper from the US for sale and caught up on world news for the first time in months. I felt I had been let out of prison – exhilaration, sheer bliss, a sense of absolute freedom. I could go anywhere, safely. I could lie on Aegean beaches, motor through Gascony, travel by vaporetto in Venice. I was free and still alive. I had survived Paraguay.

I managed to lie down across three seats on the London flight and get some sleep, for the plane was not full. I was woken for breakfast by a Brazilian stewardess. She looked down at me, and as I blinked up blearily, I saw the horrified expression on her face. She gasped, '*¿Señor, qué pasa?*' speaking Spanish as that was the language we had in common. I touched my warm, sticky face. I seemed covered in sweat. Then I looked at my hand. It was covered with blood. My head wound had burst open while I slept, and my whole face was drenched in blood. I staggered to the washroom. The guy who stared back at me from the mirror was not a pretty sight. He had aged about 10 years in a few months. There was blood and sweat all over his face, and his stubble-pocked face looked like that of a derelict on Skid Row.

I cleaned myself up as best I could, and vowed that the next travel book I wrote would be an in-depth personal account of the gastronomic restaurants of the Côte d'Azur.

Twenty-one

Charlie Carver's Gold Watch

I had seen this fabulous item when I was small boy, at my grandparents' house in Gedling Grove, Nottingham. Like the elephant's foot wastepaper basket, the oriental brass tray bought at Port Said, and the set of eight Arts and Crafts ladderback dining chairs with rush seats, it formed an integral part of the wonderland of adulthood which was their house. My grandfather Roy had a shed at the end of the garden where he used to do his stamp collection, and craft items out of wood: I used to love sitting down there watching him at work, gouging out a wooden bowl with his lathe. He used to read *The Times* every day from cover to cover, and could – and would – quote long passages of Shakespeare, Swinburne, Browning and Tennyson at long family Sunday lunches, where much burgundy was drunk, and when the roast was getting close to being finished my grandmother would whisper 'FHB', which meant Family Hold Back.

It would be nice to be able to recount that my grandparents had promised me Charlie Carver's watch, a fascinating heirloom, but, of course, they didn't. The stamp collection was sold to a shark of a dealer after Roy's death, the ladderback chairs went into an auction, and Charlie Carver's watch was borrowed by some Carvers from South Africa, who promised to pay for it to be regulated and cleaned, but then never gave it back.

Charlie Carver had interviewed the young Fawcett for his final, fatal expedition to find Paititi. Fawcett had been a personal friend of Sir Arthur Conan Doyle, author, as well as of the celebrated

Sherlock Holmes stories, of *The Lost World* in which Professor Challenger and his expedition find a plateau in the South American jungles on which the dinosaurs and pterodactyls are still alive and well. Challenger and his team are following in the footsteps of a previous expedition which has vanished without trace, led by Maple White, an American. At the base of the plateau Challenger finds the skeletons of two white men with shreds of clothing left on them and boots. They had been killed by Indians and thrown off the plateau. Conan Doyle wrote:

> A gold watch by Hudson, of New York and a chain which held a stylographic pen, lay among the bones. There was also a silver cigarette case with 'J.C. from A.E.S.' upon the lid . . . 'Who can it be?' asked Lord John. 'Poor devil! Every bone in his body seems broken . . .' Professor Challenger replied 'Maple White was not alone . . . there was a friend, an American named James Colver . . . I think, therefore, that there can be no doubt we are looking upon the remains of James Colver.'

Charles Carver, who spoke with an American accent and wore American clothes, had metamorphosed into the American James Colver – complete with gold watch from Hudson of New York. 'Anything, surely, is possible in South America,' Conan Doyle had observed, and Charlie Carver's fictional alter ego had discovered the lost world and paid for it with his life.

The past is a foreign country, as we know, and its language is notoriously open to corruption and distortion. Looking on the various websites dedicated to my ancestor John Carver, first governor of Plymouth Colony and Master of the *Mayflower*, I discovered that there is a dispute ongoing among genealogists about his relative and companion on the voyage Robert Carver. Some claim he was John Carver's brother, others his nephew – the facts are in doubt. Already the same doubt and imprecision has overtaken Charlie Carver. Andrew Johnson, a second-cousin of mine and an amateur genealogist who has done much research, informed me that the brother who had vanished in South America was in fact Bertie Carver – Charlie had stayed behind in England and inherited all the money. My grandmother, then, must have mixed up the brothers' names when she told me the story – that's what my Uncle James thinks anyway. I find it highly appropriate that even the name of the 'man with no name' who vanished, reappeared, then vanished again for ever should even now be in doubt. Perhaps it is all in the archives of long-forgotten provincial newspapers somewhere: I prefer the imprecision, the doubt; it is more suitable to Paraguay and to South America, themselves locales of fantasy, dream, vagueness and misinformation – and of the disappeared, let's not forget.

Conan Doyle's friend and fellow author Rider Haggard was given a small black stone statuette by an explorer who had come back from South America, where he had found it in a jungle ruin. Rider Haggard took it to the British Museum for identification. All their South American antiquities experts were in unanimous agreement: they knew nothing about the statuette or its origins. They could not even tell what type of stone it was carved from, for they had never seen that before either. It belonged to a completely unknown civilization. Rider Haggard believed it was from Atlantis, or a South American offshoot of that culture. Fawcett believed Atlantis had a lost colony in the South American jungle and that was what he was looking for when he disappeared.

The Incas enslaved many peoples and forced large numbers of them to move from the lowlands and jungles to the uplands of Peru, there to work on state construction projects. When the Inca empire collapsed many of these slave workers fled back to the lowlands they had originally come from, founding, it is claimed, Inca-style cities in the jungles, complete with gold and silver mines and cyclopean architecture in stone. Lost Incan-style cities are still being found in the jungles, covered with lianas and trees.

East of Titicaca in Bolivia, a city called Iskanwaya was discovered as recently as 1976. And in 2002, Mark Thomson and others found a hidden city which had not been visited since it was abandoned in about 1572. In 1971, settlers in Todos Santos were attacked by previously unknown Indians who emerged from the jungle and then disappeared back into it again. According to Dr Carlos Ponce Sangines, Director of the National Institute of Archaeology in Bolivia, 'there are still communities of the descendants of the Incas living hidden in the jungles, which certain archaeologists know about, in the north of the country, in the mountains of Apolobamba.' It was also said that these hidden people knew of an old Inca Road which led to the City of Gold – to the Paititi which Colonel Fawcett claimed to know.

Could there still be communities of people hidden in the jungles living a neo-Incan way of life? While I was writing this book there appeared an article in the British press about a previously unknown tribe of Ayoreo Indians who had emerged from the jungle in the Paraguayan Chaco to seek the help of the whites, whom normally they feared and shunned. They had only come out because they had seen these huge, new beasts, enormous, violent, and making frightening noises. Suddenly they had appeared, and were now knocking down trees and ploughing up the earth. The Indians wanted the whites to help them destroy or drive away these monsters – which were, of course, great earth-moving bulldozers. No one had even suspected the existence of this tribe before. They had known all about the whites, but the whites had not known about them.

Paraguay is much better known and explored than Amazonian Bolivia, Peru or Brazil. Aerial photos tell you nothing of the land, for it is covered with jungle, and any ruined city would be hidden underneath the foliage. Exploration in these areas is very difficult: the remains of the Fawcett expedition, like the Carver expedition, have never been found. 'East of Sacapampa are Indians living in cities of stone who guard their territory jealously and kill other

Indians who approach: these have armies of soldiers because they produce food surpluses,' wrote the explorer and author Ross Salmon in *My Quest for Eldorado*.

Myth, fantasy, romance, or a future reality waiting to be discovered by some intrepid explorer, some latter-day Carver or Fawcett? We do not know. 150 years ago Schliemann had yet to excavate Troy – the Trojan Wars were believed to be simply myth and legend by all serious historians. And 100 years ago the whole Minoan culture of ancient Crete was completely unknown – 1,000 years of Mediterranean history still waiting to be uncovered by Arthur Evans, a dilettante amateur, like Schliemann. Both of them, incidentally, were firm believers in Atlantis as a lost antediluvian culture. In the middle of the last century, the farming and obsidian-carving proto-urban culture of Çatal Huyuk in Anatolia was not even suspected. I often think how amazed Lord Byron would be, or Percy Bysshe Shelley, to be whisked to our world and shown round the museums – whole cultures on display from the ancient world which they had not even suspected existed. What odes and ballads they would compose!

What hidden wonders await us in the jungles of South America or buried under unsuspected mounds of earth as yet untouched? What will mankind know of ancient cultures 100 years from now? Is there a new Machu Picchu out there somewhere? Does Paititi, or Eldorado, actually exist? For myself I am not sure. But I am certain that Charlie Carver would say 'Yes they do', and set about equipping yet another expedition to find them.

Some Sources and Further Reading

TRAVEL

The best modern travel book on Paraguay is without doubt *At the Tomb of the Inflatable Pig* by John Gimlette (Arrow, £7.99). Published in 2003 and described as 'a riotous journey into the heart of Paraguay', it is, in fact, a serious and informative book disguised and marketed as a silly one. Gimlette has been visiting Paraguay since the 1970s and has read about and absorbed much of its history, as well as having excellent contacts in the country. At least half of his book is made up of a history of Paraguay and the region, and he manages to be as fair and neutral as one can be in such a minefield. He was able to move about in 'the good old days' when there was virtually no crime and no violence – apart from the secret services, of course. He starts his book with the fact that Asunción was gripped by a murder in the summer of 1982, then a rarity. On the Sunday I was attacked and mugged, there were five murders in Asunción alone, plus untold muggings – and that was a quiet day.

A curiosity from the depths of the *stronato* is Gordon Meyer's *The River and the People* (Methuen, 1965). This is very good and atmospheric on the Chaco and the wildlife. Meyer is a curious character, highly intelligent but deeply enigmatic, and his perspective on Argentina and Paraguay is original and unusual. A long out-of-print but worthwhile oddity to track down.

FAUNA HUGGING

The wildlife fan could start with David Attenborough's *Zoo Quest in Paraguay* (Lutterworth, 1950) and move on to Gerald Durrell's *The Drunken Forest* (Penguin, 1956). There is also Sir John Kerr's *A Naturalist in the Chaco* (CUP, 1950), a book sometimes erroneously given as *A Naturist in the Chaco*: this has led many a hopeful nudist badly astray and into the prickles.

THE JESUITS

There is an immense literature on this subject but the most accessible and romantic starter-for-ten is Robert Bontine Cunninghame Graham's *A Vanished Arcadia* (Century Classics, 1988). Voltaire's *Candide* (Penguin, 1947) gives that skeptic's amusing and not entirely inaccurate satire on the system. A serious history is Selim Abou's *The Jesuit Republic of the Guaranis (1609–1768)* (Crossroad Herder, NY, 1997).

THE TRIPLE ALLIANCE WAR

Sir Richard Burton's *Letters from the Battlefields of Paraguay* (London, 1870) is hard to get hold of – I had to order a copy from the stacks of the University of Mississippi – but well worth the effort. It is full of Burton's characteristically pungent and wildly unpolitically correct comments on 'woolly-pated negroes, high-yaller half-breeds, greasy dagoes' and all the rest. Burton was pro-López, viz: 'the bulldog tenacity and semi-compulsory heroism of a redskin Sparta.' The weasel word 'semi-compulsory' shows how little Burton actually knew of what was happening. A sample Burton prejudice: 'A revolver at night is as necessary as shoes ... personally I may state in every transaction with Paraguayans they invariably cheated and robbed me, and that in truthfulness they proved themselves to be about on a par with the Hindus.' Evidently, in Paraguay *plus ça change* ...

George Frederick Masterman's *Seven Eventful Years in Paraguay* (S. Low, Son and Marston, 1870) is a must: he served under López, and only just escaped with his life: a fascinating portrait of the country in the mid-19th century. Charles Ames Washburn, US Consul in Asunción, was another who only just escaped from López by the skin of his teeth, and his *The History of Paraguay* (Boston, 1871) in 2 volumes is as anti-López as can be, but very graphic and well-written – he was a novelist, after all, and the narrative is gripping, even if you feel you might need a pinch or three of Cerebos.

MADAME LYNCH

Oceans of ink have been spilled on the subject of this lady – the most recent account being Sián Rees's detailed and painstaking historical reconstruction *The Shadows of Elisa Lynch* (Hodder-Review, 2003). Alvin Brodsky's *Madame Lynch and Friend* (Harper and Row, NY, 1975) is highly coloured and a good read, though it aroused considerable criticism on publication for its strong anti-López and anti-Lynch stance, and also for some silly mistakes – Brodsky has toucans and flying-fish darting about the River Paraguay at one point. Those authors who have not actually been to the country often come a cropper over Paraguay. A recent British female novelist, who shall remain nameless, had the River Paraguay sparkling and glittering at Asunción – in fact it resembles thick pea-soup at the best of times. An older though still evergreen classic on la Lynch is William E. Barret's *Woman on Horseback* (Peter Davies, 1938).

THE AUSTRALIAN COMMUNISTS

The classic history is Gavin Souter's magisterial *A Peculiar People: the Australians in Paraguay* (Angus & Robertson, 1968). While researching his book Souter was arrested for photographing a lamp post with bullet holes in Asunción, and held in the police cells for a day on suspicion of . . . what one wonders? When released he was interviewed by the notorious Pastor Coronel, chief torturer to Alfie Stroessner. A 'souter', incidentally, is the old Scots for a shoemaker, and 'Pastor Coronel' means 'Colonel Shepherd' in Spanish – a good soubriquet for a man with a *picada*, or electric torture-prod, no? A more recent lengthy account is Anne Whitehead's chatty and discursive *Paradise Mislaid: In Search of the Australian Tribe of Paraguay* (Queensland University Press, 1997). This is a good travel book in its own right, as well as a retelling of the New Australia and Cosme dramas.

NUEVA GERMANIA

Ben Macintyre's superb *Forgotten Fatherland* (Picador, 1993) is an excellent, gripping read. He actually made the pilgrimage to the settlement upriver and then on horseback. Highly recommended just as an exciting and adventurous travel book alone.

STROESSNER, GENOCIDE AND HUMAN RIGHTS

Richard Aren's *Genocide in Paraguay* (TUP, 1976) is a collection of enlightening – and shocking – essays on the grim record. Norman Lewis's *The Missionaries* (Picador, 1972) has a chapter on the sinister activities of the New Tribes Mission in the Paraguayan Chaco. Isabel Hilton's interview with Stroessner 'The General' (Granta No. 31, 1990) gives a portrait of Alfie in his Brazilian exile in self-justificatory mood. Paul Lewis's *Paraguay Under Stroessner* (University of North Carolina Press, 1980) goes into the whole epoch in detail.

NAZIS

For the dedicated conspiracy theorist nothing beats H. Thomas's *Doppelgängers* (Fourth Estate, 1995). According to Thomas, leading Nazis including Hitler and Himmler had doubles killed in their place while they escaped to Argentina and Paraguay to meet up with Martin Bormann. Stalin believed this theory too – or at least pretended to – and he held the partially burnt corpses claimed to be of Hitler and Eva Braun. Gerald Posner's *Mengele* records the escape of the 'Angel of Death' from Auschwitz to Paraguay and Brazil.

LITERATURE

The greatest novel written by a European about South America is probably Joseph Conrad's *Nostromo*, much of which is based on Paraguay during the López years. Although Louis de Bernières's *The War of Don Emmanuel's Nether Parts* (Secker and Warburg, 1990) is supposed to be fantastical magical-realist fiction it is rather close to the Paraguayan reality, with *pyragues*, *caña*, torture, kidnapping, and towns called Asunción and Concepción. Before I went to Paraguay I read this book and thought it was silly, ridiculous, melodramatic and wildly overblown. Rereading it on my return I found it a rather sober and unsurprising chronicle of typical everyday *rioplatano* life.

Augusto Roa Bastos's *I, The Supreme* (Faber, 1986) is a dense, meaty, gripping read on the Dr Francia dictatorship – and by parallel with the *stronato* as well: in the same class as Gabriel García Márquez at his best. Graham Greene, alas, went to Paraguay too late, when his powers were fading. As a result, *Travels With My Aunt* (Bodley Head, 1969) and *Ways of Escape* (Vintage, 1999) are disappointing on Paraguay. Such a pity neither Ronald Firbank nor Evelyn Waugh visited the country and so never wrote about the place – it might have been created for their pens.

A more lengthy extended bibliography for those who really want to go into Paraguay in depth is given at the end of John Gimlette's *At the Tomb of the Inflatable Pig*.